Praise for Terry Teachout and

POPS

"A superb, clear, and definitive narrative biography."
— *USA Today*

"The most comprehensive and pleasurable account yet of the trumpeter's complex life and personality. Teachout's vivid and accessible portrayal of Armstrong is one of the book's great pleasures: He will make a fan of the most skeptical reader."
— *Kansas City Star*

"Teachout's sharp, often witty sentences make reading him a delight."
— *Boston Globe*

"Teachout adopts a sophisticated street-level style that mirrors what he loves best about the man known as Satchmo: Armstrong's ability (and willingness) to synthesize high and low culture for an audience as broad as his grin."
— *Time Out New York*

"Prodigious . . . Teachout's fine book brings us as close to the essential Pops as anyone."
— *Cleveland Plain Dealer*

"A comprehensive, affectionate biography of arguably the single most important figure in the history of jazz . . . and a revealing look at a broad swath of American cultural history."
— *Kirkus Reviews*

"If you like Satchmo, this book is a must-read."
— *The Oklahoman*

POPS

Also by Terry Teachout

All in the Dances: A Brief Life of George Balanchine
A Terry Teachout Reader
The Skeptic: A Life of H. L. Mencken
City Limits: Memories of a Small-Town Boy

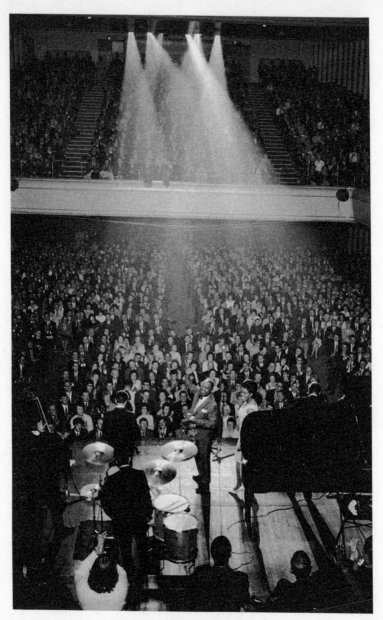

Louis Armstrong and the All Stars, 1965

POPS

A Life of
LOUIS
ARMSTRONG

Terry Teachout

MARINER BOOKS
HOUGHTON MIFFLIN HARCOURT
BOSTON   NEW YORK

First Mariner Books edition 2010

Copyright © 2009 by Terry Teachout

For information about permission to reproduce selections from this book, write to Permissions, Houghton Mifflin Harcourt Publishing Company, 215 Park Avenue South, New York, New York 10003.

www.hmhbooks.com

Library of Congress Cataloging-in-Publication Data
Teachout, Terry.
  Pops : a life of Louis Armstrong / Terry Teachout.
    p. cm.
  Includes bibliographical references and index.
  ISBN 978-0-15-101089-9
    1. Armstrong, Louis, 1901–1971. 2. Jazz musicians — United
States — Biography. I. Title.
  ML419.A75T43 2009
  781.65092 — dc22   [B]
  2009006035

ISBN 978-0-547-38637-9 (pbk.)

Book design by Victoria Hartman
The text of this book is composed in Janson.

Printed in the United States of America

DOC 10 9 8 7 6 5 4 3 2 1

Photo credits appear on page 449.

To Hilary,
"my inspirator"

Don't look for obscure formulas, nor for *le mystère*.
It is pure joy I'm giving you.

— CONSTANTIN BRANCUSI

Contents

LOUIS ARMSTRONG'S LETTERS and autobiographical manuscripts are composed in an untutored, orthographically idiosyncratic style that is part of their charm. I have left this aspect of his writing mostly untouched. All misspelled words and proper names found in direct quotations from Armstrong's writings are printed as they appear in the original documents. The only changes I have made are to replace his underscoring with italicization and to delete many of the mysterious apostrophes with which he littered his typewritten texts. (Readers wishing to see how Armstrong used apostrophes should consult *Louis Armstrong, in His Own Words*, in which Thomas Brothers describes and analyzes his orthographic practices.)

Song titles are placed inside quotation marks. The titles of longer works are italicized. All references to musical pitches and key signatures are given at concert pitch. The phrase *today's dollars* refers to the value of the dollar in 2007.

Because most of Armstrong's key recordings have been reissued countless times in various formats, this book does not contain a discography. A comprehensive listing of Armstrong's known recordings can be found in Jos Willems's *All of Me: The Complete Discography of Louis Armstrong*.

PROLOGUE

"The Cause of Happiness"

NEW YORK WAS ABOUT to rip up its cultural map in the summer of 1956, and few of the city's residents knew how dramatic the changes would be. The Guggenheim Museum was still a blueprint; Lincoln Center, an uncleared slum. New York City Ballet danced at City Center, while the Metropolitan Opera continued to perform at its decaying house on 39th and Broadway, a few steps away from the theater district. The New York Philharmonic played at Carnegie Hall, but you could also ride the subway eighty blocks north to Lewisohn Stadium in July and August and pay thirty cents to hear the orchestra. (The cheap seats at Carnegie Hall cost $1.50.) The Philharmonic's old summer home, a hulking neo-Grecian amphitheater built in 1915, is gone now, razed to make room for the North Academic Center of the City College of New York, with nothing left to mark its existence but a plaque. Only concertgoers of a certain age can remember traveling uptown to hear the orchestra accompany such soloists as George Gershwin, Marian Anderson, Van Cliburn — and Louis Armstrong, who made his Philharmonic debut at Lewisohn Stadium on July 14, 1956, playing

W. C. Handy's "St. Louis Blues" for a crowd of 22,500 with Leonard Bernstein on the podium, Handy in the audience, and a CBS camera crew and a Columbia recording team on hand to document the event for posterity. It was the first time that the most famous of all jazz musicians had played with a symphony orchestra, and it was, he said, a dream come true.

The performance, like so much else in Armstrong's life, was an inspired improvisation. *See It Now*, Edward R. Murrow's TV newsmagazine, had been following the trumpeter around Europe, filming the concerts he was giving as an unofficial "ambassador" of American goodwill. His travels had caught the eye of the *New York Times*, which ran a front-page story informing its readers that "America's secret weapon [in the Cold War] is a blue note in a minor key. Right now its most effective ambassador is Louis (Satchmo) Armstrong." To be associated with so popular a figure could do Murrow nothing but good, for his outspoken reports about McCarthyism had gotten the newscaster into trouble with his bosses at CBS, and Fred Friendly, the producer of *See It Now*, was eager to leaven the loaf with programs on less controversial topics. They had already aired "Two American Originals," a dual profile of Armstrong and Grandma Moses, and the sober-sided Murrow, though he knew nothing about jazz, had been charmed by Armstrong when the two men chatted on camera at a Paris nightclub:

MURROW: Is there any relation between gutbucket and boogie-woogie?

ARMSTRONG: Oh, I don't think so, Mr. Murrow.* They're both —rhythmatical. Did that come out of me? . . .

MURROW: Louie, I've been meaning to ask you this. What's the meaning of a "cat"?

---

*In Armstrong's diphthong-rich New Orleans accent, so similar to that of deepest Brooklyn, "Murrow" became "*MOY*-roh." It was less surprising that Murrow should have called him "Louie." "All White Folks call me Louie," he wrote in 1944. Many blacks did so, too, including several of his sidemen and at least one of his four wives, though he pronounced his first name "*LEW*-is," as can be heard on his 1963 recording of "Hello, Dolly!"

ARMSTRONG: Cat? Cat can be anybody from the guy in the gutter to a lawyer, doctor, the biggest man to the lowest man, but if he's in there with a good heart and enjoy the same music together, he's a cat.

Now Murrow and Friendly wanted to expand the *See It Now* segment into a theatrical documentary called *The Saga of Satchmo* (it was released in 1957 as *Satchmo the Great*) that would include additional footage of Armstrong's CBS-sponsored visit to Ghana, where the All Stars, his six-piece band, had played in May for a hundred thousand ecstatic listeners. All that was missing was a grand finale, and when Friendly learned that Lewisohn Stadium was planning to present its first all-jazz concert, a joint appearance by the All Stars and the Dave Brubeck Quartet, he called up George Avakian, Armstrong's producer at Columbia Records, and started peppering him with questions. "George, Armstrong was born on the Fourth of July, right?" (He wasn't, but no one, not even Armstrong himself, knew it at the time.) "Will Leonard Bernstein still be conducting at Lewisohn Stadium then? You know him — how about getting him to invite Louis to play with the Philharmonic on his birthday? Would he do it? What would they play?" Avakian hastened to assure Friendly that Bernstein, who had hosted a well-received TV show about jazz the preceding October, would be happy to share a stage with Armstrong, and that the Philharmonic would likely have an arrangement of "St. Louis Blues" in its library. He was right on both counts: Bernstein agreed at once, and the Philharmonic's librarian dredged through the files and found a version of "St. Louis Blues" arranged by Alfredo Antonini, a staff conductor at CBS. The date of the concert had to be moved to July 14, but Murrow and Friendly got everything else they wanted.

The local papers had reported that the Philharmonic would take the night off to make room for a "Jazz Jamboree" featuring Armstrong and Brubeck. Now they announced a special added attraction:

At the conclusion of the scheduled program . . . the orchestra will come to the stage to join with Louis Armstrong in "St.

Louis Blues," conducted by Leonard Bernstein. The reason for the post-program offering involves *The Saga of Satchmo*, a motion picture about the popular jazz trumpeter. Ed Murrow and his *See It Now* television crew will film the Saturday evening sequence, and it will be used as the climactic sequence of the movie. The composer of "St. Louis Blues," W. C. Handy, will attend the concert.

That, too, was Fred Friendly's idea. Avakian had told him that "St. Louis Blues" was thought to be the most frequently performed American popular song of all time. "W. C. Handy wrote that, didn't he?" Friendly asked. "Is he still alive? Do you know him? Could you ask him to come to the concert?" Once again Avakian had the answers: the eighty-two-year-old composer was living in a suburb of New York, blinded by a fall from a subway platform but more than willing to come hear the world's best-known jazzman play the world's best-known blues song with America's oldest symphony orchestra.

Armstrong's Philharmonic debut, however, was more prestigious on paper than in practice. He appeared not at Carnegie Hall but as part of a popular-priced outdoor concert, and the performance, like his trip to Ghana, was what TV viewers would learn to call a "media event," staged for the purpose of being telecast. Even before the orchestra was added to the bill, his appearance had been a grudging concession on the part of the managers of the Lewisohn Stadium concerts, who were finding it hard to sell enough tickets to fill the twenty-seven-thousand-seat amphitheater. Faced with mounting deficits for their classical and musical-comedy programs, they decided to experiment with jazz and pop — Armstrong and Brubeck were followed two weeks later by Harry Belafonte — in the hope of luring more listeners uptown.

Armstrong himself was no longer shining so brightly in 1956, though the All Stars remained among the highest-grossing nightclub acts in jazz, in large part because their leader's vocals were as distinctive as his trumpet playing. His recordings of pop songs like "Mack the Knife" and "Blueberry Hill," sung in a gratingly raspy voice (one simile-happy journalist said that it sounded like "a wheelbarrow crunching up a gravel driveway") that was easy to imitate but impossible to duplicate, kept him on jukeboxes long after most of the other musicians who came to fame in the twenties faded from view. The first jazzman to appear on the cover of *Time*, he had been in a dozen Hollywood films and had just finished shooting *High Society*, a big-budget musical remake of *The Philadelphia Story* that looked like it might do well at the box office. But Armstrong had never quite made it big on the silver screen, and while TV was now introducing him to a generation that knew little of the crucial part he had played in shaping the sound of jazz, the teenagers of 1956 had ideas of their own. Two days before the Lewisohn Stadium concert, Ed Sullivan announced that Elvis Presley had agreed to be a guest on his Sunday-night variety show. The All Stars were still playing *The Ed Sullivan Show* long after Presley turned into a reclusive self-caricature, but the writing was now on the wall: with the arrival of rock-and-roll, Armstrong's once-revolutionary music had become old-fashioned at last.

It was just as old-fashioned to many jazz aficionados, some of whom had never forgiven him for turning his back on small-group jazz. In 1929 he began to lead a series of dance bands that supplied bland backdrops for renditions of pop songs that ranged in quality from "Body and Soul" to "La Cucaracha." Though a handful of critics (and many musicians) believed his recordings of the thirties, especially his soaring remakes of such classic small-band performances of the twenties as "Struttin' with Some Barbecue," to be the high-water mark of his output, most saw them as proof that he had sold his soul to the gods of the marketplace. These skeptics had welcomed him back to the fold when he ditched his big band in 1947 and launched the All Stars, but nine years later, highbrow disfavor was on the rise again. Whitney Balliett would speak for more than a few of his colleagues when he reported in the *New Yorker* that "Armstrong has recently begun offering in his public appearances little more than a round of vaudeville antics — clowning, bad jokes — and a steadily narrowing repertory."

Even admiring musicians were known to squirm when Armstrong clowned for the mostly white audiences that packed the clubs and concert halls at which he played. He saw the eye-popping wall-to-wall grin that was his trademark as nothing more than frosting on the musical cake, a way of making innocent fun that was as much a part of his image as the handkerchief that he clutched in his left hand to mop the sweat from his face: "It's humor everywhere to me. I'm goin' get a laugh, don't care what country." For many other black entertainers, though, his uninhibited mugging was an unwelcome reminder of the old-time minstrel shows whose memory they longed to put behind them, and despite their respect for his musical achievements, they were quick to criticize his onstage behavior. The trumpeter Dizzy Gillespie, who played a more modern style of jazz, went so far as to accuse Armstrong of engaging in "Uncle Tom-like subservience." In any case jazz itself was moving in other directions by 1956. The crowd-pleasing style of the All Stars, an updated version of the collective improvisation of the New Orleans musicians from whom Armstrong had learned his trade, was now known as "Dixieland," a name that might have been calculated to put off black listeners, and most younger jazz fans thought it suitable only for consumption by middle-aged listeners in search of lost time. "Nowadays," Gillespie said, "we try to work out different rhythms and things that they didn't think about when Louis Armstrong blew. In his day all he did was play strictly from the soul — just strictly from his heart. You got to go forward and progress. We study."

But Armstrong had not lost his lifelong ability to please a crowd by playing from his heart and soul, and the prospect of seeing him do so in the company of Leonard Bernstein was especially enticing. The multitalented composer-conductor knew almost as much about popular music as he did about classical — he had two Broadway musicals under his belt and two more in the works — and the music-appreciation lectures that he was giving on *Omnibus*, the CBS series on which he had recently held forth on jazz, had turned him into something of an upper-crust media idol. His presence on the podium was thus all but obligatory, if not the summit meeting it would have been a few years later, when he had become almost as famous as Armstrong himself.

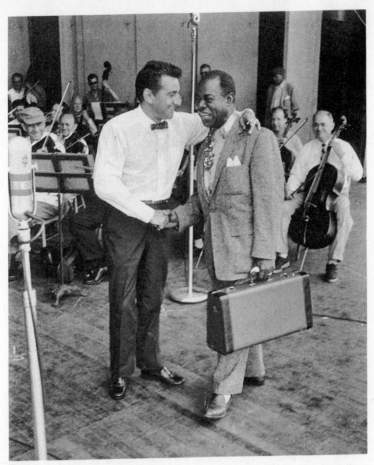

"Yeah, daddy": Armstrong meets Leonard Bernstein and the New York Philharmonic at Lewisohn Stadium, 1956.

The two men met for the first time at rehearsal. A photographer
snapped a picture of the shirtsleeved Bernstein shaking hands with
Armstrong. Both are smiling, as are all the orchestra players visible
in the photo, possibly because they had just heard the trumpeter
greet the conductor with a cheerful "Yeah, daddy." Then they got
down to business. Though Armstrong had never before worked with
so large an ensemble, he was, as always, unfazed. Indeed he was
cooler than Bernstein, who may not have known that his soloist, far

from being an unlettered primitive who played only by ear, was a fluent sight reader who liked to warm up by blowing a tune from one of his favorite Italian operas:

> He say, "Now, when you get to this cadenza and you get a little nervous or something, you know, well, just kind of shorten it or whatever it is." I said, "Okay, daddy." Well, you know, I warm up at home. I hit the stage, I'm ready, whether it's rehearsal or anything. See? From the first rehearsal on down, we wailed. Well, from then on, he got confidence. It don't take long for a person to relax once they hear me go down with the arrangement. After that, he got himself straightened.

The combination of Armstrong, Bernstein, Brubeck, and a balmy summer night had the expected effect on ticket sales. Ten thousand people were turned away. Those who got through the gates heard a superb set by the Brubeck Quartet. At intermission they read a program note by Avakian explaining that they were hearing "jazz of the thoroughly authentic kind, with no window dressing or sugarcoating or explanations or apologies." Then Armstrong and the All Stars took the stage and played an abbreviated version of their regular nightclub program. "Many of the listeners, unable to restrain their feet, bounced into the aisles," the *Times* reported the next day. "Dancing erupted sporadically throughout the stadium."

After a pause for the orchestra to set up, Armstrong and Bernstein returned to center stage. The batonless conductor gave the downbeat, and Armstrong silently fingered the valves on his Selmer trumpet as Bernstein coaxed his players into an earnest simulacrum of swing. Then he lifted his horn to his deeply scarred lips to play a cadenza, gazing skyward as he floated effortlessly up to a high note. Barrett Deems, the All Stars' drummer, laid down a heavy backbeat, and Armstrong led the band and the Philharmonic through the plaintive melody that Handy had set down four decades before. He had played "St. Louis Blues" on countless occasions and recorded it forty-odd times between 1925 and his death in 1971, but on this night he made it sound more poignant than ever. A TV camera zoomed in on Handy, who fumbled in the pockets of his summer suit, lifted his Panama hat, took a handkerchief off the top of his bald head, and dabbed tears from his unseeing eyes.

Afterward Bernstein stepped to the microphone, put an arm around Armstrong, and delivered a mellifluous homily: "Louie Armstrong has told me that his most honored ambition is being fulfilled tonight in playing with the New York Philharmonic. I should say that it is rather we on the longer-haired side of the fence who are honored, in that when we play the 'St. Louis Blues,' we are only doing a blown-up imitation of what he does, and what he does is real and true and honest and simple, and even noble." Armstrong's reply was just as characteristic: "I'd like to say thanks very much to Mister *Boin*-steen, and, uh, this [is my] first time playing with a symphony orchestra, and as we cats say, it gassed me, man, it gassed me!" It gassed the audience, too, which cheered so loudly that Armstrong and Bernstein had to fake an encore, repeating the coda of Antonini's arrangement. But John S. Wilson, the jazz critic of the *New York Times*, proved harder to gas, and his review, illustrated with a photo of Dave Brubeck, was brutally condescending:

> It is somewhat disturbing to realize that the Armstrong group's performances are being seen all over the world and are widely publicized as outstanding examples of the propaganda value of American jazz. There is no question of Mr. Armstrong's merits as an entertainer. It is natural that audiences in all countries should be drawn to him, just as the one at Lewisohn Stadium was. But, except for occasional instances, it would be misleading if the antics of Mr. Armstrong and his colleagues were to be accepted as representative of well-played jazz.

It isn't known whether Armstrong saw what Wilson wrote. "I never read no writeups," he claimed, though he owned several fat scrapbooks of press clippings and was well aware of what Gillespie and others were saying about his onstage demeanor. But even if he had read this particular review, it would have made no sense to him. He thought of himself as an entertainer first and foremost and believed that making fun was part of his job. "The people expect all that from me — coming out all chesty, making faces," he said. "That's me and I don't want to be nobody else. They know I'm there in the cause of happiness." He knew, too, that his clowning was not incompatible with being an artist, though he rarely spoke of himself in such high-flown terms: "The note's what count, even if you stand on your head. . . . I mean you don't just go around waking people up to the effect of saying, 'You know, this music is art.' But it's got to be art because the world has recognized our music from New Orleans, else it would have been dead today."

Art or not, it was just another gig. The next night the All Stars appeared on *The Ed Sullivan Show* to promote *High Society*, after which they hit the road again. That, too, was part of the job: Armstrong and his band spent three hundred nights a year on tour, playing for whoever put up the cash. To perform with the New York Philharmonic might well have been his most honored ambition, but he makes no mention of it in his published correspondence, nor does the concert figure prominently in any of his biographies (or Bernstein's). Yet Armstrong's Philharmonic debut was a pivotal moment in his long career, for it was in 1956 that his fellow countrymen started to see him as more than a mere popular musician. *See It Now*, with its footage of "Ambassador Satch" (the title of his latest album) playing for the multitudes, had shown TV viewers the esteem in which he was held elsewhere in the world. *High Society*, in which he shared the screen with Bing Crosby, Frank Sinatra, and Grace Kelly, opened shortly after the Lewisohn Stadium concert, going on to become the fourth-highest-grossing film of the year, ahead of *The Man Who Knew Too Much*, *Rebel Without a Cause*, and *The Searchers*. The All Stars still reaped their share of bad reviews, but more and more readers found themselves agreeing not with John S. Wilson but with Leonard Bernstein, and the day would come when they bought so many copies of Armstrong's recording of "Hello, Dolly!" that it pushed aside the Beatles' "Can't Buy Me Love" to become the last jazz record ever to reach the top of the pop charts. Bit by bit the familiar face of a star was evolving into something bigger, if not nearly so big, or complicated, as the private man behind the million-watt smile.

➤

It goes without saying — or should — that Louis Armstrong's music was the most important thing about him. Yet his personal story, in addition to shedding light on the wellsprings of his art, is important in its own right, and no less in need of a historically aware interpretation. He was a child of his time, not ours, and some of the things he did and said as an adult are barely intelligible to those who know little of the world of his youth. Even in his own time he was widely misunderstood, often by people who, like Dizzy Gillespie, should have known better. To understand him now, we must see him as he was, a black man born at the turn of the century in the poorest quarter of New Orleans who by the end of his life was known and loved in every corner of the earth. What manner of man succeeded in making such a journey? How did he rise above the unforgiving circumstances of his birth to become a culture-shaping giant — and what marks did those circumstances leave on him?

Everyone who knew Armstrong agreed that he was what he seemed to be. "What you saw was what you got," said Joe Muranyi, the All Stars' last clarinetist. Jack Bradley, a photographer whom the trumpeter befriended in the sixties, described him as "down-to-earth, natural, completely unpretentious, simple in the best sense of the word." It was his genuineness as much as his genius to which his fans responded. He once reacted to a radio interviewer's pronouncement that he was "a living American legend" by dropping his pants and giggling. "I don't care what company I'm in, what environment, you know?" he said on another occasion. "I just want to *be* there and enjoy it. Just as good as the average cat." Whether on stage or off, he was the embodiment of Johnny Mercer's admonition in "Ac-cent-tchu-ate the Positive": *You've got to spread joy up to the maximum / Keep gloom down to the minimum.* Louis Jordan, who played with him in 1932, recalled that "he was always happy, he would never sit grumpy." Danny Barker, the New Orleans guitarist, saw him in his dressing room after a show and remembered the sight ever after:

> He be sittin' down in his underwear with a towel around his lap, one around his shoulders an' that white handkerchief on his head, and he'd put that grease around his lips. Look like a minstrel man, ya know . . . an' laughin' you know natural the way he is. And in the room ya see, maybe two nuns. You see a street walker dressed all up in flaming clothes. You see maybe a guy come out of a penitentiary. Ya see maybe a blind man sitting there. You see a rabbi, ya see a priest, see. Liable to see maybe two policemen or detectives, see. You see a judge. All of 'em different levels of society in the dressin' room and he's talking to all of 'em. . . . And there'd be some kids there, white and colored. All the diverse people of different social levels . . . an' everybody's lookin'. Got their eyes dead on him, jus' like they was lookin' at a diamond.

He was, of course, the least average of cats, though his place in the history of jazz is harder to explain than is commonly understood. Armstrong did not invent jazz, nor was he its first significant figure, and it is not even right to call him the first great jazz soloist, as many critics and scholars have done. Sidney Bechet, the New Orleans clarinetist who was four years his senior, preceded him by a decade, and Bix Beiderbecke, the self-taught cornet player from Iowa whose playing was widely admired by jazz musicians of the twenties and thirties, started winning national recognition at the same time as Armstrong, almost to the month.

What, then, made Louis Armstrong stand out? And why is his name still known to those who know nothing else about jazz? The simplest explanation, and up to a point the best one, is that he was the first great *influence* in jazz. No sooner did he burst upon the scene than other musicians — trumpeters, saxophonists, singers — started imitating him. "I tried to walk like him, talk like him, eat like him, sleep like him," said Rex Stewart, who replaced Armstrong in Fletcher Henderson's band. Coleman Hawkins, Henderson's star saxophonist, heard him for the first time in 1924 and was stunned into speechlessness: "I stood silent, feeling almost bashful, asking myself if I would ever be able to attain a small part of Louis Armstrong's greatness." The trumpeter Max Kaminsky told of how "the combination of Louis's dazzling virtuosity and sensational brilliance of tone so overwhelmed me that I felt as if I had stared into the sun's eye." Such imagery came easily to those who heard Armstrong in his halcyon days. Philip Larkin, a part-time jazz critic and lifelong fan, called him "something inexhaustible and unchanging like the sun." Even Miles Davis, who loathed Armstrong's mugging, knew that the history of jazz radiated outward from the bell of his horn: "You can't play nothing on trumpet that doesn't come from him, not even modern shit. I can't even remember a time when he sounded bad playing the trumpet. Never."

What spoke to these artists, as it speaks to all those hearing Armstrong for the first time, is the combination of hurtling momentum and expansive lyricism that propelled his playing and singing alike. The four staccato quarter notes that he raps out at the start of "West End Blues," his most celebrated recording, proclaimed the coming of a new way of thinking about rhythm. Though the passage looks innocuous on paper, it catapulted his fellow jazzmen into a musical world in which even the simplest of phrases were charged with an irresistible forward thrust. To be sure, his internal metronome was exact enough to impress the most fanatically "rhythmatical" of classical musicians. Herbert von Karajan once told the members of the Vienna Philharmonic that he was going to an All Stars concert. "Imagine!" he said. "Two hours of music, and never once will it slow down or speed up by mistake!" But Armstrong could also toy with time, stretching it this way and that, as he does in the serene trumpet solo that ends his 1933 recording of Harold Arlen's "I Gotta Right to Sing the Blues," hovering miles above the clockwork tyranny of the beat and sounding for all the world like a lordly grand-opera tenor.

The comparison is apt, for Armstrong liked, listened to, and learned from opera. "I like that deep stuff, also — it 'gasses' me to no end," he told Orson Welles. Late in life he remembered buying his first record player, a wind-up Victrola, as a teenager in New Orleans: "Most of my records were the Original Dixieland Jazz Band . . . I had Caruso, too, and Henry Burr, Galli-Curci, Tetrazzini — they were all my favorites. Then there was the Irish tenor, McCormack — beautiful phrasing." But his style was also permeated with the rough beauty of the blues, and if it was his way to sing and play them with a smile, he knew as well as anyone that the world of which he sang could be a hurtful place: "Like when I play, maybe 'Back o' Town Blues,' I'm thinking about one of the old, low-down moments — when maybe your woman didn't treat you right. That's a hell of a moment when a woman tell you, 'I got another mule in my stall.'"

Even the classical melodies he loved took on a new tint when passed through the prism of his vast experience. "I seen everythin' from a child, comin' up," he said. "*Nothin'* happen I ain't never seen before." He was forever reflecting on the things he had seen, sometimes on paper but more often with his horn: "When I blow I think of times and things from outa the past that gives me an image of the tune. Like moving pictures passing in front of my eyes. A town, a chick somewhere back down the line, an old man with no name you seen once in a place you don't remember." That was why he never used musical terminology when speaking of his music. It was all about life:

> I'm playin' a date in Florida years ago, livin' in the colored section and I'm playin' my horn for *myself* one afternoon. A knock come on the door and there's an old, gray-haired flute player from the Philadelphia Orchestra, down there for his health. Walking through that neighborhood, he heard this horn, playing this *Cavalleria Rusticana*, which he said he never heard phrased like that before, but still to him it was as if an orchestra was behind it. Well, that what I mean by imagination. That the way I express myself because I *read* that story and I just put it in spade life — colored life — where this guy in the story, he fooled around with this man's wife and this cat finally picked up on it and stuck him in the back with a knife or somethin' like that.

These are but a few of the myriad facets of Armstrong's art, and one can go a long way toward understanding him without mentioning anything else. But it is not enough to declare him a phenomenally gifted and imaginative artist and let it go at that. The other reason why he cast so long a shadow is that his personality was as compelling as his artistry. The two could scarcely be separated, for his lavish generosity of spirit was part and parcel of his prodigal way of making music. Even in his old age, he held nothing back, and it seemed at times that nothing was beyond him. He really did perform with everyone from Leonard Bernstein to Johnny Cash. He really did end his shows (some of them, anyway) by playing 250 or more high Cs, capped with a high F. He wrote the finest of all jazz autobiographies — without a collaborator. The ranks of his admirers included Kingsley Amis, Tallulah Bankhead, Jackson Pollock, Jean Renoir, and Le Corbusier ("He is mathematics, equilibrium on a tightrope. He is Shakespearean!"). Virgil Thomson called him "a master of musical art." Stuart Davis, whose abstract paintings were full of jazz-inspired images, cited him as a "model of greatness." Is it any wonder, then, that so many musicians longed to play the way he played and sing the way he sang? It was no accident that they usually referred to Armstrong not as "Satchmo," his own favorite nickname, but as "Pops."* He was the father figure of jazz, and what his children wanted was to *be* him, or at least come as close as they possibly could.

Armstrong's openheartedness was central to his character. Though he loved the New Orleans of his childhood, he never claimed that it had been anything other than "Disgustingly Segregated and Prejudiced." Yet he never yielded to the temptation to treat white musicians as he had been treated by whites — or by the light-skinned blacks of New Orleans who looked down on their darker brothers,

---

*The source of the nickname appears to be the fact that Armstrong, like many other famous and well-traveled people, had trouble remembering proper names and fell early on into the habit of calling everyone he met "Pops."

the young Louis Armstrong included. He was pleased to play along-side Bix Beiderbecke (one of the dedicatees of his first book) and Jack Teagarden (with whom he made one of the earliest racially mixed jazz recordings). His All Stars were integrated throughout their quarter-century-long existence. "Those people who make the restrictions," he said, "they don't know nothing about music, it's no crime for cats of any color to get together and blow."

All this is part of the Armstrong legend, and thus well known. But the legend is not the whole story, just as there was more to Louis Armstrong than the grinning jester who sang "Hello, Dolly!" night after night for adoring audiences. "To friend and foe alike," the trumpeter Humphrey Lyttelton wrote, "there was, deep below the surface of companionship and bonhomie, an impenetrable wall in which every stone was an enigma." His disposition was not always cloudless, either, though he preferred not to share his occasional sorrows with strangers. Armstrong taped dozens of his private conversations during the last quarter century of his life, and these tapes, which until recently were inaccessible to scholars, show that his personality was tougher and more sharp-edged than his fans knew. He could be moody and profane, and he knew how to hold a grudge. "I got a simple rule about everybody," he told a journalist. "If you don't treat me right — shame on you!" A friend dropped in on him after a gig and asked what was new. "Nothin' new," he said. "White folks still ahead." He was as clearheaded about his own fame: "I can't go no place they don't roll up the drum, you have to stand up and take a bow, get up on the stage. And sitting in an audience, I'm signing programs for hours all through the show. And you got to sign them to be in good faith. And afterwards all those hangers-on get you crowded in at the table — and you *know* you're going to pay the check."

He also had a streak of shy passivity, a tendency to drift with the tide, that was at odds with the barely contained energy that in his youth had driven him to prowl the stages on which he played like a hungry panther. He was inclined to follow rather than lead, and when he was forced to become a leader by virtue of his inescapable talent (and the prodding of Lil Hardin, his second wife), he let white men make most of his decisions for him. It was Joe Glaser, his manager from 1935 on, who held the purse strings, choosing the musicians who worked with him and deciding where and when they would play, just as George Avakian, Milt Gabler, and Norman Granz, who produced the best of his later recordings, played a large part in determining their tone and shape. Outside of purely musical matters, most of his important career choices were made by someone else.

Armstrong's unwillingness to take charge of the direction of his professional life was in part the result of his having been born at a time when it was taken for granted by most whites that blacks were their inferiors. It was a matter of caution, and he was nothing if not cautious. Yet he guarded his hard-won star's prerogatives militantly and kept a close and suspicious eye on the competition. "Louis is real jealous of other players who put out," said Pops Foster, a longtime Armstrong sideman. "If you play bad you won't be in the band, and if you play too good you won't be there. When I'd get to romping along on the bass, he'd yell at me, 'Hey, man, if you want to play trumpet, come on down here and play.'" It wasn't that simple — he worked as often as he could with Jack Teagarden, the greatest of all jazz trombonists, and the peerless drummer Sid Catlett — but he had no use for scene-stealers. When Earl Hines, the pianist who had been his closest companion in the late twenties, quit the All Stars in 1951, Armstrong exploded, "I don't give a damn. Hines and his ego, ego, ego! If he wanted to go, the hell with him."

If the culprit happened to be a trumpeter, Armstrong would skewer him mercilessly, as Rex Stewart saw him do to Jabbo Smith. A younger player of Armstrong-like flair, Smith was appearing opposite the master at a Harlem dance and made it known that he was out for blood. At the end of his set it looked as though he might prevail. Then Armstrong took the stage:

Louis bounced onto the opposite stage, immaculate in a white suit. Somehow, the way the lights reflected off his trumpet made the instrument look like anything but a horn. It looked as if he were holding a wand of rainbows or a cluster of sunlight . . . Louis never let up that night, and it seemed that each climax topped its predecessor. Every time he'd take a break, the applause was thunderous, and swarms of women kept rushing the stand for his autograph. They handed him everything from programs to whiskey bottles to put his signature on. One woman even took off her pants and pleaded with him to sign them!

Even as he made short work of those who challenged him on the bandstand, so did he speak his mind when he thought it necessary, usually in private but on occasion in full view of the paying public. In the most widely reported of his tirades, set off by Dwight Eisenhower's reluctance to order Orval Faubus, the governor of Arkansas, to desegregate the public schools of Little Rock, Armstrong told a dumbfounded small-town newsman that the president of the United States was "two-faced" and had "no guts." (His uncensored language was harsher still.) Many were amazed by his attack on Eisenhower, especially those musicians who had previously accused him of Tomming. Popular entertainers, especially black ones, didn't say things like that in 1957 — but Louis Armstrong did.

The same man who told off a president scrawled a different set of fighting words onto a grade-school notepad as he lay in a Manhattan hospital room in 1969, sick unto death and boiling with rage. The syntax was homemade, but the meaning was as clear as a high C:

> Negroes *never* did stick together and they *never* will. They hold too much *malice* — *Jealousy* deep down in their heart for the *few* Negroes who *tries*. . . . [T]hey know within themselves that they're doing the wrong things, but expects *everybody* just because he is a *Negro* to give up everything he has *struggled* for in life such as a *decent* family — a *living*, a *plain* life — the *respect*. . . . And the *Negro* who *can't see* these *foolish* moves from some *over Educated fools'* moves — then *right* away he is *called* a *White* Folks *Nigger*. Believe it — the White Folks did *everything that's decent* for *me*. I wish that I can *boast* these *same* words for *Niggers*.

Armstrong meant for these blunt words to be published, yet three decades went by before they saw print, and to this day most scholars cite them gingerly, if at all. Granted that jazz scholarship is young, it is still noteworthy that so many writers have been so reluctant to grapple with the implications of what he had to say, then and earlier, about his life and work, which does not always mesh neatly with his carefree image. One who has done so is Dan Morgenstern, who remarked of *Satchmo: My Life in New Orleans*, his 1954 autobiography, that while its author "doesn't pass judgment on the 'gamblers, hustlers, cheap pimps, thieves [and] prostitutes' among whom he was raised, it is clear throughout this book that his values, from a very early age on, differ from theirs. . . . He was different from most of them, and the key difference was character." Armstrong was deserted by his father when he was born, raised by a part-time prostitute, and sentenced at the age of eleven to the Colored Waif's Home, an orphanage-like reform school, for firing a pistol on New Year's Eve. It was the first time his name saw print, and by all rights it should have been the last, save perhaps for another, final entry on a police blotter. Instead he wrote himself into the history of Western music, a feat so improbable that it beggars belief. But his musical talent alone, singular though it was, would not have been sufficient to pull him out of the gutter. That took something more — and he knew it.

Why did Armstrong spend so many hours scribbling on a pad or hunched over a typewriter? Partly because he was a gregarious man who enjoyed sending chatty letters to his friends and fans — he referred to the two-fingered typing he did in his dressing room between shows as his "hobby" — but also because he believed that he had something of value to say. Having been born desperately poor, he had worked desperately hard, first as a boy and then as a man. In this he had much in common with Ragged Dick, Horatio Alger's plucky bootblack, whose burning desire to "grow up 'spectable" propelled him into the ranks of the middle class. Self-discipline, self-improvement, self-reliance: these were his lifelong watchwords, and no Alger hero could have improved on his iron determination to get ahead in the world. Once he did so, he felt an obligation to tell oth-

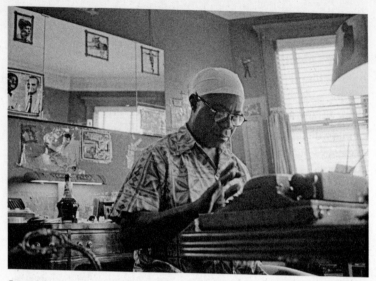

Something to say: Armstrong writing at his home in Queens, 1958. In between playing three hundred shows a year, he turned out two memoirs, several autobiographical manuscripts, dozens of magazine and newspaper articles, and thousands of personal letters to friends and fans, as well as a number of strikingly frank autobiographical manuscripts that did not see print until long after his death.

ers how to do the same. "I was determined to play my horn against all odds, and I had to sacrifice a whole lot of pleasure to do so," he wrote in *Satchmo*. A few years later he made the point more pungently in a TV interview: "The Lord will help the poor, but not the poor lazy."

Around the time that Armstrong was sent to the Waif's Home, George Bernard Shaw was writing *Pygmalion*, in which Eliza Doolittle's ne'er-do-well father mocks the then-accepted distinction between the "deserving" and "undeserving" poor: "I dont need less than a deserving man: I need more. I dont eat less hearty than him; and I drink a lot more. . . . What is middle class morality? Just an excuse for never giving me anything." Armstrong disagreed. "I think I had a beautiful life," he said not long before his death in 1971. "I didn't wish for anything I couldn't get, and I got pretty near everything I wanted because I worked for it." Those unwilling to do the same, he believed, earned their fate, whatever the color of their skin. "The *Negroes* always wanted *pity*," he wrote in his 1969 reminiscence of New Orleans life. "They did that in place of going to work ... they were in an alley or in the street corner shooting dice for nickels and dimes, etc. (mere pittances) trying to win the little money from his Soul Brothers who might be gambling off the money [they] should take home to feed their starving children or pay their small rents, or very important needs, etc." The raw note of contempt is unmistakable — and it was not reserved for his private writings. "You don't have to do a damn thing bad unless you want to," he had told a reporter nine years earlier. "Other than that, you weak-minded, you should go to a hospital or somethin'."

On occasion Armstrong has been compared to Booker T. Washington, whose long-unfashionable vision of racial redemption through self-improvement had a powerful influence on the turn-of-the-century blacks who heeded his call to "cast down your bucket where you are." Louis Armstrong was one of them. While most jazz musicians, black and white alike, now come from relatively comfortable backgrounds, those who were born poor have almost always striven mightily to join the middle class. Anyone who doubts that Armstrong filled the latter bill need only visit his home, located seven blocks from Shea Stadium in a rundown but respectable part of Queens. It is a three-story brick-covered frame house whose interior is reminiscent of Graceland, Elvis Presley's gaudy Memphis mansion. From the Jetsons-style kitchen-of-the-future to the silver wallpaper and golden faucets of the master bathroom, the Armstrong house looks like what it is: the residence of a poor boy who cast down his bucket and pulled it up overflowing. Unlike Graceland, though, the house is neither oppressive nor embarrassing, and as you stand in the smallish study, whose decorations include a portrait of the artist painted by Tony Bennett, it is impossible not to be touched by the aspiration visible wherever you look. This, it is clear, was the home of a *working* man, bursting with a pride that came not from what he had but from what he did. "I never want to be anything more than I am, what I don't have I don't need," Armstrong wrote in his old age.

"My home with Lucille [his fourth and last wife] is good, but you don't see me in no big estates and yachts, that ain't gonna play your horn for you."

In common with other self-made men, Armstrong sometimes forgot that his success was due not solely to work and pluck but also to the talent with which he had been born. He was a man of boundless generosity who preached the stony gospel of self-help, a ferociously ambitious artist who preferred when he could to do as he was told, an introspective man who exploded with irrepressible vitality when he stepped into the spotlight, a joyous genius who confounded his critics by refusing to distinguish between making art and making fun. No more than any other genius was he all of a piece. As Murray Kempton said, "[H]e endures . . . to mix in his own person all men, the pure and the cheap, clown and creator, god and buffoon." Yet all was resolved each time he raised his trumpet to his lips, for that was when the laughter stopped and the beauty began. He knew that "showmanship does not mean you're not serious," and no one who has read his writings can doubt that he was both serious and self-aware. He knew who he was, what he had done, and how far he had come, and he was fiercely proud of it all. He admitted that his music mattered more to him than anything else, even his wives: "When I pick up that horn, that's all. The world's behind me, and I don't concentrate on nothin' but *it*. . . . That my livin' and my life. I love them notes. That why I try to make 'em right. See?"

The whole world saw — and heard.

1

"BASTARDS FROM THE START"

Apprenticeship in New Orleans, 1901–1919

To the northerner New Orleans is another country, seductive and disorienting, a steamy, shabby paradise of spicy cooking, wrought-iron balconies, and streets called Desire and Elysian Fields, a place where the signs advertise such mysterious commodities as poboys and muffuletta and no one is buried underground. *We'll take the boat to the land of dreams*, the pilgrim hears in his mind's ear as he prowls the French Quarter, pushing through the hordes of tipsy visitors and wondering whether the land of his dreams still exists — if it ever did. Rarely does he linger long enough to pierce the veneer of local color with which the natives shield themselves from the tourist trade. At the end of his stay he knows no more than when he came, and goes back home to puzzle out all that he has seen and smelled and tasted. A. J. Liebling, a well-traveled visitor from up North, saw New Orleans as a Mediterranean port transplanted to the Gulf of Mexico, a town of civilized pleasures whose settlers "carried with them a culture that had ripened properly, on the tree." He knew what he was seeing, but Walker Percy, who lived and died there, cast a cooler eye on the same sights: "The ironwork on the balconies sags like rotten lace. . . . Through deep sweating carriageways one catches glimpses of courtyards gone to jungle." Unlike Liebling, he caught the smell of decay.

To the southerner New Orleans is part of the family — but a special, eccentric member, a city cousin who can't be counted on to play by the rules, French and Roman Catholic in the midst of the hardest-bitten of Anglo-Saxon Protestant cultures, politically corrupt without limit and as morally latitudinarian as the rest of the South is publicly upright. In 1897 the city fathers went so far as to legalize prostitution in the restricted district that came to be known as Storyville. (It was named after Sidney Story, the councilman who drafted the ordinances that brought it into being, though musicians simply called it "the District.") The vote supplied official confirmation of what a horrified visitor from Virginia had said six decades before: "I am now in this great Southern Babylon — the mighty receptacle of wealth, depravity and misery." No one there pretended otherwise. "You can make prostitution illegal in Louisiana," said Martin Behrman, the mayor of New Orleans during most of Storyville's existence, "but you can't make it unpopular."

Not even when it came to race did the Crescent City always toe the line. In the twenties, Danny Barker remembered, it was

> the earnest and general feeling that any Negro who left New Orleans and journeyed across the state border and entered the hell-hole called the state of Mississippi for any reason other than to attend the funeral of a very close relative — mother, father, sister, brother, wife or husband — was well on the way to losing his mentality, or had already lost it. . . . When it was decided to live somewhere other than New Orleans, Chicago was the place, and the trip there was preferably a direct one, by way of the Illinois Central Railroad.

New Orleans was no paradise for blacks, but it gave them a measure of personal safety that was harder to find elsewhere in the Old South. The same encroaching swamps that forced the city to "bury" its dead in tombs instead of graves forced its black and white citizens into closer geographical intimacy, and some neighborhoods remained racially mixed after the swamps were drained. Unlike the

African slaves who had to wait for the Civil War to bring their freedom, New Orleans's "Creoles of color," the descendants of the mixed-race slave children who were freed by their French and Spanish owner-fathers before the war, did not consider themselves black. "My folks was all Frenchmans," Jelly Roll Morton proclaimed proudly (and falsely). Some had owned slaves of their own, and long after slavery had been abolished, their descendants continued to look down on the children and grandchildren of the plantation immigrants who lived on the wrong side of Canal Street in the quarter of "uptown" New Orleans known as "Back o' Town." "The worst Jim Crow around New Orleans," Pops Foster said, "was what the colored did to themselves. . . . The lighter you were the better they thought you were."* One dark-skinned musician recalled that some Creole bandleaders "wouldn't hire a man whose hair wasn't silky." Slavery itself was a marginally more merciful affair in New Orleans, where most of the city's slaves were domestic servants and some became skilled artisans. The freedmen who crowded into New Orleans after the war, more than doubling the city's black population between 1860 and 1880, learned from the example of their urban brethren. As for the Creoles of color, they were already a full-fledged black middle class, among the first of its kind in America.

Yet such privileges as were enjoyed by New Orleans's blacks, whatever their hue, could be withdrawn at any time, a fact of which the Creoles were intensely aware. With the coming of the post-Reconstruction "Jim Crow" laws, they were pushed back across the color line. It was a Creole of color, Homer Plessy, whose attempt to ride in the first-class section of a train car led to *Plessy v. Ferguson*, the 1896 U.S. Supreme Court decision that made racial segregation legal. After an interlude of heterodoxy, New Orleans was back in the fold. "No matter how much his Diamond Sparkled," the dark-skinned Louis Armstrong wrote of the light-skinned Jelly Roll Morton, "he still had to eat in the *Kitchen*, the same as *we* Blacks." A black

---

*That was why Louis Armstrong, who came from Back o' Town, pronounced his first name "Lewis," not "Louie." As Lucille Armstrong pointed out, "He wasn't French."

man who came out of the kitchen, Armstrong knew, could end up dead: "At *ten* years old I could see — the Bluffings that those Old *Fat Belly Stinking* very *Smelly Dirty* White Folks were putting Down . . . they get full of their *Mint Julep* or that bad whisky, the poor white Trash were Guzzling down, like water, then when they get so *Damn* drunk until they'd go out of their minds — then it's Nigger Hunting time. *Any* Nigger."

In matters of sex as much as race, the city struggled with its confused heritage. Many plantation owners slept with the black women they owned, but in New Orleans such liaisons were conducted openly, and long after the half-open door of borderline acceptability slammed shut on interracial sex, the city's bordellos catered as openly to white men who shared their grandfathers' appetites. The same Basin Street celebrated in song as *the street / Where the dark and light folk meet* was also the main drag of Storyville, and when dark and light folks met there, it was often to engage in sexual commerce, sometimes accompanied by a still-unnamed style of music in which the written-out dance tunes performed by Creoles of color were infused with the rhythmically freer style of African American blacks.

Sex, race, and music: put them together and you get New Orleans at the turn of the twentieth century, a city with one foot in Europe and the other in the Deep South, committed to a tolerance bordering on libertinism yet unwilling to fully recognize the humanity of a third of its people. "I sure had a ball there growing up," its most distinguished native son would remember long after he moved away, never to return save as a visitor. He loved his hometown with all his heart — but he saw it as it was.

Until the day he died, Louis Armstrong claimed that he was born on July 4, 1900. He said so in *Satchmo: My Life in New Orleans* and *Swing That Music,* his two published memoirs, and on innumerable other occasions, and although at least one biographer found the date too pat to be plausible, it was only in 1988 that a researcher located an entry in Latin for "Armstrong (niger, illegitimus)" in the handwritten baptismal register of New Orleans's Sacred Heart of Jesus Church. According to that record, Louis Armstrong was born on August 4, 1901, the natural son of William Armstrong (known as Willie), who spent most of his adult life working in a turpentine factory, and Mary Ann Albert (known as Mayann, though her son spelled it different ways over the years), a fifteen-year-old country girl who came to New Orleans to work as a household servant. The event went unremarked by the local papers, which had more important things to cover than the birth of yet another "niger, illegitimus." The front page of the next day's *Daily Picayune* concerned itself with a lynching in Mississippi and a speech in which a South Carolina senator declared that "the 'niggers' are not fit to vote." (The latter story also made the front page of the *New York Times*.) Three weeks later Armstrong was baptized a Roman Catholic, the faith of his paternal great-grandmother, though he never practiced it and did not even know that he had gone through the ceremony as an infant. By then his father had left Mayann for another woman. In 1903 Willie and Mayann reconciled for a short time and had a second child, a daughter named Beatrice (known as Mama Lucy), but Armstrong did not live with his father, or spend any amount of time with him, until he was a teenager.

No one knows when or why Armstrong added a year to his age. He never celebrated his birthday as a boy, and it is possible, even likely, that he did not know the true year of his birth. All that can be said with certainty is that the incorrect year became a matter of legal record when he registered for the draft in 1918 and that he stuck to it with unswerving consistency thereafter. We do know, however, that it was Mayann who told him that "the night I was born there was a great big shooting scrape" in the neighborhood. Later on he claimed that it was "a blasting fourth of July, my mother called it, that I came into this world and they named me the firecracker baby." She was right about the incident but misremembered the date — it took place a month later. It is only because of surviving baptismal and census records that we now know both the date and year to have been wrong. Outside of these records, most of the rest of what we

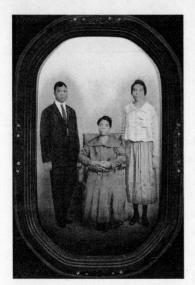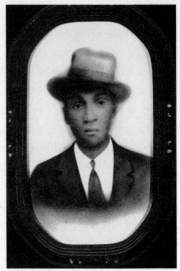

Family portraits from Louis Armstrong's personal collection, ca. 1919. On the left is the only known photograph of Mayann Armstrong (seated). The younger woman is Beatrice "Mama Lucy" Armstrong, Louis's sister. On the right is a rare photograph of Willie Armstrong, his father, who "left us the day we were born." Armstrong gave Mayann credit for teaching him "the real things" about life, but he would never speak of his father with anything other than contempt.

know of Armstrong's childhood is what he tells us in his writings, augmented by our knowledge of New Orleans and the memories of those who knew him as a boy. He wrote at length about his young years, and the picture he paints is often chaotic and sad, though he did not find it so. But he never glossed over the hardships that he faced, or left much doubt as to whom he blamed for them.

Beyond describing him as "a sharp man, tall and handsome and well built," Armstrong had little to say about his father, none of it good. From childhood onward he attached himself to older men, and it is reasonable to suppose that he was looking for some small part of what his own father had failed to give him. In the same breath that he praised Willie's looks, he added that "my father did not have time to teach me anything; he was too busy chasing chippies." That was in *Satchmo*, in which he often withheld comment about matters he otherwise described frankly, letting them speak for themselves. In later years he was franker still:

> The man who May Ann told us was our father left us the day we were born. The next time we heard of him — he had gone into an uptown neighborhood and made several other children by another woman. Whether he married the other woman, we're not sure. *One thing* — he did not marry May Ann. She had to struggle all by herself, bringing us up. Mama Lucy + I were bastards from the Start.

Armstrong was born in his parents' home, a wooden shack at 723 Jane Alley, located on the edge of "black Storyville," the separate red-light district three blocks uptown from Storyville where blacks were allowed to purchase sex. When Willie left her, Mayann gave Louis to Josephine Armstrong, Willie's mother, and moved into black Storyville proper. "Whether my mother did any hustling, I cannot say," he wrote in *Satchmo*. "If she did, she certainly kept it out of sight." In fact she was almost certainly working as a prostitute on Perdido Street, a part of town that was rough even by New Orleans standards, and when her son finally rejoined her, that was where he would live as well. For the moment he stayed with his grandmother in Jane Alley, and his memories of life there were mostly happy, though it, too, was in a rough neighborhood known to locals as "the Battlefield." It was, he later wrote, a place full of "churchpeople, gamblers, hustlers, cheap pimps, thieves, prostitutes and lots of children." Josephine kept her grandson as far away from the hustlers and pimps as she could, sending him to Sunday school and kindergarten and whipping him with switches that she made him cut from a tree that grew in the front yard. He sang gospel songs in church, rejoicing in the variegated clouds of sound emitted by a "sanctified" congregation of working-class blacks who took literally the psalmist's command to "make a joyful noise unto the Lord," worshiping loudly, jubilantly, and without any of the self-conscious decorum of their better-off brethren: "That, I guess, is how I acquired my singing tactics. . . . [T]he whole Congregation would be Wailing — *Singing* like mad and sound *so* beautiful." On weekdays he played hide-and-seek with the poor white children of the neighborhood and helped deliver the washing his grandmother took in, earning a nickel each time he carried a load.

At some point it must have been made known to Louis that his parents were living together again and that he now had a sister. Yet Willie and Mayann made no effort to reclaim their son, and it was not until 1905 or 1906 that he first saw Mama Lucy. One day Mayann sent a friend to Jane Alley to tell Josephine that Willie had deserted her once again and that she was sick and in need of help. Louis went with his mother's friend to black Storyville, riding on a segregated streetcar for the first time in his life. He found Mayann in bed with Mama Lucy in a one-room flat on Perdido Street. "I realize I have not done what I should by you," she told him. "But, son, mama will make it up." Then she sent him to Rampart Street to buy fifty cents' worth of meat, bread, red beans, and rice, the staples of her kitchen and the main ingredients of the southern-style home cooking that he would savor all his life. (As an adult he signed many of his letters "Red Beans and Ricely Yours, Louis Armstrong.") On the way he ran into a gang of bullies who called him a mama's boy and threw mud on his treasured white Lord Fauntleroy suit. He punched the ring-leader in the mouth and went about his business.

It is close to impossible for anyone not born into poverty to picture such a scene, yet Louis appears to have taken it in stride, save for a moment of panic when he first saw his sick mother. After that he adjusted to his new situation with the resiliency of youth. He looked on as one "stepfather" followed another into Mayann's bed (and remained tactfully silent as he and his sister overheard the sounds of lovemaking in their one-room home). "I couldn't keep track of the stepdaddies, there must have been a dozen or so, 'cause all I had to do was turn my back and a new pappy would appear," he recalled, adding that some of them "liked to beat on little Louis." Whenever his mother "got the urge to go out on the town" and disappeared "for days and days," he went without complaint to stay with an uncle.

Though he had only just begun to attend grade school, he took it for granted that he would also work at odd jobs to bring in extra money and was proud to help pay the bills. But he was not a passive onlooker, recording without thinking: the more he saw, the more he questioned, and his father was not the only man on whom he would someday render judgment.

Louis knew that Mayann, unlike Willie, was doing the best she could to take care of him and his sister, and he loved and admired her for it. All that remains of her is a formally posed family portrait taken around 1919 (in which the teenaged Louis can be seen to take after his broad-beamed, plump-cheeked mother) and the recollections set down by her son in *Satchmo* and his other writings. Yet it is more than enough to come away with a sense of what she was like, and why he revered her memory. A plainspoken woman who liked a drink and knew how to fight, she taught him the simple code to which he hewed ever after: "I had to work and help *May Ann*, — put *bread* on the *table*, since it was just the three of us living in this one *big room*, which was *all* that we could afford. But we were *happy*. My mother had *one* thing that *no* matter *how* much *schooling anyone has* — and that was *Good Common Sense* (and respect for human beings). *Yea. That's My Diploma* — All through my *life* I *remembered it*."

He was similarly admiring of the Karnofskys, a family of Jewish peddlers from Lithuania for whom he worked as a boy. Armstrong had little to say about them in *Satchmo*, but two years before his death, he wrote an account of his relationship with the family in which he told of how surprised he was to discover that they "were having problems of their own — Along with hard times from the other *white* folks nationalities who felt that they were better than the *Jewish* race. . . . I was only *Seven* years old but I could easily see the *ungodly treatment* that the White Folks were handing the poor *Jewish* family whom I worked for." He saw it up close, for they took him under their wing, treating him almost like a relative: he worked for them, shared meals with them, even borrowed money from them to buy his first cornet, a five-dollar instrument he saw in the window of a pawnshop.* Before that he had tooted on a battered ten-cent tin horn as he rode through the District on the Karnofskys' wagon, imitating the blues-blowing junkmen who pushed their carts up and down the streets of Back o' Town. The Karnofskys' affection made an impression so deep that it shines through every word Armstrong wrote about them six crowded decades later: "They were *always warm* and *kind* to me, which was very *noticeable* to me — *just* a *kid* who could *use* a little *word* of *kindness,* something that a kid could use at *Seven,* and just starting out in the *world.*"

He saw, too, how the Karnofskys and their fellow Jews banded together in the face of prejudice, seeking to better their lot through work, and was struck by the contrast with what he came to feel was the irresponsibility of too many of his fellow blacks — and one in particular:

> The Negroes always hated the Jewish people who never *harmed* anybody, but they stuck together. And by doing that, they *had* to have *success.* . . . Many [black] kids *suffered* with *hunger* because their Fathers could have done some honest work for a change. *No,* they would *not* do that. It would be *too* much like *Right.* They'd rather lazy around + gamble, etc. If it wasn't for the nice *Jewish* people, we would have *starved many* a time. I will love the *Jewish* people, *all* of my life.

Armstrong grew up to be an ardent philo-Semite who wore a Star of David around his neck "for luck" (his Jewish manager gave it to him) and kept a box of matzos in the kitchen "so I can *Nibble* on them any time that I want to eat late at night." His admiration for the Jews was not limited to their cuisine. Long after he consecrated himself to the art that let him give up his odd jobs and do nothing but play his horn, he gave "the *Jewish* people" credit for having taught him "how to live — real life and determination."

---

* A cornet is a stubbier, mellower-sounding version of the more familiar trumpet, invented early in the nineteenth century and primarily used in brass bands. Armstrong played it until 1926, when he switched to trumpet permanently, preferring the longer instrument's brighter upper register.

Little Louis, as his family and friends called him, was also learning other lessons about life. Black Storyville was full of music, most of it played in honky-tonks like Funky Butt Hall, located across the street from the Fisk School for Boys, to which he started going in 1907. No child in short pants would ever have been allowed inside to watch the dancers bump, grind, drink, and fight, so Louis stood on the sidewalk and listened, peering through a crack in the wall of the rickety building: "It wasn't no classyfied place, just a big old room with a bandstand. And to a tune like 'The Bucket's Got a Hole in It,' some of them chicks would get way down, shake everything, slapping themselves on the cheek of their behind." He soon learned to recognize the styles of Buddy Bolden, Joe Oliver, and Bunk Johnson, the best black cornet players in town. He liked Johnson's sweet tone, but it was the "fire and the endurance" of Oliver that stirred him most powerfully, then and later.

He was stirred in a different way by the ever-changing panorama of whores, pimps, and johns to be seen on the streets of black Storyville. Sex could be bought for as little as ten cents in Louis's neighborhood, where violence might explode at any time in a red storm of filthy words and sharp knives that left the whores mutilated or dead, sometimes at one another's hands. (Three-quarters of the arrests made at the Funky Butt involved women.) Jelly Roll Morton claimed that "many a time myself I went on Saturdays and Sundays and look in the morgue and see eight and ten men that was killed on the Saturday night." In a gentler world Louis might have been shielded from such horrors, but the child of a single mother growing up in black Storyville could hope for little in the way of insulation. He had already started to acquire a reputation as a "bad boy" when he dropped out of the Fisk School to sell newspapers, and after hours he teamed up with three other urchins to sing popular songs in the streets of the District for pennies, bringing the proceeds home to Mayann: "We'd go around to gamblers and the hustlers and pass our hat . . . a boy twelve years old bring a dollar and a half of his take home, afterwards divide it up, that's a lot of money." Older musicians took note of their barbershop harmonies. "I want you to go hear a little quartet, how they sing and harmonize," Bunk Johnson told the young Sidney Bechet. But while such recognition might have led to bigger and better things, it seems at least as likely that Little Louis was on the way to becoming another piece of urban flotsam — until he caught the eye of a policeman.

The law of unintended consequences was working overtime when Louis pried open his mother's cedar chest, stole a revolver belonging to one of his "stepfathers," loaded it with blanks, and took it along with him on his nightly tour of the red-light district. It was the last day of 1912, and the city was in its customary New Year's Eve hubbub. As Louis and his quartet strolled up Rampart Street, another boy from the neighborhood started "shooting" at them with a cap pistol. Louis promptly pulled the .38 out of his belt and fired back. All at once a policeman came up behind him and wrapped his arms around the boy. "Oh Mister, let me alone!" he cried. "Don't take the pistol! I won't do it no more!" He spent the night in a cell and went before a juvenile-court judge the next morning. What followed, unlike his birth eleven years before, was deemed worthy of coverage by the local papers: "Very few arrests of minors were made Tuesday, and the bookings in the Juvenile Court are not more than the average. . . . The most serious case was that of Louis Armstrong, a twelve-year-old [*sic*] negro, who discharged a revolver at Rampart and Perdido Streets. Being an old offender he was sent to the negro Waif's Home." The "old offender" was hauled away in a horse-drawn wagon, scared and unsure. All unknowing, he had come to the turning point of his life.

The Colored Waif's Home for Boys was as Victorian an institution as could possibly have been devised in a place like New Orleans. Located just beyond what were then the city limits, it was founded in 1906 under the auspices of the Colored Branch of the Society for the Prevention of Cruelty to Children by an ex-cavalryman named Joseph Jones (known as Captain Jones). He was a hardheaded idealist who believed that children who got into trouble belonged not in jail, where they would be at the mercy of older criminals, but in the hands of reformers determined to give them a chance to change their lives. Captain Jones ran the Waif's Home like a military school, tolerating none of the vicious excesses of latter-day "reform schools." Though the routine was rigid and the food plain — white beans, bread, and molasses were the invariable bill of fare — the young inmates knew that no harm would come to them, from each other or anyone else, so long as they followed the rules to the letter. (If they didn't, the captain beat them bloody.) They woke to the sound of a bugle and spent the day drilling with wooden rifles, cleaning the buildings, and learning the rudiments of carpentry, gardening, and music, retiring to their bare bunks at nine o'clock sharp, there to smell the honeysuckle trees that scented the evening air.

Louis, "being an old offender," may have already spent a brief stretch of time in the Colored Waif's Home for stealing newspapers, though his own memory of a previous visit was blurry at best. Whatever the truth of the matter, we know by his own account that he thrived on the predictability of life there. Except for the Karnofskys, there had never been men in his life who expected anything of him. Now there were, and he knew how to please them. No sooner did he get over the shock of being ripped away from his familiar routine than the eleven-year-old dropout became a model inmate, one whose only wish was to join the twenty-piece Waif's Home Brass Band, whose repertoire ranged from the classics to "When the Saints Go Marching In." According to Armstrong, Peter Davis, the band's manager and director, believed that "since I had been raised in such bad company I must also be worthless." But his passion for music, Davis recalled a half century later, was too evident to ignore:

> He organized quartets, singin', then he'd do dancin' out there, tap dancin'. The boys would clap and sing and he'd sing and dance. And I was playin' in a jazz band at that time, and when I'd leave [my] horn [out] intentionally, he'd sneak around there and pick up the horn and go to blowin' in it. So we had an old bugle out there, and we used to blow the police whistle [to assemble the children]. And I said, "Well, you know, that sounds too

much like jail for children and all," and next time he learned some bugle calls. . . . Louie blew the bugle for the line, the mess calls, and he blowed it so well, I tried him on the horn.

In the summer of 1913 he was permitted at last to play with the school band, first on tambourine, then drums, then alto horn. Eventually he became the band's first-chair cornetist, taking as much pleasure in the unfamiliar classical pieces to which Davis introduced him as in the spirituals that he already knew and loved: "I played all classical music when I was in the orphanage. . . . That instills the soul in you. You know? Liszt, Bach, Rachmaninoff, Gustav Mahler, and Haydn." He can be seen in a group photograph of the band, the earliest surviving picture of Armstrong, in which he looks perfectly serious, as if he knew how important it was for him to be sitting there. Perhaps he did. "Pops, it sure was the greatest thing that ever happened to me," he said in one of his last interviews. "Me and music got married at the home."

One of the unsolved puzzles of Armstrong's early life is the question of exactly when and how he started playing cornet. In *Satchmo* he says that it was Davis who first taught him to play "Home, Sweet Home," and he later told a friend that "I did learn to play the cornet in the Colored Waifs' Home for Boys. . . . The first horn I blew was in Jones's home." In his memoir of the Karnofsky family, though, he goes well out of his way to explain that they advanced him the money to buy his first instrument, on which he taught himself to play "Home, Sweet Home" and the blues: "I *kept* that *horn* for a *long* time. I *played* it *all through* the *days* of the *Honky* Tonk. People thought that my *first horn* was *given* to me at the *Colored Waifs' Home* for *Boys* (the orphanage). But it *wasn't*." He unequivocally denied Bunk Johnson's claim to have given him lessons when he was eleven, though the older man asserted no less unequivocally that "I showed him just how to hold [the cornet] and place it to his mouth and he did so and it wasn't long before he began getting a good tone out of my horn. . . . As for Waif's Home Louis did not start cornet in there because when Louis began going there he could play on cornet real good." Sidney

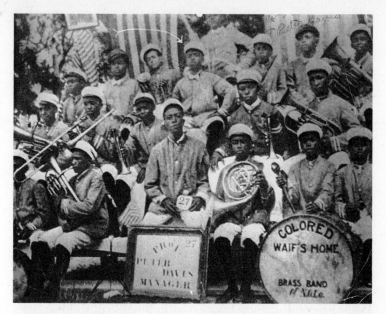

"Me and music got married at the home": Little Louis with Peter Davis and the Colored Waif's Home Brass Band of New Orleans, ca. 1913. This is the earliest known photograph of Armstrong, who is sitting directly behind Davis (the arrow points him out). The inscription at the top is in Armstrong's handwriting.

Bechet comes closest to reconciling these contradictory statements: "Of course, Louis was playing the cornet a bit before he went into that Jones school, but it was, you know, how kids play. The school helped, it really started him up."

One sign that he started playing on his own is that certain aspects of his mature technique were unorthodox. His embouchure — the placement of the mouthpiece of the cornet against his lips — was incorrect, a problem common to self-taught brass players. He seated his mouthpiece low on his upper lip and pressed it too firmly against his mouth when playing in the upper register, and he created his distinctive vibrato by shaking his hand instead of merely rocking his fingers or flexing his jaw. The result of these methods was to place excessive strain on his "chops" (as he called his lips) virtually from the start of his career. Had he demanded less of himself, the long-term results might not have been so dire, but he never held back, even as a youngster, and he split his upper lip a year or two after he started playing. It was the first of many such incidents. Technically speaking, Little Louis was living on borrowed time, and when it ran out two decades later, the price he paid would be terrible.

At the time, though, nothing mattered to him but the horn itself, which gave him a place in the world exalted above his wildest imaginings. Once he had been part of the "second line" of happy stragglers who followed the city's elaborately clad marching bands to and from the festive funerals for which they played "Nearer My God to Thee" at graveside and rowdier fare on the way home: "And when that body's in the ground, man, tighten up on them snares and he rolls that drum and they march back to their hall playing 'When the Saints' or 'Didn't He Ramble.'" The only time that Armstrong speaks admiringly of his father in *Satchmo* is when he tells how handsome Willie looked when marching in those parades. Now Willie's bastard son was leading the Colored Waif's Home Brass Band through the same streets, dressed in a brightly colored uniform of his own.

Louis was so attached to his new life that he was reluctant to leave it behind when the time came for him to return to his family. He had already come to see Peter Davis as a father figure — on occasion he spent the night in Davis's home — when, in the summer of 1914, Willie Armstrong persuaded the court to release Louis into his custody. The boy was skeptical, and not just because he was glad to be where he was: "My father had never paid me a single visit. . . . I had never lived with him, and I did not even know his wife." His suspicions were well founded. Willie's purpose in removing Louis from the home was to secure his services as an unpaid babysitter and cook, and he soon fled to Perdido Street and "that great big room where the three of us were so happy." He never again lived with his father.

As an adult Armstrong remembered the Colored Waif's Home with fondness. "I feel as though although I am away from the Waif's Home, I am just on tour from my own home, I feel just that close at all times," he wrote to Captain Jones years later. Around that time he paid a similar tribute in *Swing That Music*: "I know lots of men who are successful in life are always saying they owe their success to their hard knocks — and the harder the better. I think that's sometimes true and it sometimes isn't. But I do believe that my whole success goes back to that time I was arrested as a wayward boy . . . Because then I *had* to quit running around and began to learn something." He knew that the artisan's way to which Peter Davis introduced him had been his salvation, giving shape to his inchoate yearning for discipline. Mayann and the Karnofskys had showed him how to live. Now he knew why. Music became his reason for living, the untroubled center of his existence. He spoke of his horn as if it were an extension of himself: "Me and my horn, we know each other. We know what we can do. When I'm blowing, it's like me and my horn are the same thing." He can even be heard talking to the instrument on his 1931 recording of "Chinatown, My Chinatown": "We'll have a little argument between the saxophone and the trumpet, 'cause these cats just told me they gonna get away, and the little trumpet just said it's gonna do the same! Ain't that right, little trumpet? Say 'Yes, sir!' Ha, ha, ha, ha! Oh, that little devil."

Nothing comes easily to the poor, and it would be a few more years before Louis could devote himself solely to the pursuit of his art. His first duty was to his family, and he never shirked it: his school days, he knew, were over for good. The morning after he moved back in with Mayann, he ran into a friend who went by the name of Cocaine Buddy (many of his New Orleans friends had that kind of nickname) and said that he was looking for work as a musician. Buddy sent him to a honky-tonk across the street that was run by a man named Henry Ponce. "All you have to do," he explained, "is to put on your long pants and play the blues for the whores that hustle all night. . . . [T]hey will call you sweet names and buy you drinks and give you tips." Louis got the job, which brought in a dollar and a quarter in tips each night (about twenty-three dollars in today's money). It wasn't enough to pay the bills, so he went to his latest "stepfather," who found him a job on a coal cart pulled by a mule. For the next six months he put in ten-hour days hauling and shoveling coal at fifteen cents a load, then came home, washed up, pulled on his long pants, went to Ponce's club, and played until four in the morning. "I loved it," he said years later. "I was fifteen years old, and I felt like a real man when I shoveled a ton of coal into my wagon." On Perdido Street that made him a man, one who fed his family by driving a mule in the daytime and playing music for whores at night.

⟶

What kind of music was he playing? The first chapter of *Swing That Music* is called "Jazz and I Get Born Together," by which Armstrong meant to suggest that jazz was "born" in 1900. Jelly Roll Morton said roughly the same thing, claiming that "I, myself, happened to be creator [of jazz] in the year 1902" (when he was twelve years old). Of course no one "created" jazz, Morton least of all, but both men were right to claim that a style of music preliminary to that heard on the recordings made by the Original Dixieland Jazz Band in New York in 1917 was being played in New Orleans some time around the turn of the twentieth century. It was not called "jazz," however, nor was it the only kind of music played by the dance orchestras of New Orleans, and it was not jazz as the term later came to be defined.

Because no recordings of jazz were made before 1917, we must rely on the memories of the people who played and heard it prior to that time in order to imagine what it sounded like. Their recollections, however, are for the most part both consistent and detailed, and one point that they stressed was that the dance music played in New Orleans around 1900 could be divided into three broad categories. As Pops Foster put it, "You had bands that played ragtime, ones that played sweet music, and the ones that played nothin' but blues." "Sweet music" was the waltzes, polkas, and one-steps that were written out and played note for note at "rich people's jobs." The slow, sensual blues were mainly heard in the honky-tonks and whorehouses of the District. Somewhere in between was ragtime, with its marching-band two-four beat and "ragged" off-center syncopations. No sooner had orchestrated versions of such piano rags as

Scott Joplin's "Maple Leaf Rag" (1899) and "The Entertainer" (1902) made their way to New Orleans than they were enthusiastically taken up by local bands. Joplin's lively instrumental miniatures, like sweet music, were played as written, or with only the most self-effacing of embellishments. "[I]f you played what he wrote," Foster said, "you played enough."

It wasn't long, however, before the "musicianers" who prided themselves on their ability to read difficult arrangements at sight found that their audiences wanted to dance to something more daring than waltzes. George Baquet, a Creole clarinetist who played with the sweet orchestra of John Robichaux, heard Buddy Bolden's band for the first time in 1905, an experience that he recalled clearly thirty-five years later: "All of a sudden, Buddy stomps, knocks on the floor with his trumpet to give the beat, and they all sit up straight, wide awake. Buddy held up his cornet, paused to be sure of his embouchure, then they played 'Make Me a Pallet on the Floor.' I'd never heard anything like that before. I'd played 'legitimate' stuff. But this — it was somethin' that pulled me! They got me up on the stand that night, and I was playin' with 'em. After that I didn't play legitimate so much."

Although Bolden did not record, we know that he was less an outright jazzman than a transitional figure. Morton specifically said that he "didn't play jazz. He was a ragtime player." But Bolden also played the blues, and it may be that he was among the first musicians to learn ragtime tunes by ear, loosening up their syncopated rhythms and flavoring them with the vocalized inflections and ambiguous tonality (not quite major, not quite minor) of the blues. The distinction is a subtle one, for Joplin's rags were written-out reflections of the way in which instrumentalists of an earlier time had "ragged" the popular tunes of their day. The first jazz players referred to the music they played as "ragtime," as did their listeners. A 1913 *Times-Picayune* report of a gunfight at a Storyville club, for instance, mentions that "[h]ere a negro band . . . plays varied rags, conspicuous for being the latest in popular music, interspersed with compositions by the musicians themselves."

However it came about, it was the blending of the styles that turned classic ragtime into early jazz, and by 1912, when the word *jazz* first appeared in print, the change must have been complete. The records made by the Original Dixieland Jazz Band five years later, not long after its members left New Orleans, sound like jazz as we know it, primitive but recognizable, with the now-familiar front line of clarinet, cornet, and trombone playing the loosely woven, rough-and-ready counterpoint that would soon become known the world over. We have it on the best authority that these recordings were recognized as such in their makers' hometown, for Louis Armstrong listened to "Livery Stable Blues" and "Tiger Rag" on his first phonograph, along with the opera arias whose Italianate ardor and showy virtuosity also left their mark on his style. "Between you and me, it's still the best," he wrote of the ODJB's 1918 recording of "Tiger Rag" in *Satchmo*.

By then jazz (or *jass*, as it was then widely spelled) was popular enough to attract the disapproving attention of the *Times-Picayune*, New Orleans's biggest newspaper: "In the matter of the jass, New Orleans is particularly interested, since it has been widely suggested that this particular form of musical vice had its birth in this city — that it came, in fact, from doubtful surroundings in our slums. We do not recognize the honor of parenthood . . . Its musical value is nil, and its possibilities of harm are great." But New Orleans players continued to call it "ragtime," just as they drew a bright line between the trained "musicianer" and the self-taught semi-amateur who could play the blues only "by head." Louis had learned to do more than that in the Colored Waif's Home, but he was by no means a "musicianer." "The only thing Louis could play then was blues," Pops Foster remembered. Nor did the patrons of Henry Ponce's two-room honky-tonk want him to play anything else. The blues were what Little Louis's listeners liked to dance to between drinks, bumping and grinding their cares away.

Louis's first job lasted for only six months, coming to an abrupt halt when Ponce's club closed its doors in the wake of a shootout between the owner and another bartender. The boy dodged a bullet that day — probably not his first and definitely not his last — and considered himself lucky to have gotten away with his skin. Still, his playing had caught the ear of such first-tier jazzmen as Joe Oliver and the trombonist Kid Ory, and the interest they took in the promising teenager would serve him well. He was not yet in a position to set himself up as a full-time professional, though, and for all the pride he took in supporting his family, he found no joy in delivering coal, as we know from a song he wrote as a boy and recorded a quarter century later: *The cart was hard / And it almost killed me up.* He started looking for "a hustle that was a little lighter," even going so far as to try his hand at pimping, an occupation for which he had no aptitude. Women brought out Louis's shy streak, and he later admitted to having been afraid of the "bad, strong women" who sold themselves in the uptown district, adding that "I always felt inferior to the pimps." His lone venture into sexual salesmanship ended in an absurd combination of violence and comedy. The lady in question invited him to spend the night with her, to which he ungallantly replied, "I wouldn't think of staying away from Mayann and Mama Lucy, not even for one night." Enraged, she pulled a knife and stabbed him in the shoulder. When Mayann saw the blood on his shirt, she marched straight over to her son's whore's crib, grabbed the woman by the neck, and started choking her. By then, Louis recalled, Mayann had "got religion and gave up men," and she was in no mood to see her boy trifled with. It took several of his friends to pull her off. "Don't ever bother my boy again," she told her terrified victim. "You are too old for him. He did not want to hurt your feelings, but he don't want no more of you."

Another reason why Louis did not yet dare to concentrate exclusively on music was that he had lately assumed financial responsibility for the care of Clarence Myles Hatfield (later Clarence Armstrong), the illegitimate son of Flora Myles, Mayann's second cousin, who died not long after giving birth to the boy. It was an astonishing thing for a teenager to have done, but he thought nothing of it, for

Louis was the only member of the family who was making "a pretty decent salary," and he took it for granted that that fact obliged him to do his duty. He must have had in mind his own father, who had left Mayann, Mama Lucy, and Little Louis to fend for themselves. Then and for the rest of Louis's life, Willie was to serve as his role model — in reverse.

So he kept on hauling coal and playing as often as he could, which for a time wasn't very often at all. Not long after the United States entered World War I, the Department of the Navy, concerned for the health of its sailors, demanded that the city fathers crack down on Storyville, and on November 12, 1917, the District was officially closed. It was, historians agree, a futile gesture. The only effect its closing had on prostitution in New Orleans was to spread it throughout the remainder of the city, in the process driving down the price of commercial sex. It also put dozens of musicians out of work. The role played by Storyville in the development of jazz has long been exaggerated by those who like to suppose that jazz was born in the brothels of New Orleans. What Storyville *did* do was make it possible for some of the first jazz musicians to pursue their craft full-time. Until he started playing there, Pops Foster had taken it for granted that he would always have to work as a longshoreman to support himself. Playing bass in Storyville, he could count on making nine dollars a week — the top price for a District musician — plus tips that might run as high as twelve dollars a night. (A New Orleans carpenter made about thirteen dollars weekly.) "When all of us were playing the District," he wrote in his autobiography, "we couldn't wait for night to come so we could go to work. . . . Sometimes I didn't go home for weeks."

Louis had expected to join their ranks when he came of age. Instead the rug was pulled out from under him, and he mostly saw Storyville from the cart with which he delivered coal to its tenants. In 1947 he penned a reminiscence of the District for *True, the Man's Magazine,* and his sardonic tone does not conceal the frustration he must have felt at its closing:

I'm telling you it was a sad situation for anybody to witness. . . . [A]t that age — being around from a real young age delivering stone coal in those cribs — hanging around the pimps, Cotch players, etc., I really knew what it was all about. . . . So I had to feel sorry just like the rest of them. . . .

After Storyville closed down — the people of that section spreaded out all over the city. . . . So we turned out nice and reformed.

One measure of Louis's poverty — and his determination to do right by his family — is the Dickensian passage in *Satchmo* in which he matter-of-factly describes how he helped make ends meet by picking through the overflowing garbage barrels of the produce houses in Front o' Town, looking for "half-spoiled chickens, turkeys, ducks, geese, and so on." These leavings, however, were not for Mayann's table. Louis and his mother cut out the rotten parts, dressed what was left as carefully as possible, and "sold them to the fine restaurants for whatever the proprietor wanted to pay." It is an appalling story, and the fact that he tells it without a trace of self-pity makes it no easier to take.

But Louis's luck was changing, perhaps because he was growing more mature and self-assured. He had an affair with an older prostitute named Irene to whom he lost his virginity. Not long afterward he landed a gig at Matranga's, one of the toughest honky-tonks in black Storyville, and made a go of it. Best of all, Joe Oliver gave him one of his old cornets and started tutoring him on an informal basis. Unlike most of the older musicians that Louis met in New Orleans, Oliver was patient with the many youngsters who asked him for musical advice: "I loved Joe because he'd take more time with the younger musicians. . . . [L]ike, you were a boy, you might say, well, 'Would you show me how this passage goes?' You know, you're a little stuck with a division. Suddenly, 'Oh, boy, I ain't got time to be bothered with that!' But Joe would stop. 'Listen here! *This* is the way that goes.'" Louis became attached to the older man, as well as to Stella, Oliver's wife, who fed him red beans and rice and treated him like the son she never had.

When Oliver left New Orleans in 1918, Louis took his place in the band of Kid Ory, who later claimed to have told him that "if he got himself a pair of long trousers I'd give him a job." Working for Ory made it possible for him to give up his coal cart. Before then he had taken little note of anything that happened beyond the city limits, but November 11, 1918, stayed in his memory. He was delivering a load of coal to a restaurant that morning when he heard "several automobiles going down St. Charles Street with great big tin cans tied to them." A passerby told him that the armistice had been signed. He went on shoveling coal for a moment or two before the meaning of the news hit him: now that the war was over, the night-clubs of New Orleans would come roaring back to life. He looked at Lady, his mule, and said, "So long, my dear, I don't think I'll ever see you again." Then he abandoned Lady and the cart. "The war is over, and I quit the coal yard job for the last time," he told Mayann. Never again would he do anything but make music for a living.

It was the second of two unforgettable things that happened to him in 1918. The first had been eight months earlier, when Little Louis Armstrong took a wife.

➤

One of the most remarkable aspects of *Satchmo: My Life in New Orleans* is the candor with which Armstrong, by then one of the best-known entertainers of the Eisenhower era, describes the seamy side of life in the New Orleans of his youth. In 1954 it was no common thing for a famous man to suggest that his mother had been a prostitute, much less admit outright that his first wife was in the same line of work.

Armstrong met Daisy Parker at the Brick House, a honky-tonk across the river from New Orleans that was frequented by levee workers and prostitutes who worked the room on Saturday nights, trolling for customers. One night he noticed a shapely girl looking him over. He introduced himself and they made a "date" to meet after work at five the next morning. When she stripped, he saw that she was wearing padding on her hips and was put off as a result. But they went to bed anyway, and after a few more dates decided they were in love. Like Irene, Daisy was a few years older than her lover, and she already had a common-law husband who caught the two of them together one afternoon (in flagrante delicto, it would appear from Armstrong's poker-faced description of the encounter). Daisy's new beau ran for the nearest streetcar and went straight home, determined to give her up as "a bad job." She showed up on his doorstep a month later, full of reassuring words. They spent the night together at a hotel and were married at City Hall the next day.

"All she knew how to do was fuss and fight," Armstrong later said of his first wife. She was good at both, especially the latter, and most especially when seized with jealousy (for which she had cause — he started seeing another woman early on). Like most other New Orleans prostitutes, Daisy carried a razor and was willing to use it, and she was also known to hurl bricks at her husband's head. After one of their noisier battles, she was hauled off to jail, cursing all the way. On another occasion he awoke to find her holding a bread knife to his neck and saying, "You black son-of-a-bitch, I ought to cut your goddamn throat." For his part he claimed that her refusal to "give up her line of work" lay at the heart of their domestic disputes. Yet he spent "four years of torture and bliss" with Daisy, a prime example of his passivity in the face of provocation, which in this case he could explain only by saying that "we did love each other and tried hard — and that is the funny part of it, and the sad part."

It was an impossible situation, made worse by Armstrong's decision to take in Clarence, who was three years old and in need of a home, and worse still by what happened after that. One rainy day Louis and Daisy were listening to the Original Dixieland Jazz Band on their Victrola while the boy played by himself in the next room. Suddenly they heard him crying. Armstrong ran in and discovered to his horror that Clarence had slipped and fallen off the back gallery of their second-story apartment, landing on his head. The accident left him "feeble-minded" (Armstrong's word) and unable to care for himself in later life. Until his own death Armstrong saw to Clarence's care, adopting the child and enrolling him in "a School where they teach the Backwards Boys." He could rarely bring himself to refer other than euphemistically to Clarence's retardation, writing in 1944 that "[a]s Clarence Grew older he outgrew it all — And now is doing wonderful." But he remained devoted to his adopted son, going so far as to appear with him on a TV show during which Clarence spoke a few halting words. It would never have occurred to Armstrong to hide the boy away: Mayann's son was not one to shrink from his responsibilities, least of all the ones he assumed voluntarily. But it must have put a strain on his marriage all the same, for he was the kind of man who would have reflexively blamed himself for what happened to Clarence — unless he had reason to blame Daisy.

The marriage continued to deteriorate, and when things grew intolerable, Armstrong packed his bags and moved back in with Mayann, taking Clarence with him. Thus he was in a receptive mood when Fate Marable, the bandleader on the S.S. *Sidney*, an excursion steamer that cruised the Mississippi River, invited him to join his shipboard orchestra in the summer of 1919 for a trip from St. Louis to Minneapolis and back. Armstrong was already playing "moonlight cruises" with Marable, who had heard him with Kid Ory's band earlier that year, but this was a different matter altogether, at once a great adventure — he had never set foot outside the state of Louisiana — and a great opportunity. Marable was a stern taskmaster who insisted that his players be able to read music at sight. According to the drummer Zutty Singleton, another of his alumni, "When some musician would get a job on the riverboats with Fate Marable, they'd say, 'Well, you're going to the conservatory.'"

Though Armstrong knew how to read music, he had yet to work full-time with an ensemble that played written arrangements, and he saw in the offer a chance to hone his skills: "Fate Marable had just as many jazz greats as Kid Ory, and they were better men besides because they could read music and they could improvise. . . . I wanted to do more than fake the music all the time because there is more to music than just playing one style." For all the gaps in his training, he was "deadly serious" about his music, so much so that he considered Marable's players to be "better men" than Ory's because they could read fluently. He was well aware that a black musician had fewer career options than a white player of like ability, so it would have been natural for him to want to make the most of the ones he had. Already he was thinking of himself as a professional who could do whatever the job might require.

It was not that Armstrong didn't place the highest value on improvisation. He always remembered with pride the day that the Ory band outplayed John Robichaux's all-Creole group at a 1918 street parade: "[W]e'd proved to them that any learned musician can read music, but they can't all swing." But Armstrong's interest in becoming a better sight reader had at least as much to do with his desire to become a complete artist, a hot soloist *and* a "musicianer," an aspiration not shared by all, or even most, of his colleagues. Even a supremely exciting soloist like Sidney Bechet was content to remain musically illiterate, believing that "[t]here ain't no one can write down for you what you need to know to make the music over again." Armstrong was different. According to *Satchmo*, one of the reasons why he had originally joined Kid Ory's band was that it gave him "the chance to play the music I really wanted to play. And that was all kinds of music, from jazz to waltzes." Ory, he knew, could take him only part of the way down that road. To continue growing, he would have to move on.

Not only was he an ambitious young musician, but he was also an unhappy young husband trapped in a bad marriage, and the S.S. *Sidney*, at least for the moment, looked like his ticket to freedom. So he told Daisy of Marable's offer, explaining that it was his "one big chance to do the things I have been wanting to do all my life." And what were those things? Four decades later he claimed to have been content playing in the barrelhouses of New Orleans: "[W]e made good tips — that is, as far as tips goes, for a barrel house honky tonk. Where nothing but the lowest of guys comes into town on payday looking for anything to happen. And believe me, it did. And I was right in the middle of it all. . . . I was perfectly happy. That was my life and that was that. And I'll gladly live it all over again, so help me." But was he really as happy as that? Or did he have something else in mind for himself, a destiny that he might not yet have fully fathomed but to which he was still firmly committed? "I'm just the same as one of those people out there in the audience," he liked to say, but he also admitted that it was because he had "big things in mind as far as music's concerned" that he had wanted to join the Marable band.

Might Daisy, too, have somehow sensed that her young husband's gifts were too great to be brought to fruition in broken-bottle joints? Whatever she knew or did not know, she kissed him and let him go. Though Armstrong would come back to New Orleans — and even, briefly, to Daisy's bed — he had cast off his moorings and set sail for another, more abundant life.

2

"ALL THOSE TALL BUILDINGS"

Leaving Home, 1919–1924

THE MISSISSIPPI RIVER long ago lost the mythic significance of which Abraham Lincoln spoke when he paid tribute to General Grant's victory in Vicksburg by proclaiming that "the Father of Waters again goes unvexed to the sea." Those who live near the banks of the Mississippi know and respect its dammed-up wrath, but to the rest of us the Big Muddy is not a destination but a landmark, something to be flown over or driven across on the way from one megalopolis to another. In 1919, though, the Mississippi was still as much a legend as a river, not least because it had been the central "character" in the greatest of all American novels, *Adventures of Huckleberry Finn*, whose author also wrote a reminiscence of what it felt like for a small-town boy to have his horizons expanded by the arrival of a riverboat:

> After all these years I can picture that old time to myself now, just as it was then: the white town drowsing in the sunshine of a summer's morning; the streets empty, or pretty nearly so; one or two clerks sitting in front of the Water Street stores, with their splint-bottomed chairs tilted back against the wall, chins on

breasts, hats slouched over their faces, asleep . . . a negro dray-man, famous for his quick eye and prodigious voice, lifts up the cry, "S-t-e-a-m-boat a-comin'!" and the scene changes! The town drunkard stirs, the clerks wake up, a furious clatter of drays follows, every house and store pours out a human contribution, and all in a twinkling the dead town is alive and moving.

The boats that plied the river had already started to deprovincial-ize the Midwest by the time Mark Twain wrote *Life on the Mississippi*, and no sooner did jazz take shape in New Orleans than it, too, made its steam-powered way to sleepy towns whose citizens had never dreamed of such stupendous novelties as a dance orchestra consisting of well-dressed black men who played music as strange as the boats themselves. Most people who know something of jazz know that the riverboats helped to disseminate it, though their mental image of how this happened is often vague. (Anyone who thinks jazz steamed up the river to Chicago needs to look at a map.) Early jazz musicians fanned out in all directions from New Orleans, and the members of the Original Dixieland Jazz Band, who went to New York in 1917, played an even more far-reaching part in the music's spread by mak-ing the first jazz recordings, which within months of their release were being imitated by men who knew nothing of Basin Street, Buddy Bolden, or Joe Oliver. But the riverboats that cruised the Mississippi still have a special place in the history of American music, for they were the finishing schools in which numerous New Orleans instrumentalists, Louis Armstrong foremost among them, perfected their craft under the instruction of a man who knew little of jazz but everything about discipline.

Fate Marable was red-haired, light-skinned, and proud of his for-mal musical training. He was not, however, a Creole of color, and he didn't even come from New Orleans. He was born in Paducah, a town in Kentucky that is located at the confluence of the Ohio and Tennessee rivers, and it was there, in 1907, that he landed a job with the Streckfus Steamboat Line, a family-owned company whose elab-orately appointed excursion boats cruised the length of the Mississippi, promising infinite splendor in their newspaper ads: "One block long, 75 feet wide, 5000 passengers, three roomy decks open on all sides, 500 rockers, 2500 comfortable seats, 5000 electric lights, 1000 electric fans. Best dance music in the United States. 1500 couples can dance on the dance floor at one time!" It was Marable who kept them dancing on the S.S. *Sidney*, having first lured them onto the boat with his calliope solos. His fans included Theodore Roosevelt, who was once seen dancing to his jaunty version of "Turkey in the Straw." Marable was light enough to pass for white, and a 1916 photograph shows him leading a quintet of white instrumentalists, wearing a rakishly cocked cap and a knowing half smile. After 1917, though, he worked only with black players, and in that same year he started billing his ensembles as "jazz" bands. The expression was more than just a nod to the Original Dixieland Jazz Band, which popularized the use of the still-unfamiliar word. A ragtime pianist, Marable had been haunting the honky-tonks of New Orleans and paying attention to what he heard. "We were playing in and out of New Orleans all the time," he remembered, "and I began to notice the type of music they were playing there. It just got under my skin."

In the winter of 1917, Marable and Joseph Streckfus, a white pianist turned steamboat pilot who supervised the music played on the Streckfus Line, started hiring New Orleans musicians for their local cruises. Pleased with the results, they decided in 1919 to send a New Orleans–based group on the *Sidney*'s summer cruise. The eight-piece Metropolitan Jaz-E-Saz Orchestra included Armstrong, the drummer Warren "Baby" Dodds (pronounced "dots"), and the bassist George "Pops" Foster, all of whom would later leave New Orleans to have major careers in Chicago and New York. At the time, though, they were unknown beyond the city limits, and Streckfus, fearing that a full-strength dose of their hot music might overstimulate his patrons, ordered them to avoid the bluesy slow drags heard in New Orleans clubs. Instead the Jaz-E-Sazzers played popular songs, every fourth one a waltz, in the bouncy manner of Art Hickman's successful San Francisco dance band, seasoning them with a pinch of jazz.

According to Streckfus, the musicians "could not get the idea" at first, but as they listened to the Hickman band's recordings, they started to catch on:

> Louie Armstrong, with his trumpet in his hand, came down alongside of the Victrola and would pick up on his trumpet the notes in the several chords in the modulations, giving the saxophone section their chords, likewise the brass their changes in chords, and by repeating over and over again, all chords were down pat. . . . One headlight alongside of me began to shake, the Pilot House shook. We heard loud hollering coming from the Cabin. [I] thought something had happened and quickly went down to the Cabin Deck. The dancers were going off [the floor]. I saw Louie Armstrong coming toward me with his trumpet in hand, smiling and Louie said — "We's got it." I said, "What do you mean?" He said, "We played it slow like you wanted it, and I's put in a little swing, and did they like it!"

The band then added rags to its repertoire and, in Pops Foster's words, "started romping," though Baby Dodds recalled that it continued to play "some semi-classics and numbers like that." Marable left behind only two 78 sides cut in 1924, three years after Armstrong, Dodds, and Foster had moved on, but the band's high-stepping recording of "Frankie and Johnny" (which opens with a quote from *Lohengrin*) gives an inkling of its leader's musical inclinations. While the Jaz-E-Sazzers, as Streckfus's account makes clear, did not rely exclusively on written arrangements, they made considerable use of written-out scores in addition to playing by ear. "We had loads of fun and had an hour and a half or two-hour rehearsal almost every day, all new music," Dodds wrote in his autobiography. "That's why we learned to be such good readers." Marable was a sharp-tongued, hard-drinking martinet, and he required poor sight readers to learn on the job or pay the price. In *Satchmo* Armstrong tells how Marable made hung-over musicians play by themselves at rehearsals, a practice they called "our Waterloo." Equally important was the demeanor that Marable and Streckfus demanded of their employees, who were expected to look as sharp as they sounded — and keep to themselves. The riverboats were strictly segregated, and the black musicians sat behind a railing, never speaking to the white customers. (Blacks-only dances were held on Mondays.) In return for obeying the rules, Armstrong received $37.50 a week plus room and board, twice what Kid Ory had paid him, plus a weekly bonus of $5 paid at the end of the cruise and the chance to work alongside and learn from some of New Orleans's top musicians.

Armstrong himself was already a first-rate player by New Orleans standards when he went to work for Marable in 1919. His technique was big enough, for instance, to allow him to execute the rippling arpeggios of the clarinet solo in "High Society," a jazz tune adapted from a 1901 march that contained a "Stars and Stripes Forever"–style obbligato part originally scored for solo piccolo. "It was very hard for clarinet to do, and really unthinkable for cornet to do at those times," Sidney Bechet recalled with a touch of retrospective envy. "But Louis, he did it." He could also toss off Larry Shields's demanding clarinet breaks on "Clarinet Marmalade," which he learned by ear from the Original Dixieland Jazz Band's 1918 recording of the tune. But he had a lot more to learn, both on and off the bandstand. He dressed like a country boy, wearing a pair of overalls so faded, Baby Dodds claimed, that "it wasn't blue anymore." He had never played for a white audience, taken a train trip of any length, or seen any city but New Orleans. When he got off the train in St. Louis to board the *Sidney*, he naively asked Marable, "What are all those tall buildings? Colleges?" A musician who heard the Marable band there remembered that "Louis was so shy, as soon as he got off the stand he'd run down to the first deck — the band played on the second deck — and wouldn't talk to anyone . . . we were telling him how we loved his playing and he kept his head down, didn't want to talk."

Yet Armstrong's natural gifts were plain to see. Jess Stacy, a young pianist from Cape Girardeau, one of the Missouri river towns where the Streckfus Line stopped, heard him on an excursion cruise and was flabbergasted: "You can't imagine such energy, such musical fireworks as Louis Armstrong on that boat." Marable was determined to mold the prodigy in his own polished image. He would later recall telling him, "'Now, Louis, you are a special trumpeter but you must learn to read. I will teach you every morning at 10:00.' He needed the discipline, needed to learn it." Under the older man's tutelage, Armstrong blossomed into a potent soloist, a fairly good sight reader, and a properly dressed professional. (He can be seen wearing a three-piece suit in a 1920 photograph of the Marable band, his hair slicked into the same bangs visible in the group portrait that shows him standing next to his mother and sister.) He also caught a long-lasting cold that left him hoarse, and he gained so much weight eating the shipboard meals that he had to buy "a pair of fat man's trousers" when he came home. He would battle halfheartedly with those extra pounds, which he wore uneasily on his five-foot-six frame, until a heart attack in middle age forced him to watch what he ate. The hoarseness stayed with him, too: Baby Dodds claimed that "it was on the riverboat where Louis developed his gravel voice."

Between cruises Armstrong returned to New Orleans, where his fellow musicians — even the Creoles of color who disdained kinky-headed players from the wrong side of town — were starting to realize that the no-longer-little Louis was a very special trumpeter indeed. In 1921 he became a "permanent, full-fledged member" of the Tuxedo Brass Band, a mixed ensemble of uptowners and downtowners. Marable had taught Armstrong how to hold his own in such a group, and he marched with his new companions through the streets of the city "as proud as though I had been hired by John Philip Sousa" (whose rousing marches were part of the band's repertoire). In his earliest surviving letter, sent from Chicago in 1922 to a member of the Tuxedo Band, Armstrong told how his new bandmates in Chicago "give me H . . . all the Time because forever talking about the Brass Band And how I youster [used to] like to make those Parades." He was still talking about it a half century later: in 1968 he spoke of his association with the Tuxedo Brass Band as having been a "thrilling pleasure." Joe Darensbourg, who joined Armstrong's All

Stars in the sixties, first heard him with the Tuxedo Band in 1921. "This was before I even knew who he was," Darensbourg recalled. "You could hear that damn cornet two blocks away — I never heard a cornet like it."

Armstrong parted company with Marable around the time that he joined the Tuxedo Band. Dodds said that he and Armstrong quit because they were unwilling to stick to the rigid dance-band tempos demanded by Streckfus. Another musician who later played for Marable was told that "Louis got fired at Burlington, Iowa, for fighting on the boat. They said that [he] was a pitiful sight sitting on a box waiting for the train to come and take him home. Louis was crying rain drops and wailing, 'What will I do now?'" He was close-mouthed about what happened, but in private Marable claimed to have fired him for refusing to continue his after-hours studies. No one knows which version is true, though it is worth noting that Armstrong, who was usually lavish in praising his early mentors, wrote of Marable in *Satchmo* with respect but no great warmth. Perhaps he was nursing a grudge.

In any case he no longer needed the riverboats to make a living for himself and his extended family. By 1921 Armstrong was securely established as one of the best jazzmen in town. "I could read music very well by now and was getting hotter and hotter on my trumpet," he wrote in 1936. "My chest had filled out deeper and my lips and jaws had got stronger, so I could blow much harder and longer than before without getting tired. I had made a special point of the high register, and was beginning to make my high-C notes more and more often." His colleagues noted with wonder that he could read written-out rags as confidently as he played the blues. Whatever else Marable had failed to teach him, he was capable of running with the fastest company that New Orleans had to offer. He would later claim to have had no ambitions beyond pleasing the hometown crowds who now flocked to hear him at Tom Anderson's New Cabaret and Restaurant on Rampart Street, where he "made so much money I didn't know what to do with it."

He could have stopped there, as so many of the musicians he knew chose to do. Late in life he spoke of "an inferiority complex most all of the great musicians had in New Orleans." It was not merely a matter of racial fear, for the city's white players were also attached to its easy, seductive ways, and the clannishness of those who did leave home, black and white alike, was to become a byword in the world of jazz. As for Armstrong, he was still a mama's boy, if an unconventional one.* Even after traveling up and down the Mississippi, he was not yet ready to venture farther. But then he received a summons from the man he loved best, and within days his small world grew infinitely larger.

We know far more about Joe Oliver than we do about Buddy Bolden, but he is still a shadowy figure, visible mainly in the glimpses found in the memoirs and recollections of a handful of musicians who knew him more or less well. Today he is remembered above all for having brought Louis Armstrong to Chicago to play in his Creole Jazz Band, with which the two men cut a series of 78s that constitute the first major body of recorded work by a black jazz ensemble. A few years after that he slipped back into the shadows, dying too soon to profit from the revival of interest in early jazz that gave Armstrong's own career a second lease on life.

Born in 1885, Oliver was a dark-skinned yardman turned musician who got his start playing in brass bands. Stocky, cockeyed, suspicious by nature, and (in Kid Ory's words) "as rough as pig-iron," he kept a gun in his cornet case and threatened to use it on musicians whose conduct displeased him. Yet he was also capable of kindness, as a boy named Edmond Souchon learned when he heard Oliver playing at a Storyville honky-tonk called the Big 25. Souchon had been sneaking into the District at night disguised as a newsboy in order to experi-

---

*One of the funniest set pieces in *Satchmo* is the shaggy-dog tale of how Mayann taught her Little Louis how to hold his liquor by taking him on a night-long pub crawl, at the end of which mother and son were both falling-down drunk.

ence at first hand the new dance music of which his black nurse had told him:

> Sometimes Oliver would come outside for a breather. We wondered how we might approach him to get him to say a few words to us. Finally, I ventured, "Mr. Oliver, here is the paper you ordered." I'll never forget how big and tough he looked! His brown derby was tilted low over one eye, his shirt collar was open at the neck, and a bright red undershirt peeked out at the V. Wide suspenders held up an expanse of trousers of unbelievable width. He looked at us and said, "You know damn well, white boy, I never ordered no paper." We thought the end of the world had come. . . . Then he went on, much more friendly, "I been knowin' you kids were hanging around here to listen to my music. Do you think I'm going to chase you away for that? This is a rough neighborhood, kids, and I don't want you to get into trouble. Keep out of sight and go home at a decent time."

A few years later Oliver took Armstrong under his wing, and Little Louis, who still longed for someone to take the place of his vagrant father, responded with a filial respect whose intensity was documented in the tributes he later paid to the playing of the man he called "Papa Joe." "No trumpet player ever had the fire that Oliver had," he wrote in 1950. "Man, he really could *punch* a number. . . . Fire — that's the life of music, that's the way it should be." A photograph taken in 1922 shows Oliver seated in a chair with Armstrong standing behind him, bursting with pride and looking like nothing so much as a loyal son. By then Oliver had settled in Chicago, where his Creole Jazz Band was fast becoming one of that city's most popular dance bands. But by most accounts, including Armstrong's, he was no longer at the peak of his powers: Oliver was almost certainly exhibiting the first signs of pyorrhea, the gum disease that brought his playing days to a premature end, and seems to have felt that hiring a second cornet player, as so many other Chicago bandleaders were then doing, would be the best way to lighten the load. He had already broached to Armstrong the possibility of joining the band, and in the summer of 1922, not long after the Creole Jazz Band opened

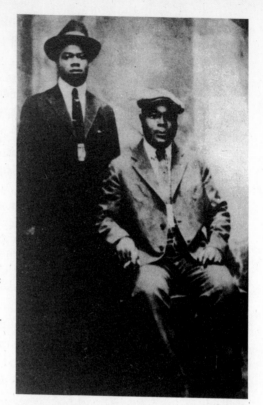

Papa Joe and his protégé: Armstrong with Joe Oliver in 1922

at Chicago's Lincoln Gardens, he sent a telegram to New Orleans saying that the time had come, followed by a one-way train ticket.

As much as Armstrong loved New Orleans, he had thought of leaving it — but only if Joe Oliver asked him. He was too careful by nature, and valued his place in the local pecking order too greatly, to do otherwise. But Oliver was no unknown character: he and his wife, Stella, were as good as family. Baby Dodds and his older, clarinet-playing brother, Johnny, also a graduate of Fate Marable's floating conservatory of music, were already working with Oliver in Chicago. The young Armstrong could not have asked for an easier transition to big-city life — or an easier way to free himself of Daisy, whom time had made no less dangerous a companion. And Oliver was offering him fifty-two dollars a week, more than he'd ever made playing in New Orleans, more even than the Streckfus Line had paid him.

Beyond all this, Armstrong had started to feel another kind of pinch. Although he assures us in *Satchmo* that he enjoyed the companionship of the hustlers of black Storyville, his patience with their wastrel ways was running thin. It wasn't that he hungered to keep company with Creoles. Throughout his life he would criticize blacks (including two of his wives) who had what he called "a sense of *'Aires.'*" But if he had no liking for the fancy manners of the black bourgeoisie, he was growing equally ill at ease with uptown blacks who chose to "lazy around + gamble, etc." while their children "*suffered* with *hunger,*" and his passion to excel as a musician was leading him down a different path. "Now when I was a teenager, I listened to the good old greats," he told an interviewer in 1961. "You know what I mean? The boys around my crowd wanted to go into the next neighborhood and fight and all that, you know what I mean, so I thought they were stupid. See? I wanted to hear the elegant people, and what they talked about in music and everything like that."

In *Satchmo* Armstrong has much to say about Black Benny Williams, a six-foot-six thug who played bass drum with brass bands in between stretches in jail. Black Benny had befriended him when he was still in short pants — Sidney Bechet and Kid Ory both credited Benny with having drawn their attention to his playing — and Armstrong would always speak admiringly of the courage of the older man, whom he regarded as a mentor: "He would not bother anyone, but God help the guy who tried to put anything over on him. . . . Not scared of anyone and so great on the bass-drum, a good heart — he was my star." But toward the end of *Satchmo* he also makes a point of telling how Black Benny greeted him on his return from his first riverboat cruise. The great man asked Armstrong to stand him a drink. Everyone else in the saloon ordered one as well. Armstrong threw a twenty-dollar bill down on the bar, and Black Benny kept the change for himself:

> I smiled all over my face. What else could I do? Benny wanted the money and that was that. Besides I was so fond of Benny it did not matter anyway. I do believe, however, if he had not

strong armed that money out of me I would have given him lots more. I had been thinking about it on the train coming home from St. Louis. But since Benny did it the hard way I gave the idea up. I sort of felt he should have treated me like a man.

That was one of the reasons why Armstrong decided to quit his well-paid job at Tom Anderson's cabaret and go north to seek his destiny. To Black Benny and his New Orleans friends, he would always be Little Louis, the shy, plump boy who played the blues in honky-tonks and was good for a touch. The riverboats, on the other hand, had shown him a world far removed from the one into which he had been born, a place where hard work might bring a serious musician "a *living*, a *plain* life — the *respect*." That was what he wanted, and Black Benny could not show him how to get it any more than Kid Ory could have shown him how to read music. The time had come for him to find a new teacher, and once Oliver's telegram came, there was no wavering. Though the members of the Tuxedo Brass Band did their best to talk Armstrong out of leaving, he remained adamant: "Joe Oliver is my idol. I have loved him all my life. He sent for me and whatever he's doing I want to do it with him." On August 8, 1922, he played a jazz funeral with the Tuxedo Brass Band. Afterward he went home, packed his "glad rags" in a single suitcase, and pulled on a pair of long underwear. Even though it was midsummer, Mayann insisted that he wear long johns — she feared that her boy would catch cold in the Windy City — and knowing that there were no dining cars for blacks on the eight-hundred-mile train ride, she made a trout-loaf sandwich to tide him over. Mother and son then left for the station, where a teary-eyed crowd had gathered to send him off. The next time he saw New Orleans, nine years later, he would be famous.

Armstrong had taken a later train in order to play with the Tuxedo Band one last time, so instead of meeting him at the station, Oliver tipped a porter to put the nervous newcomer in a cab bound for Lincoln Gardens, where the Creole Jazz Band was playing. A policeman spotted him first, saying, "You are the young man who's to join King Oliver's band." Armstrong noticed the use of the unfamiliar nickname: "In New Orleans it was just plain Joe Oliver." Already Chicago intimidated him, and his first impression was identical to the one that St. Louis had made on him three years earlier. "I'd never seen a city that big," he later said. "All those tall buildings. I thought they were universities." Similar scenes can be found in the novels of Willa Cather and Theodore Dreiser, whose characters were knocked off balance by their initial glimpses of the sprawling lakeside city, where new skyscrapers seemed to sprout from the sidewalks every week or so, contract killers were treated like crowned royalty, and even a colored cornet player from down South could dream of someday being called "King" by the cop on the beat. "It was a wonderful place when I was a kid," a local newspaperman told A. J. Liebling. "Guys would be shot down every day on the busiest street corners. It was romantic." Carl Sandburg's poetry is no longer in critical favor, but the lines he wrote about Chicago a few years before Armstrong stepped off the train from New Orleans still convey something of what the city was like back then: *Stormy, husky, brawling, / City of the Big Shoulders.* Lil Hardin, a pianist who had moved there a few years earlier, put it more prosaically: "I made it my business to go out for a daily stroll and look this 'heaven' over. Chicago meant just that to me — its beautiful brick and stone buildings, excitement, people moving swiftly, and things happening."

For blacks who came there from Louisiana and Mississippi, Chicago was the terminus of the Great Migration that brought hundreds of thousands of them north to seek better, freer lives, swelling the city's black population from 44,000 in 1910 to 233,000 in 1930. Not only were Chicago blacks encouraged to vote by the local machine politicians, but they even had a daily newspaper of their own, the *Chicago Defender,* which touted the city as "the promised land" and urged its southern readers to make the long voyage and "join the ranks of the free. . . . Anywhere in God's country is far better than the Southland." Oliver and Jelly Roll Morton had shifted their activities to Chicago, and other musicians were making their way there as well. For now they were mostly black, but curious white teenagers were also sneaking into the nightclubs and dancehalls of the South Side to listen to jazz, and some of them, including Bix Beiderbecke, Bud Freeman, and Benny Goodman, would become famous jazzmen in their own right. Freeman never forgot the bouncer at Lincoln Gardens, one of the spots they frequented: "The big, black doorman weighed about 350 pounds, and every time he saw us he would say, 'I see you boys are here for your music lessons tonight.'"

Lincoln Gardens, the South Side's largest dancehall, was the hottest spot in town, though there wasn't much to the place. Baby Dodds remembered it as "a hall with benches placed around for people to sit on. There was a balcony with tables on one side and the whole interior was painted with lively bright colors." George Wettling, one of the boys who went there for "music lessons," was more specific:

> The thing that hit your eye once you got into the hall was a big crystal ball that was made of small pieces of reflecting glass and hung over the center of the dance floor. A couple of spotlights shone on the big ball as it turned and threw reflected spots of light all over the room and the dancers. . . . The ceiling of the place was made lower than it actually was by chicken wire that was stretched out, and over the wire were spread great bunches of artificial maple leaves.

Once Armstrong got there, he lingered nervously outside, listening to Oliver's band "really jumpin' in fine fashion." Then Oliver burst through the door. "Come on IN HEAH, you little dumb sombitch, we've been waiting for your black ass all night," he shouted. Armstrong listened to the rest of the show from inside the hall, after which Oliver took him around the corner to his flat, where Stella served the hungry men a huge dish of red beans and rice and a bucket of lemonade to wash it down. (Like his chubby protégé, Papa Joe was a big eater.) Then they went to the boarding house where Oliver had arranged for him to live. His room had a private bath, an amenity with which Armstrong, who had grown up scrubbing himself in galvanized backyard laundry tubs, was unacquainted.

The next day he took a bath, strolled around town, put on his grubby tuxedo, and headed for Lincoln Gardens, which was filling up with musicians eager to hear the new kid in town. "The news spread like wildfire," one of them remembered. "It wasn't that Louis' name was then known, but the musicians were aware of the fact that a young trumpet player had just arrived from New Orleans and was playing with Oliver." He didn't cut an impressive figure, though, at least not to Lil Hardin, who was about to join the band and met him the next night: "Everything he had on was too small for him. His atrocious tie was dangling down over his protruding stomach and to top it off, he had a hairdo that called for bangs, and I do mean bangs. Bangs that jutted over his forehead like a frayed canopy."

Armstrong made no attempt to wow the crowd, preferring as always to lay back and let Oliver shine: "I never tried to go over him, because Papa Joe was the man and I felt any glory that should come to me must go to him — I wanted him to have all the praise." But toward the end of the evening someone in the audience called out, "Let the youngster blow!" Oliver stood aside and let Little Louis play the blues. The last page of *Satchmo* describes that moment of triumph, and the last sentence sums it up in eight perfect words: "My boyhood dream had come true at last."

~

For the next year or so, he was as happy as he would ever be. Joe and Stella Oliver continued to cosset their hometown boy, who was now living in a city where (as he later wrote) there was "plenty of work, lots of Dough flying around, all kinds of beautiful women at your service. A musician in Chicago in the early twenties were treated and respected just like — some kind of a God." And he was sharing a bandstand with six friends who were, Baby Dodds said, earning a living doing what they liked best: "Nobody took the job as work. We took it as play, and we loved it. I used to hate when it was time to knock off." The pleasure of which Dodds spoke is evident in the thirty-seven sides recorded by Oliver and the Creole Jazz Band in 1923, though the performances themselves are not always pleasurable to hear. Of their significance, however, there can be no doubt: they are the first recordings in which a black jazz band can be heard in a representative cross section of its repertoire, as well as the earliest surviving sonic documentation of the greatest jazz musician of the twentieth century. All we know about the way that Louis Armstrong played prior to his first visit to a recording studio is what he and those who heard him said and wrote about it years later. Starting on April 5, 1923, we can hear for ourselves — after a fashion.

The Creole Jazz Band's recordings predate by two years the earliest use of electric microphones in the making of commercial phonograph records. The members of the band huddled around a megaphone-like horn that transmitted the acoustic vibrations generated by their playing to a stylus that etched them into thick platters of hot wax spun by a gravity-powered turntable. The ovens that warmed the platters made the studios so hot that, according to Baby Dodds, "perspiration as big as a thumb dropped off us." Each ten-inch platter held only three minutes of music, and if anything went wrong in the course of recording a selection, be it musical or mechanical, the musicians had to start from scratch. Unlike most New Orleans–style jazz groups, this one featured not three but four front-line players — the leader and Armstrong on cornets, Johnny Dodds on clarinet, and Honoré Dutrey on trombone — whose closely knit ensembles were reduced by the primitive recording apparatus to a thick sonic sludge. Nor could the acoustic recording method reproduce the deep, booming tones of Baby Dodds's bass drum (the engineers restricted him to wood blocks and an occasional whack on a cymbal) or Bill Johnson's upright bass (he played banjo instead). It was a frustrating, nerve-racking business, made all the more stressful by the fact that the Creole Jazz Band had to go to Richmond, Indiana, home of the Gennett Record Company, to cut its first nine 78 sides. They were recorded in a single marathon session, after which the band took the milk train back to Chicago, overnight accommodations not being available for blacks in Richmond, a hotbed of Ku Klux Klan activity.

All this helps to explain why the records, at least as far as Edmond Souchon was concerned, "miss conveying the way that Oliver was playing in Chicago when I heard him." Certainly their tinny, congested sound is far removed from Eddie Condon's near-ecstatic memories of his visits to Lincoln Gardens:

> As the door opened the trumpets, King and Louis, one or both, soared above everything else. The whole joint was rocking. Tables, chairs, walls, people, moved with the rhythm. It was dark, smoky, gin-smelling. People in the balcony leaned over and their drinks spilled on the customers below. . . . Oliver and Louis would roll on and on, piling up choruses, with the rhythm section building the beat until the whole thing got inside your head and blew your brains out.

Even less do the Creole Jazz Band's records hint at the stylistic range reported by a dancer who told how the band would sometimes play "seven, eight, nine minutes of a gorgeous tune, a waltz, a ballad." But Baby Dodds thought that they were "very much like the Oliver band sounded when it played in the Lincoln Gardens," and the records also impressed the New Orleans musicians who heard them. Danny Barker, for one, recalled that "those other [jazz] records that had come before seemed like there was something in them empty. They didn't have that kind of beat, and they didn't have all the improvisation that was going on in Oliver's and Louis'."

Today, of course, what matters is not that so many of Oliver's recordings are so dim and distant, but that some of them, played in digital transfers and listened to with a sympathetic ear, do seem to suggest what his band might have sounded like in person. In order to better appreciate the Oliver band's recorded legacy, though, it helps to listen to other recordings of jazz made around the same time. A handful of proto-jazz vocalists, most notably Ethel Waters, a black blues singer with a feel for jazz who later became a pop-singing Broadway star, had already broken out of the rhythmic straitjacket of ragtime when Kid Ory, then living in California, became the first black jazz instrumentalist from New Orleans to make commercial recordings. "Ory's Creole Trombone" and "Society Blues," recorded in 1922, may well be closer in style to the music that Oliver played in the honky-tonks of New Orleans than the more polished dance music that he was playing at Lincoln Gardens. The recordings of the Friars Society Orchestra, the band of white New Orleans émigrés that later became known as the New Orleans Rhythm Kings, are of like interest. These sides, also cut in 1922, preserve a gentler ensemble style than that heard on the recordings made after 1917 by the Original Dixieland Jazz Band and other white groups, and Armstrong admired them greatly ("Oh *what* a band *they* had"). After them, the deluge: Oliver, Sidney Bechet, and Jelly Roll Morton all made their recording debuts in 1923, and from that moment on it becomes possible to track the stylistic evolution of twenties jazz almost from week to week.

Modern-day listeners, however, are unlikely to be dazzled by their first hearing of any of these recordings, least of all those of the Creole Jazz Band. On record Oliver and his musicians stick to a danceable jog, and the most ear-catching moments are the cornet duets during which the rest of the band falls silent and Oliver and Armstrong leap out into space, flying through the air with the greatest of ease. Everyone who heard them was mystified by these two-cornet breaks. "I don't know how they knew what was coming up next," George Wettling said, "but they would play those breaks and never miss." Armstrong explained the secret years later: "While the band was just swinging, the King would lean over to me, moving his valves on his trumpet, make notes, the notes that he was going to make when the break in the tune came. I'd listen, and at the same time, I'd be figuring out my second to his lead. When the break would come, I'd have my part to blend right along with his."

In addition to the breaks, what is most satisfying about the Creole Jazz Band is its smooth, consistent swing, a commodity never to be taken for granted in early recordings of jazz, many of which are rhythmically stiff by modern standards. The moderate tempos that Oliver chose allowed his musicians to stay within their technical

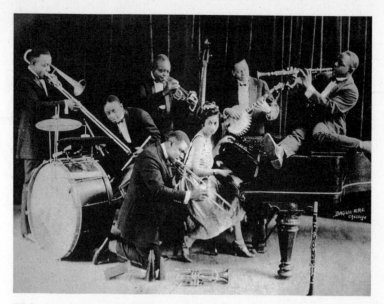

"Nobody took the job as work": A publicity photo of King Oliver's Creole Jazz Band, 1923. Oliver, standing behind Armstrong and Lil Hardin (who married the following year), is as sober as a hanging judge, but everyone else appears to be having a ball. The drummer and clarinetist are Baby and Johnny Dodds.

means, and unlike the Original Dixieland Jazz Band, which could sound frenetic to the point of jerkiness, they played with a relaxed ease that more than made up for their harmonic blunders. (Armstrong was the only member of the band capable of negotiating the chord changes of popular songs with absolute accuracy, and the exactitude of his ear was to be a hallmark of his mature style.) To hear a performance like "Dipper Mouth Blues," whose pungent three-chorus solo by Oliver would become one of the first great set pieces of jazz, copied by every trumpeter who played the song, is to grasp the truth of what Baby Dodds said about the Creole Jazz Band: "The Oliver band played for the comfort of the people. . . . The music was so soothing and then when we put a little jump into it the patrons just had to dance!" The results attracted the attention of OKeh Records, a white-owned label known for its "race records" cut by black artists and marketed to black listeners. In June OKeh, which was based in New York, started making records in Chicago, and the first ones were by the Oliver band, a fact of which the *Defender* took note: "For years, King Oliver's Band has served up jazz to thousands at the Lincoln Gardens, Chicago's dazzling cabaret, but man alive, can't these boys play it, say it in true blues harmony. Why, they are the ones who put jazz on the map."

Though it cannot be right to use the word *innocent* in connection with the music of men who had seen so much of life, there is still something about their records that speaks of the high spirits of youth. It can also be seen in a publicity photo that shows the members of the Creole Jazz Band hamming it up for the camera. Lil Hardin, pretty and slender, sits at the piano, while Johnny Dodds sprawls atop it, his legs askew. Baby Dodds is hunched over his drums, a slight smile on his face. Armstrong kneels in front of the band, playing not cornet but an absurd-looking slide trumpet. Only Oliver seems wholly sober, as well as older than his frisky colleagues. He was too serious a man to go in for such foolishness. Once he went so far as to prepare a leaflet of instructions for his sidemen: "This is a matter of business. I mean I wants you to be a band man, and a band man only, and do all you can for the welfare [*sic*] of the band in the line of playing your best at all times."

The best-remembered number in the band's repertoire is "Dipper Mouth Blues," jointly credited to Oliver and Armstrong and recorded twice, for Gennett in April and again for OKeh two months later. (The title came from one of the many nicknames inspired by Armstrong's large mouth.) He was the first of scores of jazzmen to learn Oliver's climactic solo by heart and, later, to record it himself. "Everything I did, I tried to do it like Oliver," he said. Even in 1923, however, that was no longer true. Oliver used mutes to alter the timbre of his cornet, making it cry like a baby or curse like a man, whereas Armstrong rarely used anything but a simple straight mute and never indulged in the tonal trickery for which Oliver was renowned. It was not for lack of trying: Lil claimed that he spent a whole week trying without success to imitate Oliver's "wah-wah" muted inflections on "Dipper Mouth Blues." "Louis never could play that solo like Joe," she said. "And I think it kind of discouraged him because Joe was his idol and he wanted to play like Joe." But thereafter he cultivated a shining tone that dwarfed the smaller sound of his mentor, just as his studies had given him a foundation of formal knowledge that Oliver, who readily confessed to being a poor sight reader, could not hope to rival.

The gulf that already separated the two men is evident in "Chimes Blues," cut at the Creole Jazz Band's first recording session. "It was just a little light solo, but I like the phrasin' in it," Armstrong remarked in 1956. It was a good deal more than that. He plays two solo choruses, both of which begin with a raggy arpeggiated figure that was worked out in advance. The first chorus, however, ends with a sharp upward rip, the second with quarter-note triplets that float freely and excitingly above the steady 4/4 beat, a pair of devices soon to be recognized by musicians everywhere as Armstrong trademarks. No less recognizable is his firmly shaped tone, warmed by a shake of vibrato at the end of each phrase. It is a sumptuous, arresting sound, much larger than that heard from Oliver in "Dipper Mouth Blues," and it points to the accuracy of a detail Armstrong mentioned whenever he spoke of the Creole Jazz Band's recording sessions: "To show you how much stronger I was than Joe, those were acoustical records, with those big horns; Joe would be right in the horn blowing and I would be standing back in the door playing second trumpet." (Lil remembered him as "looking so lonesome. He thought it was bad for him to be away from the band.") The individuality of his solo on "Chimes Blues" was no fluke. Six months after recording it, Armstrong ripped off a string of two-bar breaks in "Tears" that foreshadow his classic "Potato Head Blues," recorded three years later. So far as can now be known, only one other person in the world could play like that: Sidney Bechet, who was just back from Europe and whose 1923 recordings of "Wild Cat Blues" and "Kansas City Man Blues," made in New York that July, are as daring as "Tears" and even more formally coherent.

Armstrong meant what he said when he called Oliver "my inspiration and my idol." The simplicity and directness of the older man's playing were not lost on his protégé, who forever after would stress the central place of melody in his own style, and the role that Oliver had played in teaching him that invaluable lesson: "Joe Oliver tell me, play the lead, boy, play the lead so people can know what you're doing. . . . Any time you play straight lead, you just as hot as anybody." In later years he would bemuse interviewers by expressing affection for the saccharine whinnyings of Guy Lombardo and His Royal Canadians, with whom he sat in on occasion and whose performances he attended whenever he could. To Armstrong, though, their virtues were obvious. Like Joe Oliver, they played the melody: "You can't find another band that can play a straight lead and make it sound that good."

But the admiring pupil had now surpassed his faltering teacher, and the teacher knew it, going so far as to admit as much to Lil Hardin. "As long as I keep him with me, he won't be able to get ahead of me," Oliver told her. "I'll still be the king." He was not the only one who knew. "There's a kid down there in New Orleans, if he ever comes up here you're dead," a fellow émigré had warned him as early as 1920. "A green looking country boy, with big forehead, thin lips and robust physique, this newcomer brought us an entirely different style of playing than King Joe had given us," Dave Peyton recalled a few years later in the *Defender.* "He was younger, had more power of delivery and could send his stuff out with a knack." The white press, too, was starting to take note of Armstrong. A reporter who covered the Creole Jazz Band's 1923 appearance at a trade convention in Chicago singled out "the little frog-mouthed boy who played the cornet."

Armstrong had heard the same talk. Even before he came to Chicago, his colleagues in the Tuxedo Band told him that he was good enough to lead his own group. He modestly demurred. Yet "Chimes Blues" and "Tears" showed that he could do things with his horn of which Oliver could only dream, and he was uncomfortably aware of the decline in his mentor's technique, which he took great pains to conceal when they played together:

> Knowin' that my tone was stronger than his, see, I would never play over [i.e., higher than] Joe. That's the respect I had for him, you know? But if he would have thought of it, he would have let me play the lead. You notice, all these records you hear more harmony . . . Joe's lead is overshadowed.

It is no accident that Armstrong is featured so stingily on Oliver's recordings — he plays a total of five solo choruses on three tunes — or that his name appears in none of OKeh's newspaper ads for the Creole Jazz Band. His lack of prominence in the studio reflected what was happening on the bandstand. According to Tommy Brookins, who saw the band at Lincoln Gardens, "On [an] evening when he was sick, Oliver played as a member of the ensemble [and] let Louis solo and, believe me, Louis really played, showing everyone present all he knew, all his tricks, and he received after each song tremendous acclamations." Such occasions remained rare. When Oliver first told the members of the band that Armstrong was coming north to join them, they asked "whether he'd let Louis play first or second. And Joe said, 'It's my band. What am I going to do, play second?'"

Left to his own devices, Armstrong might have played second indefinitely. "I never cared to become a band leader: there was too much quarrelling over petty money matters," he wrote in *Satchmo*. "I just wanted to blow my horn peacefully." Like so many men, he needed a woman to spur him to action.

Lil Hardin Armstrong, as she later preferred to call herself, is one of jazz's most underappreciated figures. It was her own fault, for she never succeeded in turning herself into anything more than a fair jazz pianist, and the solos that she played on the recordings she made with Armstrong between 1923 and 1927 range in quality from passable to embarrassing. The record producer John Hammond, never known for his tact, dismissed her as "a ragtime pianist who always reminded me of Minnie Mouse's playing in the early Disney movies." She was better than that — just — but her contribution to the history of jazz arose not from the quality of her playing but from the nature of her relationship with Louis Armstrong. Not only did she pull him out of Papa Joe's nest, but she played as important a part in his musical maturation as had Fate Marable.

Lillian Hardin, like Daisy Armstrong, was older than her husband-to-be. She was born in Memphis in 1898, and her mother set her to studying organ and piano from the third grade onward. Not ragtime or the blues, though: like so many other middle-class blacks, Dempsey Hardin thought them "wuthless immoral music," so her daughter played hymns and classical music instead, purchasing the sheet music to "St. Louis Blues" behind her back. The minor-key cadenza in the style of Beethoven that Lil plays as an introduction to Armstrong's 1926 recording of "You're Next" shows that her acquaintance with the classical piano literature was more than casual, if perhaps not so extensive as she pretended. In 1914 she became a music major at Nashville's Fisk University, home of the Fisk Jubilee Singers, whose polished concert performances of spirituals had helped to make the school one of America's best-known black colleges. Though she would claim to have graduated as valedictorian, Lil actually spent only a year at Fisk, dropping out in frustration when her earlier training proved inadequate to the demands of college-level musical instruction.

The Hardins then moved to Chicago, where Lil got a job demonstrating sheet music for the customers of a music store whose owner booked dance bands on the side. One night she sat in with the Creole Jazz Band:

> When I sat down to play I asked for the music and were they surprised! They politely told me they didn't have any music and furthermore never used any. I then asked what key would the first number be in. I must have been speaking another language because the leader said, "When you hear two knocks, just start

playing." It all seemed very strange to me, but I got all set, and when I heard those two knocks I hit the piano so loud and hard they all turned around to look at me. It took only a second for me to feel what they were playing and I was off. The New Orleans Creole Jazz Band hired me, and I never got back to the music store — never got back to Fisk University.

From then on "The Hot Miss Lil," as she was billed, was a full-time jazz musician, one of a handful of female instrumentalists to be accepted by her male colleagues, though her understanding of the music she played was limited. "I liked the numbers we were playing, but if you'd tell me he was good or that was good . . . I wouldn't know the difference," she admitted. In 1969 Armstrong summed up her limitations with unanswerable brevity: "Read music — yes. As an improviser — *Hmm* — terrible." But she was good enough to satisfy Oliver, and at the time Armstrong found her more formidable. Twenty years later he described her as "a Big High-powered Chick . . . Right out of Fisk University — Valedictorian of her Classes." He never knew that she lied to him, and everyone else, about her academic career, calling her "the master mind of the two . . . Lil with the better education and experience, she only did what any wife that's interested in her husband would do."

Though Louis and Lil were both married, their friendship ripened into romance, and they made other kinds of music together as well. After hours they practiced in private, playing "classical trumpet music" (his phrase) along with the popular songs that were Armstrong's usual fare. It was probably at her urging that he took lessons from a German teacher who tried without success to introduce him to the new "non-pressure system" that made it possible for trumpeters to play high notes without putting excess strain on the lips. They even collaborated on a ragtime-flavored cornet showpiece called "Cornet Chop Suey" that they jointly registered for copyright on January 18, 1924. The Creole Jazz Band is not known to have played "Cornet Chop Suey," and Oliver was incapable of executing so demanding a piece, whose nimble-fingered introduction is reminiscent of the clarinet solo on "High Society" that Little Louis had taught himself to play on cornet.

By then Lil had decided that her beau was more talented than their boss, and she was shrewd enough to know why he let his surrogate father dominate him: "As long as he's with Joe he would never bring himself out. . . . He's a fellow who didn't have much confidence in himself to begin with." So she took his affairs in hand:

> Oliver was keeping Louis' money. He was saving part of his salary for him. So after I started going out with Louis, I said, "No, no." I said, "You don't look right." I said, "You've got to change your clothes." So he said, "What's the matter with my clothes? I bought this from a guy." Everything he had on was second hand. . . . So I said, "Where's your money?" He said, "Joe keeps my money." I said, "Well, Joe doesn't need to keep your money. You keep your own money. . . . I'm gonna look out for you from now on."

Lil bought him a new wardrobe, found him a lawyer, and arranged for a pair of divorces. On August 30, 1923, *Louis Armstrong v. Daisy Armstrong* was filed with the Circuit Court of Cook County, alleging that "on or about the 15th day of February A.D. 1921" Daisy Armstrong "willfully and without any reasonable cause deserted and abandoned your orator, and wholly refused to live and cohabit with him any longer as husband and wife." The case went to trial on November 15, at which time Armstrong swore that Daisy had deserted him. "I went to work," he told the judge, "and when I got home she was gone. . . . I asked her to come back to me but she would not." A divorce was duly granted, and though Daisy petitioned the court to vacate the decree, laughably claiming that she had lived "in a manner well becoming a good, true and virtuous wife," nothing came of it. Mayann came to Chicago and gave her blessing to the couple, after which Lil Hardin married the second cornet player of the Creole Jazz Band on February 5, 1924. Their photographs were printed atop the *Defender*'s wedding announcement: "Miss Lillian Hardin, daughter of Mrs. Dempsey Miller, 3320 Giles Ave., was married to Louis

Armstrong of New Orleans, La. They gave their reception at the beautiful Ideal Tea room . . . The bride was beautifully attired in a parisian gown of white crepe elaborately beaded in rhinestones and silver beads." Present at the wedding, the paper reported, were "John Dodds," "Warren Dodds," and "Joseph Oliver."

From then on Lil devoted herself to persuading her husband to go it alone. At first it was a tough sell. Not only was he happy where he was, but working for Oliver had not diminished his respect for the older man. "Every other page in my story is Joe Oliver," he said years later. "Whenever Joe came to the house you'd think God had walked in," Lil said. "Louis never seemed to be able to relax completely with him around because he was so afraid of doing something that might upset him." But even the starry-eyed Armstrong could see that the Creole Jazz Band was coming apart at the seams. According to Lil, Johnny Dodds found out that Oliver had been skimming his sidemen's salaries, collecting ninety-five dollars for each member and paying them only seventy-five. As Baby Dodds remembered it, Oliver refused to show the band the royalty checks he was receiving from Gennett. The result was the same: everyone except Louis and Lil quit. The good times were over.

Though Armstrong would claim not to have been troubled by the complaints of his former bandmates, he began to pay heed to his bride's repeated assurances that it was time for a change: "I listened very careful when Lil told me to always play the lead. Play second trumpet to no one. They don't come great enough. . . . You know how much I loved Joe Oliver regardless of all that other crap, but still and all, he did make a statement to Lil during a conversation. He said, 'As long as Little Louis is with me, he can't hurt me.'" Lil immediately told Armstrong what Oliver had said, adding that "as much as you idolize him, daddy, you must leave him immediately. Because King Oliver and his ego and wounded vanities . . . may hurt your pride." At length she gave him an ultimatum. "You can't be married to Joe and to me," she said, and in June Armstrong handed in his notice. "You made me quit," he told her afterward. "Now what do you want me to do?"

What he did was start looking for work, at first unsuccessfully. Then he joined the band of Ollie Powers, a singing drummer who was performing at the Dreamland Café, a popular Chicago nightspot. Armstrong was the only cornet player in Powers's band, which pleased Lil: "That's when Louis started playing and showing what he had in himself, because as long as he was with King Oliver he was playing second to Joe and trying to play Joe's solos, which he couldn't play, because it wasn't his style at all." It was a small step in the right direction, soon to be followed by a giant one. Fletcher Henderson, the leader of Harlem's best-known dance orchestra, sent Armstrong a telegram inviting him to join his brass section. Henderson had tried to hire him two years before, but Armstrong was unwilling to leave New Orleans for anyone other than Oliver. Now he said yes. Henderson was offering only fifty-five dollars a week, not the best money he'd made, but enough to make the venture worth the risk, so he parked Lil in Chicago and went to Manhattan to see what it had to offer a promising young jazzman.

The offer was timely in ways that Armstrong could not have imagined. A month after he came to Chicago, F. Scott Fitzgerald published *Tales of the Jazz Age*, giving a name to the period of upheaval that was changing American culture. In 1921 Alfred Stieglitz held the first public showing of his nude photographs of Georgia O'Keeffe; in 1923 Ernest Hemingway's first book was published; in 1924 Paul Whiteman, the leader of a hugely successful jazz-flavored dance band with symphonic aspirations, premiered George Gershwin's *Rhapsody in Blue*. Jazz, too, was being discussed widely and taken seriously in America as well as in Europe, where Igor Stravinsky, Paul Hindemith, and Darius Milhaud had incorporated its jagged rhythms into their music. By 1925 W. J. Henderson, the most discerning American music critic of the day, was informing his readers that jazz embodied "our care-free optimism, our nervous energy and our extravagant humor."

Yet even then most white Americans thought of Whiteman (who billed himself as "King of Jazz"), Gershwin, ragtime, or the Original Dixieland Jazz Band and its many imitators when they thought of jazz. John O'Hara, that most sensitive of social observers, chose Whiteman's 1923 version of Gershwin's "I'll Build a Stairway to Paradise" as the music to which Julian English, the drunken antihero of *Appointment in Samarra*, listens as he prepares to commit suicide. Hearing it, O'Hara wrote, left English "screaming with jazz." Whiteman's "Parade of the Wooden Soldiers" was the most popular record in America when the Creole Jazz Band cut "Dipper Mouth Blues." *Shuffle Along*, the first all-black Broadway musical, had opened three years earlier, but the music of Joe Oliver was unknown outside the urban ghettos, save to the handful of nervy white boys who went there to listen, learn, and buy his records. Unless you happened to live in certain parts of Chicago or New Orleans, Louis Armstrong wasn't even a half-remembered face, much less a paid-up member of the modern movement in American art. You had to look closely to find his name on the labels of Oliver's 78s:

DIPPER MOUTH BLUES

(Oliver–Armstrong)

KING OLIVER'S JAZZ BAND

Lil was right. Second trumpets don't come great enough — not until they go out on their own.

3

"A FLYING CAT"

Harlem and Chicago, 1924–1927

HARLEM WAS HOT in the summer of 1924, in more ways than one. Once it had been a quiet, isolated Dutch farm town at the northern end of Manhattan, but the building of the subway system made it possible to live there and work downtown, and by the Roaring Twenties it was home to two hundred thousand black New Yorkers who sought to turn their piece of the island into a redoubt of which they could be proud. Many were artists — the flowering of artistic and intellectual activity known as the Harlem Renaissance was just getting under way in earnest — and many of the artists were musicians. The music never stopped playing in Harlem, and it was so varied and imaginative that people from all over the globe came to listen. Darius Milhaud had already woven his memories of what he heard there into a ballet score called *La création du monde* that gave European concertgoers their first glimpse of a new musical world:

> Against the beat of the drums, the melodic lines criss-crossed in
> a breathless pattern of broken and twisted rhythms. A Negress

whose grating voice seemed to come from the depths of the centuries, sang in front of the various tables. With despairing pathos and dramatic feeling, she sang over and over again, to the point of exhaustion, the same refrain to which the constantly changing melodic pattern of the orchestra wove a kaleidoscopic background. . . . Its effect on me was so overwhelming that I could not tear myself away.

Splendid as the musicians of Harlem were, though, there was more to jazz than they knew. Ethel Waters recalled with amusement how one of her first accompanists in New York, a university man named Fletcher Henderson who had majored in chemistry before taking up music, found it hard to "give me what I call 'the damn-it-to-hell bass,' that chump-chump stuff that real jazz needs." After leaving Waters, the young man started a dance band of his own, modeling it after Paul Whiteman's orchestra. Like Whiteman, Henderson played a mixture of popular songs, light classics, and jazzy instrumentals, and his musicians were capable of reading written arrangements at sight. That was just what the management of the Roseland Ballroom, located on Broadway at 51st Street, had in mind when it placed an ad in the *New York Clipper* in February of 1924 announcing an opening for "[t]wo high-grade Dance Orchestras . . . Jazz bands will not be considered." The purpose of the second sentence was to weed out groups that were too noisy to please the all-white clientele attracted by the newspaper ads promoting the "matinee tea dances" at "America's foremost ballroom." But every high-grade dance orchestra worthy of the name also felt obliged to employ at least one hot soloist to spice up its music, and so when Henderson brought his band to Roseland, he sent for Louis Armstrong.

Armstrong's new boss had more in common with Fate Marable — or Lil Hardin — than with Joe Oliver. Henderson's father, a Georgia schoolteacher, spoke both Greek and Latin, and he himself cut a figure that a Creole might well have envied. He was tall, slender, and light-skinned, and his upper lip was decorated with a dapper little mustache. "He was a pleasant man, gentle and thoughtful," said Rex Stewart, who succeeded Armstrong as Henderson's solo trumpeter. "He could be frivolous or serious, according to his mood. However, even in his zany moments, there would be overtones of gentility." Harlem's middle-class blacks believed in keeping up appearances, and the leader of so ungenteel an institution as a dance band could only profit from carrying himself with a cultivated air. He expected his musicians to do likewise. "He'd look at your hair, your face, see if you shaved, your shoes, see if they're shined," one of them said. "You had to be perfect to suit him."

Henderson's Harlem was a long way from the South Side of Chicago, not to mention Perdido Street, and Armstrong felt a draft when he showed up for his first rehearsal: "I said to myself, 'These boys look like a nice bunch of fellows, but they seem a little stuck up.'" It didn't help that Henderson was so cool a customer. Armstrong later said that he looked "all sharp as a Norwegian," an image that is both clever and telling. Henderson and his men left behind their own descriptions of that first encounter. Kaiser Marshall, the drummer, said that Armstrong "had on big thick-soled shoes, the kind policemen wear, and he came walking across the floor, clump-clump, and grinned and said hello to all the boys." Don Redman, the band's chief arranger, noticed that he was still wearing "long underwear down to his socks." Having spent the past year blowing the blues with Joe Oliver at Lincoln Gardens, Armstrong was (in his own words) no longer "used to playing in bands where there were a lot of parts for everybody to read." He made several mistakes, joking to hide his nerves, though Marshall noticed that "[a]fter he made one mistake he didn't make it again."

What happened next is best told by Henderson himself:

One passage began triple fortissimo, and then it suddenly softened down on the next passage to double pianissimo. The score was properly marked "pp" to indicate the pianissimo, but when everybody else softened down, there was Louis, still blowing as hard as he could. I stopped the band, and told him — pretty sharply, I guess — that in this band we read the marks as well as the notes. I asked him if he could read the marks and he said he could. But then I asked him: "What about 'pp'?" and he answered, "Why, it means *pound plenty!*"

The musicians broke up, and from then on Armstrong was home free, though he would never feel wholly comfortable in the Henderson band. In public he was tactful, but toward the end of his life he taped a reminiscence in which he called his fellow bandsmen "bighead motherfuckers" and "prima donnas." That sounds right, if not altogether fair. Some of Henderson's men, like Coleman Hawkins, the band's star saxophone soloist, came from middle-class families, and all of them were making a living playing music at a time when most of Harlem's other residents were forced to do menial jobs to pay the rent. It was as important to such men to dress well as it was for them to be able to play whatever their leader put in front of them. One can scarcely blame them for looking askance at a rube in long johns who dared to share their bandstand.

At first Armstrong found his new job challenging. Henderson claimed that he "*really* learned to read in my band, and to read in just about every key. Although it's common today, it wasn't usual at that time to write in such keys as E natural, or D natural, so that Louis had to learn, and did learn, much more about his own horn than he knew before he joined us." And he was as shaken by New York City as he was by his better-schooled, stylishly clad colleagues. "In that big town," he wrote in *Swing That Music*, "I was just a little small-town boy, and nobody much on Broadway had ever heard of me." No less troubling to him was the fact that Henderson's men indulged in undisciplined behavior on the bandstand. About that, too, he was tactful, saying only that the Henderson band was "gettin' a little lackin'." His private reminiscences were a good deal sharper: "After a while the cats in Fletcher's band would drink so much, and they'd come out on the stand and goof, wouldn't keep time, didn't hit notes on time — and figured 'so what?'" Such conduct was bound to enrage a serious-minded young man from Back o' Town who not so long ago had shoveled coal to put food on his family's table.

Armstrong was also puzzled by his bandmates' lack of musical curiosity. At Roseland they played opposite Sam Lanin's dance band, and Armstrong was fascinated by the technical agility of Red Nichols, Lanin's cornet soloist. "Louis and I used to play for each other in the musicians' room downstairs," Nichols recalled. "He was very interested in the false-fingering ideas I was working out and I showed him how it was done." But the other musicians couldn't be bothered to listen, preferring to play cards between sets. Armstrong found their attitude inexplicable: "I could see all these musicians down there playing poker and all *this* goin' on, and I couldn't understand it! I'd just come from New Orleans, where the musicians were very serious about their music. . . . All of my life in music, whatever happened to me that's right today come from observin' other musicians that was playing something."

Before long, though, Armstrong saw that his new bandmates were taking *him* seriously, and that his reputation had preceded him. Not only were New Orleans expatriates talking him up, but the Creole Jazz Band's records had made their way to New York. Once he realized that "Harlem had heard a little bit about me," he relaxed and started to enjoy himself. "What he carried with him," Rex Stewart said, "was the aroma of red beans and rice . . . he conveyed this to the world by the insouciant challenge of his loping walk, the cap on his head tilted at an angle, which back home meant: 'Look out! I'm a bad cat — don't mess with me.'" None of it would have mattered, of course, had it not been for the ace tucked up Armstrong's sleeve: he could outplay anyone in town. That included Henderson's big-headed sidemen, whose tentative solos were put in the shade by Armstrong's lustrous tone and unerring swing. "I was always hitting them notes that them cats couldn't hit," he bragged. No sooner did he make his debut at Roseland than the word went out that he was something special. "Louis played that opening night at Roseland, and my goodness, people stopped dancing to come around and listen to him . . . The next night you couldn't get into the place. Just that quick." So said Howard Scott, who sat next to him in Henderson's trumpet section, and there is no shortage of corroborating testimony, starting with Armstrong's own account of the same occasion: "I *Cut Loose* one night while we were down at the Roseland ballroom and all of the Band Boys just couldn't play for watching me." Coleman Hawkins told of another night when he played Don Redman's "Shanghai Shuffle" so sensationally that "I think they made him play ten choruses. After that piece, a dancer lifted Armstrong up onto his shoulders."

We need not take these stories entirely on faith, for the Henderson band went into the recording studio a week after Armstrong's arrival in New York, and one of the first sides it cut was "Shanghai Shuffle." The band's playing of Redman's arrangement, a coy piece of pop *chinoiserie*, is bouncy but square (if no more so than most of the other records cut in 1924 by dance bands of both races). Then Armstrong crashes out of the starting gate with a syncopated phrase that leads into a blistering-hot chorus in which he pulls one of his favorite musical tricks out of his hat for the first time on record: he plays eighteen Cs in a row, avoiding monotony by varying the accentuation of each one. To modern ears his solo contains no surprises, for the rhythmic language that he was forging on Henderson's bandstand was to become the lingua franca of jazz. But in Armstrong's case familiarity breeds no contempt, and "Shanghai Shuffle" remains listenable to this day.

So does "Copenhagen," adapted by Redman from a stock arrangement that in turn had been based on a recording made in May by the Wolverine Orchestra, a combo led by the twenty-one-year-old Bix Beiderbecke. The cover page of the published version proclaimed it to be "RED HOT as written. Play what you see and the horns will start smoking." Though Armstrong does not echo Beiderbecke's recorded solo in his fiery blues chorus — he probably never heard it — it is touching to think that the two young men who did more than anyone else to determine the sound of early jazz recorded the same arrangement of the same piece within five months of one another. Once again, though, it is no longer possible for us to respond to Armstrong's solo with the amazement of his contemporaries, so it is worth taking note of the words of the trumpeter Louis

Metcalf, who heard him play it at Harlem's Apollo Theater: "Louis' solo was *so* good. But different, and the audience didn't know about how much to applaud."

What is most remarkable about these solos, and the others that Armstrong contributed to Henderson's recordings, is that they *are* solos, brief but potent monologues in which he steps into the spotlight and speaks his musical piece, often accompanied by the rhythm section alone. He had been raised in a different kind of tradition, one in which it was taken for granted that the individual artist, however gifted, would subordinate himself to the needs of the ensemble. In New Orleans solos were the exception, not the rule, and even after moving to Chicago, Joe Oliver would continue to stress ensemble playing over individual improvisation, his own included. As the New Orleans clarinetist Albert Nicholas put it, Oliver "didn't want to hear any one person, [he] wanted to hear the whole band. He wanted everyone to blend together." But the more Armstrong grew as a musician, the harder he found it to stay within the narrow compass of the time-honored New Orleans style. He still loved his Papa Joe — he always would — but he wanted to be heard.

In May of 1925 Armstrong showed Redman "a little book of manuscripts, some melodies that he and the famous King Oliver had written in Chicago. . . . He asked me, 'Just pick out one you may like and make an arrangement for Fletcher's orchestra.'" Redman chose "Dipper Mouth Blues," renaming it "Sugar Foot Stomp" and arranging it in a way that fused Oliver's loose, swinging sound with the yelping clarinets and quacking brass of the Henderson band. Armstrong's contribution was a reasonable facsimile of his mentor's three-chorus blues solo. The results were both recorded and published as a stock arrangement in which Armstrong's interpretation of the Oliver solo was transcribed note for note by Elmer Schoebel, the New Orleans Rhythm Kings' pianist, the first of many occasions on which an Armstrong solo was reduced to musical notation for lesser men to play and ponder. Redman claimed that "Sugar Foot Stomp" was "the record that made Fletcher Henderson nationally known."

In the process it helped spread the word about Armstrong. "From the time Louis catapulted onto the New York scene, everybody and his brother tried to play like him," Rex Stewart wrote. That included Stewart himself, whom Henderson ordered to "play like Louis" when he joined the band in 1926. Henderson later admitted that Armstrong had made the band "really swing-conscious with that New Orleans style of his." Redman agreed, saying that he had "changed our whole idea about the band musically."

Yet Lil Armstrong, whose eye rarely wandered far from the main chance, had noticed when she visited New York that "in Fletcher's billing there was nothing but 'Fletcher Henderson's Orchestra.' Nobody else's name. . . . I cared less about Louis playing with a big-name band if his name wasn't anywhere to be seen." Not only was his name absent from ads for the band's New York performances, but he does not seem to have been written about in any newspapers, black or white, save for the odd item in the *Chicago Defender* and, surprisingly, a passing mention in *Variety:* "There is considerable discussion among colored musicians as to who ranks the highest in the east as cornetists. It is claimed by many that the best two are Joe Smith and Louis Armstrong." (Smith, a talented but more conventional soloist, joined Henderson a year after Armstrong.) Unmoved by the fact that her husband's performances and recordings with the Henderson band were bringing him to the attention of a larger audience, Lil decided that it was time for another change. She went to the manager of the Dreamland Café and told him, "I want to put a band in, I want to bring my husband back from New York, and I want him to be featured, I want $75 a week [$800 in today's dollars] for him, and I want his name out there in front." As if that weren't enough, she then demanded that he be billed as "the world's greatest trumpet player." As soon as her conditions were met, she wrote to her husband and told him to come home. He balked, which didn't surprise Lil: "He wasn't anxious to be a star, you know? He just enjoyed playing." So she fired off a telegram telling him to "COME BY STARTING DATE OR NOT AT ALL."

Two decades later Armstrong told his first biographer that "I had to choose between — My Wife + Fletcher's Band." The choice was made easier by Henderson's refusal to let him sing with the band. In 1922 he had seen Bill "Bojangles" Robinson, the great black tap dancer, perform in Chicago, an experience that persuaded him that there was more to being an entertainer than merely playing well. After that Armstrong danced on occasion with the Creole Jazz Band, but Oliver allowed him to sing only at out-of-town performances: "Although I was a Singer when I joined the King's outfit, and he knew that I could sing . . . he didn't seem to bother. And I did not feel that I should — *force* the issue." Henderson was similarly reluctant to feature him as a vocalist, though he did let him sing in public from time to time. "About three weeks after he joined us, he asked me if he could sing a number," the bandleader recalled. "I know I wondered what he could possibly do with that big fish horn voice of his, but finally I told him to try it. He was great. The band loved it, and the crowd just ate it up." Henderson even unbent to the extent of allowing him to speak a few words at the end of the band's 1924 recording of "Everybody Loves My Baby": "Ow, brother, don't play me that! Ah, now you come to do it! Oh, that's it, boy!" It was the first time that Armstrong's voice had been heard on record, and he bragged about "the compliments Fletcher received, when the recording was released." But the experiment was not repeated, and it irked him that Henderson "had a million dollar talent in his band and he never thought to let me sing." It was then unusual for jazz instrumentalists to double as singers, and it occurred to Armstrong that Oliver and Henderson might not have thought him up to the task: "I gathered that those two Big shot Boys, Joe + Fletcher, just was afraid to let me sing thinking maybe, I'd sort of ruin their reputations, with their musical public. They not *knowing* that I had been singing, all of my life. In *Churches, etc.* I had one of the finest All Boys Quartets that ever walked the streets of New Orleans. So you see? Singing was more *into* my Blood, than the trumpet."

Armstrong might also have been fearing the consequences of an extramarital entanglement. Before he left New Orleans for Chicago,

Black Benny Williams gave him a piece of advice that he later handed down to posterity in a letter to one of his managers:

> He said to me, "You're going out into this wide wide world. Always remember, no matter how many times you get Married. — Always have another woman for a Sweetheart on the outside. Because, *Mad* day might Come, or she could be the type of woman whose Ego, After realizing that you *Care* deeply may — for no reason at all, try giving you a hard time. And with no other Chick whom you're Just as fond of — on the out side — two Chances to one you might do Something '*Rash*' which is a *Mild Word*." I find — the advice — Benny gave me — turned out, to be very logical.

Logical or not, Armstrong lived by it: he started going out with a Harlem chorus girl named Fanny Cotton not long after Lil, who had come to New York to check on him, returned to Chicago and left her husband to his own devices. Little more is known of the affair than that it took place, but the world of jazz, then as now, was a small one, and it is possible that Lil got wind of the dalliance and decided to force his hand.

Armstrong's memories of his break with Henderson muddy the waters still further:

> Fletcher only let me play third cornet in his band the whole time I was in his band. Dig that shit. He'd only give me sixteen bars, the most, to get off with. . . . Every time he'd give me credit for hittin' a note, he always had a little pep talk for me. He'd say, "Boy, that was wonderful. Say, you know one thing? You'd be very good if you go and take some lessons." I'd say, "Yessir!" But in my head I'm saying, you can go fuck yourself. . . . So you can imagine how glad that I was to join my wife Lil and her fine band. She had a damned good band. To me, it was better than Fletcher's. Other than those big arrangements that Don Redman were makin', I wasn't moved very much with them too much. Too much airs and all that shit.

This has the ring of truth, in part because the best of his New York recordings were made under other auspices. Shortly after Armstrong's Roseland debut, Henderson had introduced him to Frank Walker, the head of Columbia's race-records division, and Walker began using him to back up blues singers. Many of these singers, like Maggie Jones and Virginia Liston, are now remembered only because Armstrong happened to play on their records — he cut several dozen blues sides in 1924 and 1925, many of which show him off to excellent advantage — but he also played for Bessie Smith, who had recently been dubbed "Empress of Blues Singers" by the *Chicago Defender*, on nine 78 sides to which he contributed fills and solos. The best known of them is a stately "St. Louis Blues" that remains to this day the quintessential vocal version of the song, even though the two artists didn't get along very well: "I was there to make the records, didn't get to talking to her too much, don't think we spoke the same kind of language."

Better still were the duets that Armstrong recorded with Sidney Bechet for OKeh and Gennett around the same time. Here he really lets himself go, especially on the earthy "Texas Moaner Blues" and two versions of a minstrel-show tune called "Cake Walkin' Babies from Home" in which he and Bechet come out of their respective corners swinging (Bechet wins the first round, Armstrong the second). As fine as he sounds on his recordings with the Henderson band and the blues singers that he was accompanying, it is in the company of Bechet that we first hear the roar of the young lion, who had never before recorded with a peer capable of giving as good as he got. After that he must have found it harder than ever to settle for the "sixteen bars to get off with" that Henderson offered him.

In the end he decided once again that Lil knew best, sent her a telegram that read "I WILL BE THERE," and handed in his notice. The Henderson band threw him a going-away party at Small's Paradise, one of Harlem's fanciest clubs, and Armstrong got drunk and embarrassed himself: "I said — 'Fletcher Thanks for being so kind to me.' And — er — wer — er — wer — And before I knew it — I had 'Vomit' ('*Puked*') directly into Fletcher's '*Bosom*.' All over his Nice Clean Tuxedo Shirt." (It was part of his charm that he could tell such a story on himself.) He went home to sleep it off and caught the morning train to Chicago the next day, there to take up his new duties as the World's Greatest Trumpet Player.

❧

Armstrong had more than a wife and a job waiting for him. He had signed an exclusive contract with OKeh, and within days of his return to Chicago he was in the studio, making records that would be — for the first time in his life — released under his own name.

Ralph Peer, the OKeh executive who signed Armstrong before he left New York, appears to have been primarily responsible for the label's decision to record him as the leader of a five-piece band. It would not be Peer's only major contribution to the history of American popular music. Not long after signing Armstrong, he moved to the Victor Talking Machine Company, where he led a field-recording expedition from which he brought back the first 78 sides of Jimmie Rodgers and the Carter Family. Later on he would work with such noted blues singers as Furry Lewis and Blind Willie McTell. But Peer had no great liking for the music he recorded, dismissing it as "hillbilly and nigger stuff." What he liked was money, and by cutting himself in on the copyrights to the songs that his artists recorded at a time when no one else appreciated their value, he made himself rich.

According to Peer, who met the Armstrongs in Chicago in 1923 or 1924, Lil approached him about recording her husband immediately after he agreed to join the Henderson band. Peer tried him out a couple of weeks after he hit town, with predictably successful results:

> Whenever we needed a New York trumpet player our first choice would be Louis Armstrong . . . So this went on for a year or so and finally [Lil] came to see me again and said, "[Louis] can't stand it in New York." And I said, "Well, now, if he goes back to Chicago, I will do this for you. We will create an Armstrong orchestra so that we can give you some work." . . . [He] went back to Chicago and we sent a recording outfit out to an old warehouse there . . . I'd really set up the dates around Louis. I really did it to get him enough money so he could pay his way up there.

"That," Peer added, "was the beginning of Louis Armstrong." So it was, though no one knew that in 1925, Armstrong least of all. His eye was still on the sign posted in front of the Dreamland Café that proclaimed the presence within of "Madame Lil Armstrong's Dreamland Syncopators," featuring "Louis Armstrong, the World's Greatest Cornet Player." (He wasn't a trumpeter just yet.) Lil had promised him star billing, and she had delivered the goods. "Girl, are you crazy?" he asked her incredulously. "What do you mean, calling me the world's greatest trumpet player? And I *bet* you I don't get $75 a week." But he did, and after hours, usually around nine or ten in the morning, he augmented that sum by recording for OKeh. Lil's band opened at the Dreamland on November 6, and three days later he was once again backing up blues singers in the studio. Then, on November 12, it was Armstrong's turn to shine. He and Lil, accompanied by Johnny Dodds, his old boss Kid Ory, and Johnny St. Cyr, a New Orleans banjo player and another of Fate Marable's alumni, cut three 78 sides whose Cherokee-red labels identified them as the work of "Louis Armstrong and His Hot Five," the first chapters in what was to become the Old Testament of classic jazz.

"Gut Bucket Blues," the third of the four dozen small-group sides that Louis and Lil recorded together between 1925 and 1927 and the first to be released, starts out with a twangy banjo solo over which Armstrong shouts a few words of encouragement in the same high-pitched voice heard on "Everybody Loves My Baby": "Aw, play that thing, Mr. St. Cyr, lawd! You know you can do it — everybody from New Or-*leans* can really do that thing. Hey, hey!" He lifts his cornet to his lips and starts to blow, and the rest of the band tumbles in behind him. They play two choruses of the blues, after which the other musicians solo, with Armstrong introducing each one in turn: "Ah, whip that thing, Miss Lil! Whip it, kid! Aw, pick that piano, yeah . . . Blow that thing, Mr. Johnny Dodds! Ah, toot that clarinet, boy." Then Armstrong takes center stage with a penetrating solo in which he returns repeatedly to a flatted third, the same "blue" note around which King Oliver built the first chorus of his "Dipper Mouth

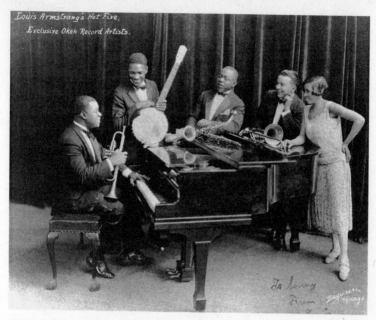

Louis Armstrong's Hot Five,
Exclusive Okeh Record Artists.

The Hot Five, 1926. From left: Armstrong, Johnny St. Cyr, Johnny Dodds, Kid Ory, and Lil Armstrong. Though they performed together only once in public, their recordings for OKeh made them the most significant band in the history of jazz.

Blues" solo. The other horn players come back for a final ensemble chorus, to which Armstrong appends a two-bar break prefaced by one of his now-familiar upward rips.

That's all there is to "Gut Bucket Blues," and according to St. Cyr, it didn't take much longer to come up with the number than it did to play it. Elmer Fearn, who produced the session, had asked for a blues:

> So we made a short rehearsal and cut the number. When Mr. [Fearn] asked, "What shall we name it?," Louis thought for a while and then said, "Call it 'The Gut Bucket.'" Louis could not explain the meaning of the name. He said it just came to him. But I will explain it. In the fish markets in New Orleans the fish cleaners keep a large bucket under the table where they clean

the fish, and as they do this they rake the guts in this bucket. Thence "The Gut Bucket," which makes it a low down blues.

Armstrong was allowed to pick his own sidemen, but because OKeh was still using acoustic equipment to record its Chicago sessions, the Hot Five included neither a bassist nor a drummer, and Lil's commonplace accompaniments were a far cry from the stodgy but sure backing of Henderson's four-man rhythm section. Even so, the little band works up a rocking swing that conceals the anxiety felt by its members. Armstrong spoke of it in an article he wrote for *Esquire* in 1951: "[W]hen we went down to the Okeh Recording Company for the first time, we were all Mike Fright. We did not realize just how much we were frightened—until the day we recorded the 'Gut Bucket Blues.'" By session's end, though, they had the hang of it, and from then on "we began to really get into the groove, the New Orleans groove."

As well as playing with the Hot Five, Armstrong seized the opportunity to sing, and on "Heebie Jeebies," recorded at the band's third session for OKeh in February of 1926, he introduced a novelty with which he would thereafter be identified. Instead of singing the words to the second verse, he replaced them with improvised nonsense syllables: *Eeeff, goff, oomff, dee-buht, deedle-la-bahm,* rrrip-*bip-di-doo-di-doot.* He had been singing that way since childhood, though his decision to "scat" (as it was known in New Orleans) on "Heebie Jeebies" was an improvisation born of necessity. He loved to tell how it happened: "I dropped the paper with the lyrics—right in the middle of the tune...And I did not want to stop and spoil the record which was moving along so wonderfully...So when I dropped the paper, I immediately turned back into the horn and started to Scatting...Just as [if] nothing had happened...When I finished the record I just knew the recording people would throw it out...And to my surprise they all came running out of the controlling booth and said—'Leave That In.'"

Armstrong didn't invent scat singing, but it was his version of it that caught on. "Heebie Jeebies" is said to have sold some forty thousand copies, a high number for a race record by a little-known artist, and though OKeh made no mention of his singing in its advertisements for the record, many who heard it were moved to imitation. A clipping preserved in Armstrong's scrapbooks reports that "Louis Armstrong sure has the loop cornetists [i.e., the cornetists of Chicago's Loop] working hard to imitate him. Some time ago we heard one trying to imitate Louis singing 'Heebie Jeebies.'" "You would hear cats greeting each other with Louis's riffs when they met around town," Mezz Mezzrow, a white musician who later befriended Armstrong, wrote in his memoirs. Mezzrow also described Bix Beiderbecke's reaction to hearing "Heebie Jeebies" for the first time: "'Ha! Ha! Ha!' Bix kept chuckling as the record played over and over, and his long bony arms beat out the breaks, flailing through the air like the blades of a threshing machine."

Beiderbecke's laughter reminds us that Armstrong's music, like his personality, was fundamentally optimistic. "You're crying in your horn, all right, but it's the audience that should cry, not you," Joe Oliver had told him. "You have to learn to never wear the trouble in your face." It was a piece of advice that he never forgot, perhaps because it suited him better than it did Oliver. Armstrong was a major-key artist who would always be disinclined to lament the woes of the world, aware of them though he was, and because comedy came so naturally to him, it was no less natural for him to incorporate it into his music. From the beginning OKeh advertised the Hot Five in black newspapers, and the copy is often revealing, as in the case of the ad for "Big Fat Ma and Skinny Pa," one of the band's many recordings of minstrel-style comic songs: "There's a world of amusement in store for you, when you hear Louis Armstrong sing this comical tune. Louis' Hot Five sure do blow a mean fox trot accompaniment. You won't know whether to let your feet do their stuff — or just sit down and shake yourself with laughter." In addition to singing such songs, Armstrong often incorporated miniature comedy skits into the Hot Five's recordings, and OKeh's newspaper ads suggest that his listeners shared his taste for the broad-brush ethnic humor on which he had been raised.* To be sure, there was nothing out of the ordinary about such Hot Five sides as "Don't Forget to Mess Around," whose lyrics pay tribute to a Charleston-type dance step of the twenties, or "Big Butter and Egg Man," on which Armstrong can be heard "courting" May Alix, a now-forgotten Chicago nightclub singer: *I'll play you a little minor in G / And if you say it's necessary, baby, why, I'll even hit high C!* Jelly Roll Morton's recordings, as well as many others of the period, are full of the same sort of hokum. The difference is that Armstrong, unlike Morton, lived long enough to be criticized for his sense of humor by younger blacks who were unaware (or unwilling to admit) that their parents had found it uproariously funny.

Armstrong's contract with OKeh stipulated that he would "not make records for any company other than our own organization or as a part of any other musical unit." Later that year Elmer Fearn heard him on a record released by another label and called him on the carpet. "Do you know who is singing, Louis?" Fearn asked. "I don't know, sir," he replied, "but I won't do it again." The story points to another important aspect of his early recordings, which is that the inclusion of his voice, whether singing or speaking, helped to humanize them. Even before his face became known to the readers of newspapers and illustrated magazines — and, later, to filmgoers and TV viewers — Armstrong was the first jazz musician whose voice was heard by large numbers of people. In this way he emerged from behind the anonymity of the recording process and impressed his personality on all who heard him, even those who found most instrumental jazz to be unapproachably abstract. It was the secret of his appeal, and he knew it. So did the many singing instrumentalists who followed in his footsteps, hoping to lure some of the same listeners

---

*Armstrong's record collection contained numerous 78s by Bert Williams, the black vaudevillian whom W. C. Fields called "the funniest man I ever saw." In 1938 he made his own commercial recordings of two comic monologues, "Elder Eatmore's Sermon on Generosity" and "Elder Eatmore's Sermon on Throwing Stones," originally recorded by Williams in 1914.

who smiled at the sound of his gritty tenor voice, which deepened as he grew older but was always as recognizable as a fingerprint.

Kid Ory remembered the Hot Five sessions as freewheeling and companionable. "Our recording sessions," he wrote, "would start this way: the OKeh people would call up Louis and say they wanted so many sides. They never told him what numbers they wanted or how they wanted them. . . . After we'd make a side, Louis would say, 'Was that all right?' And if one of us thought we could do it over and do it better, why Louis would tell them to do it again, and so we would do it over." Though Armstrong was the leader, he gave his sidemen plenty of leeway, and they had no trouble meeting his demands, especially since, as Ory pointed out, they were all old friends who "knew each other's musical styles so well from years of working together." Baby Dodds, who played with the band a year and a half later, recalled its rehearsals, held in the Armstrongs' living room, in the same way: "He would tell each of us when to take a solo or when not to, and who would come in at different times. We weren't a bunch of fellows to write down anything. That would have made it too mechanical. We would stop and talk it over more than anything else. If there was any writing involved Lil would write down what the musicians were supposed to do."

No longer strapped into Henderson's tightly organized routines, Armstrong was free to experiment, and his creative resourcefulness grew from session to session. He was not infallible: he drops the ball in the eleventh bar of an otherwise superb solo on "Savoy Blues," for instance, blotting his copybook with a couple of fumbled notes. But even on an off day no one in the band could touch him (though Johnny Dodds's more conservative style was compelling in its own way). "Cornet Chop Suey," recorded the same day as "Heebie Jeebies," is one of the many sides on which his sidemen fade into the woodwork, leaving the prodigy alone at center stage. For such feats of musical derring-do, he accepted a flat fee of fifty dollars a side, the same way that he took one-time cash payments for the tunes he wrote for the Hot Five to record: "We used to sit on the back stairs with Lil and write five or six numbers at a time and take 'em downtown and sell them to OKeh, ya know, right quick. We weren't payin' attention to the royalties and all that [in] those days." It was, all things considered, the deal of the century. Not only did the Hot Five's 78s, priced at seventy-five cents each, sell well, but they continue to be reissued to this day.

Even without royalties, though, it was a better deal for Armstrong. In 1925 he was an admired sideman with a modest following. By the end of 1927 he was the most important soloist in jazz, the man to whom other musicians looked for inspiration, and it was his records that showed them the way. "You couldn't buy his records [in Chicago] when they first came out, because they were selling like hotcakes," the trumpeter Doc Cheatham later recalled. "All the stores that sold records, even grocery stores, were selling his records." The New Orleans trumpeter Wingy Manone played the Hot Five's "Oriental Strut" for a young trombonist named Jack Teagarden one day in New Mexico, and the two men decided on the spot to pay homage to its maker. "We had heard that if you buried things out there on the mesa they would be petrified like all the old trees and stuff that had turned to stone," Manone wrote in his memoirs. "So one day Jack and I took Louis' record of 'Oriental Strut' and drove out on the mesa with it. We dug a big hole and laid that record away, and as far as I know it is still there today."

The original Hot Five performed together in public only once, at an "OKeh Cabaret and Style Show" presented by the record company at the Chicago Coliseum on June 12, 1926. The *Chicago Defender* reported that the group "broke up the big ball . . . with their hot playing," but it was nothing more than a publicity stunt, for Armstrong, like his sidemen, was too busy with his regular gigs to make personal appearances with the Hot Five. The *Defender* had already treated his return to Chicago as news: "Mr. Armstrong, the famous cornetist, will grace the first chair in the Dreamland Orchestra sometime this week." Two weeks later it proclaimed "the feature man in Lil's new band at the Dreamland" to be "the jazz cornet king . . . the king of them all." By then he was keeping a scrapbook, and the *Defender* gave him plenty of stories to clip.

In addition to playing at the Dreamland, Armstrong joined the "Little Symphony," the fifteen-piece ensemble that played under the violinist-conductor Erskine Tate at the 1,300-seat Vendome Theater, the South Side's biggest movie house, whose orchestra pit was outfitted with a ten-thousand-dollar pipe organ. Like most such groups, the Vendome band not only accompanied the silent films shown at the theater but played pop tunes and light classics between screenings. It is unlikely that Armstrong kidded about "pounding plenty" when the conservatory-trained Tate (whom he addressed, not ironically, as "Professor") was on the podium. He had long been eager "to get the experience of playing Classic and Symphony Music," and Tate gave it to him. One of his featured numbers was the "Intermezzo sinfonico" from Mascagni's *Cavalleria Rusticana*, the resplendent operatic interlude on which he later liked to warm up. Tate also encouraged him to show off his jazz chops: "I was at home then, 'cos that's what they hired me for, anyway, them hot numbers. That's when I could hit 50 high C's and more, maybe pick up a megaphone and sing a few choruses on 'Heebie Jeebies' or sump'n." Doc Cheatham said that "whenever Louis would play, stand up and play that solo at the Vendome, the people would start screaming. You couldn't hear what he was playing for a few bars." He recorded two numbers with the Vendome band, and "Stomp Off, Let's Go" shows that it was a bristlingly hot group, one of the best with which he played in the twenties.*

Armstrong was as proud of his stint with Tate as Bix Beiderbecke was of the two years he spent playing in Paul Whiteman's brass section, and for much the same reason. It showed that he had become a "musicianer," capable of playing anything the job required, be it Mascagni or "Heebie Jeebies." But he also continued to work with

---

*It was at the Vendome that Armstrong made the switch from cornet to trumpet, the instrument played by the orchestra's first-chair trumpeter. He later explained that he did so because Tate thought his "stubby little cornet" looked out of place.

Lil at the Dreamland, and the awkward fact that his wife was his boss did not go unnoticed by his fellow musicians. They dubbed him "Henpeck," a nickname he affected not to resent: "The guys who called me 'Henpeck,' all the time they did it, I know they were broke all the time and I always had a pocket full of money. . . . Lil saw to that." One may take leave to question his sincerity. Armstrong was not the first man to marry an ambitious, determined woman, then grow tired of letting her run his life, astute though her suggestions might be — and he would never cease to acknowledge how valuable they had been. He was grateful, for instance, when Lil seized the initiative and bought an eleven-room house for the young couple (and for Clarence, Armstrong's adopted son, who had come north to live with them, much to Lil's displeasure). He saw it for the first time on his return from New York and was agog. "You're a magician!" he told her. But he no longer cared for her hectoring, and their marriage became an on-and-off affair. "Whenever we'd break up," he remembered, "we'd draw all of our money out of the bank and split it up."

Early in 1926 he started seeing a pretty teenager named Alpha Smith who came to the Vendome regularly, always sitting in the front row. Armstrong had firm views on what made a woman desirable: "First thing I look at is her general shape. It must be sharp and full of nice curves. Then I dig her clothes, the way she wears them and how they fit her and her personality. Then I dig her lips. I like kissable lips. A woman's lips must say, 'Come here and kiss me, Pops.'" Alpha's lips filled the bill, and soon the two of them "began to get Thicker + Thicker," especially after it came to Armstrong's attention that Lil was "Running Around with one of the Chicago 'Pimps' while I was at work." Unlike Lil, of whose *"Aires"* he had had enough, Alpha made no pretense of gentility: "She was a poor girl — not near as Fortunate as Lil was when I First met her — Maybe the one reason why Lil + I didn't make a good go of married life together. . . . We were always Fussing and threatening to Break up if I sat on the Bed after it was made up." Lil knew that she was partly to blame. "Poor Louis never had a chance," she said. "I was on him for breakfast, dinner and supper, as the saying goes. No wonder he soon sought the companionship of less exacting women. But I was in love and I wanted him to be a great man." Her love was not enough to hold him: he and Clarence moved in with Alpha and her family in the spring of 1926, and in April he quit the Dreamland band. Louis and Lil were not done with one another — they continued to record together through the end of 1927, and there would be intermittent attempts at reconciliation for a few years after that — but their marriage was for all intents and purposes over.

Armstrong went to work for Carroll Dickerson, the bandleader at the Sunset Café, a "black-and-tan" club with a racially mixed clientele. This put him in competition with Joe Oliver, whose new band, the Dixie Syncopators, was playing across the street at the Plantation Club. Armstrong had considered rejoining Oliver, but Dickerson's keyboard man, a pianist from Pittsburgh named Earl Hines, talked him out of it. "Why don't you come on over with us young fellows?" he suggested. Armstrong had jammed with Hines and liked his playing. He also liked the idea of working with Zutty Singleton, Dickerson's drummer, with whom he had been friendly ever since his New Orleans days. Dickerson sealed the deal by offering him ten dollars a week more than Oliver was willing to pay, and he made up his mind to go with the young fellows.

Oliver was furious to find himself up against his protégé. "Close those windows," he warned Armstrong, "or I'll blow you off Thirty-Fifth Street!" One night, according to the cornetist Wild Bill Davison, the two men dueled on the bandstand of the Sunset Café, playing "125 choruses of Tiger Rag — exchanging choruses. People went insane — they threw their clothes on the floor — it was the most exciting thing I ever heard in my life." The fact that the younger man had become so popular must have made the encounter all the more galling. "Wasn't long before all Joe Oliver's crowds was coming to hear me," Armstrong said. "Wasn't nothing to be done about it but ask Joe Oliver if there was anything I can do for him. The Sunset was packed every night." Eddie Condon later wrote that there was so much hot music to be heard in that part of town that a passerby standing on the corner of 35th and Calumet "could hold an instrument in the middle of the street and the air would play it."

Joe Glaser, the manager, soon saw that Armstrong was the club's main draw, so when Dickerson got in trouble for flirting with one of the white patrons, Glaser fired him, renamed the band "Louis Armstrong and His Sunset Stompers," and put Armstrong's name in lights, billing him as "The World's Greatest Trumpeter." The gesture made a deep impression on Armstrong: "I couldn't help thinking I had travelled pretty far since I'd left the Waif's Home, a little more than ten years before." So did Glaser himself, a lower-tier gangster who made no secret of his ties to Al Capone, whose syndicate controlled the Sunset. Armstrong had known such men since childhood, and he and Glaser hit it off: "I always admired Mr. Glaser from the first day I started working for him. He just *impressed* me different than the other Bosses I've worked for. He seemed to understand Colored people so much. And he was wonderful to his whole show and Band—Would give us nice presents etc. And don't you think for once that Mr. Glaser didn't *Pitch a Bitch* when things aren't Jumping Right."

Armstrong remembered Capone as "a nice little cute fat boy— young—like some professor who had just come out of college to teach or something." But it was Glaser whom he trusted, especially after the manager of the Sunset Café stood up to Capone on his behalf:

> When one of Capone's Boys told Joe Glaser that he must take the name *Louis Satchmo Armstrong* down from the *Marquee* LIGHTS because this is a small world and very few *people*— "*know Louis Armstrong*" and his *greatness*, Mr Glaser *still* standing at the door of the *Sunset Café* (Chicago) sharp as a tack *TACK*— "29" years old, THREE "YEARS" older than *ME* at that time. When this *ugly Gangster* told Joe Glaser that he *must* take the *name* of ARMSTRONG down— off of the *Marquee* and it was an "order from *Al Capone*" Mr Glaser *looked* this *Cat* straight in the face, and *told* him *these* words— I think that *Louis* Armstrong is the *world's greatest* and *this* is *my place* and I *defy* *any*body to take his *name down* from there. And *that* was *that*.

The Sunset Café offered its customers not just the World's Greatest Trumpeter but a floor show complete with chorus girls, comedians, and a tap-dancing master of ceremonies (plus a brothel upstairs). The musical fare was stylish for a mob-run joint: Bud Freeman recalled hearing Armstrong blow "twenty or more improvised choruses" on Noël Coward's "Poor Little Rich Girl." In addition to singing and playing, he took part in the floor show, hurling himself into the proceedings with the same happy abandon he brought to the comedy routines heard on the Hot Five's records: "Zutty . . . would dress up as one of these real loud and rough gals, with a short skirt, and a pillow in back of him. I was dressed in old rags, the beak of my cap turned around like a tough guy, and he, or she, was my gal."

The crowds loved it all, and so did Armstrong. "I was young and strong, a flying cat, and God, I blew the people right out of that place," he remembered. Musicians flocked to hear him, too, among them Bix Beiderbecke and Wingy Manone, to whom he confided the "secret" of how he improvised lengthy solos without seeming to repeat himself: "Well, I tell you . . . the first chorus I plays the melody. The second chorus I plays the melody round the melody, and the third chorus I routines." Like so many of Armstrong's quips, this one turns out on closer inspection to be less amusing than true. Comparatively straightforward theme statements, subtly varied melodic paraphrases, and climactic set-piece "routines" were the building blocks of his best-known solos, and he assembled them not piecemeal but with a cumulative continuity that caught the ear of younger players. For the trumpeter Roy Eldridge, it was this continuity that set Armstrong's solos apart from those of his contemporaries: "He started out like a new book, building and building, chorus after chorus, and finally reaching a full climax . . . He was building all the time instead of just playing in a straight line."

The Stompers made only one record, a strutting version of Jelly Roll Morton's "Chicago Breakdown," but it is enough to suggest the band's quality. Armstrong's onstage merriment, however, was too much for Dave Peyton, a black bandleader of Whiteman-esque inclination who covered the local music scene for the *Defender* and sniffily assured its readers that the Sunset Café band was "noisy, corrupt, contemptible, and displeasing to the ear. You have to put your ear muffs on to hear yourself talk in the place. Louis will learn in time to come that noise isn't music." In fact Peyton admired Armstrong, covered him in the pages of the *Defender*, and even played with him on occasion. When it came to black bands, though, he was as fussy as Fletcher Henderson and believed Armstrong's cavorting to be incompatible with the dignity he thought appropriate to "the greatest cornet player in the country." He was the first of countless high-minded critics who would prove incapable of coming to terms with Armstrong's artistic populism, though it was as much a part of him as his gravelly voice.

Not long after going to work for Glaser and Capone, Armstrong quit Professor Tate's Little Symphony and started gigging around town after hours. In between shows he visited the OKeh studios as often as he could, passing miracles at fifty dollars a throw. "I never had any time to be at home, except just for a few hours' sleep," he recalled in *Swing That Music*. "I met myself coming and going." Somewhere along the way he "wrote" *Louis Armstrong's 125 Jazz Breaks for Cornet* and *Louis Armstrong's 50 Hot Choruses for Cornet*, a pair of folios published by Melrose Music whose contents consisted of notated solos transcribed from specially made cylinder recordings of his playing. The volumes sold for a dollar apiece, and the fee Armstrong received for them was large enough to pay for his first car, "a cute little Hupmobile." The cover of *125 Jazz Breaks for Cornet* bore the following "publisher's note": "Throughout the world the name of Louis Armstrong is known to thousands of musicians. It is accepted by interpreters of jazz and commands at all times a place of honor." As indicative of Armstrong's local celebrity was Dave Peyton's coverage in the *Defender* of the publication of *125 Jazz Breaks* and *50 Hot Choruses*, which he described in language that the earnest young man whose face was emblazoned on their covers must have appreciated: "Louis Armstrong is a fine example for ambition and thrift. . . . The finest white musicians from the finest orchestras in Chicago and elsewhere wend their way to the Sunset café where Louis plays nightly, just to hear him play things that they want to learn."

This is one of the first clippings preserved in Armstrong's scrapbooks, and it illustrates the generosity that would mark his later career. Even as Joe Oliver had gone out of his way to show Little Louis the ropes, so did Armstrong go out of his way to pass on what he had learned, both in print and in person. He later said that the young white musicians who came to hear the Creole Jazz Band at Lincoln Gardens were merely doing what he had done as a boy when he hung around Funky Butt Hall. One of the enduring legends of early jazz tells how the New Orleans cornetist Freddie Keppard passed up the chance to make the first jazz recordings. "Nothin' doin,' boys," he allegedly told the members of his Creole Band in 1916. "We won't put our stuff on records for everybody to steal." The Original Dixieland Jazz Band then took Keppard's place in the Victor studios, and in jazz history. Though the story is now thought to be apocryphal, it remains illustrative of the narrow-minded attitude of many New Orleans musicians — the same attitude of which Armstrong's career was a living refutation.

In May of 1927 the Hot Five returned to the studio after a six-month hiatus. OKeh had switched to electrical recording in the interim, so the group was expanded to include Pete Briggs on tuba and Baby Dodds, Armstrong's old bandmate, on drums. Never before had he made small-group recordings accompanied by a four-piece rhythm section, and he relished the fuller, fatter sound of the new lineup, which OKeh dubbed the "Hot Seven." Not only is his playing strikingly extroverted throughout the Hot Seven's four sessions, but the second of them yielded up a masterpiece. "This particular recording really 'gassed me,'" Armstrong wrote of "Potato Head Blues," adding that "every note that I blew . . . I thought of Papa Joe." Yet his solo owes little to Oliver, or anyone else. The climax of "Potato Head Blues," written by Armstrong, is what jazz musicians call a "stop-time" chorus, meaning that the band marks the downbeat of every other measure with a staccato chord, falls silent for two bars, then plays another chord. Against this sparse background Armstrong flings a tune that links the chords together like a cable strung along a row of telephone poles. Starting with the first bar, which he prefaces with one of the crisp syncopated figures that launch so many of his solos, he gradually lengthens his phrases until he is leaping boldly across the band's chords, forging a line so seamless that it sounds as if it were composed rather than improvised. Very likely it was: Armstrong, like Joe Oliver before him, worked out set-piece solos on many of the songs that became regular parts of his repertoire.* However "Potato Head Blues" came to be, it is one of the greatest solos recorded by a jazzman, a landmark of modern music that long ago achieved iconic status, both musical and cultural. In addition to being included in the *Smithsonian Collection of Classic Jazz* and the first set of transcriptions published by Jazz at Lincoln Center as part of its "Essential Jazz Editions" series, it was cited by Woody Allen in *Manhattan* as one of the things that make life "worth living," along with Marlon Brando, Groucho Marx, Willie Mays, Frank Sinatra, "Swedish movies," the slow movement of the *Jupiter* Symphony, Gustave Flaubert's *L'Education sentimentale*, and Paul Cézanne's apples and pears.

With "Potato Head Blues" Armstrong came into his full maturity, an event that coincided with the death of his mother. Mayann had lived in Chicago for a year or so after Louis and Lil were married, then gave in to homesickness and returned home to New Orleans, content in the knowledge that her older child was settled and successful. In 1927 arteriosclerosis laid her low, and Louis brought her back to Chicago, where she died that summer. He claimed to have cried only once in his life, when Mayann's coffin was closed for the last time, and as long as he lived he remembered her dying words: "Son — Carry on, you're a good boy — treats everybody right. And

---

*Then and for years to come, many successful bandleaders, Armstrong among them, played set solos on their most popular numbers and expected their musicians to do likewise. "Don't play anything you can't play twice," Louis Jordan told a sideman in 1947. "Because if I like it you've got to keep it in. . . . [I]f you're experimenting with your solos, some nights you're not going to be able to invent and we're going to have a sad show. But if you play the same thing all of the time it will always sound right."

everybody—White and Colored Loves you—you have a good heart.—You can't miss."

Toward year's end he went back to the studio for one last set of recordings with Lil and the Hot Five. Briggs and Baby Dodds were sent packing, and the higher fidelity made possible by the introduction of the microphone makes their absence all the more conspicuous. Perhaps for this reason, Armstrong added an extra musician, the New Orleans guitarist Lonnie Johnson, who plays a key role in the best of these performances, a variation on "Tiger Rag" called "Hotter than That." Johnson's propulsive strumming goads him to new heights of creative audacity. His scatted vocal chorus, accompanied by guitar and banjo alone, contains an electrifying passage in which he bounds across the beat like a flung pebble skipping over choppy waters. "I just played the way I sang," he would later say. More than any of his other recorded vocals, "Hotter than That" suggests the truth of this remark.

Johnson lays out on "Struttin' with Some Barbecue," a song over whose copyright Louis and Lil quarreled four decades later (she sued him, he settled). Armstrong said that he wrote it himself, and the first phrase ascends to the major seventh of the tonic chord, a harmonic twist of which he was fond, though one rarely encounters it in so exposed a position in a late-twenties jazz composition, suggesting that the classically trained Lil might have had a hand in composing the melody. By now she had resumed her studies, earning a diploma from Chicago Musical College, where she took lessons from Louis Victor Saar, a pupil of Brahms. Her solo repertoire, the *Defender* reported in an announcement of one of her recitals, included works by Mozart, Weber, Chopin, Debussy, and Scriabin.

What Armstrong thought of Lil's classical studies is not known, but he admitted to having sought her counsel when he, Hines, and Zutty Singleton struck out on their own. After the Sunset Café was briefly shuttered (the police raided it every week or so), the three friends formed what Hines called "a little corporation . . . we agreed to stick together and not play for anyone unless the three of us were hired." The "Unholy Three," as they called themselves, made a hapless attempt to set up shop as club owners, taking a year-long lease on a South Side hall. None of them was equipped to undertake such a venture, and they lost their shirts. "I don't know what happened," said Hines, "but we like to starve to death, making a dollar or a dollar and a half apiece a night." Unconvinced of their total lack of business savvy, they rented a second hall and put on another dance, the results of which were, Armstrong ruefully confessed, even more disastrous:

> Comes Intermission time — Just as the people were deciding what to do during that period in walks a Drunken *Darkie* — pulled out a 45 Pistol and Leveled it, directly at the direction of us on the Bandstand. . . . The Crowd Scattered *Everywhere* — that left the Hall rather Clean — so this *Drunken* Darkie could get a good view at us on that little Bandstand. — Now when he raised his pistol again as if he was really going to shoot at us. — *LAWD TADAY* [today] — We were so Scared until Earl Hines *tried* to go through his *UPRIGHT* piano. — And Heaven knows where Zuttie + I went.

Fortunately, fate had other plans for the Unholy Three. Six months later they were holed up at OKeh's studios, making the most influential records in jazz history.

4

"IT'S GOT TO BE ART"

T HE TIES THAT BOUND Armstrong and his youthful companions did not survive the combined stresses of flying bullets and misbegotten business ventures. Not long after Hines went to New York for a short visit, Armstrong and Singleton broke their one-for-all pledge and signed up for a second tour of duty with Carroll Dickerson, who was now in charge of one of the bands at a brand-new hall, the Savoy Ballroom, whose half-acre dance floor could hold four thousand people. The money was good, making it possible for the two men to pay off the lease on the South Side hall that had threatened to bankrupt them, but there was no place in the Savoy band for Hines, so they left him in the lurch.

One day the pianist ran into his faithless friends on the street. "What are you doing to me?" he asked. "Here I'm mighty near starving to death!"

"It's rough out here," Armstrong replied, "and I gotta make them payments on the house. I had to get me a gig, so I went to work at the Savoy. Carroll Dickerson took Zutty, too. We tried to talk you in, but we stuck with you a pretty good while there, didn't we?" Hines soon landed a job at the Apex Club, playing in the band of the clarinetist Jimmie Noone, another New Orleans émigré. Still, it irked him to have been deserted, and when he rejoined Armstrong and Singleton, it was not in public but in a recording studio.

Even then "Fatha" Hines (as he would later be known) was a character and a half, slick and ingratiating and ever quick to flash the toothpaste grin that became as well known to music lovers as his foul cigars and bad toupee. He was, like Armstrong, a fervent believer in pleasing a crowd by any means necessary, though he preferred to do so by playing solos of the utmost unpredictability. But unlike his colleague, Hines was a middle-class black from a musical family who had attended integrated public schools in Pennsylvania and spent his childhood studying piano with a German teacher who drilled him in Chopin and Czerny, in the process giving him a technical command unrivaled by any other jazz pianist of the twenties. Under other circumstances he might have aspired to a concert career, but that, he knew, was impossible. "What future was there for a black classical pianist?" he asked himself. Instead he turned to jazz.

"A lot of people have misinterpreted the whole thing and said that I just got my style from Louis," Hines said, "but I was playing it when I met him." Recordings bear him out — his style was substantially formed at least three years before they met — but the two men had clearly been thinking along the same lines, even though their approaches were dissimilar in detail. Hines had no feel for the blues ("I'm too technical to play the blues") and only a modest gift of melody. He packed his solos with a mixture of cascading filigree work and the bright, hard-edged octave passages that gave his "trumpet-style" playing its nickname: "I got sick of playing a lot of pretty things and not being heard, and I figured that if I doubled the right hand melody line with octaves, then I would be heard as well as the trumpets and clarinets." Long before the introduction of the microphone put jazz pianists on an even footing with their colleagues, Hines had no trouble cutting through the clamor of a horn section in full cry. What he had in common with Armstrong was a rhythmic adventurousness so pronounced that his bandmates found his wilder

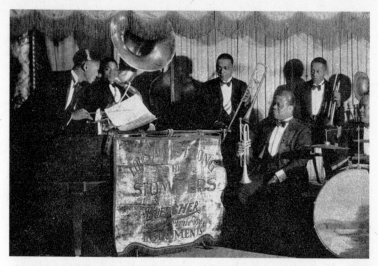

Castor and Pollux: Louis Armstrong and His Stompers at Chicago's Sunset Café, 1927. A rare photograph of Earl Hines (far left) and Armstrong (fourth from left) on the bandstand in the twenties. A few months after it was taken, they would record "West End Blues" and become immortal.

flights of fancy all but impossible to follow. Teddy Wilson, a Hines disciple whose own playing was neat and well turned to a fault, admiringly described his sense of rhythm as "eccentric." He liked nothing better than to dart off in unexpected directions: "I'd be sitting there playing and grinning and thinking and saying to myself, 'How am I going to get out of this?'"

It was Hines's insistence on going his own way that was to be his chief contribution to Louis Armstrong's stylistic development. Armstrong had already done much to break with his musical past, but so far he had had to do it alone. He needed a sympathetic companion to serve as a sounding board, and he couldn't have asked for a better one. Hines, too, was in need of musical companionship when he arrived in Chicago in 1924, an eighteen-year-old whiz kid looking for another youngster quick-witted enough to test his mettle. He looked in vain until the day when he jammed with Armstrong at the black union hall: "I always remember that first tune we played together. It was 'The One I Love Belongs to Somebody Else.' I knew right away that he was a giant." Castor had found Pollux, and now they would light up the skies.

Armstrong and Hines had recorded together for the first time in April of 1927, backing up Johnny Dodds on four performances in which the pianist's subdued but authoritative playing revealed him to be infinitely more adept than Lil Armstrong. In May the two men cut "Chicago Breakdown" with the Sunset Café band. By that time they were fast friends. "Louis was wild and I was wild, and we were inseparable," Hines said. Thirteen months later, after the breakup of the Unholy Three, they were reunited in the studio, where they accompanied the insipid-sounding pop vocalist Lillie Delk Christian. The next day they returned for the first of four Hot Five sessions recorded by a six-man band (OKeh was never picky about niceties of nomenclature) with Singleton on drums and three other members of Dickerson's band — Jimmy Strong, Fred Robinson, and Mancy Carr — in place of Johnny Dodds, Kid Ory, and Johnny St. Cyr. Nine sides came out of these sessions, all memorable and one immortal.

"West End Blues," recorded on June 28, starts with a surprise, an unaccompanied cadenza in which Armstrong snaps out four biting quarter notes by way of fanfare, then vaults upward through a chain of interlocking triplet arpeggios to a fiery high C embellished with a touch of vibrato. It was the most technically demanding passage to have been recorded by a jazz trumpeter up to that time, and for this reason alone it was bound to displease the old-school New Orleans musicians of Armstrong's youth, one of whom grumbled that "because Louis was up North making records and running up and down like he's crazy don't mean that he's that great. He is not playing cornet on that horn; he is imitating a clarinet. He is showing off." Armstrong admitted that he had aspired when young to the facility of the great New Orleans clarinetists: "I was just like a clarinet player, like the guys run up and down the horn nowadays, boppin' and things." But his introduction to "West End Blues" has at least as much in common with the florid *bel canto* cadenzas he had heard in the recordings of Amelita Galli-Curci and Luisa Tetrazzini, and listeners acquainted with turn-of-the-century American band music will also spot the mark of the elaborate unaccompanied passages in the solos of Herbert L. Clarke, John Philip Sousa's star cornetist, several of whose records Armstrong owned and cherished. "I've heard trumpet solos from 1908 up to the present day—Herbert Clarke and all those boys that really used to blow them horns and it sounds like it was recorded yesterday," he told Leonard Feather in 1954. Armstrong probably became acquainted with Clarke's playing during his own tenure with the Tuxedo Brass Band—the 78s that he owned were made then—and it is possible that such cornet showpieces as Clarke's "Bride of the Waves" or "The Debutante" were the "classical trumpet music" at which he had tried his hand with Lil.

Even if Armstrong did have Clarke in mind, his "West End Blues" cadenza has a propulsive momentum altogether unlike the freer ebb and flow of classical rubato. He is on the move from the first note onward, raising the rhythmic stakes still further with a shift of gears known to contemporary classical composers as a "metric modulation," in which he turns a single beat in the second measure of the cadenza into two-thirds of a beat in the third measure. This instinctive, almost imperceptible change of tempo allows him to slip without a hitch into the spiraling triplets that lead to the high C, from which he skitters back down to a low A-flat in a tricky flurry of triple-tongued notes. Then the band enters and Armstrong plays the theme, composed by Joe Oliver and named after a lakeside resort in New Orleans. Oliver and his band had recorded "West End Blues" two weeks earlier for Vocalion. The Hot Five play the song in the same key and at the same tempo, but the effect is wholly different, especially when Armstrong ends the first chorus by spiraling upward once more in a variant of the triplet arpeggios of the cadenza. The refulgent splendor of his tone is worlds away from Oliver's staid playing.

For the second chorus Fred Robinson serves up a trombone solo enlivened by Hines's throbbing tremolo background. Jimmy Strong then steps to the microphone and repeats the melody in the deep-toned *chalumeau* register of his clarinet, while Armstrong echoes each phrase in sweet-sounding, tenderly sung scat syllables: *Wah-dwa-dwa . . . wah-dwa-dwa-doh . . . waaah-dwa-dwo-loh . . . wa-da-dee-dee-da.* It is a lovely touch of fantasy, and Hines preserves the mood with a frilly piano solo interrupted by a brief interlude of sparkling trumpet-style octaves. Then Armstrong picks up his horn and tiptoes to a high B-flat, holding it for four shimmering bars before descending majestically from the firmament in what Gunther Schuller describes as "an impassioned, almost stammering repetitive phrase that seems to float, completely unencumbered rhythmically, above the accompaniment." After such eloquence there is nothing more to be said: Hines releases the pent-up tension with a mock-classical tag, and Armstrong and the band answer with a teasingly fulsome amen-brother cadence.

Though it was recorded in a studio rather than unfurled before a cheering crowd, "West End Blues" is very much a public utterance, not confiding but grand. Armstrong had been playing it at the Savoy, where Artie Shaw, a young saxophonist from New York, heard him one night: "I sat on a rug-covered bandstand and just waited and he came on. And the first thing he played was 'West End Blues.' And I heard this cascade of notes coming out of a trumpet. No one had ever done that before." Even his gentle duet with Strong sounds like an audience-tested routine, and his trumpet solos, for all their freedom from rhythmic constraint, have a similar air of premeditated formality, suggesting that they might have been prepared, in whole or in part, prior to the recording session — an inference supported by considerable evidence, circumstantial and otherwise. The triple-tongued passage in the cadenza, for instance, is prefigured by a two-bar break that he took on Margaret Johnson's recording of "Changeable Daddy of Mine," made four years earlier, and the last chorus echoes his repeated descents from a high B-flat on the Hot Seven's "S.O.L. Blues" and "Gully Low Blues." No alternate takes survive to show how "West End Blues" might have evolved in the studio, and Armstrong is not known to have left behind any detailed account of the session, but Hines talked about it in an interview in which he said that the arrangement, which took at least four takes to record successfully, was mapped out in advance, including the cadenza, the clarinet-voice duet, the piano solo, and the final chorus. Only the coda was left to chance: "Now how the ending was going to be we didn't know. We got to the end of it and Louis looked at me and I thought of the first thing I could think of, a little bit of [a] classic thing that I did a long time ago and I did it five times and after I finished that I held the chord and Louis gave the downbeat with his head and everybody hit the chord on the end."

In the days of 78s, recording engineers were unable to play back a take without rendering the wax master unusable for commercial release, so the band did not hear the final version of "West End Blues" until it was issued by OKeh a few weeks later. "Earl Hines, he was surprised when the record came out on the market, 'cause he brought it by my house, you know, we'd forgotten we'd recorded it," Armstrong recalled in 1956. But they liked what they heard. "When it first came out," Hines said, "Louis and I stayed by that recording practically an hour and a half or two hours and we just knocked each other out because we had no idea it was gonna turn out as good as it did." Nor were they the only ones who were impressed. Within days of its release, Ethel Waters cut a cover version whose penultimate scat-sung chorus is similar in style to Armstrong's wordless vocal. That same vocal was revelatory to the young Billie Holiday when she heard it for the first time: "I heard a record Louis Armstrong made called the 'West End Blues.' And he doesn't say any words, and I thought, this is wonderful! And I liked the feeling he got from it. . . . Sometimes the record would make me so sad I'd cry up a storm. Other times the same damn record would make me so happy."

Another musician who listened closely to "West End Blues" was Joe Oliver, who re-recorded the song for Victor in 1929, this time in a version in which the solos of Armstrong and Hines, including the opening cadenza, are reproduced as exactly as possible. That is sad enough — a master should never have to ape his protégé — but what is sadder still is that Oliver, though his name appears on the label, does not play on the record. Unable to execute the trumpet solos, he left the thankless task to Louis Metcalf, who had heard Armstrong soloing with Fletcher Henderson's band on "Copenhagen" five years earlier. Though Armstrong claimed to have been "flattered" by the recording, he must have been dismayed by the results. Metcalf does his best to duplicate Armstrong's golden tone and easy swing, but he overshoots the first note of the cadenza and never regains his composure, and his playing on the rest of the record is a blurry copy of the real thing. Another decade and a half would go by before the art of jazz reached the point where the entire Charlie Barnet band could blast out the "West End Blues" cadenza in unison on a 1944 recording that offers a dramatic demonstration of how much the jazz musicians who came after Armstrong owed to his example.

Armstrong himself returned to "West End Blues" at least twice on record, in both cases playing solos that track the ones on the 1928 performance closely but not slavishly, his customary practice when playing the songs for which he was famous: "And always, once you got a certain solo that fit in the tune, and that's it, you keep it. Only vary it two or three notes every time you play it." The first remake is a big-band version from 1939 in which the cadenza is flabby-toned (though the scat chorus is more adventurous than the quasi-canonic repetitions of 1928). In the second, a 1955 All Stars recording, the cadenza, while firm in tone, sounds overblown, almost gross, next to the lapidary elegance of the original. It was inevitable that these later versions would fail to come up to the mark, not because Armstrong had become a less compelling player but because he had evolved into a different *kind* of player, sparer in his choice of notes and less unabashedly virtuosic (though he would always enjoy showing off for an audience). The change was in part the result of the lip damage that he sustained over the years, which affected both his flexibility and his stamina. He could still play with undiminished force in 1939, but he had to pace himself so as not to exhaust his resources, and by 1955 his control had been compromised by decades of overwork. In 1928, by contrast, he was still a flying cat, rising effortlessly to the challenges posed by Hines, and in "West End Blues" we hear him in his absolute prime.

⤚

Hines is less in evidence on "West End Blues" than on "Skip the Gutter," recorded the day before.* Here the band drops out after a forgettable opening ensemble and the pianist goes head to head with Armstrong in a musical joust whose results are, if anything, more exhilarating than the two versions of "Cake Walkin' Babies from Home" that Armstrong had recorded with Sidney Bechet. Yet their shared chorus of can-you-top-this breaks, each tossed off with insolent ease, is no duel to the death: what we hear this time is not a battle for supremacy but a friendly game, though Hines was not beyond trying to throw his playmate off the scent by deliberately jumping in one count too soon at the end of the sixteenth bar of their duet chorus. Instead of rising to the bait, Armstrong pauses for a breathless instant, then bats back a syncopated figure that reestablishes the beat with unflappable precision.

"Skip the Gutter" shows how far Armstrong had pulled away from the New Orleans tradition. The ensembles on the Armstrong-Hines Hot Fives are often little more than bookends (most of which are in any case arranged rather than improvised) that serve only to frame the solos that are now the point of the performances. This is why Strong and Robinson sound so unprepossessing by comparison with Johnny Dodds and Kid Ory. Though neither pair was as accomplished as Armstrong and Hines, Dodds and Ory had the advantage of working within a tradition that they had known all their lives. They function not as virtuoso showmen but as parts of a larger whole, playing their modest roles with a grace that helps to conceal their limitations. Strong and Robinson, by contrast, are on their own, and unable to fall back on the conventions of the New Orleans style, they betray their lesser gifts. But Armstrong didn't care: he was

---

*The title of the song, written by Spencer Williams, is a now-obsolete slang phrase that means "hurry up."

indifferent to the defects of the second-rate musicians with whom he too often worked. "I don't even hear them," he told Singleton. Later on he would tell a story that illustrates the kindness of heart that led him to ignore their lapses:

> Always remember — Louis Armstrong never bother about what the other fellow is playing, etc. A musician's a musician with me. Yea — I am just like the *Sister* in our church in N.O. [New Orleans], my home town. One Sunday our pastor whom we all loved happened to take a Sunday off and sent in another preacher who wasn't near as good. The whole congregation frowned on him — except one Sister. She seemed to enjoy the other pastor the same as she did *our* pastor. This aroused the Congregation's curiosity *so much* — until when Church service was over they all rushed over to this *one Sister* and asked her *why* did she enjoy the substitute preacher the same as our regular one? She said, "Well, when *our pastor preach*, I can look right through him and see *Jesus*. And when I hear a preacher who's *not* as good as ours — I just look *over* his *shoulder* and *see Jesus just the same*."

In Hines's case, of course, no allowances were necessary — he could hit anything Armstrong pitched — and Chicago clubgoers had been privileged to hear the two men working together under more musically favorable circumstances. So were record collectors, for on July 5, the day of the last Hot Five session, Carroll Dickerson's Savoyagers came to the OKeh studio to record "Savoyagers' Stomp" and "Symphonic Raps" with Hines sitting in on piano. These sides, like "Stomp Off, Let's Go" and "Chicago Breakdown" before them, contrast fascinatingly with the Hot Fives, giving us a precious glimpse of what Armstrong sounded like in the nightspots where he worked. Here we see him not as the leader of a small group but as featured soloist with a well-rehearsed big band, playing arrangements into which his solos fit as smoothly as a diamond in a costly setting. He knew how good the band was: "If I have to say it myself — We made up one of the Damnedest bands, there were." He must have known, too, how good he sounded with it, for it was the

Savoy band that would accompany him when he began to appear in public as the leader of an orchestra that performed under his name.

The twin sessions were notable for another reason, which is that Bix Beiderbecke happened to be in another studio down the hall, cutting two sides for OKeh. He and Louis had met for the first time when the S.S. *Sidney* stopped at Davenport, Iowa, in 1919. "He was a cute little boy," Armstrong recalled. "He'd come down to hear the bands, and then go home and practice what he heard. He and I became friends the first time we met—he was the type of youngster I admired all the way." Beiderbecke had joined Paul Whiteman around the time that Armstrong became Carroll Dickerson's featured soloist, and Whiteman's records now were bringing him to the attention of the same audience that was also discovering Armstrong. The Whiteman band was in Chicago that month for a three-week run of theater engagements. Armstrong had heard the group at the Chicago Theater three days earlier:

> I had been diggin' [Beiderbecke] in small combos and stuff. Now my man's gonna blow some of these big time arrangements, I thought . . . and sure enough he did . . . as soon as I bought my ticket, I made a beeline to my seat because the band was already on, and they were way down into their program, when the next number that came up, after the one they were playing when I came in, was a beautiful tune called "From Monday On". . . . My, my, what an arrangement that was.
>
> They swung it all the way . . . and all of a sudden Bix stood up and took a solo . . . and I'm tellin' you, those pretty notes went all through me.*

Armstrong went backstage to say hello, and that same night Beiderbecke and three of his bandmates returned the compliment by paying a visit to the Savoy. After the last show, when all the cus-

---

*In 1956 Armstrong played the Whiteman-Beiderbecke recording of "From Monday On" as part of a Voice of America radio program devoted to his favorite jazz records by other musicians.

tomers had gone home and the doors were locked, the two men jammed together. As Armstrong described it, "Now you talking about jam sessions. . . . huh. . . . those were the things . . . with everyone feeling each other's note or chord, et cetera . . . and blend with each other instead of trying to cut each other . . . nay, nay, we did not even think of such a mess . . . we tried to see how good we could make music sound which was an inspiration within itself." Izzy Friedman, another member of the Whiteman band who came to the Savoy with Beiderbecke that night, felt the same way, saying that "it wasn't a cutting session, not in the least. It was a real blending of ideas. We just played with these guys like old friends."

Beiderbecke also sat in with Joe Oliver at the Plantation Club, and a member of the audience recalled that "tears rolled down Oliver's face and Oliver said that Bix was the greatest he had ever heard." Armstrong expressed his own admiration for the younger man's playing on many occasions: "I was thrilled to death with whatever Bix did. . . . Bix had a way of expressing himself — his music would make you want to go right up to the bandstand, shake his hand and make yourself known." He doubtless appreciated the fact that Bix, like Hines, had arrived at a conception of the jazz solo that departed as radically from the New Orleans tradition as did his own, though Beiderbecke's softer-spoken style could not have been further removed from Armstrong's slashing, searing arcs of melody. Their personalities were as dissimilar as their styles: Beiderbecke was already drinking to excess, and in 1930 he quit the Whiteman band and entered a sanitarium that specialized in the treatment of alcoholics. A year later he was dead. Armstrong grieved at his passing but was not surprised by it: "Half the time he didn't eat properly and a whole lot of things like that. . . . I'd say, 'Well, man, you got to have your own mind sometimes, man. Them cats, they don't mean you no harm or nothing like that.' But Bix, he never would say 'no,' and that's what hurt him." That was a mistake the self-disciplined Armstrong would never make. He liked his pleasures, but he knew when to say no.

Five months went by before Armstrong and Hines recorded again. During that time the Dickerson band continued to pack the

Savoy Ballroom, making a series of radio broadcasts that spread the name of its principal soloist far and wide. Armstrong became so closely identified with the Savoy that when he brought the Hot Five back into the studio, it was renamed "Louis Armstrong and His Savoy Ballroom Five." It also acquired a new member, Don Redman, who had left the Henderson band to become the musical director of McKinney's Cotton Pickers, a Detroit-based dance band that was working out of Chicago during the second half of 1928. Redman sat in on several of the Savoy Ballroom sides, playing clarinet and alto saxophone and helping to give the band the richer sound heard on "Beau Koo Jack," an original composition by Alex Hill whose arrangement drew retrospective praise from Hines: "Even then they were already writing overloaded arrangements that the guys couldn't swing, but this one did, and the group sounded like a big band." Armstrong's fleet, fluent solo is but one of the highlights of the best-played small-group record he cut in the twenties, a tour de force of early ensemble jazz fit to be ranked alongside Jelly Roll Morton's equally masterly Red Hot Peppers recordings.

Yet "Beau Koo Jack" must yield pride of place to a pair of performances recorded in December, "Muggles" and "Weather Bird." Considered as a whole, "Muggles" is not nearly so impressive as "Beau Koo Jack," amounting as it does to a string of solos by Hines, Robinson, Strong, and Armstrong, the first of which is atypically aimless and the next two of indifferent musical quality. It is because of Armstrong's climactic two-chorus explosion that "Muggles" belongs to the ages. He charges in on Strong's heels with a two-bar break in which he doubles the tempo, proceeding directly to the most memorable of his many fantasias on one note, a chorus in which he rocks back and forth between a B-flat below middle C and the same note an octave higher, screwing up the tension to a pitch reminiscent of the last chorus of "West End Blues," then releasing it with a dark-blue phrase borrowed from Joe Oliver's solo on the Creole Jazz Band's 1923 recording of "Jazzin' Babies Blues."

The word *muggles* was one of many synonyms for marijuana used by jazz musicians in the twenties. It was also called "tea" and "shit," and those who smoked it were "vipers." According to one witness, Armstrong became a viper earlier that year when a white arranger visited him backstage at the Savoy Ballroom. "I got a new cigarette, man," the man said. "It makes you feel so good." It seems improbable that Armstrong would have been unfamiliar with marijuana, since it was widely used in New Orleans, but all that is known for sure is that he started smoking it on a regular basis in 1928 and continued to do so for the rest of his life. He would later explain to an acquaintance that it "makes you feel good, man. It relaxes you, makes you forget all the bad things that happen to a Negro. It makes you feel wanted, and when you're with another tea smoker it makes you feel a special kinship." It was also, unlike alcohol, legal, though by 1931 twenty-nine states had outlawed its use and sale, a development that was soon to get Armstrong into trouble.

It became customary for Armstrong and his sidemen (except for Hines, who disliked marijuana) to get high before making a record, which probably explains how "Muggles" got its name. But it is unlikely that Armstrong was anything other than clearheaded when, two days earlier, he and Hines sent home the rest of the Savoy Ballroom Five, which had just cut "Beau Koo Jack," and recorded "Weather Bird," the most forward-looking of the three dozen 78 sides they made together in 1927 and 1928. It was the sole occasion on which they went it alone in the studio, and they took full advantage of their freedom, sailing through a duet that resembles "Skip the Gutter" sped up and writ large. Again one gets the feeling that Hines is trying to give his partner the rhythmic slip, but never quite successfully. The strongest impression left by "Weather Bird," though, is of an airy lightness made possible by the absence of a rhythm section, combined with a sense of awe at the incisiveness of musical argument. Armstrong called the recording "our vir-tee-o-so number," and Hines claimed that the trumpeter spun it out of thin air. "We had no music," he recalled. "It was all improvised, and I just followed him." Perhaps the pianist was unaware that the song, a multithemed rag composed by Armstrong, had been recorded by the Creole Jazz Band in 1923, but the first half of the Armstrong-Hines version follows the earlier recording fairly closely, suggesting that their performance, for all its seeming spontaneity, may in fact have been rehearsed with some care. Nor was "Weather Bird" the first recorded jazz duet: Joe Oliver and Jelly Roll Morton had already cut two. It was, however, the first such recording of any musical significance, and its quicksilver brilliance has yet to be surpassed.

One puzzling aspect of "Weather Bird" and the other recordings Armstrong made with Hines is how infrequently he spoke of them in later years. He does not mention them in *Swing That Music* and has nothing to say about Hines himself beyond remarking that the pianist "could swing a gang of keys" and that the two men "liked each other from the first and were to see a lot of each other afterwards." The stock anecdotes that he trotted out for journalists included no stories about the pianist, and though he praised their recordings whenever asked, he rarely brought them up on his own, save during the period between 1948 and 1951 when Hines was a member of the All Stars: "Of course, everybody knows that Earl was really in his prime in those days." Then Hines quit the band in a dispute over billing, provoking an untypically spiteful outburst from Armstrong, who rarely spoke ill of his fellow musicians. "He's good, sure," Armstrong said, "but we don't need him. . . . Earl Hines and his big ideas. Well, we can get along without Mr. Earl Hines."

What was the wedge that drove them apart? In private life Armstrong was the most welcoming of men, but except in the early years of the All Stars, when he shared a bandstand with Hines, Sid Catlett, and Jack Teagarden, he preferred as a rule not to consort with his fellow giants. Sometimes he would employ musicians who were deservedly well known in their own right—Henry Allen, Barney Bigard, Cozy Cole, J. C. Higginbotham, Billy Kyle, and Trummy Young all played with him for extended stretches—but for the most part his bandmates were journeymen who could be trusted not to hog the limelight. Hines was different: not only was he as influential among piano players as Armstrong was among trumpeters, but he was also a showboater whose onstage antics antagonized more than one colleague. "I like to listen to him," Coleman Hawkins said, "but I ain't particular about playing with him." One sure way to enrage Armstrong was to try to steal his thunder, and it is hard to picture Hines taking a back seat to him, or anyone else.

All this was far in the future, though, when they recorded the last three Savoy Ballroom Five sides, "Hear Me Talkin' to Ya," "St. James Infirmary," and "Tight Like That," on December 12, 1928. Hines had cut his first solo recordings in New York the week before, and he made two more that morning while Armstrong and Don Redman retired to the men's room to smoke a joint. Two weeks later, on his twenty-fifth birthday, the pianist opened at the Grand Terrace, a mob-run nightclub which in 1937 would move to the same building where the Sunset Café had previously operated. He spent the next decade working for gangsters and leading one of the liveliest big bands of the Swing Era. Armstrong was about to become a bandleader as well, though his road to stardom was a little longer and a lot bumpier, and made him far more famous.

For both men 1928 was their floruit, a year of triumphs to which all their subsequent undertakings would forever after be compared. The time was ripe for such prodigies, with modernism at its apogee and mass-produced popular culture in its first flower. It was the year of *Lady Chatterley's Lover* and "Makin' Whoopee," Evelyn Waugh's *Decline and Fall* and Walt Disney's "Steamboat Willie," the Stravinsky-Balanchine *Apollo* and the Brecht-Weill *Dreigroschenoper.* Jazz, too, had by 1928 won a measure of acceptance in highbrow circles that in retrospect is striking, even startling, given its recent origins in the honky-tonks of New Orleans. George Gershwin, who thought it to be "the only musical idiom in existence that could aptly express America," made use of jazz-derived musical techniques in *An American in Paris*, premiered by the New York Philharmonic that December to general acclaim. When Maurice Ravel came to New York earlier in the year to play his jazz-flavored violin sonata with Joseph Szigeti, he assured reporters that American classical composers would do well to take jazz seriously: "I am waiting to see more Americans appear with the honesty and vision to realize the significance of their popular product, and the technic and imagination to base an original and creative art upon it." Aaron Copland, soon to emerge as America's leading classical composer, felt the same way. He had already written two large-scale pieces influenced by jazz, *Music for the Theatre* and the Piano Concerto, and in 1927 he declared that jazz might someday become "the substance not only of the American composer's fox trots and Charlestons, but of his lullabies and nocturnes. He may express through it not always gaiety but love, tragedy, remorse." But he later changed his mind, deciding that jazz "might have its best treatment from those who had a talent for improvisation."

Copland was right. For jazz to reach its fullest expressive potential, as well as a truly popular audience, it would first need to find embodiment not in a composer, however gifted, but in a soloist of genius with a personality to match, a charismatic individual capable of meeting the untutored listener halfway. Such a man existed, and there were those who sensed his potential. When Bix Beiderbecke and Hoagy Carmichael first heard Louis Armstrong playing with King Oliver in 1923, they were staggered. Carmichael set down his reaction in his memoirs: "'Why,' I moaned, 'why isn't everybody in the world here to hear that?' I meant it. Something as unutterably stirring as that deserved to be heard by the world." Five years later it was being heard by the patrons of the Savoy Ballroom, the buyers of race records, the lucky listeners who happened to tune in to Carroll Dickerson's broadcasts — and no one else. Musicians, to be sure, received Armstrong's records as life-changing revelations. When Artie Shaw first heard them, he became "obsessed with the idea that this was what you had to do. Something that was your own, that had nothing to do with anybody else." At least one of the Hot Five sides appears to have caught the ear of a somewhat wider audience as well. Eli Oberstein, who signed Armstrong to an exclusive contract with Victor Records four years later, recalled that "West End Blues" was his "first record that really made any wide inroads ... When I say, made him well known, I mean to the country at large. In Chicago he was quite an artist, and in New Orleans he was quite an artist, but he was not known anywhere else in the country." But Oberstein hastened to point out that the people who bought his records in 1928 consisted mainly of Armstrong's fellow musicians and "college students, who right now are crazy about 'hot' music . . . the average layman does not understand his type of work."

What if the Hot Fives had circulated more widely at the time of their release? It is unlikely that they would have gone over very well with the country at large, consisting as they do of ordinary jazz and blues tunes played by a scrappy combo dominated by two titans. Even on the sides that featured Armstrong's appealing voice, he was almost always restricted to wordless scat vocals, vaudevillian novelties, or blues-drenched songs like "St. James Infirmary," the folk ballad about a man who goes to the morgue to behold his lover on a slab: *I went down to St. James Infirmary / Saw my baby there / Stretched out on a long white table / So sweet, so cold, so bare.* Of the sixty-five songs recorded by the Hot Five in its various incarnations, no more than a half dozen continue to be played with any regularity. In order for the world to hear and embrace his art, Armstrong needed a more accessible repertoire and a more flattering setting — and both were close at hand.

5

"THE WAY A TRUMPET SHOULD PLAY"

On the Move, 1929–1930

THE MAN WHO MADE Louis Armstrong a pop star was tone-deaf. Tommy Rockwell, OKeh's New York–based recording director, was a "burly, rough-looking character" (as George Avakian remembered him) who started as a salesman and worked his way up through the corporate ranks. One of his closest associates claimed, by all accounts without exaggeration, that he "couldn't carry two notes of a melody." But tone-deafness has never stopped anyone from making money out of popular music, and if Rockwell didn't know one note from another, he still knew a good thing when he heard it. Among other good things, he was responsible for persuading Bix Beiderbecke to record on piano as well as cornet, and he also made the first recordings of McKenzie and Condon's Chicagoans, a group of young white instrumentalists whose music, a revved-up variant of the style of collective improvisation that was born in New Orleans, came to be known as "Chicago-style jazz." A shrewd executive who booked dance bands on the side, Rockwell sensed that Armstrong could appeal to a significantly wider audience, and in 1929 he acted on his intuition.

By then the Savoy Ballroom was floundering, and the management had gone so far as to stop paying its musicians regularly. "Mr.

Fagan the owner would come to us with a *hard luck 'story'* every week," Armstrong remembered. "And the way he would *'lay'* this Story on us, we Just couldn't leave him that's all. After all we were all Troopers." But even the most loyal of troupers must eat, and Armstrong, who was still paying off the mortgage on the house that he and Lil had bought, was looking for work. Rockwell asked him to come to New York to record as a single act, and on March 5 the two men spent a long day in the studio that would prove both fruitful and fateful. The plan was for Armstrong to be accompanied by the dance band of Luis Russell, a pianist who had worked with Joe Oliver in Chicago before moving to New York and putting together a group of his own that featured such New Orleans émigrés as Paul Barbarin on drums, Albert Nicholas on clarinet, and Pops Foster, Armstrong's old friend from the S.S. *Sidney,* on bass, plus a ringer from Georgia, a trombonist named J. C. Higginbotham. It was an eminently logical pairing. Not only was Russell's medium-sized band the only black ensemble of its kind on OKeh's roster, but it played semi-arranged music with plenty of hot solos and a strong New Orleans flavor, a recipe well suited to Armstrong's robust tastes: "It's just as though they could see right through my back and know what's coming next almost as soon as I do."

Rockwell booked a morning session at OKeh with Armstrong and the Russell band, who had "rehearsed" by performing together at Harlem's Savoy Ballroom the previous night. The trumpeter's return to New York was triumphant. "Long before [the] time of opening," Dave Peyton reported in the *Chicago Defender,* "long lines were seen along Lenox Avenue, eager to get in, but thousands were turned away." Among those present was Joe Oliver, who had moved to New York two years before. In 1956 Armstrong recalled their reunion:

> It's the last time Joe Oliver prob'ly heard me play, and the man just stood up and cried.... [H]e came up and he stood right across from the bandstand, and that's where he stood, and he could see all the moments when I was a kid, running errands for his wife, and he'd give me those lessons, you know, and we'd eat red beans and rice together. I'll never forget it.

After the show Armstrong's colleagues feted him at a banquet. Rockwell was on hand, as was Eddie Condon, a white banjo player from Chicago (he later switched to guitar) who had admired Armstrong ever since hearing him at Lincoln Gardens. A fast-talking, publicity-savvy hustler who loved hot jazz and whiskey, usually in that order, Condon had no use for the color bar that kept black and white musicians from playing together other than at informal jam sessions. Struck by the presence at the banquet of so many good players of both races, he said to Rockwell, "You ought to make a record while Louis is here." Rockwell decided then and there to record a racially mixed combo that same morning, postponing the date with Russell until after lunch.

Condon showed up at the studio a few hours later, accompanied by Joe Sullivan, another Chicagoan who played Hines-style piano, and Jack Teagarden, who had come to New York from Texas in 1927 and soon was one of the busiest trombonists in town. Armstrong brought along Kaiser Marshall, whose drumming he knew well from his stint with Fletcher Henderson, and a tenor saxophonist named Happy Caldwell. Rounding out the band was Eddie Lang, a pioneer of jazz guitar who had already recorded with blacks and whose single-string solos were admired by musicians of both races, including Armstrong, who knew his innovative playing from Bix Beiderbecke's records. Instead of going to bed after the banquet, Armstrong, Caldwell, and Marshall had spent the night driving around town, breakfasted at six, and picked up a jug of whiskey before meeting their colleagues at the studio. The musicians emptied the jug, then threw together a string of blues solos whose nonchalant air suggests a late-night (or early-morning) jam session. Marshall recalled how Armstrong gave a title to the improvised "tune":

After we recorded that number the studio man came around with his list to write down the usual information, composer, name of tune and so on. He asked Louis what the tune was called, and Louis said "I don't know!" Then he looked around and saw the empty jug sitting in the middle of the floor and he said: "Man we sure knocked that jug — you call it 'Knockin' a Jug.'"

"Knockin' a Jug" was Armstrong's first recording with a mixed band, as well as the first of innumerable occasions on which he would perform with Teagarden. Their paths had crossed a decade before in New Orleans, where the trombonist heard Armstrong on a Streckfus riverboat: "The boat was still far off. But in the bow I could see a Negro standing in the wind, holding a trumpet high and sending out the most brilliant notes I had ever heard. . . . It was Louis Armstrong descending from the sky like a god." Armstrong felt the same way about the slow-moving, hard-drinking virtuoso with patent-leather hair who played and sang the blues in an easygoing yet idiomatic style rarely heard from white musicians in the twenties. "The first time I heard Jack Teagarden on the trombone," he wrote in *Satchmo*, "I had goose pimples all over." It was fitting that their first encounter on record should also be one of the earliest mixed-race recording sessions, since both men were devoid of racial prejudice. "He was from Texas," Armstrong said, "but it was always, 'You a spade, and I'm an ofay. We got the same soul. Let's blow.'"

That afternoon Armstrong returned to the studio to cut two sides with the Russell band, augmented by Condon on banjo and Lonnie Johnson on guitar. The first was "I Can't Give You Anything but Love," a ballad by Jimmy McHugh and Dorothy Fields from *Black-birds of 1928*, the longest-running all-black Broadway revue of the twenties. This version, which opens with a doleful instrumental chorus split down the middle by Armstrong (who uses a straight mute) and Higginbotham, appears at first glance to have little in common with the daredevil small-group sides that had made the trumpeter's name a byword among jazz musicians. It almost sounds as if he were sitting in with Guy Lombardo. But then he puts down his trumpet and croons an ingeniously oblique half-scatted paraphrase of the melody accompanied by three gently mooing saxophones and Pops Foster's bowed bass, followed by a trumpet chorus that sheers daringly away from the tune and soars off into the blue, ascending toward (but not quite hitting) a climactic high D. The results exemplified his recipe for a three-chorus solo: "The first chorus I plays the melody, the second chorus I plays the melody round the melody, and the third chorus I routines." They also showed that he could make a ballad sound as jazzy as a blues, a lesson not lost on his contemporaries. Ethel Waters paid homage to him yet again in 1932 with a recording of "I Can't Give You Anything but Love" in which she reproduces Armstrong's vocal chorus note for note, a knowing tribute that also serves as a sign of the spread of his renown.

What inspired Armstrong to record so sentimental a song in so original a manner? "Tommy Rockwell knew it had to be different," he later told a colleague. "The song had been on the radio for almost a year, and everybody did it like cheerful — 'One day I'll buy you diamond rings, baby,' and all that. Rockwell thought I should do it like life really is — the guy really *can't* give her anything but love. So he had Brother Higginbotham and the saxophones play it way down low, and I sang it that way, too." And whose idea was it for him to record a show tune in the first place? Armstrong's writings shed no light on the matter, but three months earlier he had accompanied Lillie Delk Christian on her OKeh recordings of "I Can't Give You Anything but Love" and "I Must Have That Man," another song from *Blackbirds of 1928*. Though he had never before recorded such fare under his own name, he had been playing it in public since his Sunset Café days. Thus he might have suggested "I Can't Give You Anything but Love" to Rockwell, and he would certainly have been responsible for picking the third song recorded that day, an instrumental named after a Storyville whorehouse whose madam he remembered fondly: "Lulu White was a famous woman of the sporting world in Storyville . . . She had a big house on Basin Street called Mahogany Hall . . . The song was written after her house had gotten so famous." "Mahogany Hall Stomp" shows off the Russell band at its rocking best: Pops Foster beats out a fat-bottomed bass line as Armstrong romps through three muted choruses, one of which consists of a sunlit high B-flat stretched out for ten breathtaking bars. Their pellucid simplicity would be echoed by virtually every other jazz trumpeter of the thirties.

Even if it was Armstrong's own idea to record both "I Can't Give You Anything but Love" and "Mahogany Hall Stomp," he could not have done so without Rockwell's approval, and it was probably the OKeh executive's idea to team him with Luis Russell's band as well. The success of their collaboration sealed Armstrong's artistic fate: from 1929 to 1947 he would lead a big band that crisscrossed the country playing show tunes and pop songs for dancers and theater audiences. Many jazz fans later came to feel that Armstrong had "sold out" by switching to big-band accompaniment, but he had been working with such groups ever since he quit the Creole Jazz Band in 1924. Had he done otherwise, he would never have become a star, though it would not have occurred to him, or the other well-known jazz instrumentalists of his generation, to do anything else. Dancing was where the money was. Even such stalwarts of the New Orleans style as Joe Oliver and Jelly Roll Morton eventually bowed to the inevitable and added saxophone sections to their bands. Not until World War II did small-group jazz become a bigtime business, and even then the cautious Armstrong waited until two years after the war was over to dispose of his expensive orchestra and start working with a six-piece combo. He loved the Hot Five, but he saw no reason why he couldn't make equally good music with a big band — and he was right.

➤

Armstrong went back to Chicago to appear as a single act at the 3,500-seat Regal Theater, a fancy South Side variety house whose stage curtain was spangled with rhinestones. He shared the bill with MGM's first talkie, *Alias Jimmy Valentine*, in the process earning his own first mention in the *Chicago Tribune* — in a tiny ad that billed him as "The World's Greatest Cornetist." (Chicago's most widely read newspaper would not mention Armstrong by name in its news columns until 1931.) He remained loyal to Carroll Dickerson, Zutty Singleton, and the rest of his old bandmates, all of whom enjoyed one another's company so much that they rented a flat and started their own after-hours club. But companionship pays no bills, and when Rockwell sent Armstrong a telegram in May telling him to return to New York to play in a Broadway show, he obeyed — and brought his band along with him: "I told them — 'Well fellows — you all know how well I love you all — And you Boys love me too — What say if we have our Cars fixed up and Mr. Rockwell has just sent me enough money — And I can give each man in the band $20 to eat off of and help Buy Gas, and we'll all go to New York together?'"

It was a quixotic proposal, since the job Rockwell had lined up for Armstrong required him to rejoin Fletcher Henderson's orchestra, which Vincent Youmans had hired to play in the pit of his new show, *Great Day*, a mixed-race musical about life on a Louisiana plantation whose score contained such standards-to-be as "More Than You Know" and "Without a Song." But the trumpeter stuck to his guns, and a few weeks later his ragtag four-car caravan pulled out of Chicago, bound for glory with a side trip to Niagara Falls. Armstrong heard his records being played in black neighborhoods all along the way. "We were popular all through the Towns we passed through — Toledo Ohio — Cleveland — Detroit — Buffalo," he wrote. "They all had been hearing our Broadcasts from the 'Savoy' Ballroom in Chicago the whole time we were there." According to Singleton, he was "surprised" that anyone outside Chicago and New York knew who he was.

The band barely made it to Manhattan in one piece. Dickerson crashed his secondhand vehicle along the way and had to abandon it, and no sooner did Armstrong's Hupmobile pull into Times Square than the radiator boiled over. A passing policeman noticed the car's Chicago tags and asked Armstrong and Singleton whether they were carrying any shotguns. The trumpeter went straight from there to the OKeh office, where he sprang his surprise on Rockwell:

> He said "'Louie' — I've just arranged to put you in The 'Great Day Show.'" I said — "Oh fine Mr. Rockwell — But — er, wer — I brought my band with me and you'll have to Book us Some place." Mr. Rockwell Hit the Ceiling saying — "Band? I did not send for your Band — I sent for you only." I said, (very calmly) "Just the same Mr. Rockwell, we're here now — I just couldn't leave my Boys that's all — I know you can Book us Some place. Another thing we all need money — so you'll have

to let me have about $_Dollars to keep us eating — Room Rent and our Laundry until we go to work."

After Rockwell climbed down from the ceiling, he advanced Armstrong enough money to take care of the musicians' immediate needs. Within two days they had lined up a job subbing for Duke Ellington at Harlem's Audubon Theater. "The pit band looked pretty surprised when the curtain went up and there we were on stage," Singleton wrote. Then Armstrong trotted out "St. Louis Blues," a "good ol' good one" (the phrase that he used to introduce one of his greatest hits) with which he never failed to please a crowd. Singleton remembered for the rest of his life what happened next: "When he finished, even the band in the pit stood up and applauded for him." But Rockwell's decision to back Armstrong and the Dickerson band while they found their footing in New York was no act of charity. On May 18 the trumpeter signed a one-year management contract with Rockwell, who agreed to secure for him a minimum of twenty-five weeks' worth of work. In return Armstrong agreed to pay Rockwell $75 out of the first $250 he earned each week, plus 50 percent of all additional net profits. (Record royalties were split evenly.) It wasn't slavery, but it wasn't generous, either.

Shortly after signing with Rockwell, Armstrong left his band behind and went to Philadelphia to join the company of *Great Day*, which was already in previews. It should have been another triumph. Instead it turned into one of the few occasions on which he was publicly humiliated. Youmans added white string and wind players to the Henderson band, expanding it to the size of a regular Broadway pit orchestra, and brought in a white conductor to replace Fletcher Henderson. As for Armstrong, the *New York Age* reported that

Louis Armstrong was supposed to be the first cornetist in the orchestra, and Russell Smith, second cornetist. In fact it is alleged they were so seated at a rehearsal, and after a number had been played, either Dr. Felix, who is said to have arranged or composed the music, or the conductor, is alleged to have told Armstrong to change chairs with Smith. This placed Russell as first trumpet, Armstrong second. The number was replayed and the decision was made that Armstrong was not adapted to the show business and his seat was declared vacant.

Great Day flopped in Philadelphia and underwent extensive doctoring before it finally opened on Broadway in October, by which time the rest of the blacks in the orchestra had been sent packing as well. Robert Benchley's *New Yorker* review was unsparing: "Almost as much work was put in on *Great Day* as on the Panama Canal, and with nowhere near as much to show for it." The show closed after just thirty-six performances. If Armstrong was hurt by what happened, he never admitted it — he says nothing about *Great Day* in *Swing That Music* and mentions it only in passing in his other writings — and Rockwell gave him no time to lick his wounds. Instead he returned at once to New York and the Dickerson band, which had been hired by Connie and George Immerman, the white proprietors of a Harlem nightclub called Connie's Inn, to play for a black revue called *Hot Chocolates*.

Such shows had been popular ever since Eubie Blake's *Shuffle Along*, the first all-black Broadway musical, opened in 1921 and ran for 504 performances, and in recent years Harlem's top cabarets had started getting into the act. Some of them, like Connie's Inn and the Cotton Club, where Duke Ellington's band was in residence, were for whites only — and only for whites with money to burn. According to the *New York Age*, "Immerman's is opened to Slummers; Sports; 'coke' addicts, and high rollers of the White race who come to Harlem to indulge in illicit and illegal recreations." In *Swing That Music* Armstrong described the crowds that filled the five-hundred-seat club, which was located in a basement on the corner of 131st Street and Seventh Avenue:

In the audience, any old night, would be famous actresses and critics and authors and publishers and rich Wall Street men and big people of all kinds, being gay and enjoying the hot swing music and the fast stepping floor shows. Everybody, of course, was in evening clothes. They had to "dress" to get in. My, the money they spent in those days in those Harlem Clubs! A gentleman and lady would have to spend from forty to sixty dollars for one evening, without spending money for wine.

For a $60 tab — $650 today — the high rollers who came to Connie's expected to be well and truly entertained. The management did its best to oblige, putting on floor shows consisting of light-skinned, scantily clad chorus girls (some of whom were female impersonators) accompanied by red-hot jazz. The club went out of its way to make downtowners feel at ease, and by 1928 the "Goings On About Town" section of the *New Yorker* was regularly citing Connie's as "among the better places for first visitors [to Harlem] not under expert guidance." Later the magazine dispensed with euphemism, warning that Harlem's "most lowdown and amusing places do not welcome unknown whites."

In February of 1929 the Immermans brought in Fats Waller and Andy Razaf to write a score for their spring floor show. According to the *Pittsburgh Courier*, *Hot Feet* was "the first floor show of New York's exclusive night clubs to be entirely the work of men of color," and the opening night was so well received that the Immermans decided to beef up the show and turn it into a Broadway revue bankrolled by Dutch Schultz, one of New York's most vicious gangsters, who was already supplying Connie's with bootleg liquor. *Connie's "Hot Chocolates,"* as the downtown version of *Hot Feet* was officially known, was previewed at a Bronx theater on June 3. Not long after that, Rockwell talked the producers into adding Armstrong to the show. By then it was clear that the Immermans would need a second group to perform uptown at Connie's while LeRoy Smith's house band played for *Hot Chocolates* on Broadway, so Leonard Harper, the show's director, worked out a plan: Armstrong would play in the pit each night for *Hot Chocolates*, then rush uptown to join the Dickerson band for the late show at Connie's.

Armstrong had already met Fats Waller during his stint with the Henderson band, and they hit it off instantly. He was, the trumpeter said, "the most jolliest musician I ever met in my life." More important, Waller was Armstrong's kind of musician, a chubby, gin-guzzling stride pianist who liked every kind of music but boogie-woogie. The two men worked together in Erskine Tate's Vendome band when Waller paid a visit to Chicago in 1926. "We used to play for the films, and during the intermission, we would play a big Overture and a Red Hot Number afterwards," Armstrong remembered. "And folks, I'm telling you, we used to really romp." Waller had cut several records and was considered one of Harlem's top jazz pianists, but like Armstrong, he would not become famous until he learned how to package himself as a popular entertainer. But the success in 1928 of *Keep Shufflin'*, the first Broadway show to which he contributed original material, helped to establish him as a professional songwriter, and in the two weeks that separated the Bronx tryout of *Hot Chocolates* from its Broadway opening, Waller and Razaf, the pianist's trusty lyricist, came up with a pair of showstoppers. "Ain't Misbehavin'," which the two men knocked out in a single forty-five-minute sitting, is a swinging ballad whose riffy, unmistakably pianistic tune has the chiseled quality of a classic. Leonard Harper decided to "plug" it, arranging for the song to be sung by Edith Wilson in the first act, then reprised as an entr'acte by Armstrong, who played and sang it from the orchestra pit after intermission. "From the first time I heard it, that song used to 'send' me," he wrote in *Swing That Music*. "I wood-shedded it until I could play all around it." The second number written by Waller and Razaf for *Hot Chocolates* was a minor-key song of social significance called "(What Did I Do to Be So) Black and Blue." It was, amazingly enough, Dutch Schultz who had the idea for the song, telling Razaf that the show needed a comic number in which a "colored girl" sang about how hard it was to be black. When Razaf balked, Schultz pulled a gun and told him to get to work.

Hot Chocolates opened at Broadway's Hudson Theatre on June 20. Though Charles Brackett claimed in the *New Yorker* that it had "everything a revue should have except some good new music," his colleagues disagreed. *Time* capped its enthusiastic one-paragraph notice with a sentence that summed up the consensus view: "Best tune:

'Ain't Misbehavin'.'" But it was still customary in 1929 for the drama critics of New York's morning papers to leave shows at intermission so that they could write and file their reviews in time to appear the following day, and only one, the anonymous reviewer of the *New York Times*, stayed in his seat long enough to take note of Armstrong's contribution: "One song, a synthetic but entirely pleasant jazz ballad called 'Ain't Misbehavin'" stands out, and its rendition between the acts by an unnamed member of the orchestra was a high light of the première."

That Armstrong went unnamed in the review was no oversight. His name did not appear in the opening-night program, presumably meaning that his entr'acte was added to the bill after the program had gone to press. But his rendition of "Ain't Misbehavin'" must have made an immediate impression on audiences, for by July 8 it was listed in the program, and eleven days later he and the Dickerson band recorded the song for OKeh. The arrangement follows the pattern set by "I Can't Give You Anything but Love": Armstrong plays a muted half-chorus theme statement accompanied by saxophones, followed by eight bars of Dickerson's dainty violin. The sax section wraps up the first chorus, after which Armstrong sings a breathless paraphrase of Waller's melody. Then he pulls out his straight mute and cuts loose with a full-chorus trumpet solo that makes only glancing reference to the theme. The solo was clearly worked out in rehearsal and burnished to a high gloss by repeated performances on Broadway — it pivots on a two-bar break in which Armstrong tosses off with seeming nonchalance a quote from *Rhapsody in Blue* — but like all of his set pieces, it sounds as fresh as if it had been made up on the spot.

If Rockwell had any lingering doubts about Armstrong's commercial potential, "Ain't Misbehavin'" erased them. The trumpeter returned to the studio with the Dickerson band on July 19 to record the song. OKeh rushed it into stores, and the ads heralded his star quality: "Here it is as New York Audiences hear Louis play it in 'Connie's Hot Chocolates.'" Unmentioned in the earliest ads was the

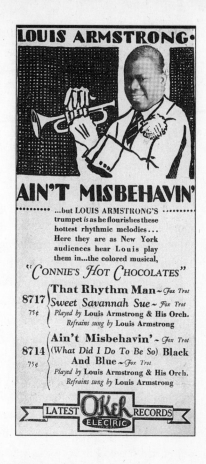

A 1929 advertisement for Armstrong's OKeh recording of "Ain't Misbehavin'," released while he was performing the song on Broadway in *Hot Chocolates*. Ads such as these, which appeared in black newspapers, helped to spread Armstrong's fame — but only to the buyers of "race records." It was not until his music started to be marketed to a more ethnically diverse audience that he became a true star.

flip side, "Black and Blue," with which he would later come to be as closely identified even though he had not sung the song in the show. In *Hot Chocolates* Razaf's lyric was prefaced by a verse in which a dark-skinned woman complains of intra-racial prejudice. On record Armstrong dropped the verse and turned the chorus into a threnody for blacks of every shade. Yet there was nothing lugubrious about the way he sang "Black and Blue," to which he brought a touch of wry humor that made its closing lines all the more telling: *My only sin is in my skin / What did I do to be so black and blue?* For the narrator of Ralph Ellison's *Invisible Man*, it was an anthem whose stark honesty pointed to the possibility of deliverance:

I'd like to hear five recordings of Louis Armstrong playing and singing "What Did I Do to Be so Black and Blue" — all at the same time. Sometimes now I listen to Louis while I have my favorite dessert of vanilla ice cream and sloe gin. I pour the red liquid over the white mound, watching it glisten and the vapor rising as Louis bends that military instrument into a beam of lyrical sound. Perhaps I like Louis Armstrong because he's made poetry out of being invisible. I think it must be because he's unaware that he is invisible.

For the rest of the year Armstrong ping-ponged between Broadway and Harlem, and a week after the show opened, he even managed to work in a few extra performances next door at the Lafayette Theater. "Didn't exactly feel I had the world at my feet, but was very nice everybody was picking up on the things I was doing and all the band leaders wanted me," he said four decades later. As usual his self-appraisal was realistic: *Hot Chocolates* had not made him a superstar, but it did give him a toehold in the white world, and it also gave him a pop song that was the perfect vehicle for his ebullient singing and playing. He would continue to perform "Ain't Misbehavin'" for years to come. "I believe that great song, and the chance I got to play it, did a lot to make me better known all over the country," he wrote in 1936. That was putting it mildly. Better than anyone, he knew how well it had served him.

"Chicago's own Louis Armstrong and his orchestra are the current rage in New York," Dave Peyton reported in the *Chicago Defender* in July. In a detail guaranteed to please his black readers, Peyton told how "[t]he white musicians of New York tendered Louis a banquet several weeks ago and presented him with a handsome wrist watch, engraved thusly, 'To Louis Armstrong, the World's Greatest cornetist, from the Musicians of New York.'" The musicians who threw the party included Eddie Lang, Joe Venuti, and Jimmy and Tommy Dorsey, the best white jazzmen in town, and the inscription, according to Armstrong, read GOOD LUCK ALWAYS TO LOUIS ARMSTRONG

It was a singular tribute, coming as it did at a time when it was unthinkable for black and white players to share a stage.

Yet the banquet also pointed to the distance that still separated Armstrong from true fame. To bridge that gap he would have to make hit records, so Tommy Rockwell put him to work. Between September of 1929 and the end of 1930, Armstrong recorded twenty-eight different songs in eighteen recording sessions, all but two with big-band accompaniment and many issued both as race records and as part of OKeh's regular line, meaning that they would also be distributed to stores in white neighborhoods. Nor was he recording commercial fluff. Most of the songs he sang, then and for the next few years, became standards that continue to be performed today — it was Armstrong who introduced many of them into the jazz repertory — and some, like "Body and Soul," were harmonically complex to a degree that would have defeated most of his New Orleans contemporaries. "After You've Gone," "Blue Turning Grey over You," "I Ain't Got Nobody," "I Can't Believe That You're in Love with Me," "Memories of You," "Rockin' Chair": such was the fare that he now offered his fans. Except for the already-familiar "St. Louis Blues" and "Tiger Rag," he was careful to steer clear of explicitly jazzy material, but that hardly mattered, since everything he did came out jazzy, even "Sweethearts on Parade," a footling ditty by Carmen Lombardo, Guy's brother, that Armstrong, in one of his most stupendous feats of alchemy, turned into a three-minute trumpet concerto of the utmost splendor.

It was Armstrong's singing that gave these records their commercial appeal, and on many of them he can be heard assimilating the distinctive style of a new mentor whose music he had discovered the year before:

> I remember the first time a friend of mine in Chicago, he came to my house and said, "Man, there's a little cat comin' up singin', you got to dig him! His name is Bing Crosby. See, you got to dig him on Paul Whiteman's records." And that was my boy, Papa Bing.

By 1929 Crosby was well on the way to becoming the most famous pop singer in America, one who had learned much, as Rudy Vallée would point out, from Armstrong's improvisational freedom and rhythmic ease: "Compare a record by Crosby, in which he departs from the 'straight' form of the melody and lyric, and then listen to an Armstrong record and discover whence must have come some of his ideas of 'swinging.'" Though Vallée believed that Crosby's embrace of Armstrong's style was unconscious, Crosby knew very well what he was doing. "I'm proud to acknowledge my debt to the Reverend Satchelmouth," he said in a 1950 interview. "He is the beginning and the end of music in America." Armstrong returned the compliment by paying close attention to the younger man's balladry. "Bing's voice has a mellow quality that only Bing's got," he said. "It's like gold being poured out of a cup." No one in his right mind would call Armstrong's voice mellow, but listening to him croon "I'm Confessin'" or "When Your Lover Has Gone," with their delicately fluttering ornaments, shows that he aspired to Crosby's lyricism. In place of the shouting of the acoustically recorded Hot Five sides, he now sang with a warmth whose source is self-evident. Later on he would even record three of Crosby's signature ballads — "I Surrender, Dear," "Star Dust," and "Wrap Your Troubles in Dreams" — in strongly individual performances that nonetheless owe much to Bing's example.

The oft-noted problem with Armstrong's vocal records is that their accompaniments and accompanists are mostly undistinguished. Even Crosby admitted as much. "Louis never had a very good band," he said in his autobiography. "I don't know why. He always was great himself but he never seemed to have very many good men playing for him." Nowhere in his records of the period, or for long afterward, is it possible to hear arrangements comparable in craftsmanship to the ones that can be heard on the contemporary recordings of Henderson, Duke Ellington, Paul Whiteman, or the Casa Loma Orchestra, to name four big bands that aspired to an ensemble polish that Armstrong's groups never achieved. At least one of his musicians thought that he was getting what he wanted: "It's ridiculous to think that Louis couldn't have used fancier arrangements. If he'd wanted them, he'd have bought them. . . . [H]e wanted simple riffs, hot but simple, behind his solos." Yet that preference, if such it was, does nothing to explain his equally puzzling willingness to work with second-rate players. Did he think they made him sound better by contrast? Or was he afraid to insist that his white managers hire a higher class of sidemen? Instead he chose to make do with gray competence, just as he accepted without demur the stylized three-chorus format first heard on "I Can't Give You Anything but Love" and repeated with only minor variations on most of the big-band records he cut for OKeh.

The simplicity of this format was the very thing that recommended it to Armstrong. As a young man he had learned from Joe Oliver to worship at the altar of melody, and that lifelong belief was never displayed more systematically than in the records that he made in 1929 and 1930. "When You're Smiling," indeed, is nothing but melody, first stated by Carroll Dickerson's violin and the band's unctuous saxophones, then sung with unlicentious freedom by Armstrong, followed by a clarion trumpet recapitulation. Significantly, his solo was inspired not by a jazz musician but by B. A. Rolfe, a now-forgotten white trumpet soloist and dance-band leader who was known in the thirties for his perfectly controlled upper-register playing. Armstrong had first heard him playing opposite the Henderson band at Roseland: "Vincent Lopez came in there as guest one time. B. A. Rolfe was with him, and he would play a tune called 'Shadowland' an octave higher than it was written. I observed that, and it inspired me to make 'When You're Smiling.' The way I look at it, that's the way a trumpet should play."

After hearing Rolfe, Armstrong began pushing harder at the accepted upper limits of the trumpet's range. Soon he was comfortable with the high E-flat that had once been accessible only to classically trained players, and in October of 1930, on Eubie Blake's "You're Lucky to Me," he nailed (barely) his first recorded high F. "I started blowin' all them high notes to impress folks," he later admitted, "but I never intended to keep it up." He had no choice. After 1930 audiences took for granted his access to the highest possible notes. Even Joe Oliver was impressed. "Louis Armstrong . . . is some cornet player now Bunk," he wrote to Bunk Johnson early that year. "That bird can hit F and G with ease." Others were dipping into the same bag of tricks. Jabbo Smith, a daring young virtuoso from Georgia who had set up shop in Chicago around the time that Armstrong moved to New York, could play as high as Armstrong and was in some ways even more facile. What Smith lacked, however, was Armstrong's ability to use the upper register of the trumpet to *expressive* effect, soaring above the staff in a manner reminiscent of the 78s of Caruso and John McCormack that he had heard in New Orleans. The 1929 recording of "When You're Smiling" is our first glimpse of this technical triumph, which became central to his identity as a soloist in spite of the fact that it had nothing to do with jazz per se, though other trumpeters were quick to emulate it — if they could.

Nowadays Armstrong's playing on "When You're Smiling" no longer surprises listeners, but in 1929 it floored all who heard it. Taft Jordan, then a fourteen-year-old novice trumpet player from Norfolk, Virginia, never forgot hearing him play the song at a local dance:

> Well, right after intermission [Armstrong] went into "When You're Smiling," and the house was in an uproar. And just as suddenly it quieted down, because everybody wanted to hear this. After Louis got through singing it, the saxes came in for eight bars, and then he played, and they screamed again — and came right back down. Then he really got into playing "When You're Smiling"! He had a great big Turkish towel around his neck, and perspiration was coming out like rain water. When he got to the last eight bars, he was getting stronger and stronger.

The bandstand was surrounded by musicians, some of whom suspected that Armstrong was playing a trick instrument on which he could play higher than normal. One of them asked to see his trumpet between sets. "So the guy put his mouthpiece in and sounded C on Pops' horn and C on his own," Jordan recalled. "He ran the scale on his, and he ran the scale on Pops'. It was all the same. It was no trick horn. It was just the man, the difference of the man." No musician who heard him play "When You're Smiling" could fail to grasp the difference. Yet the squarest of dancers needed no road map to pick out the tune, or to be struck by the luster with which he played it. That was the way he wanted it, then and later, though his own contributions to the records he made during this period never want for the transforming touch of his imagination. While nothing could be more "conservative" than his straightforward version of "If I Could Be with You One Hour Tonight," the ingenuity with which he reshapes the song's melodic line is (in Gunther Schuller's words) "a dazzling lesson in how to mix primary thematic material with purely ornamental passages without ever losing the sense of the overall melody."

What is missing from most of Armstrong's early big-band records is the element of contrast that had been provided in 1928 by the piano playing of Earl Hines. On the rare occasions when it is present, it becomes clear what he gave up by choosing to put himself forward as a soloist pure and simple. The spirited ensemble work of Luis Russell's band, for instance, adds immeasurably to the total effect of "St. Louis Blues," one of the few records of this period in which the playing of Armstrong's sidemen, especially J. C. Higginbotham, is worthy of note. Philip Larkin described it with glee: "Armstrong shouts a couple of blues choruses not to be found in the original [W. C.] Handy song sheet, then after twelve bars of Higgie's trombone Louis leads the ensemble in four blistering choruses of solid riffing. By the third chorus the whole building seems to be moving." Larkin's friend Kingsley Amis was similarly transported by Armstrong's singing on "Bessie Couldn't Help It," another Russell-accompanied side in which the band's bouncy playing inspired him to emit what Amis called "a kind of gurgle of indescribable lasciviousness."

Most of Armstrong's early big-band recordings are flecked with such flights of spontaneity. A particularly endearing one is the moment in "I'm a Ding Dong Daddy (from Dumas)" when he launches into a choice bit of scat, then admits in midphrase that "I done forgot the words." He had never been more creatively vital, and that burgeoning vitality was almost always sufficient to make up for the absence of the competing voices that had helped to make his earlier records so exciting. Even on the simplest of the big-band sides, his playing is charged with an expressive depth that seizes the ear. Darius Milhaud, whose visits to the nightclubs of Harlem a few years earlier had filled him with awe, now heard in "Exactly Like You" a note of pathos that casual listeners might well overlook. "The impression is heart-rending," Milhaud wrote. "One is overwhelmed at the pain and the despair." *Despair* is not the right word — Armstrong's music is as free of that grim emotion as it is of self-pity — but there is an underlying seriousness to his lighthearted art that recalls a remark made by the film director Howard Hawks, who claimed that "the only difference between comedy and tragedy is the point of view."

Armstrong himself came to feel that his playing was overstated, and as he grew older he pared away its excesses. Even in his youth, though, he leavened his virtuosity with charm. "Louis Armstrong, the hottest trumpet player in America conducts the hottest, and most rhythmic dance record on sale," read OKeh's ad for "I Can't Give You Anything but Love" and "Mahogany Hall Stomp." *Variety*, however, was at least as astute when it assured its readers that the hottest trumpet player in America also had "a very ingratiating manner." It had as much to do with his success as his genius.

The stock market crashed in October, but Armstrong didn't notice. He was too busy racing from gig to gig and having fun afterward. In those days he cut so fine a figure that a young trumpeter named Buck Clayton, who ran into him on the street a year later, never forgot the sight of him: "He had just come out of the hotel and he looked awfully sharp. His hair looked nice and shiny and he had on a pretty gray suit. He wore a tie that looked like an ascot tie with an extra-big knot in it. . . . I only saw him for a few minutes but he sure impressed me just by his appearance." The days of high-top shoes and long johns were over: the world's greatest trumpeter had learned to dress the part.

For all the sharpness of his tailoring, Armstrong was still the same kindly man he had always been. Mezz Mezzrow, who got to know him around this time, noted that he "looked at the humorous side of life and if he saw anybody angry he'd look the situation over and say gently, 'Well, he hasn't dug life yet but he's a good cat at heart.'" He was, in short, a happy man, and he had plenty to be happy about. *Hot Chocolates* ran all the way through the middle of December. White listeners were buying his records. For the past year or so he had been subscribing to a clipping service, and now Alpha Smith, the pretty young girl from the South Side of Chicago who had broken up his marriage to Lil and become his regular consort, spent her spare time pasting stories that proclaimed his virtues into his scrapbooks. In November the *Melody Maker*, an English magazine for dance-band musicians whose editors took jazz seriously, featured him in an article about New York's top jazzmen: "Louis has everything about 100 per cent. . . . In addition he is in every way a charming, honest, unassuming fellow."

Armstrong had a setback when the Immermans fired the Dickerson band after *Hot Chocolates* closed: "[T]he Guys in the Band Commenced to making Late Time etc. . . . [T]he boys, (the lushies) commenced to messin' up (with a Capitol F) and Mr. Connie who was a very nice man to us said — 'I just can't stand it any longer.'" But he had already figured out that "I had to get in front of my own band," and Tommy Rockwell was ready to send him out on the road. The most far-reaching consequence of the firing was that it ended his friendship with Zutty Singleton. The two men had never been entirely at ease with one another, for Singleton was a proud and prickly man who resented his younger colleague's popularity, and this may explain why he now accepted the Immermans' offer of a job with the new house band at Connie's Inn. "Friendship is one thing and business is another," he told Armstrong. Singleton claimed that he had offered to continue working with the trumpeter, but Mezz Mezzrow disputed that version of the quarrel: "He was a great artist himself, and felt maybe he'd get further on his own, and some day have his own band, so he stayed in Connie's." Armstrong responded by putting Singleton on his drop-dead list. He said nothing about their break in public, but on one of his private tapes, made after Earl Hines had quit the All Stars in 1951, he can be heard telling a girlfriend that "there's two musicians I ain't never supposed to play with again, and I made that very clear to Joe Glaser, and I don't think he'll go over my will, over my, over my demands, when he see I'm serious. And that's Earl Hines and Zutty Singleton. . . . You're supposed to stick together, that's them hardships, and [Singleton] didn't. He didn't stick with nobody. He insulted me. And that's what puts the son of a bitch behind the eight-ball." The ban was not absolute — the two men played together on a few occasions — but only at the end of their lives did they reconcile.

Armstrong worked as a single act throughout the first six months of 1930, fronting a string of bands and stopping the show wherever he went. The difference was that his activities were now deemed worthy of note by the white press. On his return to New York, he made it into Walter Winchell's widely read Broadway column for the first time: "Louis Armstrong, the most torrid of the horn-tooters and blues-shooers is at the Cocoanut Grove and his delightful specialties serve to entice the bored-with-Broadway diversion seekers, on Sunday eves particularly, when Armstrong offers an endless routine of terrifically-tempoed tunes." Even the *New Yorker* deigned to take note of him, reviewing "After You've Gone" and "St. Louis Blues" in the snooty manner it assumed when speaking of black entertainers: "New conceptions of familiar Senegambiana, and there is nothing quite so smoky as Mr. Armstrong's singing of vocal choruses." Yet despite the attention he was getting in New York, he had little choice but to play out of town. The Depression had put the bite on the local club scene, and musicals like *Hot Chocolates* were becoming riskier to mount. The best money was in Hollywood, so in July he went there to look for work. By now he had started recording with the Blue Rhythm Band, a Harlem group managed by Irving Mills, the entrepreneurial wizard responsible for Duke Ellington's commercial success. According to Lionel Hampton, Mills thought it might be profitable for Armstrong to go to California on his own and front the house band at the Cotton Club, the top nightspot in Culver City, the Los Angeles suburb where MGM was based.

Armstrong remembered it differently: "I had a friend who ran on the [railroad] from New York to California . . . And would always tell me he could get a Pass for me any time I should see fit to go out there . . . And always I would ask him, 'What's out there?' . . . Not knowing that I was as popular as I actually was in California." In his version, he took a train out West "with nothin in particular to look for or forward to either." On his arrival he ran into a fan who took him to the Cotton Club, whose band, in which Hampton played drums, impressed him. So did the club itself, a sprawling faux-Tudor building located up the street from MGM. Frank Sebastian, the proprietor, was a tall, well-dressed sharpie with a "welcoming, infectious smile" and a manner that one of his employees recalled as "majestic." Sebastian's club was widely thought to be mobbed up, and even if it wasn't, its owner must have been playing fast and loose with the law, since the Cotton Club openly permitted gambling and the local police looked the other way at the bootleggers who supplied its all-white movie-star clientele (George Raft was a regular) with liquor. Marshal Royal, a member of the house band, described Sebastian as "the big man in Culver City. The tops in the police department. The police all came in there and ate for free, you know." The Cotton Club may be the unnamed nightspot where Raymond Chandler recalled that "two policemen were always on duty — not to keep you from getting liquor, but to keep you from bringing in your own instead of buying it from the house."

Armstrong's version of how he came to California appears to be slightly embroidered. On July 11 a local black newspaper reported that he had just arrived in Los Angeles "to open at Sebastian's Cotton Club," indicating that he had already been engaged before leaving New York. One way or another, though, he became the titular leader of what was now billed as "Louis Armstrong and his New Sebastian Cotton Club Orchestra." (The "new" was a nod to Harlem's better-known club of the same name.) He brought along a companion: Armstrong had left Alpha behind in Chicago, and Lil joined him for a short-lived reconciliation. It was in Los Angeles that they made their last record together. On July 16 Louis and Lil met Jimmie Rodgers in a Hollywood studio and cut "Blue Yodel No. 9 (Standin' on the Corner)," a Rodgers-penned variation on "Frankie and Johnny." The singer-guitarist, who had signed with Victor three years earlier, was so popular that the patrons of general stores were said to ask for "a sack of flour, a slab of bacon, and the latest Jimmie Rodgers record." Nobody knows how the date came to pass, but it isn't hard to guess: Ralph Peer, who had brought the Armstrongs to OKeh in 1925, was now producing country records for Victor, and Rodgers was his number-one star. "I'd been knowin' Jimmie for a long time," Louis later claimed. Now that he was looking for work, it seems probable that he met up with Peer after arriving in California and agreed to play on the session, his first on the West Coast.

Neither Armstrong is credited on the label of "Blue Yodel No. 9," but their joint presence is unmistakable. Louis fires off a no-nonsense introduction, and Lil supports him in her best barrelhouse style. Then Rodgers enters, telling one of his timeless tales of romantic mischance, complete with yodeling. The accent may be that of a hillbilly from Mississippi, but the sensibility is straight out of Storyville, and Armstrong backs up Rodgers with the same down-home fills he had supplied for Bessie Smith and Ma Rainey. Like other country-blues singers, Rodgers freely dropped and inserted beats at will: the last stanza of "Blue Yodel No. 9" consists of three bars in 4/4 time, a bar of 2/4, two more bars of 4/4, and another 2/4 bar, after which the singer continues to switch unpredictably between two and four. But the Armstrongs followed him without too much difficulty, and the resulting performance was far more than a cross-cultural novelty. Not that Louis's ability to adapt to Rodgers's style should have come as a surprise: the record collection with which he traveled in later years contained everything from Bix and Bing to Bartók's *Concerto for Orchestra*. In 1970 he would startle his purist fans by recording an album of country songs. "No change for me, daddy, I was doing that same kind of work forty years ago," he blithely told a friend.

The day after Armstrong recorded with Rodgers, he opened at the Cotton Club, whose art-deco table cards variously billed him as "King of the Trumpet," "The World's Greatest Cornetist," and "Star of Connie's 'Hot Chocolates.'" At first he had been skeptical about playing jazz with an ensemble of Californians, but they easily overcame his qualms. "Louis fell in love with us," Lionel Hampton said in his memoirs. On another occasion Hampton spoke of a performance at which Armstrong cut loose in a way that showed how he felt about the Cotton Club band: "We were on the air one night, and he said, 'Look out, man, we're gonna open up with "Dumas." I feel good tonight, and if I'm going well, Hamp, you sit on those cowbells with me, and I'll play another chorus.' Well, man, I was sitting on those cowbells, and Louis played about ninety-nine choruses on 'I'm a Ding Dong Daddy from Dumas.'" In later years Armstrong wrote of Hampton and his colleagues in a way that is indicative of the depth of his disillusion with Carroll Dickerson's "lushies" and Fletcher Henderson's "big-head motherfuckers":

> I had already heard some of the greatest men on their instruments, yet, these boys sort of had a little something on the ball (musically) that I had not witnessed . . . Such as endurance — tones, perfect sense of phrasing, and the willingness and the spirit that the Eastern Musicians or the Southern Musicians used to have before they got to Broadway and became stinkers, looking for power and egotisms, the desire to do practically anything but enjoy their first love — which is their instrument. . . . Lionel used to get so Enthused over my playing Trumpet he would get "*Soakened Wet.*"

The band was even more impressed by its new leader. The trombonist Lawrence Brown, who was to spend the remainder of his long career playing for Duke Ellington, singled out Armstrong as "the only man that ever made me enjoy coming to work. . . . [He was] the kind of musician you could sit there all night and listen to and be amazed at the technique, the poise, and just everything." The critics agreed. "Louis Armstrong is the most extraordinary trumpeter I have ever heard," W. E. Oliver of the *Los Angeles Evening Herald* wrote of Armstrong's Cotton Club debut. "In addition, he is one of the best showmen I have seen at the head of an orchestra." A letter sent by Johnny Mercer to his wife, Ginger, hints at the way Armstrong was perceived by a jazz-savvy listener: "The great Louis Armstrong was at his youthful peak, his prime, but those dumb customers at the Cotton Club didn't want to hear 'Struttin' with Some Barbecue' or the 'Heebie Jeebies' or 'Knockin' a Jug' or 'Monday Date.' What they loved was the suggestive 'Golfin' Papa, You Got the Nicest Niblick in Town.'" Even then his penchant for catering to the crowd was starting to make knowledgeable fans uncomfortable.

OKeh hastened to record Armstrong with the Cotton Club band. On July 21 they went into the studio for the first of six sessions at which they cut several of his best-remembered sides, including "Ding Dong Daddy," "Sweethearts on Parade," and Eubie Blake's "Memories of You," the last of which Lionel Hampton had good reason to recall. Armstrong saw a strange-looking instrument in the studio and asked the drummer what it was. "Oh, that's a new instrument they're bringing into percussion, into the drum department," he replied. The trumpeter asked if Hampton could play it, and he responded by picking up a pair of mallets and rattling off "Cornet Chop Suey" note for note. "Come on, we going to put this on a record," Armstrong said, and a few minutes later Hampton was backing him up on "Memories of You." It was the first time that jazz had been played on a vibraphone.

By then Armstrong must have decided that his future lay on the West Coast, for in September he canceled his contract with Tommy Rockwell, who was trying to get him to return to New York for another stint at Connie's Inn. He preferred to stay in California, in part because he had been invited to perform in a movie. *Ex-Flame*, an updated screen version of the Victorian novel *East Lynne*, sank without trace, and no prints of the film have survived, though Armstrong is known to have appeared with the Cotton Club orchestra in a nightclub sequence. It was an inauspicious debut for a man who would costar with Bing Crosby in one of the top-grossing films of 1936. Otherwise he had nothing to complain about. He was filling the Cotton Club every night, and his live broadcasts were being heard up and down the West Coast. "Hottest of the hot trumpeters, model of innumerable collegiate orchestras, a consistent recorder and good seller," *Variety* called him in November. A month later he made it into *Time*, which took note of "Memories of You" in its record column: "For those who like hot jazz with husky singing, husky trumpets."

Mayann Armstrong's deathbed prophecy had come true at last. Everybody loved her Louis — except the Los Angeles Police Department.

6

"DON'T LET 'EM COOL OFF, BOYS"

On the Run, 1930–1932

LOUIS ARMSTRONG WAS NEITHER the first nor the last jazz musician to use marijuana. Since his death, though, he has become the one with whom it is most closely identified, for he left behind two posthumously published accounts of his experiences with the intoxicant herb in which he admitted to having enjoyed it enormously. The least hypocritical of men, he saw no reason to conceal the fact, known to all his friends, that he smoked pot nearly every day: "I felt at no time when ever I ran across some of that good shit, that I was breaking the law, or some foolish thought similar to it . . . There isn't one person in the whole wide world — white — black — grizzly or gray who ain't breaking the law of some kind, for their kicks — contentment."

In the first of these accounts, Armstrong discusses "gage" (his preferred nickname for marijuana) in connection with his mother's advice to take a laxative daily. She had given him a potion concocted out of "Pepper Grass, Dandelions, and lots of weeds similar to gage" that she picked by the railroad tracks, brought home, and boiled up into a "physic." Later he saw young white musicians looking "fresh — neat and very much contented" after their gigs, and learned that they were smoking marijuana instead of drinking alcohol. Again Mayann's counsel came to mind: "I never was born to be a Square about anything, no matter what it is . . . My mother always told me, to try anything at least once." He did so and became an ardent advocate. At one point he started writing a book in which he called for the legalization of marijuana, declaring it to be "an Assistant — a friend a nice cheap drunk" and claiming that it was both "a thousand times better than whiskey" (which in the age of bootleg liquor was very likely true) and safer than "Heroin — Cocaine — etc. — or some other unGodly shit. . . . Show a dope fiend a bucket of water and they'll run like hell to keep it from touching them. But a viper would gladly welcome a good bath, clean underwear, top clothes, stay fresh and on the ball."

Armstrong's preference for marijuana over alcohol was known to jazz musicians everywhere, as well as to fans who shared his tastes. One "club" of St. Louis smokers presented him with a joint the size of a baseball bat, accompanied by a card dubbing him "King of the Vipers." Many younger players later said that it was Armstrong who first got them high. "The first person I ever saw smoke marijuana," Charlie Barnet wrote in his memoirs, "was Louis Armstrong. . . . During an intermission we all went over to hear Louis. He was down in the basement rolling the stuff and I know I had some that night." Buck Clayton, who met him backstage at the Cotton Club, liked to tell how Armstrong offered him a toke before showing him how to execute the impossible-sounding glissandi that the younger man had heard on his radio broadcasts. They finished the joint together, after which Clayton went home, got down on his knees, and prayed, "Oh God, now that I am a dope addict, please forgive me. Please don't let me become a real habitual dope addict. I just did it one time, please stop me now."

Few jazz musicians shared Clayton's short-lived fear of marijuana. "Every one of us that smoked the stuff came to the conclusion that it wasn't habit-forming and couldn't be called a narcotic," Mezz Mezzrow wrote in *Really the Blues*, the 1946 autobiography in which he told how he supplied the jazz-playing "vipers" of the thirties with their drug of choice. He was careful not to name Armstrong as one of them, but it isn't hard to guess the identity of the "fine musician" whom he quotes at length in *Really the Blues:* "Man, they can say what they want about us vipers, but you just dig them lushhounds with their old antique jive, always comin' up loud and wrong, whippin' their old ladies and wastin' up all their pay, and then the next day your head feels like all the hammers in the piano is beatin' out a tune on your brain. Just look at the difference between you and them other cats, that come uptown juiced to the gills, crackin' out of line and passin' out in anybody's hallway. Don't nobody come up thataway when he picks up on some good grass."

Marijuana was still legal in most states when Armstrong started using it. Mezzrow remembered how the two of them would "roll our cigarettes right out in the open and light up like you would on a Camel or a Chesterfield." But its use was already a felony in Louisiana, and by 1930, when the Federal Bureau of Narcotics came into being, a dozen additional states, including California, had passed antimarijuana laws. Harry Anslinger, the head of the Treasury Department's new bureau, was a hard-line Prohibition enforcer who had sought to criminalize the purchase of liquor and was now determined to make marijuana illegal throughout America. In 1937 he wrote a widely read magazine article called "Marijuana: Assassin of Youth" in which he called it "as dangerous as a coiled rattlesnake. How many murders, suicides, and maniacal deeds it causes each year, especially among the young, can only be conjectured." Such heavy rhetorical breathing was a staple of Anslinger's campaign, and it was echoed in antidrug films like *Reefer Madness* that portrayed the use of marijuana as the first step on a road that led to promiscuity, madness, and death. At length Anslinger got his way, and Armstrong stopped rolling joints on the sidewalks of Harlem. "At first you was a mis-do-meanor," the trumpeter recalled in an apostrophe to "Mary Warner" that he taped late in life. "But as the years rolled by you lost your misdo and got meaner and meaner, jailhousely speaking." He knew whereof he spoke. The "special kinship" of vipers got him into the worst scrape of his career — one that put his life at risk.

It started in the parking lot of the Cotton Club, where Armstrong went on the night of November 14, 1930, to smoke a joint between sets with the white drummer Vic Berton, one of Bix Beiderbecke's old compatriots:

> While Vic and I were blasting this joint, having lots of laughs and feelin' good, enjoying each other's fine company, we were standing in this great big lot in front of some cars. Just then, two big healthy dicks (detectives, that is) come from behind a car, man, nonchalantly, and say to us, "We'll take the roach, boys." Mmmm! Vic and I said nothin'. So one dick stayed with me until I went into the club and did my last show. He enjoyed it, too. Because when he and I were on our way down to the police station, he and I had a heart-to-heart talk. The first words that he said to me were, "Armstrong, I'm a big fan of yours and so is my family. We catch your programs every night over the radio."

The detective went on to explain that another local bandleader who was jealous "because you were doing bigger business" had informed on him. "When we found out that you was the one that we must nab," he added, "it broke our hearts." That didn't stop him from taking Armstrong to the downtown city jail, where the trumpeter spent a night behind bars. A week after praising Armstrong as the "hottest of the hot trumpeters," *Variety* got wind of his plight and published another story pointing out that his offense was "a felony punishable by not less than six months and no more than six years in the penitentiary." Black newspapers across the country took note of his arrest, but in 1930 the white public at large knew little of marijuana, or of Louis Armstrong. The arrest went unreported by the *Los Angeles Times*, and it wasn't until ten months later that *Time* got around to mentioning it in a story about the growing popularity of "muggles": "In California, Cornetist Louis Armstrong ('world's greatest Negro cornet player') was sentenced to jail for 30 days for taking poison when caught smoking a 'reefer.'"

Why was he let off so easy? According to Charlie Barnet, the police had "no substantial legal precedent, because marijuana wasn't classified as a narcotic then, and they were afraid of being sued if they interfered with performances at the club." That may have been part of it, but Ralph Berton, Vic's younger brother, later claimed that Abe Lyman, who led the band at the Ambassador Hotel's popular Cocoa-nut Grove nightclub, put the fix in:

> Abe Lyman, Vic's leader at the Coconut [*sic*] Grove, with his brother Tommy, who was a wheel in L.A. County politics (ru-mored to be the bootlegger & procurer of the Democratic party boss), met with His Honor in chambers and explained the facts of life to him. . . .
>
> His Honor was a rational man. Court was reconvened, the two felons brought back upstairs, and, in view of "new evi-dence," given modified sentences that wouldn't interfere with their working hours.

In those days the local authorities were accustomed to cutting deals with celebrities in trouble — especially when the mob took an interest in their trouble. Armstrong wasn't quite a celebrity, but he was successful enough that Frank Sebastian made a point of coming to at least one of the trumpeter's court appearances, where he pre-sumably pulled a string or two of his own. Regardless of who did what to whom, the King of the Vipers went back to work at the Cot-ton Club with the utmost promptitude. He played there until the fol-lowing March, when he pleaded guilty and was sentenced by Judge William Tell Aggeler, who preached him a starchy little sermon: "So you leave [marijuana] alone. Don't deal in it at all. If you have a nice home and a good wife, and you are getting along all right, don't be cultivating evil habits. You and all of us have enough naturally to overcome without tagging ourselves with something that only causes trouble." Armstrong then served nine days of his thirty-day term, after which the judge obligingly suspended the remainder of the sen-tence so that he could "leave the state of California and go to the state of Illinois, not for any improper purpose, but for the purpose of receiving a valuable salary for at least the term of the next six months, with which he can support his wife and child." He had a job in Chicago — and a new manager to go with it.

After Armstrong's death John Hammond spoke of "the vultures who surrounded Louis in the most creative days of his career." None was more vulturine than Johnny Collins, the squat, mustachioed scoundrel who replaced Tommy Rockwell as his manager. Little is known of Collins, who vanished without a trace after he and his client parted company in 1933, but everyone who met him in the thirties seems to have disliked him. "He was a gangster," Armstrong said, and no one could explain how he became the trumpeter's personal manager, not even Armstrong himself. "Mr. Johnny Collins [became] my Manager in California through some Deal he made with Mr. Tommy Rockwell my other manager — *Damn* — Come to think of it — I sure had a Manager's Fit," he wrote in 1944. Budd Johnson, one of Armstrong's sidemen, believed that Collins had "tricked" him into signing a management contract. All we know for sure is that Armstrong had canceled his original contract with Rockwell in September of 1930, which may explain how Collins, who moved to California in August, was able to persuade him to put his affairs in the hands of a different manager. But Rockwell and the Immerman brothers, who were eager to bring Armstrong back to Connie's Inn, had no intention of giving up without a fight — and they knew how to play rough.

➤

For the moment Armstrong remained unaware of the dire implications of the "manager's fit" in which he was caught up. As soon as his sentence was suspended on March 19, he headed straight for Chicago, leaving Lil behind in Los Angeles. According to Armstrong, his semi-estranged wife had cuckolded him there:

> I was still married to Lil Armstrong — she was also out in California with me the whole time I was out there. Also the man she claimed she had him travel with her from New York everywhere she would go to Massage her Hips. — Keeping them from getting too large. — UMP — She sure must have thought I was a Damn fool Sho Nuff. As if I didn't know her Hips are sure to Ignite from the Friction.

Armstrong spent a week playing at the Regal Theater, after which Johnny Collins booked him into the Showboat, a mob-owned nightspot that one of his sidemen described as "all glitter and glass, a very high-class operation." Unable to bring his beloved Cotton Club band with him, he worked instead with a handpicked ensemble of local players that he put together himself, the first such group to be assembled specifically for the purpose of accompanying Armstrong, and a few weeks later he hired a second trumpeter, Zilner Randolph, to write arrangements and serve as the band's music director. He fussed over the onstage appearance of his new musicians, buying them fancy uniforms and warning them to return promptly to the stand after their breaks: "Don't let 'em cool off, boys, keep that audience hot!" He later spoke of them as "a Band that Really deserved a *whole lot* of *Credit* that they *didn't* get," and his colleagues in turn found him to be a caring leader. "He didn't let much ruffle him," said George James, one of the band's saxophonists. "He was the same from day to day, a genteel person. He was like a father to us."

Kindness and discipline do not always go hand in hand, however, and while one hopes that Armstrong's band sounded better in person than on the records that he made for OKeh after opening at the Showboat, it seems more likely that his new sidemen played pretty much the same on the bandstand as in the studio. "There was never much fooling around during recording sessions," James assured an interviewer sixty-one years later. "We were always very professional, and we knew the arrangements well. All of it was material we were using every night. Do you know that Louis made us memorize each new arrangement when we rehearsed it?" But most of the charts were stocks that had been doctored in a futile attempt to make them sound more interesting, and the band's playing of them too often failed to rise above plodding mediocrity. More than ever before, Armstrong himself was all that his records had to offer, and it is a tribute to his genius that the sides he cut that April remain listenable today.

The best known of them is "When It's Sleepy Time Down South," a tribute to the joys of southern life written by Leon and Otis René, a pair of Louisiana Creoles who now lived in California.

They had met Armstrong the preceding year and played the song for him. He responded enthusiastically, untroubled by the fact that the lyrics make conspicuous reference to "darkies," a word that most blacks found as offensive then as they do today. "That's my song, give me that copy, I'm going to feature it every night at the Cotton Club," he told the Renés. "Just give me three saxophones to hold me under, I'll hit the melody, man." He was as good as his word, making "Sleepy Time Down South" his theme song. From then on he played it twice a night all over the world, and there is no reason to think that he did so reluctantly, though in the fifties he would replace "darkies" with "people." Such niceties meant nothing to Armstrong, who made the change solely to keep his audiences happy. For him the song's lyrics evoked the land of lost content, part real and part imagined, that he had left behind in New Orleans: *You hear the banjos ringin', the darkies singin' / They dance till the break of day.* Armstrong was not the only black émigré who felt that way, though the instrumental version of "Sleepy Time Down South" that he recorded in 1941 suggests that he found the song's shapely, handsomely harmonized melody to be as appealing as its nostalgic lyrics. He and Charlie Alexander, the band's pianist, introduce the 1931 recording with a snippet of spoken by-play meant to remind their listeners of the Great Migration that had brought so many of them northward: "How long you been up here, boy?" "Oh, I been up here 'bout, about a year and a half." "A year and a half? Well, man, I been up here a long time myself. I'm goin' back home."

In "You Rascal You (I'll Be Glad When You're Dead)," a novelty about a man whose best friend is dallying with his wife, Armstrong sings with seeming relish about a situation not unlike the one in which Lil had placed him. Once again the spotlight is on his vocal choruses, half-sung, half-spoken, and wholly frisky, and while the heavy-handed playing of the Showboat musicians cannot begin to compare to the way in which the Cotton Club band, propelled by Lionel Hampton's snappy high-hat work, danced through "Ding Dong Daddy," Armstrong manages to light a fire under them well before the last chorus: "Boy, what make you so no good? You come to my house and eat up all my vittles — you *know* what I mean, that's somethin' to eat." His friends appreciated that touch of naughtiness, not to mention the stanza in which he promised to be *standin' on the corner high / When they bring your body by.* But only the members of his band would have known that the song might also have been intended to send a different message, one of distress. Mere days before recording "You Rascal You," their leader found himself standing in a phone booth with a pistol shoved in his side, wondering if his journey from Jane Alley to the brink of stardom was about to come to a bloody end.

Armstrong liked nothing better than to tell a good story on himself, and the story of what happened to him one April night at the Showboat was one of his best, trotted out regularly and retold with the same consistency that he brought to the playing of his favorite solos. According to Armstrong, a "big, bad-ass hood" named Frankie Foster paid him a visit backstage after the show and told him that he had a show to play in New York the next night. The trumpeter told him that he already had an engagement in Chicago, to which Foster responded by pulling out his revolver and cocking it. "*Jesus*, it look like a cannon and sound like death!" Armstrong recalled. "So I look down at that steel and say, 'Weeelllll, maybe I *do* open in New York tomorrow.'" Foster took the trumpeter to a phone booth and handed him the receiver. In later years he was chary about admitting who was on the other end of the line, but in an affidavit filed a few weeks after the fact, he stated unequivocally that the caller was Connie Immerman.

"When are you gonna open here?" Immerman asked.

Looking straight at Foster, Armstrong replied, "Tomorrow A.M."

Another detail that Armstrong omitted when telling reporters the story of his brush with death was that he thought Tommy Rockwell to have been responsible for it. On one of his private tapes he can be heard explaining to his wife Lucille and a group of friends what really happened at the Showboat: "I knew it was [Rockwell] that did it. Was signed up to him at the time, and he wanted me to go and play at Connie's Inn. . . . So he send this gangster, which was the toughest man in Chicago at that time, Frankie Foster, and this cat hadn't

shaved for six months. . . . This Frankie Foster, he's a killer man!"
On this occasion Armstrong said that the caller was George Immerman, not his brother, but the point of the story was the same: Rockwell and the Immermans were prepared to have him murdered if he
didn't cooperate.

Armstrong would later claim to have been initially unaware that
Rockwell and Johnny Collins were "having a 'Feud' (fuss) over my
contract. Why — And for what — I've never found out until this
day." But shortly after his arrival in Chicago, he found out that it was
a blood feud. On April 25 the *Defender* ran a story stating that three
men had been arrested for trying to extort money from Armstrong.
The men claimed in their defense that they were "only trying to get
him to change managers." Later that summer Armstrong claimed in
a court filing that Rockwell and a gang of toughs approached Collins
at the Showboat and demanded that he give them six thousand dollars. Otherwise, one of them told Collins, they would "burn off" his
mustache. On yet another occasion, Armstrong said that "the Gangsters started a fight in the Show Boat in Chicago, right in front of
where I were standing . . . One of the Gangsters took a chair and hit
a woman over the head with it — And the Chair Crumbled up all in
a lot of pieces. Some of the pieces hit my horn."

For a musician raised in black Storyville, such shenanigans were
old hat. Nor were Chicago's black musicians necessarily inclined to
regard their white bosses with reflexive disfavor. "We looked on Al
Capone as more or less a Robin Hood in the black community," the
bassist Milt Hinton remembered. Being threatened face-to-face by a
"bad 'sommitch'" with a gun, however, was different. Johnny Collins
may have looked like a tough guy, but when it came to the likes of
Frankie Foster, he was punching far above his weight. Foster was
thought to have killed Jake Lingle, a crooked reporter who suppos-
edly made the mistake of trying to blackmail Capone. Collins and
Armstrong both understood that a threat from a man like that could
not be shrugged off. At the same time, Armstrong resented the Immermans for having fired him after *Hot Chocolates* closed, and he had
no wish to go back to work for them now that his star was on the rise:

"I felt that—as dirty as Connie Fired me and my Band, I did not want any parts of those people ever again—I am just that way. If you Kick my Ass Once you can bet I won't come back if I can help it, so you can Kick it again."

What to do? His first response was to ask his own gangster friends for help, and they obliged. One of them even went so far as to pay a visit to Tommy Rockwell, who just happened to be in Chicago. On more than one occasion Rockwell would claim that he, too, had been called on by a local tough guy who warned him to catch the next train out of town and "stop fooling around with other people's artists." But he always denied that he was behind Foster's visit to Armstrong, going so far as to threaten to sue Robert Goffin for ostensibly claiming in *Horn of Plenty*, his 1947 Armstrong biography, that Foster had informed the trumpeter that he "was now working for Rockwell." Rockwell assured *Down Beat* that "[t]he incidents involving Frankie Foster concerned Connie's Inn and Foster himself, and did not involve him [i.e., Rockwell] directly."

Was Rockwell telling the truth? Armstrong was open in later years about the role that mobsters had played in his early career, but he could tell only what he knew, and he knew nothing about the rivalry between Rockwell and Collins beyond what he had seen at first hand. It may well be that the Immermans and Dutch Schultz decided on their own to use muscle to bring Armstrong back to New York. Certainly Rockwell's next move was that of a businessman, not a criminal: he filed a grievance with the American Federation of Musicians, the union to which all professional musicians belonged, alleging that Armstrong was refusing to fulfill a contractual commitment to perform at Connie's Inn. Rockwell then played his hole card, producing a contract between Armstrong and Connie's Inn dated July 25, 1930, two months before the trumpeter fired him. The contract was signed by Rockwell, who had tucked a power of attorney into their original agreement. It was — or seemed to be — conclusive evidence. Joseph Weber, president of the AFM, sent Armstrong an admonitory telegram on May 14: "T. G. ROCKWELL HAS SUBMITTED CONTRACTS CALLING FOR YOUR SERVICES AT CONNIES INN AND

DEMANDS THAT YOU IMMEDIATELY START TO FULFILL SAME STOP YOU WILL MAKE ARRANGEMENTS TO DO SO OR SUBMIT REASONS WHY YOU SHOULD NOT BE HELD IN VIOLATION OF SAID CONTRACTS."

This was more than just a shot across the bow. If Armstrong's original contract with Rockwell was still in force, the AFM could suspend or expel him for failing to abide by its terms, thus making it impossible for him to continue working. Collins responded the same day by sending Weber a telegram signed by Armstrong in which he claimed that the trumpeter had canceled his contract with Rockwell. Weber, not surprisingly, chose to believe Rockwell and sent Armstrong a second telegram three weeks later informing him that he had been expelled from the AFM. In the meantime, though, Armstrong and Collins had come to the conclusion that the Chicago mob was more of a threat to them than the New York union, so they departed on a tour that would put them beyond the reach of Foster and Schultz. Armstrong had lived in Chicago long enough to know that "it's no trouble at all for a Gangster to pull the Trigger — especially when they have you Cornered and you Disobey them." Thus he needed no urging to skedaddle, and on May 23, less than two weeks after wrapping up his run at the Showboat, Armstrong and his band played a dance at Detroit's Greystone Ballroom. The world's greatest trumpeter was on the lam.

Collins's next move was to book the band into the Suburban Gardens, a whites-only dancehall in New Orleans. No one knows why he decided to send Armstrong south, though it seems probable that he thought his client would be farther out of harm's way there. Armstrong had not been back to New Orleans since going to Chicago in 1922 to play with Joe Oliver, and he later claimed to have been unsure of the reception that he would receive there: "I did not know whether they had forgotten about me in all the time I'd been away, because I was just 'Little Louie' Armstrong when I left and not too much account." In 1931 he was still capable of being surprised by his popularity, and it is perfectly possible that he didn't expect his home-town to give him a welcome that he would never forget.

The Armstrong band made its way to New Orleans by private railroad car, a mode of transportation that was less romantic in prac-tice than it sounds. While it was easier for black bands to sleep and eat on board than to search out such segregated hotels and rooming houses as were open to them on the road, the cramped, noisy berths in which they slept were often not much more comfortable than the rooms on the wrong side of the tracks to which they would otherwise have been relegated. Still, a private Pullman car had a certain cachet about it, and George James was one of many black musicians who thought such trains "the best way to travel, especially through the South."

Armstrong described the band's arrival in *Swing That Music:*

> When our train pulled into the old L. & N. Station out by the Mississippi, at the head of Canal Street, I heard hot music play-ing. I looked out the car window and could hardly believe what I saw. There, stretched out along the track, were eight bands, all swinging together, waiting to give us a big welcome. As soon as I got off the train the crowd went crazy. They picked me up and put me on their shoulders and started a parade down the center of Canal Street.

One might suspect him of exaggerating were it not that every other contemporary account of his reception says more or less the same thing. According to James, "They had Canal Street all lit up, with crowds, and marching bands, and balloons, and so forth, like Mardi Gras." A local newspaper reported that "the train of automo-biles and the milling thousands of enthusiastic worshippers held up traffic on Canal Street, the busiest street in New Orleans, for more than 30 minutes." From there Armstrong and his musicians were es-corted to a banquet at the Elks Lodge — not, of course, the whites-only Lodge No. 30, but the local headquarters of the all-black Im-proved and Benevolent Order of Elks of the World — then taken to the segregated Patterson Hotel, to which the crowd had carried their baggage and instruments. The fatherless waif in short pants was now the toast of New Orleans, the most famous musician ever to be born and raised in the cradle of jazz, then or later. No other victory would be so sweet.

Armstrong and the band went straight from the party to the Suburban Gardens, where two cheering throngs awaited them. The black crowd, he recalled, "gathered outside right along the levee, hoping to catch the music through the open windows. I'll never forget that sight. And the club was just as packed inside, five thousand people or more they said." WSMB, New Orleans's oldest radio station, was broadcasting live from the club, but a last-minute hitch threatened to scuttle the show. "I just haven't the heart to announce that nigger on the radio," the announcer said, so Armstrong took over the chore. It was, he claimed, "the first time a Negro *spoke* on the radio down there. . . . For the rest of that night and the rest of that gig I did my own radio announcing. That other announcer? They threw him out the same night . . . ain't that something?"

Much had changed in New Orleans since Armstrong went north. Many of the city's best musicians had either left town or would soon do so. Funky Butt Hall was now the Greater St. Matthew Baptist Church, though Buddy Bolden was still living in the same insane asylum to which he had been committed in 1907, suffering from what his doctors described as alcohol-induced schizophrenia. He died there in November, unaware that the music he had helped to create was now known throughout the world. But the Colored Waif's Home remained in business, and Armstrong went there for a visit shortly after his arrival, accompanied by a newspaper reporter who told his readers the tale of Little Louis's youthful struggles, ultimate triumph, and continuing devotion to his birthplace: "'Your home is in Chicago now?' Armstrong was finally asked. 'No indeed, sir,' he replied instantly. 'I only live in Chicago. My home's New Orleans.'"

Armstrong spent the rest of the summer playing for packed

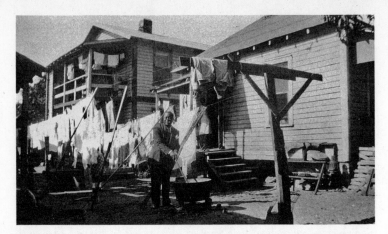

Hometown boy makes good: Armstrong pays a visit to 723 Jane Alley, the one-room shack where he was born. This previously unpublished snapshot from Armstrong's personal collection was unknown to scholars until it was identified by the author in 2008.

houses at the Suburban Gardens, and after hours he played the gratifying part of hometown boy made good. He sponsored a local baseball team called Armstrong's Secret Nine, endorsed a cigar called the Louis Armstrong Special, was photographed standing outside the shack where he was born, and showered gifts in all directions. "I remember, too, when we was staying at the hotel in New Orleans, at 6 o'clock—he wouldn't let anybody bother him until then—he'd come out of the rooms and there's a queue of people about half a block long on both sides of the hallway, and he's passin' out money just like that," one of his musicians recalled. "This happened the whole three months we was there. He bought 'em baseball suits and caps, bought 'em radios, and he bought radios and things for the Waifs' Home." The only thing he was unable to do was play for his own people, who could listen to him on the radio but were barred from the Suburban Gardens. At the end of Armstrong's stay in New Orleans, Johnny Collins tried to put on a blacks-only farewell dance at an army supply base, but the performance was canceled at the last minute for reasons that remain unclear. The fiasco was written up in newspapers as far away as San Antonio:

Dressed up in their party clothes, several thousand New Orleans negroes were disappointed Monday night when Louis Armstrong, home town negro orchestra leader who made good in Northern night clubs, and his band went from pillar to post without finding a place to play. . . . Armstrong and the band did the best they could. They struck up a minor chord and there was a shuffling of feet and a swaying of bodies while they were deciding what to do. The promoters of the dance sent word that rules forbade renting the warehouse.

It was not the only blot on Armstrong's return to the Crescent City. He had already admitted to a reporter that he had "recently aroused the ire of leading Chicago gangsters and caused that infamous population to threaten the musician's life," and in July Collins filed a suit on his behalf against Tommy Rockwell, the Immerman brothers, and the American Federation of Musicians, charging that they were "conspiring and confederating to interfere with, hinder or prevent the plaintiff in the exercise of his vocation." An affidavit decorously described his encounter with Frankie Foster: "Being compelled to enter the said telephone booth, your deponent spoke to someone on the telephone, whom he believes was Connie Immerman, and the said party desired to know when your deponent would come to New York, since he desired to build a show around him." Collins's lawyer produced a handwriting expert who testified that Immerman's countersignature on the trumpeter's contract with Connie's Inn was only a few days old, meaning that it had not been executed until after Armstrong had canceled his agreement with Rockwell, thus invalidating any subsequent contract with the Immermans. To top it off, Armstrong swore that the Immermans had offered to pay him only $250 a week, less than half of what he had been making at the Cotton Club.

As if all this weren't vexing enough, Lil came to New Orleans to harass him still further. (Daisy, his first wife, looked him up as well but made no trouble.) He had brought Alpha Smith along with him, perhaps to show Lil that the amenities would no longer be observed. "You don't need me now you're earning a thousand dollars a week,"

Lil later claimed to have told him. "We'll call it a day." It seems unlikely that she was that high-minded — she did not consent to a divorce until 1938 — but in August she agreed to a legal separation, and from then on Alpha had him all to herself.

Tommy Rockwell settled out of court the following year, perhaps because the New York papers had started running stories about the case that tied him to the mob: "In consequence of the colored trumpeter's hair-raising experiences, several indictments have been found by a Chicago Grand Jury, and both Armstrong and Manager Collins are hiding in either Philadelphia or Washington under a strong police guard." But until the case of *Louis Armstrong, Plaintiff, against Thomas G. Rockwell, Joseph N. Weber, et al., Defendants* was resolved, Armstrong had little choice but to stay away from Manhattan, where Rockwell and the Immermans were waiting with writs in hand. Instead he embarked on a tour of vaudeville theaters and movie houses whose details he could no longer remember clearly in later years: "There was so much happenin' during my life and travels, etcetera. And they were happenin' so fast until they ran through my head just like water on a duck's back." He may have considered New Orleans his home, but now he lived out of a trunk, traveling not in private Pullman cars but in unheated buses that whisked him from Houston to Oklahoma City, St. Louis to Cincinnati, Cleveland to Baltimore. And though newspaper ads billed him as the leader of "the highest paid colored band in the world," no amount of money could buy Armstrong and his men the respect they deserved but rarely got:

> Why, do you know I played ninety-nine million hotels I couldn't stay at? And if I had friends blowing at some all-white nightclub or hotel I couldn't get in to see 'em — or them to see me.... [M]ost of the time while touring the South, we used to stock up in a grocery store. We'd come out with a loaf of bread, a can of sardines, big hunks of bologna, cheese and we'd eat in the car. Sometimes we'd go to the back doors of restaurants where there were Negro chefs. They'd give you what you wanted. Many are the times I've eaten off those big wooden chopping blocks.

Even when they played by the rules, black musicians who ventured south of the Mason-Dixon Line could never count on staying out of trouble. In October the Armstrong band, accompanied by Johnny Collins's wife, pulled into a Memphis bus station and was told by a dispatcher to switch to a smaller, less comfortable vehicle for the next leg of its endless voyage. When Mary Collins pointed out that her husband had paid for a bigger bus, the Memphis police, who must have been outraged by the fact that Armstrong was traveling with a white woman, responded by throwing the whole band in jail. "You're in Memphis now, and we need some cotton-pickers," they were told. Not until Armstrong agreed to play a benefit concert were they released. The show was broadcast — Mezz Mezzrow heard it in New York — and Armstrong acknowledged the presence of his erstwhile captors by stepping to the mike and saying, "Ladies and gentlemen, I'm now going to dedicate this tune to the Memphis Police Force: 'I'll Be Glad When You're Dead You Rascal You.'" Preston Jackson tells what happened next: "Now whether Louis meant well by it or meant it as a slur, I don't know. We did play the song and after the broadcast they all made a dash towards us, 'bout ten or twelve of them. There was nowhere for us to run or we would have ran, you know. But they told us, says: 'You're the first band that ever dedicated a tune to the Memphis Police.' So we got out of that and finished the tour."

Three weeks later Armstrong, none the worse for his latest encounter with the law, was in a Chicago recording studio for the first in a five-month-long series of sessions at which he cut sixteen songs. The heat was temporarily off in the Windy City, where Al Capone, who was defending himself against a federal tax-evasion rap, had more important things to worry about than a black trumpeter's feud with his white manager. Armstrong's contract with OKeh would expire the following spring, and the company's executives must have wanted to get as much out of him as they could before he moved on. It was a good time to squeeze him for all he was worth, not only because he was at the peak of his powers but also because long hours on the bandstand had finally whipped his accompanists into shape. Between November 3 and March 11, the Armstrong band knocked out one important side after another. "Between the Devil and the Deep Blue Sea," "Georgia on My Mind," "Keepin' Out of Mischief Now," "Lazy River," "I Got Rhythm," "Star Dust," "Wrap Your Troubles in Dreams": these were the records that introduced him to a generation of listeners who had never heard of the Hot Five, much less Joe Oliver, and knew little more about jazz than that Louis Armstrong played it.

It is no accident that so many of these performances were of ballads. Few jazz musicians were recording — the Great Depression had caused record sales to drop from 104 million discs in 1927 to 6 million in 1932 — but Armstrong was still in demand, in part because he had turned himself into a pop crooner who also played trumpet. That his Crosby-inflected vocals were as rhythmically alive as his trumpet solos was beside the point: what mattered was that they helped to define him as a personality. Eli Oberstein, who was to persuade Armstrong to move from OKeh to Victor, described him as "the largest selling artist making records today, bar none," mentioning his "sensational-type" trumpet solos but making clear that his singing had sealed the deal: "Louis Armstrong recently did some vocalizing which was a little different than the run. Other artists have taken up that same kind of thing, but Armstrong was really the first to bring it out on records where it meant anything."

Of all the ballads Armstrong recorded that winter, the one that best displays the evolution of his singing style is Hoagy Carmichael's "Star Dust," cut on November 4, 1931, the same day that Buddy Bolden died and three months after the death of Bix Beiderbecke. The latter is an especially interesting coincidence, since the melody of "Star Dust" is a knowing evocation by Carmichael of Bix's cornet playing (though it also bears an equally coincidental resemblance to "Potato Head Blues"). Fortunately for students of Armstrong's approach to improvisation, two complete takes of "Star Dust" survive and have been released. Both are based on a routine that must have been worked out in advance on the bandstand, since measures nine through fifteen of the first-chorus trumpet solo are identical on both takes, as is the opening phrase of the vocal chorus, in which Armstrong flattens out the descending arpeggio of Carmichael's melody into a string of repeated D-flats. The takes differ in detail, however, and while the overall effect is similar, the first is more effervescently spontaneous.

Richard Sudhalter, Carmichael's biographer, called Armstrong's interpretation of "Star Dust" "a singular, and incomparable, event. . . . It is an aria, trumpet and vocal proceeding from the same broadly operatic conception, at once a transfiguration of Carmichael's melody and a reaffirmation of its hot jazz origins." He singled out the vocal chorus for special mention:

> It does no disservice to two exemplary trumpet choruses to suggest that the performance's most startling feature lies in the vocal. . . . Armstrong attenuates, foreshortens, extends and compresses, words and entire phrases, sometimes almost into incomprehensibility — only to emerge with a dramatic impact far greater and more immediate than [Mitchell] Parish's lyric, however manifold its virtues, could ever have dreamt of attaining.

As Sudhalter's description indicates, Armstrong's vocal is a paraphrase of Carmichael's tune *and* Parish's lyric, whose words he reshapes with a desentimentalizing freedom that delighted the composer: *SometimesIwonderwhyIspendsuchlonelynight (oh, baby, lonely nighnnmmmm) / Dreaming of a song (melody, memory) / And I am once again with you.* Even for him it was a daringly imaginative transformation, much more so than the instrumental portion of the record, in which he mostly stays within earshot of the tune. The fact that he takes the song at a danceable lope suggests that he was regularly tossing off similar musical miracles on the bandstand in the winter of 1931.

Not all of Armstrong's "miracles," however, were nearly so musical. Around the same time that he recorded "Star Dust," he also began incorporating into his stage act a marathon version of "Shine" in which he squeezed out 250 high Cs in a row (his sidemen counted them). Early in 1932 he starred in a one-reel Paramount short called

A Rhapsody in Black and Blue, his first surviving movie appearance, filmed in Astoria at the time of his abortive attempt to return to New York. In *A Rhapsody in Black and Blue* he is seen in a dream sequence in which a henpecked husband envisions himself as the king of Jazzmania, an imaginary African kingdom where Armstrong, clad in a leopard skin and little else, performs "Shine" and "You Rascal You" for him alone. The sequence is at once preposterous and racially condescending, but Armstrong comes on less like Uncle Tom than Superman, and though he limits himself to a truncated version of the codas that he played on stage, the film hints at the ruckus he raised each time he splattered a cheering crowd with one high note after another.

Armstrong's 1930 recording of "Tiger Rag," with its clinching E-flat and interpolated snippets from such other numbers as E. E. Bagley's popular "National Emblem March" and "Vesti la giubba," the familiar tenor aria from *Pagliacci*, was one of the first recorded examples of the stunt work that had been an important part of his live performances long before "Shine." In March of 1932 he topped it with "New Tiger Rag," a longer version of the same routine that includes his introductory stage patter: "Now, ladies and gentlemen, we have a little novelty here for you this evening. We're gonna take a little trip through the jungles, you know, and we want you all to travel with us, because that tiger's runnin' so fast, takes about seven choruses to catch that baby, so I want you all to count with me." His recording of "I Got Rhythm" is similarly exemplary of his dynamic stage presence, and it is a pleasure to hear — once. But the climactic solo, like the set-piece routine definitively enshrined on "New Tiger Rag," is of no great musical interest, consisting as it does of simple riffs stapled together with little regard for logical development. For all his virtuosity, Armstrong was rarely at his best when playing at fast tempos. It was in ballads, swinging medium-tempo numbers, and the blues that he did his most creative improvising. If he had recorded nothing but "Star Dust" and "St. Louis Blues," he would still be remembered as the greatest jazz soloist of his time; if he had recorded nothing but "I Got Rhythm" and "New Tiger Rag," he would be remembered only as a high-note specialist with a funny voice.

Jazz criticism barely existed in 1932, and so there was no one to say that he had "sold out" by making such records or by turning away from the small-group format of his late-twenties sides, though there were already those who thought so. A year and a half after "New Tiger Rag" was recorded, Charles Edward Smith published an article in the *Daily Worker* in which he claimed that Armstrong's big-band recordings represented "the white man's notion of Harlem jazz." But his exhibitionistic streak cannot be ignored, for had he lacked it, he would never have dared commit to record such explosions of virtuosity as the introductory cadenza of "West End Blues" or the tongue-twisting triplets he tosses off so casually in "Beau Koo Jack." We must take him, like all great artists, as he was, and it is no sacrifice to do so, for even when he was at his most trivial, seriousness kept breaking in. The same session that produced "New Tiger Rag" also gave us "Lawd, You Made the Night Too Long," a Tin Pan Alley pseudo-spiritual that he turned into a paradoxically exuberant minor-key lament that opens with ecstatic shouts of "Hallelujah! Hallelujah!" and closes with one of his most riveting trumpet solos.

"Lawd, You Made the Night Too Long" is noteworthy for another reason, which is that it brought Armstrong's seven-year stint at OKeh to an end. The label was now paying him $1,000 a side, nearly $13,000 today. In 1932 you could buy a brand-new Packard for $1,750, a two-sided 78 for seventy-five cents, and a carton of eggs for fifteen cents — if you had the cash. Armstrong's ability to command such fees could be one of the reasons why he left OKeh, which was on the brink of financial collapse (the company stopped placing ads in black newspapers at the end of 1931) and may not have been able to meet his price. He wasn't allowed to leave without a fight, though: OKeh's lawyers took Armstrong to court in an unsuccessful attempt to keep him under contract for one more year. The suit was newsworthy enough to make it into *Time*, which ran a story called "Black Rascal" that was one of the first pieces about the trumpeter to appear in a national magazine. The manner in which it was written says much about how Armstrong was perceived by white America, as do the many other stories about him that *Time* would publish in years to come:

> "Ladies & Gentlemen, this is the Reverend Satchelmouth Armstrong. . . ." He gets his head up to an amplifier. His natural voice is almost whisper-small. "Chinatown, My Chinatown, Chinatown, Chinatown. . . ." He rarely has more than a rough idea of the words. "All right, boys, I'll take the next five bars." He throws back his head, raises his trumpet, bleats noisily but marvelously. He has struck 200 high C's in succession, ended on high F. . . .
>
> The Negroes behind Louis Armstrong are carrying the tune, when it can be detected behind his raspy, comical singing, his fancy trumpeting. Their rhythm is flawless, thanks to their leader who may smoke Muggles to make his own performance hot but who realizes perfectly the need for tireless rehearsing. Louis Armstrong may have developed a fancy man's taste for clothes, travel with 20 trunks full of them. But no black man works harder than he does.

The publication of "Black Rascal" was one sign of Armstrong's growing popularity.* Another was the frequency with which other musicians were imitating him. Joe Oliver had already re-recorded "West End Blues" in the style of his protégé in 1929, the same year that Earl Hines's big band recorded "Beau Koo Jack" in a stock arrangement that featured a harmonized version of Armstrong's solo played by two trumpeters. A year earlier Jelly Roll Morton recorded "Mournful Serenade," an uncredited rewrite of "Chimes Blues" that ends with a pair of ensemble choruses based on Armstrong's first recorded solo. Ethel Waters's "I Can't Give You Anything but Love" was followed by a 1932 Mills Brothers performance of "St. Louis Blues" that made reference to Armstrong's big-band version, and a

---

*It also appears to have been the last time that Armstrong's use of marijuana was mentioned in a general-circulation publication until after his death, save for a 1967 interview in which he falsely claimed that "[m]any years ago I quit messing around with that stuff."

Chick Webb recording of "On the Sunny Side of the Street" in which Taft Jordan parroted his interpretation of the same song. White musicians were listening to Armstrong just as closely: the Boswell Sisters, a close-harmony vocal trio whose members swung so hard and had such strong "N'Awlins" accents that they were often taken for black, cut a version of "Heebie Jeebies" in 1931 that alluded briefly but unmistakably to Armstrong's scat solo. In 1934 Louis Prima, another New Orleans musician who had come north to New York, recorded the first in a long series of trumpet-and-vocal sides that were meant to evoke his master's voice.

The master himself was still keeping his distance from the Big Apple, and the grueling months he had spent on the run were taking their toll on his lip. George James recalled a night in Philadelphia when Armstrong was unable to play at all: "First we noticed a blister on his chop, and every day it got worse until he couldn't put his mouthpiece on it." A smart manager would have pulled his star attraction off the road at once. Instead Collins dispatched Armstrong to England to play for throngs of puzzled Britons who had never heard — or seen — anyone like the King of the Vipers.

7

"I DIDN'T BLOW THE HORN"

Crisis, 1932–1935

AMERICA'S NEW MUSIC was brought to the Old World by Sidney Bechet and the Original Dixieland Jazz Band, who arrived in England — separately — in 1919. Several classical composers, Claude Debussy and Igor Stravinsky among them, had already written pieces influenced by ragtime and its precursors, and by 1913 the sound of American syncopation had circulated so widely that the *New York Times* could run a story headlined "AMERICAN RAGTIME SWEEPING EUROPE." Five years later Jim Europe's "Harlem Hellfighters" band was playing peppy versions of "Clarinet Marmalade" and "Memphis Blues" for French audiences. But it was the arrival of New Orleans–born musicians that lit the fire, and Ernest Ansermet's hats-off review of a Bechet performance conveys something of the way in which open-eared Europeans greeted the sounds of jazz: "There is in the Southern Syncopated Orchestra an extraordinary clarinet virtuoso who is, so it seems, the first of his race to have composed perfectly formed blues on the clarinet. . . . I wish to set down the name of this artist of genius; as for myself, I shall never forget it — it is Sidney Bechet."

Such receptivity was rare among the first European critics of jazz. More common was the reporter who heard the ODJB at the London Palladium and declared that the group was "doing its best to murder music." Before long, though, jazz found its way into British night-clubs and dance halls in the form of Whiteman-style dance bands like the Savoy Orpheans, who in 1925 accompanied George Gershwin in the English premiere of *Rhapsody in Blue*. These well-meaning but prim-sounding ensembles were favored by the BBC, whose announcers were advised to avoid using the vulgar expression *jazz* on the air. That same four-letter word is nowhere to be found in Evelyn Waugh's *Vile Bodies*, the 1930 novel that was to England's "bright young things" what *Tales of the Jazz Age* was to America's flappers. Still, Waugh and his contemporaries were aware of jazz, or what passed for it in England, and when recordings of the real thing began to go on sale in Europe, some started to play it themselves. Bandleaders Fred Elizalde, Bert Firman, and Jack Hylton had all recorded more than creditable versions of such authentic jazz tunes as "Clarinet Marmalade," "Sugar Foot Stomp," and Jelly Roll Morton's "Milenberg Joys" by 1927. A handful of noted American players, including Buster Bailey, Jimmy Dorsey, and Adrian Rollini, paid brief visits to England around the same time. But no major jazz soloist had performed there since Sidney Bechet was run out of the country five years earlier after getting into a fistfight with a whore and spending two weeks behind bars. For most British jazzmen, it was Louis Armstrong, not Bechet, who showed them the reality behind the records.

In Europe as in New York, Armstrong's reputation — and his records — had preceded him. A letter sent to Elmer Fearn from the New York office of OKeh in 1926, only a year after the trumpeter first recorded under his own name, indicates that several Hot Five sides had just been released in Italy by Fonotipia-Odeon. The letter, preserved in Armstrong's scrapbooks, was accompanied by an Italian catalog with his picture on the cover, captioned "Le ultime novita" (The latest novelty). The writer went straight to the point: "We would suggest your giving these to Louis, showing him the tremendous amount of publicity he is securing by means of his OKeh contract, so that any time he sees fit to go to Italy, they will welcome him with open arms." Not long afterward Armstrong's records began to be issued in England by Parlophone, OKeh's European outlet. Within a few years some three dozen of them were in circulation there, along with other recordings by the likes of Bix Beiderbecke, Duke Ellington, Jelly Roll Morton, and Red Nichols; and two new English magazines, the *Melody Maker* and *Rhythm*, were covering jazz, as was the *Gramophone*, an influential classical-music monthly.

At first the critics of the *Melody Maker* found jazz hard to grasp, in part because so much of it was played by blacks. In 1927 one of them praised Fletcher Henderson's recording of "Whiteman Stomp" as a model of "really good nigger style." But soon they started getting the hang of it, and by 1929 they knew enough to single Armstrong out in a story about "New York's 'Star' Musicians": "The king of all trumpet players — without any exception — and all the other trumpet players willingly admit it — is Louis Armstrong, the negro." Though Armstrong had yet to perform in England, Nat Gonella, who played trumpet in Billy Cotton's dance band, was impersonating him as part of Cotton's stage act, wearing a brown-colored mask and a kinky-haired wig. Tasteless though his outfit may sound to modern ears, Gonella was by his own admission a "raving fan" with nothing but admiration for Armstrong. In 1932 he wrote an article for the *Melody Maker* called "Imitation without Apology" in which he called his idol the "greatest dance trumpeter on earth." His sincerity is made manifest on the recording of "Bessie Couldn't Help It" that he cut with the Cotton band in 1930, a mixed bag that says much about the state of pre-Armstrong British jazz. It opens with a muted trumpet solo, followed by a vocal chorus sung in "vo-do-de-o" style by a male trio. The rhythm section jounces along amiably but unswingingly, pushing at the beat like a fat man trotting downhill. Then Gonella returns to sing a chorus in a clumsy evocation of Armstrong's steel-wool voice, and the record lurches to a close with an open-horn solo whose good intentions bring it no closer to the mark.

What is more interesting about "Bessie Couldn't Help It," however, is not that Gonella's version of Armstrong's style was so approximate but that a British trumpeter was capable in 1930 of imitating him at all. What was missing from Gonella's record, as it was from most of the jazz, semi-jazz, and pseudo-jazz recorded in England prior to 1932, was the deeper comprehension available only through direct exposure to the playing of great jazz musicians.* Spike Hughes, an Anglo-Irish bassist-bandleader-critic, later pointed out in his memoirs that European jazzmen "learnt all we knew about jazz at second hand, from gramophone records and a very occasional short-wave broadcast." The experience of listening to an Armstrong 78 through the horn of a hand-cranked Victrola is not to be despised, but the boxy sound of an acoustic phonograph could no more convey the force of his physical presence than a TV screen can suggest the visual impact of a CinemaScope Western. In order for the British to fully understand what he had done to jazz, they would have to hear him in person.

➤

Armstrong's first trip to Europe was cobbled together with minimal forethought. Unable to book the trumpeter in New York because of his battle with Tommy Rockwell and the Immermans, Johnny Collins broke up his band in Chicago after its final recording session for OKeh, then sent its leader west to Los Angeles to front the Cotton Club band once more. In July Armstrong returned to New York, then sailed for England with Alpha and Collins on the S.S. *Majestic*. Nine days later, on July 18, 1932, he opened at the London Palladium, accompanied by a pickup ensemble of expatriate blacks and French musicians who were shipped over from Paris to play for him. The editors of the *Melody Maker* barely had time to shoehorn the news into the July issue: "For some time past, idle rumours have been afoot that Louis Armstrong was coming to London. . . . Now

---

*The American trumpeter Jack Purvis (who was, like Gonella, white) had managed to suggest somewhat more of Armstrong's essence in a 1929 small-group recording called, appropriately enough, "Copyin' Louis."

that the visit is really to take place it will come as a complete surprise, for no such rumour has heralded the engagement." Another sign of the trip's catch-as-catch-can nature is that *Time*'s profile of Armstrong, published on June 13, did not mention that he would be leaving for England less than a month later.

Alerted to his imminent arrival by ship-to-shore radio, the staff of the *Melody Maker* threw together a welcoming banquet and dispatched Dan Ingman to the Paddington station to meet the midnight boat train from Plymouth. Armstrong himself remembered being met at the dock earlier that day by Percy Mathison Brooks, the editor of the *Melody Maker*, who "shook my hand and said to me 'HELLO, SATCHMO.' I had never heard the name before. Satchelmouth, yes." The nickname "Satchelmouth" was, like "Dippermouth," an allusion to the size of his capacious mouth, and it would have been known to British jazz buffs in 1932, since he had used it two years earlier in the introductory patter to his recording of "You're Driving Me Crazy" ("Look out there, Satchelmouth"). According to Armstrong, he took a liking to Brooks's abbreviated version — which was almost certainly "Satchelmouth" pronounced with a stiff upper lip — and began using it himself. Doubt has since been cast on the literal accuracy of the anecdote, but something more or less like it must have happened, for he stuck with the story to the end of his life, by which time the nickname had become as much a part of his image as his white handkerchiefs.

When Ingman met Armstrong's train in London later in the evening, he was surprised to see how short the trumpeter was, though he recognized his speaking voice at once. Ingman established that Collins had neglected to reserve rooms for the Armstrong party and called up "eight famous hotels" before finding one that would accommodate blacks. The next day Armstrong was wined and dined by a roomful of British jazz musicians and journalists, among them Nat Gonella and Spike Hughes. On Saturday afternoon he went to Victoria station to collect the members of his band, where he was met by Robert Goffin, a Belgian poet, criminal lawyer, and jazz critic whose newly published *Aux frontières du jazz*, one of the first book-length studies of the music to appear in Europe, was dedicated to "Louis Armstrong, the True King of Jazz." Goffin picked Armstrong out of the crowd and introduced himself. "He does not know who I am, but that does not matter," he wrote in a memoir of their first meeting. "He assumes I am some sort of musician or manager or pugilist, a good pal anyhow whoever I am. When I give him my book he dances with pleasure, takes me in his arms, overwhelms me with cigarettes, threatens to have a shave in my honour."

A few hours later Goffin looked on as Armstrong rehearsed his new band:

> I scrutinise him more closely: he is smaller than he appears in his photographs but his trumpet is bigger; he talks and gags with the ten musicians; continual use of the mouth-piece has put a tuck in his lips; he produces a few vertiginous notes, sees that his players are where he wants them, executes a pirouette, snatches off his coat and opens a huge trunk packed with bundles of music. . . . Louis plays, conducting with his eyes, sudden jerks of his hands, capers and contortions of his whole body, as though he wanted to terrify the three saxophonists who find themselves called on for a "hot" ensemble.

Armstrong's body language was indispensable, for some of his players spoke no English, forcing him to communicate with them through an interpreter. He claimed in *Swing That Music* that "all swing men can talk together and understand each other through their music, so we got along fine." But he found it necessary to spend the rest of the weekend putting them through their paces, by all accounts to little avail, though no one seems to have been bothered by the fact that the band was (according to Leonard Feather) "sloppy" and "makeshift" when it made its debut on Monday. All eyes and ears were on the "King of the Trumpet and Creator of His Own Song Style," as posters referred to the American at the top of "Vaudeville's Biggest Bill!!!"

It is hard to imagine Louis Armstrong sharing a bill with such quintessentially English vaudevillians as Max Miller, the "cheeky chappie" whose loud suits and blue humor were as familiar to his

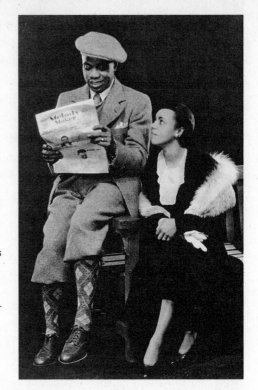

"Come here and kiss me, Pops": A previously un-published studio portrait of Armstrong with Alpha, his third-wife-to-be, in London. The newspaper that Armstrong is reading is the *Melody Maker,* a British publication that had praised him in 1929 as "the king of all trumpet players — without any exception."

audiences as Armstrong's handkerchiefs and high Cs were to his — but, then, it is as hard for most of us to imagine what the London Palladium was like in 1932, three-quarters of a century before it passed into the hands of Andrew Lloyd Webber and became the home of high-tech musical-comedy extravaganzas. Nowadays the Edwardian music hall, with its galloping comic songs, sentimental ballads, and flamboyantly costumed clowns, is known only to viewers of such films as *The 39 Steps* and *The Entertainer.* In the thirties, though, it was still an immensely popular and vital institution, much more so than America's fast-fading vaudeville circuit, and the 2,300-seat Palladium (on whose stage the hapless Mr. Memory is shot dead in the last scene of *The 39 Steps*) was the city's most celebrated "variety house." In any case Armstrong had nowhere else to go. The British musicians' union was adamantly opposed to letting foreign musicians work in England, and the Ministry of Labour accordingly refused to grant permits for the members of American bands to perform in hotels, restaurants, or nightclubs. Alien though its culture was to a black jazzman from New Orleans, the music-hall circuit was the only place where Armstrong could introduce himself to the British public.

On opening night he served up four of his most trustworthy crowd pleasers, "Them There Eyes," "When You're Smiling," "Chinatown, My Chinatown," and "You Rascal You." He had played them repeatedly for American audiences, and Dan Ingman reported in the *Melody Maker* that they went over well at the Palladium: "Each one was received with tumult. The packed house absolutely rose to it. There is no doubt, of course, that musicians preponderated in the house — familiar faces were everywhere — but members of the lay public, once they had got over their astonishment, were equally enthusiastic." The difference was that for the first time since *Hot Chocolates* opened on Broadway, Armstrong was playing for an audience heavily salted with journalists, some of whom were well-informed jazz fans who understood the significance of what they were hearing and were determined to convey it to their readers.

Ingman's account was the longest and most detailed:

Top *F*'s bubble about all over the place, and never once does he miss one. He is enormously fond of the lip-trill, which he accomplishes by shaking the instrument wildly with his right hand.

His singing is — well, words just fail me. It's like it is on the records, only a thousand times more so! He works with a microphone and loudspeakers — except for his trumpet playing, which varies from a veritable whisper to roof-raising strength — mostly the latter. His style is peculiarly his own, mostly long, high notes . . .

All the time he is singing he carries a handkerchief in his hand and mops his face — perspiration positively drops off him. He puts enough energy in his half-hour's performance to last the average man several years.

What struck Spike Hughes most forcibly was "the extreme economy of means by which Armstrong achieves his effect, and the light and shade he uses to build his climaxes," though he, too, was fascinated by "the electric, incessant energetics" of the trumpeter's on-stage conduct. So was Robert Goffin, who compared him to a boxer in the ring: "His face drips like a heavyweight's, steam rises from his lips; he holds his trumpet in a handkerchief, passes into a kind of excruciating catalepsy and emerges Armstrong the sky-scraper, rockets aloft into the stratosphere, blows like one possessed and foams at the mouth." Everyone agreed that he was even more thrilling in person than on record, but some musicians were disturbed by his extroverted behavior, and at least one of them described his debut in terms suggestive of discomfort with the color of his skin: "His actual presence gave me, in a sense, a shock, and I much regret to have to admit to finding something of the barbaric in his violent stage mannerisms." Nor was the behavior of what Philip Larkin was later to call "the stageshow Armstrong" pleasing to certain jazz fans who knew and loved his earlier recordings. "The sweating, strutting figure in the spotlight hitting endless high notes had only a tenuous and intermittent connection with the creator of the intensely moving music of 'West End Blues' and 'Muggles,'" Iain Lang remembered. Then and later his opinion was shared by a small but vocal minority — one that would grow more influential in the years to come.

Press reports indicate that Armstrong toned down his act over the course of the run. One account claimed that he "worked a little more piano [i.e., softly] than last week and was, consequently, more acceptable to English audiences." But he was still too wild for many of the Palladium's patrons. Dan Ingman was being tactful when he praised the "lay public" for its enthusiastic response. Long after the fact he admitted that "not all of the 28 houses were full by any means. And every time I was there, which was often, I saw people walking out." Another musician claimed that tomatoes were thrown at Armstrong: "He laughed, like he laughed at everything. But inside, he was sad. He told me, 'They don't understand. . . . They don't like me. I wonder why? In America they like me.'"

If the lay public was skeptical about Armstrong, so were the lay journalists who wrote about him. Hannen Swaffer reported in the *Daily Express* that "five out of six people seated in a row in front of me walked out while [Armstrong] was on; so did two people on my right — and several others at the back." Who stayed behind? Swaffer said that "pale aesthetes were lily-like when he appeared, and the young Jewish element at the back was enthusiastic." As for Armstrong himself, he was "the ugliest man I have seen on the music-hall stage. He looks, and behaves, like an untrained gorilla." Another, slightly less offensive *Daily Express* column described Armstrong's singing in a way that was just as revealing, albeit unintentionally, of its author's prejudices: "This savage growling is as far removed from English as we speak or sing it — and as modern — as James Joyce." *Rhythm* responded with a squirmingly self-conscious editorial called "The Armstrong War," which argued that Swaffer's piece "adequately describe[d] the whole show as it must have appeared to anybody who did not understand how perfectly amazing is Armstrong's trumpet work."

No less illustrative of establishment attitudes toward Armstrong was a sniffy memo written by Roger Eckersley, Controller of Programmes for the BBC, which had broadcast one of his Palladium shows: "I, myself, am entirely against the kind of stuff that Louie Armstrong plays, and should deprecate the introduction of it into the programmes." It is easy to mock such prissy snobbery now that Armstrong's genius is universally acknowledged. In 1932, however, he was still a part of the musical avant-garde — the newspaperman who compared him to James Joyce spoke more truly than he knew — and British listeners were understandably less well prepared than their American counterparts to grapple with his musical innovations, much less his onstage conduct. Even Max Jones, who later became a trusted friend, was disconcerted by his first sight of the man whom he remembered as "a lithe, smallish but power-packed figure prowling the stage restlessly, menacingly almost . . . I remember doubting if he was in full control of himself." If that was the way that Armstrong struck an onlooker so favorably disposed as Jones, perhaps one can forgive a buttoned-down bureaucrat like Eckersley for finding his hot jazz incomprehensible.

Far more illuminating was the response of the composer-critic Constant Lambert, who in 1927 had written *The Rio Grande*, a work for piano, chorus, and orchestra that makes idiomatic use of the language of jazz-based popular music. His comments merit serious consideration: "An artist like Louis Armstrong, who is one of the most remarkable virtuosi of the present day, enthralls us at a first hearing, but after a few records one realizes that all his improvisations are based on the same restricted circle of ideas, and in the end there is no music which more quickly provokes a state of exasperation and ennui." If Lambert heard only the songs that Armstrong played at the Palladium, it is possible to see how he might have failed to recognize the full extent of the trumpeter's imaginative resources, especially since he praised Duke Ellington as "a real composer" on the same occasion. Perhaps he would have responded more warmly had he heard "Beau Koo Jack" instead of "You Rascal You." Or not: other critics would prove no more able to see that the virtuoso-clown and the fertile improviser were one and the same man.

~

"I'll never forget England and its people, so nice to me," Armstrong said not long before his death. He had reason to remember them. The ranks of his English admirers included such classical musicians as William Walton, the country's most promising young composer, and William Primrose, already a rising star on the viola. Even those artists who, like Lambert, had their doubts about Armstrong did him the honor of taking him seriously. While he was aware of the controversy that his performances were stirring up — he saved all his clippings, even Swaffer's tirade — what seems to have impressed him most about the press coverage of his visit was that there was so much of it. He was now fairly well known in America but had yet to receive that kind of attention from the white newspapers of his native land, and it took him by surprise. "I didn't see how all of these people over there could have come to hear about me, let alone want to make so much fuss over me," he wrote in *Swing That Music*.

Not only did England open Armstrong's eyes to the extent of his renown, but it gave him a clearer perspective on the limitations of his manager. Dan Ingman went backstage before a performance and was disturbed by what he saw:

> Collins suddenly said, "Where's the dough? If I don't get the dough, Louis don't play." The promoter had a huge crowd and there was no problem. He offered a cheque but Collins was adamant — no cash, no Louis. It must have been humiliating for Louis, though he showed no sign of it. He just looked at the floor and went on swinging his trumpet in his hand . . . He was docile, this world-famous musician, subservient in the presence of Collins.

While Ingman could not have begun to appreciate the ingrained caution that kept a black man like Armstrong from speaking his mind about a white man like Collins, he was right about who held the whip hand. On another occasion he casually mentioned to Armstrong that the trumpeter "must be worth a lot of money. He replied that he wasn't. . . . [H]e had pocket money and all the clothes he wanted, that was the lot." Yet he had been barnstorming up and down England, playing to full houses in Birmingham, Glasgow, Liverpool, London, Nottingham, and York. For all his docility, Armstrong's temper must have been growing frayed, especially now that he had caught sight of a different style of life.

Come November, though, he said farewell to England, sailed back to New York with Collins and Alpha, and resumed the old grind. "Louis was now a star of the first magnitude in the brilliant constellation of [British] music-hall celebrities," Robert Goffin later claimed in *Horn of Plenty*. "On his return to America he received fantastic offers." Not so. Instead of accepting one of the stateside offers that Goffin conjured out of thin air, he spent a month appearing in what John Hammond called "a pretty poor revival of *Hot Chocolates*" at the Lafayette Theater. "It is a fact," Hammond told the readers of the *Melody Maker*, "that when [Armstrong] came back from Europe there was not one line in any paper about it. Although famous now in England, he is virtually unknown to the theater public here." That was an exaggeration, too, but not by much. Though Armstrong's records were solid sellers, he was a second-tier celebrity, worthy of a half page in *Time* on a slow news week but not nearly so famous as Bing Crosby, or even Rudy Vallée. His name did not appear in the news columns of the *New York Times* until 1935, or in the *Reader's Guide to Periodical Literature* until 1944. It would take something more than a tour of British music halls to make him a full-fledged star.

The problem is clear in retrospect: Collins was incapable of supplying the firm and intelligent direction that Tommy Rockwell had previously given to Armstrong's career. After *Hot Chocolates* closed, the trumpeter went out on the road for a few dates with Chick Webb's band, which also accompanied him on his first recording session for Victor, a scrappy affair at which he cut four unmemorable songs, one of them a knockoff of "Sleepy Time Down South" called "That's My Home," which he played and sang with far more conviction than it deserved. The days of "Body and Soul" and "Star Dust" were over, at least for now: the recordings he made for Victor in 1932 and 1933 are a mismatched assortment of variably worthy pop tunes, forgettable novelties, and remakes of such now-familiar standbys as "Basin Street Blues" and "St. Louis Blues." To make matters worse, Armstrong's lip was in fragile shape, though he still had his good nights, such as the performance of *Hot Chocolates* attended by Irving Kolodin, a classical-music critic who also liked jazz: "His trumpet virtuosity is endless — triplets, chromatic accented eerie counterpoints that turn the tune inside out, wild sorties into the giddy stratosphere where his tone sounds like a dozen flutes in unison, all executed with impeccable style and finish, exploits that make his contemporaries sound like so many Salvation Army cornetists." But he was heading for a fall, and it came when he split his lip at a New Year's Eve dance in Baltimore, with results so appalling that his musicians wept to see them. Mezz Mezzrow described the grisly spectacle in *Really the Blues:* "A shock and a shiver ran through the theater. The whole house shuddered, then rocked with applause. Louis stood there holding his horn and panting, his mangled lip oozing blood that he licked away, and he managed to smile and bow and smile again, making pretty for the people."

After a too-short layoff to rest his bruised chops, Armstrong returned to Chicago, where Zilner Randolph put together a new band for him. On January 26 the group gathered in a Chicago studio for a marathon six-side session that produced, against all odds, a pair of classic recordings that stood out amid the chaff. "I Gotta Right to Sing the Blues" and "I've Got the World on a String" were both written by Harold Arlen, the house composer for Harlem's Cotton Club and one of the first white songwriters to successfully incorporate jazz and the blues into his style. In "I've Got the World on a String," a soon-to-be-standard rhythm ballad that Bing Crosby recorded on the same day in New York, the emphasis is on Armstrong's vocal, in which he sticks closely to Ted Koehler's lyric but reshapes the contours of Arlen's wide-ranging melody with casual deftness. It is a lovely piece of work that would be better remembered were it not for the fact that the next song on the session, "I Gotta Right to Sing the Blues," was one of Armstrong's immortal masterpieces, as worthy of comparison with "West End Blues" as it is different from that riot of virtuosity. Here it is the trumpet solo that seizes our attention, for Armstrong, in a departure from his customary practice on ballads, dispenses almost completely with Arlen's melody, substituting instead a series of rhythmically free phrases that lead upward to a high B-flat. Four times he falls off from that shining note — and then comes the fifth fall, at the bottom of which he changes course and swoops gracefully upward to a full-throated high D whose vibrancy was perfectly caught by Victor's recording engineer. It is a showstopping stroke, yet there is no trace of overstatement about it: Armstrong seems to have broken through to a realm of abstract lyricism that transcends ordinary human emotion. Only then does he condescend to ease back into the vicinity of the tune, returning the bedazzled listener to the everyday world.

Armstrong's solo is so phenomenal that one can listen to it a half-dozen times without realizing how bad the band sounds. The only exception is the uncredited pianist, who tosses off a glittering pair of two-bar breaks that suggest Earl Hines without being derivative of him. The prodigy in question was a slender, fine-featured alumnus of Booker T. Washington's Tuskegee Institute, of whose English department his father was chairman. Though the young man at the keyboard had classical training, the records of Armstrong, Hines, Fats Waller, and Bix Beiderbecke had filled him with an even stronger love for jazz, and so the twenty-year-old Teddy Wilson made his way from Alabama to Chicago, where he signed up for a hitch with Armstrong's band and spent three months playing for the musician whom he admired above all others. "It was a privilege to hear that man play every night," Wilson later said. "He was such a master of melodic improvisation, and he never hit a note that didn't have a great deal of meaning. Every note was pure music."

Wilson, who went on to become one of the best-known jazz pianists of the thirties, was as dismayed by the playing of the Randolph band, which he described as "no good at all" (another member of the group called it "putrid"), as he was impressed by Armstrong. Under the circumstances, one of the things about the trumpeter that struck Wilson most forcibly was that "he was always right and he was not at the mercy of the drummer or the saxophones, the rest of the band, and he never complained to any musician. . . . [H]e just went right straight ahead and played in that world of his own." Off the bandstand he was a considerate leader, "always friendly with the band, but not buddy-buddy with anybody." He was already spending much of his spare time answering fan mail and writing letters to friends "all day in the bus . . . he'd be typing, typing, typing." He also appears to have been bringing in a good deal of money: Wilson was told that he earned $1,500 a week, $21,000 in today's dollars. Nobody knows how much of the take went to his manager, but even if Collins kept half of it for himself, the other half was still a tidy sum for a black man in Depression-era America.

Wilson and his fellow musicians got forty dollars a week and thought themselves lucky to be paid so well. "You could still get a room for fifty or seventy-five cents a night, and a meal for seventy-five cents," recalled the tenor saxophonist Budd Johnson, after Wilson the best sideman in the band. "And of course, Louis kept us high!" The effects of that fringe benefit can be heard on their recording of "Laughin' Louie." Written by Clarence Gaskill, who is better remembered for "Sweet Adeline," the song is a miniature vaudeville skit that opens with a frenzied nonsense vocal (*I wake up every morning and I have to laugh / 'Cause I look on the wall and I see my photograph*). From that point onward Armstrong lets his imagination run wild, throwing together a comedy routine inspired by the once-popular, now-forgotten "OKeh Laughing Record" of 1922, in which two people laugh hysterically at a sappy trumpet solo. First comes a brief monologue: "Y'all won't let me play some hot riffs for you this evening, and you won't let me sing for you, but you must listen at this beautiful number, one of them old-time good ones. Listen at this!" Then, after some raucous kidding from the band, he plays a formal-sounding cadenza based on a piece of silent-movie music that he must have remembered from his Vendome days. The effect of the juxtaposition is surreal, and it is no surprise to learn that he had gone out of his way to get the band in the mood. As Johnson remembered it: "We made one particular record called 'Laughing Louie.' And Louie used to get up there and we wouldn't allow anybody on the recording sessions, you know, unless they were real personal friends, because Louie would like to get high, and he'd like for the band to get high. . . . So he says, 'We going to record "Laughing Louie" today, gentlemen.' And he says, 'I want everybody to smoke a joint.'"

In between recording sessions the band played one-nighters in midwestern towns where Armstrong was comparatively little known and so felt obliged to overwhelm his audiences with repeated demonstrations of his superhuman powers. He was still playing 250 or more high Cs at the end of "Shine," and Harry Dial, his drummer, recalled a string of "Tiger Rags" that went on for so long that "my collar was all down, my feet were wet, and my suit looked like I slept in it. That guy worked me to death." One night at a dance in Oklahoma City where the members of the band were higher than usual, Budd Johnson overheard a little old lady saying, "My, my, they all look so tired and sleepy — but the music is good!"

Not everyone agreed. John Hammond, for one, dismissed "That's My Home" as "saccharine" (he was right about the song, wrong about the performance) and told his readers that "Louis' future discs should be made with a small group of virtuosi, as in the old Hines days." Hammond, a coupon-clipping Ivy League dilettante whose love of jazz had led him to become a critic and part-time record producer, wrote columns for the *Melody Maker* and *Rhythm* in which he laid down a standard of artistic purity that was alien to the applause-hungry Armstrong. In 1933 the sternly uncompromising great-great-grandson of Cornelius Vanderbilt was known only to a small circle of music lovers, but within a few years he became an influential figure in the music business, playing key roles in the careers of Count Basie, Benny Goodman, Billie Holiday, and Teddy Wilson. As Hammond's fame grew, his jaundiced view of Armstrong, whom he saw as an artist who went astray when he started presenting himself "as a soloist, as a performer, rather than as an ensemble musician," would be taken up by other jazz critics for whom the word *entertainer* was a near-obscenity.

While Armstrong continued to play with unrivaled power and intensity, his high-register work was occasionally unsteady, a sign that he had yet to recover from the effects of his split lip. (His discomfort is plain to hear in the coda of "Laughin' Louie.") Nor had he emerged from the shadow of violence that had followed him since he fled Chicago in 1931. When he came east to Philadelphia in July to play a theater date, two hoods muscled their way into his dressing room and offered to "protect" him from trouble. After they left, Armstrong told his valet to collect the box-office receipts and take them straight to the bank. "I went on stage and played my last show," he later said. "Then instead of coming back to my dressing room where these guys were, I went out the stage door and down the street to the police station. I said, 'Lock me up. There's a couple of guys in my dressing room and they want to kill me.' Then I sent for my manager, Mr. Collins, and I told him, 'Let's catch the first boat for England.'"

By the time Armstrong and Collins docked in Plymouth, their partnership was on the rocks. The *Melody Maker* broke the news in a front-page story accompanied by a picture of Collins that made him look like a B-movie hood: "When Louis Armstrong completes his present European tour, now likely to extend into October in England, with several Continental bookings to follow, he and his manager, Johnny Collins, will sever their connection." The parting was not nearly so polite as the story made it sound. John Hammond, who sailed to England on the same ship, saw the two men quarreling and described the results in his autobiography:

> One night [Collins] got very drunk in Louis' stateroom while I was upbraiding him for using the word "nigger" and for his shabby treatment of Armstrong, who was, after all, Collins' bread and butter. The manager became so furious he took a swing at me. Somehow, for I am certainly no fighter, I managed to counter his punch and knock him on his behind. I think Louis never forgot that fight. It was probably the first time a white man had thought enough of him to fight someone who abused him.

Hammond's version of the quarrel may sound too self-serving to be taken at face value, but in a 1953 conversation with George Avakian that was taped for posterity, Armstrong confirmed it and added further details. He and Collins had been arguing about what songs the trumpeter should play at his English performances. "Listen, cocksucker, you might be my manager and you might be the biggest shit, booking the biggest business in the world," Armstrong told him. "But when I get on that fucking stage with that horn and get in trouble, you can't save me." It was then that Collins called him a "nigger," the first time he had used the word in Armstrong's presence. "I could bash his fucking brains out," he told Avakian. "See what I mean. But it's a different story. It's a white man. So I don't fuck with Johnny." The drunken Collins then took a swing at Hammond, who responded with "a short, hard jab in his fucking chops. Zoom! And I'm standing right behind him, seeing he's falling. . . . I still let him fall and bash his fucking brains out. Boom!" Armstrong was already angry with Collins, mainly because he'd gotten the trumpeter into trouble with the mob, though there were plenty of other reasons: "Always something would be wrong, always in trouble with the promoters — trying to make me declare bankruptcy. Fantastic stuff." The shipboard quarrel was the last straw, and the two men parted company in London. A few days later, on August 17, Armstrong learned of the death of his father in New Orleans, an event that left him (so he said) unmoved. Not long afterward he played a command performance for King George V, shocking the crowd by gesturing to the royal box, growling "This one's for you, Rex!" and launching into "You Rascal You." The king responded by presenting him with a gold-plated Selmer trumpet.

From there he went to Copenhagen, where the largest crowd he had seen in his life was waiting for him: "All I remember is a whole ocean of people all breaking through the police lines and bearing down on us until I got afraid we were going to get stomped underfoot. They pushed a big trumpet, all made out of flowers, into my hands and put me into an open automobile and started a parade." Once again Armstrong's records had preceded him, creating an audience for his music whose size and enthusiasm startled him. A few days later the trumpeter and his latest band, a mixed-race group, were filmed on a Danish sound stage for inclusion in *København, Kalundborg og —?*, a *Big Broadcast*–style feature film about a radio station. He performs "I Cover the Waterfront," "Dinah," and "Tiger Rag," the latter two in versions similar to the ones he had recorded for OKeh. The three-song sequence, shot by a single camera and intercut with footage of a cheering audience in order to suggest that

Armstrong was playing at an actual concert, is the first extended visual document of his performance style that has come down to us. While it is more sedate than a group of off-the-air live recordings made a week later in Stockholm, the sequence nonetheless testifies to the accuracy of the contemporary newspaper stories that describe his onstage behavior. As the film rolls, the veil of the past is lifted and we are brought face-to-face with the stage-show Armstrong: the white handkerchief, the crouching and springing, the dancing in place during the band's instrumental interludes, the sudden stillness and concentration each time he puts his horn to his mouth. We even witness his oft-reported tic of repeating the titles of the songs he is introducing: "Now, good evening, ladies and gentlemen, I'm Mr. Armstrong, and we're gonna swing one of the good ol' good ones for ya. Beautiful number. 'I Cover the Waterfront,' 'I Cover the Waterfront.' I *like* it. Look out now, cats, look out there. One, two . . ." He plays and sings with his eyes closed, rapt and transported, a study in ecstasy.

Armstrong made the rounds of Europe that winter, performing in Denmark, Norway, the Netherlands, and Sweden, then returning to England for more music-hall dates, the most eagerly awaited of which failed to come off. Coleman Hawkins had left Fletcher Henderson to seek fame and fortune in Europe, and Jack Hylton, under whose auspices Armstrong and Hawkins were touring England, hoped to present the two men together in what the *Melody Maker* called "a new act, which will be devised to allow the world's two greatest individual musicians to co-star." What Hylton did not know was that Hawkins had disliked Armstrong ever since the ill-dressed bumpkin from New Orleans had joined Henderson's band and stolen his thunder. The feeling was mutual. "Hawk didn't think that I was big enough to share a concert . . . top billing, you know," Armstrong later told Max Jones. "So he and his handlers, whoever they were, they did nothing more than mention the concert and that was all that happened to that shit." To the *Melody Maker* he said only that "I've figured it out, and it seems it ain't going to do me any good." The concert was scrapped, and the paper's fickle editors now accused him of "wrecking" it as the result of "an acute attack of artistic temperament."*

Armstrong was as subject to such attacks as the next man, but it seems more likely that his chops were at fault. He left London for Paris in May of 1934, and in *Swing That Music*, written two years later, he describes the trip in the evasive manner of a man with something to hide: "We had had a very hard year and I wanted to rest, so [the band] broke up and I went to Paris and got an apartment where I could be quiet for a little. I didn't want to do any more work just then, so I just lazed around for three or four months, meeting the swing musicians and critics and taking it easy." All true, but he had first canceled a week's worth of performances at London's Holborn Empire, and in 1966 he was honest about why he did so: "In England on the stage . . . my lip split, blood all down in my tuxedo shirt, nobody knew it." Reports in the British press indicate that he had been up to his old tricks again, shocking the prudes by playing dozens of high Cs on "Shine." Given the state of his lip, that was asking for trouble.

In Paris he made the rounds of the local nightspots and the acquaintance of Hugues Panassié, the critic and promoter who was, after Robert Goffin, his most assiduous European advocate. Panassié had been one of the first French journalists to write about Armstrong, and in 1934, shortly before the trumpeter's arrival in France, he published *Le jazz hot*, an intelligent but opinionated critical survey that revealed him to be, like John Hammond, self-confident to the point of arrogance. At first he had preferred the white jazzmen of the twenties to their black counterparts, but he kept on listening, and in *Le jazz hot* he declared Armstrong to be "the greatest of all hot soloists . . . I do not think I am making too strong a statement when I say that [he] is not only a genius in his own art, but is one of the most extraordinary creative geniuses that all music has ever known."

---

*The two men later smoothed over their differences, and in 1938 Hawkins spoke admiringly to a Swiss journalist of Armstrong's recording of "Jubilee": "That's just *great!* You see, about ten, fifteen years ago Louis was so much ahead of everybody that he became *the* inspiration for all of us."

Panassié, unlike Goffin, was not a blind enthusiast, and he criticized Armstrong's "deplorable virtuoso playing" on "New Tiger Rag" and "High Society," worrying that "when he first plays in our country, he will think he must bring the public the actor and instrumental virtuoso, instead of the great creative musician." But the two men hit it off anyway, and their friendship lasted for the rest of the trumpeter's life.

Armstrong's first encounter with Django Reinhardt, the illiterate gypsy who was Europe's first major jazz soloist, was less auspicious. Reinhardt had idolized Armstrong ever since hearing his recordings of "Indian Cradle Song" and "Savoy Blues" in 1931, which caused the guitarist to put his head in his hands and cry, "My brother! My brother!" Though Reinhardt was eager to play for his new hero, Armstrong had no particular interest in hearing an obscure French jazzman, and an encounter set up by Panassié's friend Charles Delaunay fell flat: "Armstrong, preoccupied by his toilet, kept rushing across the room to fetch a shirt or a tie: only once did we hear a 'Very good! Go on!' emerge from the dressing-room. Django was mortified. Beads of sweat stood out on his forehead." But a few days later, Ada Smith, the redheaded American expatriate known as "Bricktop" whose Montmartre nightclub was famous enough to make it into F. Scott Fitzgerald's "Babylon Revisited," called the violinist Stephane Grappelli, Reinhardt's musical partner, to tip him off that Armstrong had dropped into her *boîte*. "It must have been about five in the morning, and she asked Django to come and accompany Armstrong," Grappelli recalled. "Naturally, Django and I set off at once, and for the only time in my life I heard Louis sing, accompanied only by Django's guitar. There were no discussions to decide what key they'd play in or what tunes they'd choose. Louis began and Django followed him in the twinkling of an eye."

Armstrong's lip was still out of order, and it was not until November 7 that he took up his horn again and recorded six songs for French Brunswick. Though it was the first time in a year and a half that he had set foot in a studio, he made a lively impression on his first recording of "On the Sunny Side of the Street" (whose set-piece solo had long been a regular part of his stage performances) and an

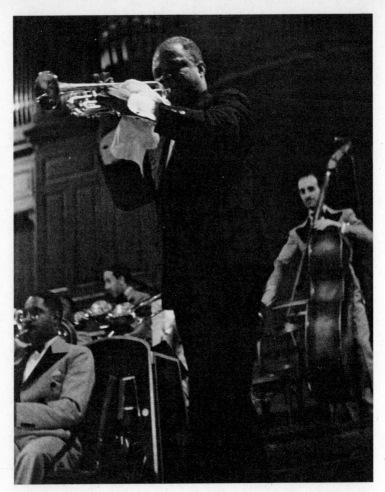

"A brilliant meteor flourishing his trumpet": A previously unpublished photograph of Armstrong performing at the Salle Pleyel in Paris, 1934. A few weeks later he returned to America with his lip in tatters and his career at a standstill.

original number called "Song of the Vipers" in which he alternated between slightly shaky trumpet solos and wordless scatting and shouting. Two nights later the band of Paris-based musicians that accompanied him in the studio joined him on stage for a pair of concerts at the Salle Pleyel, the Paris hall where he made his long-delayed French debut. Hugues Panassié was there: "The entrance of

Louis on stage was something unforgettable: as the first measures of his band resounded he made his appearance running, like a brilliant meteor flourishing his trumpet. . . . Contact was immediately established, one was irresistibly captured by the incredible dynamism that was released by his entire being." Also present was a correspondent for the *New York Herald*, who reported that "the rubber-mouthed and consummately rhythmic American Negro . . . led his 11-piece band through a jazz program which was crystal-clear, honest and occasionally profound." So were many musicians and other artists, including the classical composer Georges Auric, who told Panassié that the concert had been "overwhelming," and Jean Renoir, who recalled it as a "triumph" at which the audience "wildly applauded a performer of a kind quite new to them playing music that was utterly strange." Django Reinhardt was just as excited: "My friend, there is nothing more to say; there is only one musician; it is Louis Armstrong."

As always there were dissenters. One of them, surprisingly, was Darius Milhaud, who strolled around the lobby at intermission saying, "Very 1920, very 1920." The composer of *La création du monde*, it seemed, had lost interest in jazz, and some of the critics who came to the concert had never had any use for it. Lucien Rebatet wrote a review for *Action Française*, the Fascist paper, whose language had an ominous ring: "It could be rather curious to see negroes roll their wild eyes, gyrate, and shake with the pulsations of the drum, like the ancestral beat. . . . But one discovered afterwards that, beneath the appearances of scary trances, it is all blatant fakery, bad acting, pretty much unchanging." The classical composer Gösta Nystroem struck a similar note when he reviewed one of Armstrong's Stockholm concerts: "Mr. King of Jazz and man-eater offspring, Louis Armstrong, shows his clean-shaven hippopotamus physiognomy." Those who imagine prewar Europe to have been a haven for black musicians would do well to read and reflect on such notices.

In *Swing That Music* Armstrong said that his Paris debut was a triumph: "I got such a big hand I had to come out of my dressing room in my bathrobe for the curtain calls." It went so well, he added, that a French impresario, Jacques Canetti, had agreed to book a tour of the Continent, on which he and Alpha embarked the following month. But Armstrong was not ready to resume so demanding a schedule. He had asked too much of himself, not just in the past year but for the past quarter century, and now he would pay the price.

Arthur Briggs, a black trumpeter who went to Europe in 1919 with Sidney Bechet and the Southern Syncopated Orchestra and later settled in Paris, observed Armstrong up close in 1934 and was alarmed by what he saw. A well-trained player who recognized at once that his colleague's embouchure had been compromised by too much pressure and too many high notes, Briggs noticed that the sharp, precise attack heard on recordings like "Cornet Chop Suey" had given way to a softer sound that was "a push, and not an attack." Armstrong's lips, he recalled, "were as hard as a piece of wood and he was bleeding and everything else. We thought he had — well, we didn't say cancer because in those days we wouldn't have thought of it — but we thought he had some very sad disease." In the past he had chosen to bulldoze his way through such crises, for once he established himself as king of the high Cs, he saw no choice but to continue his lip-shredding ways, much like an aging gunfighter who must kill all comers or be killed himself. But his aim was no longer true, and when his chops gave out yet again at a concert in Turin, he packed his bags, went back to France, and caught the next boat to America.

The editors of the *Melody Maker* ran a front-page story written by the furious M. Canetti whose headline told the whole sad tale: "Armstrong Flees to U.S.A. / Breaks Contract and Leaves France in Secret / Allegations of Resentment and Jealousy towards Fellow Coloured Artists." The resentment, it appears, was mainly on Canetti's part, and he took his revenge by airing every piece of dirty laundry on which he could lay his hands: "In addition, fresh troubles are known to await him in New York, where he must answer a suit by his lawful wife, Lilly [*sic*] Armstrong, and where he must explain to both Brunswick and Victor his reason for signing an exclusive contract with the former when he was in no position to do so, and for breaking his exclusive contract with the latter."

Armstrong, of course, left far more than resentment and jealousy in the wake of his travels. He also left his mark on a generation of European musicians who drank deeply from the well of his genius. Spike Hughes went to New York in 1933 and recorded ten of his own compositions with an all-star "Negro Orchestra" whose members, in addition to Coleman Hawkins and Benny Carter, included such past and future Armstrong sidemen as Henry Allen, Sid Catlett, Kaiser Marshall, and Luis Russell. A month after the Salle Pleyel concerts, Django Reinhardt and Stephane Grappelli launched the Quintette du Hot Club de France, an Armstrong-influenced band that was the first European jazz group to make recordings comparable in quality to those of their American counterparts. At their debut recording session they cut two of Armstrong's staples, "Dinah" and "Tiger Rag." Other instrumentalists, Nat Gonella in particular, cracked the code of swing after hearing Armstrong in person and started playing with a rhythmic certainty not unlike that of their mentor. Even the BBC launched a series of live big-band performances called *America Dances!* transmitted from America to England via shortwave.

But none of these things, however gratifying, could help Armstrong climb out of the hole in which he found himself. Not only was Lil suing him for six thousand dollars in unpaid "maintenance" that Johnny Collins had neglected to remit, but Collins, having tried and failed to lure the trumpeter back into his fold, was threatening to sue him for breach of contract. "Never, never, never," Armstrong said after reading a telegram from Collins begging him to kiss and make up. Now it seemed that he might have to go back to work for a man he despised and distrusted—assuming that he could first square things with the gangsters who stalked him. Worst of all, his lip was in tatters, and nothing but a long, expensive layoff could restore it to working order. He glossed over his plight in *Swing That Music:* "From January of 1935 to May I took myself a good rest in Chicago." Thirty years later he came clean: "When I come back to America I didn't blow the horn for about six months. I'd thrown it out of my mind. Couldn't go no further with all them shysters yiping at me." Holed up in Chicago, besieged by lawyers, and unable to play the horn that was his life, he turned in desperation to the one man he thought could help him, a hot-tempered boxing promoter who was flat broke and mobbed up to the eyeballs. He could not have found a less likely savior — or a more effective one.

8

"ALWAYS HAVE A WHITE MAN"

With Joe Glaser, 1935–1938

AFTER JOE OLIVER, Joe Glaser was the most important person in Louis Armstrong's life, and Armstrong knew it. He would never be shy about praising the man who managed his career from 1935 on, often so lavishly that it made his listeners ill at ease. Glaser's *New York Times* obituary cited an interview in which the trumpeter described him in language that might have come out of the mouth of Uncle Remus: "Asking me about Joe is like askin' a chile 'bout its daddy." In private Armstrong was less fulsome, but no one who heard him talk about Glaser came away doubting the strength of his feelings for the man whom he called "my dearest friend." Glaser claimed to feel the same way. "I'm Louis and Louis is me," he told a journalist in 1949. "There's nothing I wouldn't do for him." Yet there was no intimacy to their friendship. According to Lucille Armstrong, "They couldn't be in the same room together two minutes. They were two different people." What bound them together was not so much affection as gratitude: each was responsible for the other's success.

"You don't know me," Glaser liked to tell people when meeting them for the first time, "but you know two things about me: I have a terrible temper and I always keep my word." He was a teetotaler who raised dogs, liked sports, hated nightclubs, and did his best to be in bed each night by ten o'clock. He was also a bullying vulgarian who spewed obscenities in all directions and called his black clients "shines" and *schwarzes*. Nat Hentoff once saw "a painting of the antebellum South with happy darkies playing the banjo and singing" on the wall of his office. One night he paid a rare visit to Café Society, Barney Josephson's jazz club, and chided the owner because so many of the customers were black. "Now look," he said, "don't get me wrong. Nobody likes a little nigger pussy better than Joe Glaser. But in business it's another matter." Many who met him came away suspecting that failure to do his bidding could get your leg broken — or worse. "He acted like a crook," said Andy Kirk, whose band Glaser managed in the thirties. "If you cursed him out, he liked you." Max Gordon, the owner of the Village Vanguard, called him "the most obscene, the most outrageous, and the toughest agent I've ever bought an act from." To Noël Coward, whom he booked into a Las Vegas casino, he was "a brisk little Jewish go-getter. . . . shrewd, sentimental, noisy and generous." But Coward and Gordon, unlike Kirk, liked and trusted Glaser, as did many of those with whom he did business. "If I have Joe Glaser's word," Ed Sullivan said, "I can go to sleep. And the performer he is booking can go to sleep, too." The trick was to know what his word was.

While Glaser was forthright about having worked for Al Capone, no one held that against him — everyone in Chicago who had anything to do with jazz in the Roaring Twenties, it seemed, had *something* to do with Capone — and he lived long enough and made enough money to be thought respectable by those who knew no better. The *Times* obituary skated over his early days: "Born in Chicago, the son of a prominent physician, Mr. Glaser went to medical school but dropped out, because he said he continually became ill in the dissecting room. Mr. Glaser then went into the used-car business, became the manager of several fighters and then branched out into the nightclub and saloon business." It omitted the fact that the manager of the world's most famous jazz musician had twice come close to doing hard time for raping teenage girls. Born in 1897, Glaser went to work for the mob in the mid-twenties and within a few years was running Capone's South Side nightclubs and whorehouses, a job that allowed him to give his sexual interests free rein. In 1928 he was sentenced to a ten-year prison term for attacking a fourteen-year-old. "She wore make-up and seemed to be in her twenties," Glaser assured the judge. "In fact, it was her mother who pointed her out to me and encouraged my interest in her." He married the girl, but a month later he was in trouble again, this time with a seventeen-year-old, and Capone had to send a fixer to get him off the hook. Ernie Anderson, a publicist who worked with Glaser and Armstrong, looked into the matter years later and was informed that "all the court records . . . had been 'lost or destroyed.'"

Glaser returned to managing boxers, but he continued to run afoul of the law, and it was said that he had been imprisoned at one time for committing murder. Budd Johnson heard that "he killed a guy over this black prostitute, and was sent to the penitentiary." This, however, appears to have been nothing more than a rumor, one that Glaser himself may have spread in order to heighten his reputation for being a dangerous man to cross. Whatever the truth of the matter, he was on his uppers when Armstrong retreated to Chicago in 1935 to figure out his next move. Tommy Rockwell, who was now co-owner of the Rockwell-O'Keefe Theatrical Agency, which represented Bing Crosby, the Casa Loma Orchestra, and the Mills Brothers, was offering Armstrong a five-thousand-dollar advance to sign another management contract. He was still under contract to Johnny Collins, though, and had no wish to tie himself up yet again with the man who he thought had turned the mob loose on him four years earlier. What Armstrong needed was a tough guy of his own, one whom he could trust. Glaser had treated him honorably and well when they worked together at the Sunset Café eight years earlier, so Armstrong looked his old boss up.

As Glaser told it, the trumpeter was "broke and very sick. He called me up from New York and he said, 'Mr. Glaser, I don't want to be with nobody but you. Please Mr. Glaser, just you and I. You understand me, I understand you.'" In Armstrong's version, Glaser needed help as well: "He had always been a sharp cat, but now he was raggedy ass." That was part of what made him attractive. "I'm going to get Joe Glaser, because he ain't got nothing," Armstrong told Budd Johnson. "We both can start out together." Either way, though, the bottom line was the same. Not only was Armstrong looking for someone who could settle his mob-related problems, but he wanted above all to be relieved of responsibility for his tangled business affairs. "Pops, I need you," he told Glaser. "Come be my manager. *Please!* Take care of all my business and take care of me. Just lemme blow my gig."

The proposition Armstrong made to Glaser was straightforward: "You get me the jobs. You collect the money. You pay me one thousand dollars every week free and clear. You pay off the band, the travel and hotel expenses, my income tax, and you take everything that's left." (The arrangement was eventually restructured as a fifty-fifty split in which Glaser continued to pay Armstrong's expenses, both professional and personal.) Armstrong knew that his new manager might end up making more than he did, but that didn't matter: "I never tried in no way to ever be *real real* filthy rich like some people do, and after they do they *die just* the same." Glaser, on the other hand, wanted nothing more than to die filthy rich, and saw in Armstrong his last best hope of doing so. They shook hands on the deal, and Glaser gave up his other business, such as it was, and devoted his formidable energies to making Armstrong a star. For a time there were lean stretches when he was unable to hit the target — as late as 1937 Armstrong sometimes made as little as seventy-five dollars a night — but the trumpeter's faith in Glaser never wavered.

Today most people cannot help but see Armstrong's behavior toward Glaser as too close to subservience for comfort. He told an interviewer that one of the reasons why he approached Glaser in 1935 was that he had "always admired the way he treated his help." On the same occasion he remarked that "I never called him Joe in my life." But it is easy to forget that Armstrong came from a world in which a black man who treated a white man any other way was dicing with

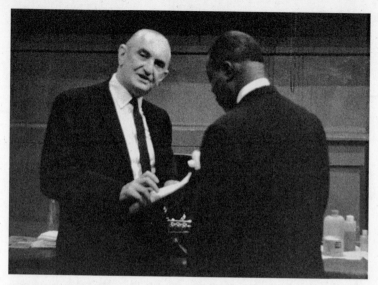

"I'm Louis and Louis is me": Joe Glaser and Louis Armstrong. This previously unpublished backstage photograph, taken in the fifties by Armstrong's close friend Jack Bradley, suggests the complexity of the relationship between the shy trumpeter and the foul-tempered manager who (in Armstrong's grateful words) "saved me from the gangsters."

death. In 1955 he shared with Glaser a piece of advice given to him by Black Benny Williams, the New Orleans tough who had looked after him when he was a boy: "*Dipper*, As long as you live, no matter where you may be — always have a *White Man* (who like you) and can + will put his Hand on your shoulder and say — '*This is "My" Nigger*' and, Can't Nobody Harm Ya." By 1935 he had seen more than enough to know the value of such protection, and he believed that Glaser could give it to him.

Though the two men rarely socialized after hours, they were close in a way that few outsiders could appreciate. "I always said I didn't believe either one of them could live without the other," said Trummy Young, who played trombone for Armstrong for twelve years and saw his relationship with Glaser up close. What Young could not have seen, though, was that Armstrong had always been looking for a father, and that Glaser, for whatever reason or reasons, was willing to play the part. "Louis has never failed to take my advice, never failed to respect me, and has been one of the most honorable and faithful guys to me in the world," he said. "I guess to me he's like a son. . . . He's always called me 'Pops.' He's never called me 'Joe.'" In fact Armstrong talked back to Glaser on occasion, but never in public and only in the way that a loyal son might quarrel with his stern father. Beyond that he followed orders, secure in the knowledge that no one would harm him: "There ain't but one guy can protect that horn, 'cause he love music himself. Nobody knows Mr. Glaser was a violin player at eleven years old. That's why he knows music. . . . Our first contract was for ten years, after that we didn't bother, don't know whether I was right or wrong, but I was happy."

Barney Bigard, who played clarinet for Armstrong in the forties and fifties, summed up what was known to everyone who passed through his bands:

> Joe hired and fired everybody. Whatever he did it was alright with Louis. If he fired someone Louis wouldn't say anything, even if he liked the guy real well. It wasn't on account of that he was frightened of Joe, or that Joe was a white guy handling him. It was just that Louis long ago figured that he did best out of the world if he didn't get involved in the business side. He didn't want to tread on anyone's toes or hurt anyone's feelings. . . . They really were plain old-fashioned friends. Louis wasn't just saying that for business reasons.

Did Glaser feel the same way about Armstrong, or was he simply looking out for his golden goose? No one knew for sure. "Joe Glaser, the way he'd talk, you figure he didn't care about Louis or nobody else, but he did. . . . Joe cared more for Louis than he did for his own family," Trummy Young said — but then went on to add that "Glaser used to tell everybody, he said, 'Look, I might give anybody a screwing, but not him. See, he's my man. He put me where I am today.'" As for Armstrong, he would later write a lengthy reminiscence of his New Orleans days in which he placed special emphasis on his "long time admiration for the Jewish people." He had just learned that Glaser had suffered a stroke and was in a coma. This is the dedication:

> I dedicate this book
> to my manager and pal
> Mr. Joe Glaser
> The best Friend
> That I've ever had
> May the Lord Bless Him
> Watch over him always.
>
> His boy + disciple who *loved* him *dearly*.
> Louis
>   Satchmo
>   Armstrong

Glaser started by taking out a six-figure insurance policy on his disciple's life. Then he paid off Lil and bought out Johnny Collins for five thousand dollars, seventy-three thousand in today's dollars, a not-ungenerous sum for a musician thought to be damaged goods. It is safe to assume that he also used his gangland connections to ensure that Armstrong would no longer receive backstage visits from pistol-packing thugs. Such favors never come cheap, and the question begs itself: what did a washed-up small-timer like Joe Glaser have to offer in return? For the rest of his life, the precise nature of Glaser's post-1935 relationship with the mob would be his deepest, darkest secret. All Armstrong ever knew for sure was that he had "saved me from the gangsters," and it was not until both men were in their graves that the price of his freedom finally became known.

After establishing a clear title to Armstrong's services, Glaser set up a temporary beachhead at the Rockwell-O'Keefe office in Chicago and spread the word that the trumpeter was ready to resume his career. In June *Down Beat*, a new music magazine that aspired to be an American counterpart to England's *Melody Maker*, published an interview in which Armstrong announced that he would be hitting the road the following month. "My chops was beat when I got back from Europe," he said, but added that "I'm all rested up and dying to get going again." While the piece claimed that he had been sitting out his contract with Collins, it also acknowledged that his absence from the scene had caused gossip: "His inactivity and seclusion has started a score of rumors that he had 'lost his lip,' that he had a split lip, that his former wife, now leading her own band, had tied up his earnings to satisfy the demands of her suit for alimony, and so on. Musicians all over the world wondered what the real truth was in Louis' 'solitude.'" Armstrong denied nothing, but he also made it clear that he was now raring to go — and that he had put his affairs in the hands of "Joe Glaser, Louis' newly acquired personal manager."

Armstrong spent the next couple of months working with yet another Zilner Randolph–directed band, accompanied this time by Glaser, who learned the ropes of the band business by traveling with the trumpeter. He also received a firsthand education in the realities of life on the road: Glaser, Armstrong said, "would buy food along the way in paper bags and bring it to us boys on the bus who couldn't be served" whenever the band traveled through the Deep South. In September he booked the trumpeter into Connie's Inn for a four-month run. (By then the club had moved to Times Square and the Immerman brothers were no longer running it, having sold out after George Immerman was kidnapped and held for ransom.) When Local 802 of the musicians' union barred Glaser from bringing Armstrong's Chicago-based sidemen into a New York nightclub, he sent them home and made an offer to Luis Russell, whose once-successful band was on the ropes. Armstrong took over the group at the end of September, and Russell stayed on as pianist and musical director. Though the band had expanded from ten to thirteen players since last working with Armstrong in 1930, some of the charter members, including Pops Foster on bass and Paul Barbarin on drums, were still with Russell in 1935, and Armstrong reveled in their homey style. "I enjoyed all the moments that I spent with Luis Russell and his band — well, maybe because there were mostly New Orleans boys in that band," he said. "The warmth, the feeling, the swing, the beat, the everything, were there. . . . I was very proud 'n' happy to have played in that band every night." He liked it so much that he was willing to overlook such musical flaws as Bingie Madison's out-of-tune clarinet solo on the remake of "Struttin' with Some Barbecue" that he cut with the Russell band in 1938: "That [solo] was a half a tone off, but it sold all right. . . . Them cats know that a guy got to blow the way he feels and sometimes he hits them wrong."

But Glaser had no intention of returning to the days when Armstrong and Russell had recorded "Mahogany Hall Stomp" and "St. Louis Blues" for OKeh. Like Tommy Rockwell before him, he planned to present his new client not as a purveyor of hot jazz for black dancers but as a middle-of-the-road popular entertainer capable of appealing to white listeners as well. In 1932 Eli Oberstein had claimed that college students and musicians were Armstrong's biggest fans, a point that Charles Edward Smith reiterated in an article published two years later in *Esquire:* "The substantial following enjoyed by Louis Armstrong is due largely to jazz enthusiasts at prominent universities — Yale, Princeton, etc. — who began collecting his records five years ago." Glaser was sure that Armstrong could please an even wider audience if he made a few changes in the way he presented himself. "An entertainer, singer, and musician can make 10 times as much money as an ordinary trumpet player," he later explained. "So I used to say, 'Louis, forget all the goddamn critics, the musicians. Play for the public. Sing and play and smile.'" Armstrong understood that kind of talk, and he was impressed by Glaser's willingness to take a chance on reaching out to a new crowd: "Joe Glaser could realize I could play with white boys! You know? And play for white people! When I first signed up with him, he didn't just book me in colored dances." So he rethought his approach, starting with the lip-busting extravaganzas that had gotten him into trouble. "For many years I blew my brains out," he said. "Hitting notes so high they hurt a dog's ears, driving like crazy, screaming it. . . . Joe Glaser told me, 'Play and sing pretty. Give the people a show.'"

Singing pretty meant singing intelligibly. Even Armstrong's most fervent admirers praised his mush-mouthed, heavily accented vocals in terms that made them sound impenetrable. Hoagy Carmichael, who recorded "Rockin' Chair" with him in 1929, wrote in his autobiography of how "[t]hose big lips of his, at the mike in front of my face, blubbering strange cannibalistic sounds, tickled me to the marrow." Rudy Vallée, the megaphone-wielding crooner who was hipper than he looked, contributed an introduction to *Swing That Music* in which he reassured his readers that the "utterly mad, hoarse, inchoate mumble-jumble that is Louis' singing" was in fact "beautifully timed and executed." Glaser probably told him to clean up his diction, but whoever was responsible for the change, Armstrong's records began to reflect his newfound determination to sing prettier for the white people whose favor he sought to curry.* So, too, did his toned-down stage act, which Leonard Feather, a British-born jazz critic who had last seen him on stage in 1934, now described as "a subtle mix of showmanship and artistry. There were no wild gesticulations to the band, no exhibitionism of the kind that had brought him boos and catcalls two years earlier."

Armstrong's new record label was run by a musical populist who had an exquisitely well-honed appreciation of the commercial value of pretty singing. "I know how to keep my pulse on the multitude," said Jack Kapp, who first made a name for himself as the general manager of Brunswick Records, whose stable of artists included Bing Crosby, the Boswell Sisters, Duke Ellington, Fletcher Henderson, Al Jolson, Guy Lombardo, Ted Lewis, and the Mills Brothers. In 1934 he struck out on his own and started a new label, Decca Records, to which most of the musicians with whom he had worked at Brunswick followed him. At a time when pop records retailed for seventy-five cents apiece, Decca's releases sold for thirty-five. In addition to cutting prices, Kapp posted admonitory signs in his studios that read

---

*In 1936 and again in 1937 Armstrong underwent surgery on his vocal cords, presumably in an attempt to remove the nodular growths that were responsible for his raspy voice. The operations were unsuccessful, and thereafter his voice grew increasingly gravelly.

WHERE'S THE MELODY? His handling of Crosby exemplified the Decca approach: the jazz-conscious, scat-singing balladeer now embarked on a recording program that also included, in addition to the standard pop tunes of the day, such unlikely fare as "Aloha Oe," "Home on the Range," "I Love You Truly," "Silent Night," "Swanee River," and "Swing Low, Sweet Chariot," accompanied by everyone from the Dorsey Brothers to the Andrews Sisters. The goal, Kapp told Crosby, was to establish him as "the John McCormack of this generation.... [T]he masses want melody combined with soul, which is yours." To everyone's surprise but Kapp's, the plan worked, and by the time Crosby died in 1977, thirty-eight of his Decca singles had hit the top of the charts. (The Beatles, by comparison, recorded twenty-four number-one hits.)

That was just what Glaser wanted for Armstrong, so he took him to Decca, put him in Kapp's hands, and gave the producer free rein. It helped, of course, that Armstrong, for all his swinging instincts, liked nothing better than a "good ol' good one" played straight and sweet. "He loved melody," said Milt Gabler, who encouraged him to record similarly commercial fare for Decca after World War II, and his OKeh sides had already shown him to be willing to experiment with such eclectic-sounding additions to his big bands as the steel guitar on "I'm Confessin'," the castanets that punctuate "The Peanut Vendor," and the violins and vibraphone that augment the Russell band on "Song of the Islands."

What Kapp had in mind was clear from the moment that Armstrong walked into Decca's New York studios on October 3, 1935, for his first recording session in more than a year. The date began with "I'm in the Mood for Love," a new ballad by Jimmy McHugh and Dorothy Fields, the authors of "I Can't Give You Anything but Love," and it sent an updated version of the same message that the older song had sent to record buyers six years earlier. "I'm in the Mood for Love" is arranged in a faceless but impeccably professional school-of-Lombardo style that was worlds away from the haphazard accompaniment that Zilner Randolph's musicians had supplied for "I Gotta Right to Sing the Blues." Like "I Can't Give You Anything but Love," it starts with a muted trumpet solo, after which Armstrong sings Fields's lyric more or less straight, interpolating an *oh, baby* here and a bit of scat there but otherwise sticking to the text as written. The record ends with an open-horn solo whose climax is a lone, unspectacular high B-flat. The effect is so placid-sounding that it is possible to overlook the freedom with which Armstrong reworks McHugh's melody, loosening up its phrases so that it sounds as if he is spinning them off the top of his head. The rest of the session was given over to swinging versions of two more pop tunes, "Got a Bran' New Suit" and "You Are My Lucky Star," and "La Cucaracha," a featherweight novelty that Armstrong tossed off with every sign of pleasure.

That first date set the tone for six years' worth of Decca sessions at which Armstrong would cut well over a hundred 78 sides, most of them conceived along lines broadly similar to Bing Crosby's recordings of the same period. Pop songs from Hollywood and Tin Pan Alley, ephemeral novelties, nineteenth-century ballads, black spirituals, Hawaiian songs, even the odd big-band update of a chestnut like "Dipper Mouth Blues": such was the fare that Jack Kapp encouraged him to sing in the hope of making him accessible not just to what Kapp called "the evergrowing Armstrong cult" but to a broad-based, ethnically diverse audience. Like Crosby, Armstrong was paired from time to time with such other Decca artists as Jimmy Dorsey, the Casa Loma Orchestra, and the Mills Brothers, and on occasion the two men even recorded the same songs. If the novelties were fatuous, the pop tunes were often the best that the publishers of the day had to offer, and once in a while he got to record a gem like George Gershwin's "Love Walked In" or Hoagy Carmichael's "Jubilee," the second of which the Russell band turns into a portrait of a New Orleans street parade over which the trumpeter flings two piping-hot solos.

Similarly reminiscent of days gone by was a pair of 1937 sessions at which Armstrong and the mellow-toned Mills Brothers, a vocal quartet whose members knew their colleague's work well, recorded "Carry Me Back to Old Virginny," "In the Shade of the Old Apple Tree," Stephen Foster's "Old Folks at Home," and a gently swinging version of "Darling Nelly Gray," the century-old abolitionist ballad about a slave whose lover is sold to another owner: *Oh, my darling Nelly Gray, they have taken you away / And I'll never see my darling anymore.* It is unlikely that many white listeners knew what Armstrong was singing about, or caught the dig of irony in his spoken coda to Foster's paean to plantation life: "Well, look-a here, we are *far* away from home! *Yeah*, man." The collaboration must have reminded him of the quartet with which he had sung on the streets of Storyville, for he recorded seven more sides with the Mills Brothers, among them a jaunty rendering of Irving Berlin's "My Walking Stick" of which Fred Astaire would surely have been proud.

No matter what he was given to record, he gave his best in return, and his alchemic ability to turn dross into gold was undiminished. If his new style was less spectacular, it was also purer, shorn of the excesses that had obscured the lyricism at the heart of his artistry. To some extent this purity may have been imposed by the cumulative effects of the string of split lips that he suffered in the early thirties, but if that was the case, it would not have been the first time that a great artist has been freed to follow his inner impulse by technical limitations arising from physical decline. He could still thrill: "Struttin' with Some Barbecue," whose stupendous glissandi pop like flags in a high wind, is even more exciting than the 1928 original. More often, though, he opted for the simplicity that is a sign of maturity, a process that reached its apex in his 1941 remake of "Sleepy Time Down South." Max Harrison summed up this journey of self-refinement as follows:

> Armstrong's small-group recordings of the 1920s have nearly monopolized critical attention and this is understandable because he was then innovating almost constantly. During that period he was one of a tiny group of men who were drastically expanding the musical language of jazz: an exciting state of affairs. Later, innovation became unnecessary, because he had won all the territory he needed and his next task was that of discovering its full potentialities. . . . Beyond this lies "Sleepy Time Down South," which contains not a superfluous note and whose almost classical focusing on essentials distills all the qualities he brought to music.

Hugues Panassié put it more poetically: "Before, he was seeking — and finding. Now, he *knows*."

＜━━＞

Armstrong and the Russell band opened at Connie's Inn on October 29, 1935, and remained in residence for the next four months, broadcasting regularly over CBS. It was a good time for a jazzman to be making remote broadcasts from a big-city nightclub, for Benny Goodman's band had blown the roof off Los Angeles's Palomar Ballroom two months earlier, ushering in the decade that came to be known as the Swing Era. Demography was having its way with American culture: sixteen years after the doughboys of World War I came home from Europe and started impregnating their wives, a new cohort of teenagers had found a new kind of music to call their own. It was no coincidence that *Esquire* and *Vanity Fair* both ran pieces about Armstrong that winter, or that he signed a contract to write his autobiography shortly thereafter. Never before had jazz been as popular as it was soon to become.

The title page of Armstrong's *Swing That Music* makes no mention of a ghostwriter, and he claimed that "every word of it was my own." In fact it sounds in places like a heavily edited version of the Louis Armstrong whom we know from *Satchmo: My Life in New Orleans* and his later autobiographical manuscripts, and in other places like the work of a different hand altogether. The culprit was Horace Gerlach, an obscure pianist-songwriter who is credited as "editor" of the last section of the book, a nonsensical discourse on jazz incorporating ten transcribed solos by such Swing Era jazzmen as Benny Goodman, Tommy Dorsey, Bud Freeman, and Red Norvo. All are based on an Armstrong-Gerlach song called "Swing That Music," which the trumpeter had recorded twice for Decca in the preceding year, once with his own band and again three months later in a more polished remake accompanied by Jimmy Dorsey. (The first version incorporates an abridged version of his "Shine" routine, in which he plays forty-odd high Cs topped with an F.)

The manuscript of *Swing That Music* has not survived, making it impossible to know the extent to which Armstrong was directly responsible for its composition. What is not in doubt, though, is that he could have written the book on his own had he been encouraged to do so. His earliest known letter was sent less than a month after he moved to Chicago from New Orleans, by which time he owned a typewriter and knew how to use it. His surviving letters from the early forties (some of which are quite long) reveal him to have been a witty correspondent with an eye for detail. He described himself as "a two-fingered blip on my portable typewriter" in a radio interview conducted around that time, adding that he was "really proud" of his ability to "speak and write straight English" and that he had bought a dictionary of synonyms and antonyms to help him in writing *Swing That Music*. As early as 1933 his letters began to be printed in the *Melody Maker* and other jazz magazines, and after World War II his byline appeared frequently in American and British magazines, including such mainstream publications as *Holiday* and the *New York Times Book Review*. All this suggests that *Swing That Music* was based on a manuscript that Armstrong wrote himself, presumably at Glaser's urging, then gave to Gerlach to rewrite.

Reviewers mostly overlooked the book, which was published in November of 1936, but Otis Ferguson, one of the few jazz critics to comment on *Swing That Music*, caught its quality well when he described it as "a nice easy book, talking as naturally as Louis himself about early life in New Orleans and on the river, and covering up the actual work of his job and career like a maiden aunt in a stiff breeze." Yet for all its omissions and evasions, *Swing That Music* was significant by definition in that it was the first autobiography to be written by a jazz musician, and while it is now of limited interest save as a historical curiosity, it does contain a valuable (if guarded) firsthand account of the period between Armstrong's move to Chicago and his decision to sign with Glaser thirteen years later.

Of greater long-term significance to his career was the release that same month of *Pennies from Heaven*, his earliest surviving feature

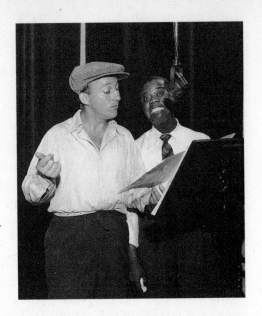

Reverend Satchelmouth meets the Boss of All Singers: Bing Crosby and Louis Armstrong in the recording studio, 1936. Though Crosby never invited Armstrong to his home, he went out of his way to give the trumpeter star billing in *Pennies from Heaven*.

film, in which he shared top billing with Bing Crosby, the first time that a black performer received star billing in a Hollywood movie. Armstrong and Crosby had gotten to know one another in 1930, when they appeared concurrently at the New Cotton Club and the Cocoanut Grove. "Every night between their outfit and our outfit," Armstrong recalled, "we used to *Burn up* the air, *every* night.... [T]hey would haul ashes over to the Cotton Club where we were playing and swing with us, until Home Sweet Home was played." In private life Crosby was a distant man who rarely socialized with his colleagues, and he made no exception for Armstrong. "I've never been invited to the home of a movie star, not even Bing's," the trumpeter remarked years later. But Crosby genuinely liked him, and if they were more warm acquaintances than close friends, their mutual affection is still evident from the by-play preserved on surviving airchecks of Armstrong's appearances on Crosby's radio shows. "I never met anybody that didn't love him that ever saw him work or ever has encountered him, had any connection or any business with him," Crosby told the British trumpeter-critic Humphrey Lyttelton. As for their mutual admiration, it was boundless, so much so that

Armstrong once went so far as to record a special version of "Happy Birthday" as a present for the man he called "the *Boss of All Singers.*"

In 1936 the Boss of All Singers was also America's number-one entertainer, a triple threat whose movies and radio appearances were as popular as his records, putting him in a position to reach over the color bar and lend a helping hand to the man who had taught him how to swing. Armstrong had already appeared on *Kraft Music Hall*, Crosby's hugely successful new Thursday-night series on NBC. When Crosby struck a deal with Paramount that allowed him to make one independent film each year, his first project under the new contract was a Jo Swerling screenplay about a singing ex-con who opens a nightclub in an allegedly haunted house. Crosby, who co-produced *Pennies from Heaven*, stipulated that Armstrong be cast in the role of the ignorant but lovable sidekick who helps the singer out by offering to play in his club. Armstrong's part, like the rest of the film, is now a period piece. His big number, "Skeleton in the Closet," is an eye-rolling look-out-fo'-dat-boogie-man specialty: *The spooks were havin' their midnight fling / The merry-making was in full swing.* (The "spooks" in question were ghosts, not blacks.) Even more creakingly dated is his "comic" by-play with Crosby:

ARMSTRONG: I got the boys together and I told them you wanted us to play the music at the restaurant. And for that we'd get ten percent of the business. And that's where the trouble started. . . . [T]here's seven men in the band. And none of us knows how to divide ten percent up by seven. So if you could only make it seven percent?

CROSBY: Seven percent, Henry, it's a deal.

ARMSTRONG: Oh, *thank* you, Mr. Poole! I *told* them cats you'd do the right thing.

But both men had grown up with that kind of humor and found it harmless. Five months before the trumpeter's death, he and Crosby appeared on *The David Frost Show* and reminisced about the making of *Pennies from Heaven*, and Armstrong recited the 7 percent scene from memory. "Those scenes I had with Bing in that picture were Classics," he had previously written in a 1967 letter. Classic or not, the film was a hit, and most of the reviews singled out Armstrong for favorable comment. Frank Nugent's *New York Times* notice mentioned him only in passing, but *Time* proclaimed "Skeleton in the Closet" to be the "best bit" in *Pennies from Heaven. Variety* was even more enthusiastic: "Best individual impression is by Louis Armstrong, Negro cornetist and hi-de-ho expert. Not as an eccentric musician but as a Negro comedian he suggests possibilities."

The success of *Pennies from Heaven* was fueled by the popularity of the title song, which became one of Crosby's biggest hits. It gave Armstrong an opening through which Joe Glaser unhesitatingly pushed him: between 1937 and 1945 he appeared in seven more Hollywood feature films, often playing comic roles similar to the one in *Pennies*. He took them seriously, enough to become a founding member of the Negro Actors Guild. "Each year I also have a fine part in a moving picture," he bragged in a 1946 letter to the *Melody Maker*. Not only did he share the screen with Crosby, Jack Benny, Danny Kaye, Ida Lupino, Ann Miller, Dick Powell, Ronald Reagan, Ethel Waters, and Mae West, but he also introduced Harry Warren's Oscar-nominated "Jeepers Creepers," which Alec Wilder praised as "a wonderful rhythm song. . . . It pretends to nothing clever or ingenious or elaborate. But it swings and is its own marvelous salty self."* And Armstrong, as *Time* and *Variety* noted, was an immensely warm and appealing presence onscreen, a natural actor whose lively facial expressions were a cameraman's dream. He had the purest, most potent kind of star quality: no sooner did he walk into a shot than the eyes of the audience went straight to him and stayed there.

Yet only one of Armstrong's first eight films, Vincente Minnelli's *Cabin in the Sky* (1942), is now widely remembered, and his role in that pioneering all-black musical shrank to insignificance when his

---

*Both in *Going Places* (1938) and in his bubbly Decca recording of the song, Armstrong personalized Johnny Mercer's lyric to charming effect: *Where'd you get those eyes, Gate? / Where'd you get those eyes, Satch?*

featured number, "Ain't It the Truth," was left on the cutting-room floor. Elsewhere he appeared in purely musical cameos or as wince-making characters of one kind or another—he is actually referred to as "Uncle Tom" in *Going Places*—and though he always read his lines, such as they were, with zesty self-assurance, his performances embarrassed more than a few of his fellow blacks, then and later. Nor did white liberals of the day look with favor on the pictures in which he appeared: James Agee, writing in *Time*, claimed that the blacks in *Cabin in the Sky* were "regarded less as artists . . . than as picturesque, Sambo-style entertainers." Even *Down Beat* took unfavorable note of the film's "Uncle Tom slant."

The lone picture from this period in which Armstrong manages to convey something more is Raoul Walsh's *Artists and Models*, released in 1937. In "Public Melody Number One," written by Harold Arlen and Ted Koehler and staged by Vincente Minnelli, he makes a brief but unforgettable appearance as a mysterious trumpet-wielding gangland type from Harlem who materializes from out of nowhere to serenade Martha Raye, whose body was darkened with makeup in an attempt to make her duet with a black man more acceptable to white viewers. It didn't help, for Armstrong made it surpassingly clear that his intentions were strictly dishonorable: *Ain't no use hidin' / I'm going to take you ridin'.* Not surprisingly, *Variety* didn't care for *Artists and Models:* "While Miss Raye is under cork, this intermingling of the races isn't wise, especially as she lets herself go into the extremest manifestation of Harlemania torso-twisting and gyrations. It may hurt her personally." An Atlanta newspaper critic was blunter: "Martha Raye, thinly burnt-corked, does a Harlem specialty with a fat Negro trumpeter and a hundred other Negroes. It is coarse to the point of vulgarity. I have no objection to Negroes on the screen. I like them from Bill Robinson down the line. Their stuff is usually good. But I don't like mixing white folk—and especially a white girl—in their acts."

After that Armstrong stuck to playing trumpet and being funny. It was very much to his professional advantage to do so: the producers of *Cabin in the Sky* paid him $7,500 for two weeks' work. Not only

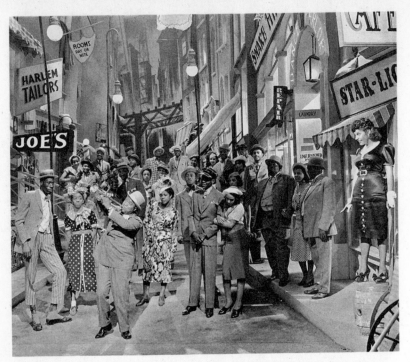

"A fine part in a moving picture": A 1937 publicity still of Armstrong and Martha Raye (at far right) in "Public Melody Number One," staged by Vincente Minnelli for Raoul Walsh's *Artists and Models*, one of the few Hollywood films that hints at the trumpeter's sexual allure. Raye darkened her skin in order to appear onscreen with a black man.

did his screen appearances help introduce him to the white public, but they also brought him to the attention of newspaper and magazine editors who were more likely to go to his movies than see him in person. They were even likelier to tune him in on the radio, and in the summer of 1937, four months before the release of *Artists and Models*, he vaulted over yet another barrier by becoming the first black to host his own network-radio variety show. Rudy Vallée, whose series was one of NBC's longest-running programs, went on a three-month vacation that April and turned his microphone over to Armstrong, who hosted a summer-replacement series called *Harlem* that ran each Friday on NBC's Blue Network. Vallée had long booked black artists on his show, and though his career was in decline, he was still famous enough to impose his will on the network, making it possible for him to take the next step and invite Armstrong to sub for him. "Sponsored by the makers of Fleischmann's Yeast," *Billboard* reported, "this new series is notable in that it is the first big all-colored show bought by a national account."

Harlem also included comedy routines by Eddie Green and Gee Gee James and guest shots by such well-known black musicians as the Mills Brothers and Cleo Brown, but the bulk of each program was devoted to Armstrong and his band, and the star of the show did his own announcing, just as he had at the Suburban Gardens in 1931. The reviews were mixed, and *Variety* said that the series "could only be recommended to the most incurable addicts of Harlem stomp music . . . Armstrong's throaty, almost unintelligible announcements do not help, either, and he should refrain from singing." But at least *Harlem* had a sponsor — *The Nat "King" Cole Show* vanished from America's TV screens two decades later when no one on Madison Avenue would touch it — and though Armstrong never again hosted his own show, he continued to perform on radio until the fifties, when the rise of television made the older medium obsolete.

The part played by Armstrong in helping to open up radio to black performers has long been unknown save to specialists. He was, however, well aware of what it meant at the time. Asked by Leonard Feather in 1941 to list the key events in his career, he started by mentioning "when Pops [i.e., Joe Glaser] booked me for my first commercial program over the — N.B.C.," then went on to cite his first four feature films, *Pennies from Heaven*, *Artists and Models*, *Every Day's a Holiday* (for which Hoagy Carmichael wrote "Jubilee"), and *Going Places* (in which Armstrong sings "Jeepers Creepers" to a racehorse). Next came *Hot Chocolates* and "Ain't Misbehavin'." Only then did he finally get around to listing six of his favorite records, "I'm Confessin'," "Lazy River," "Memories of You," "Old Man Mose," "Swing That Music," and "West End Blues." Those who think of Armstrong solely as a jazz musician may find his priorities puzzling, but it was in 1936, not before, that he began turning up in the mainstream press on a more or less regular basis, and it was his films and radio appearances, not his public performances, that put him there. A month after *Harlem* went on the air, Warner Bros. released "Clean Pastures," Friz Freleng's animated spoof of *The Green Pastures*, the Pulitzer Prize–winning play by Marc Connelly in which a stageful of happy darkies enacts the Old Testament. Armstrong was affectionately caricatured in the cartoon, along with Fats Waller, Cab Calloway, and the Mills Brothers, a sure sign that he had finally won a place in the pantheon of pop culture. Rudy Vallée, Bing Crosby, Jack Kapp, and Joe Glaser had done what once seemed impossible: they had made Louis Armstrong a true star.

◆

Popular renown brought few changes in his daily life. He had always been a workhorse, and Glaser rode him harder than ever now that he was starting to make serious money. "Once we jumped from Bangor, Maine, to New Orleans for a one-nighter, then on to Houston, Texas, for the next night," Pops Foster recalled in his autobiography. Armstrong lived in the continuous present, playing pretty for the people, grabbing a bite to eat between shows, signing autographs after the last set, answering a stack of fan letters before bedtime, then starting from scratch the next day. After each dance he peeled off his sweat-soaked clothes and cleaned himself as best he could. "I mean, you see, places did not have them fine dressing rooms and showers and things then," said Charlie Holmes, who spent five years in his saxophone section. "You just waited until everybody got out of the place, and then he could change his clothes after everybody had gone, and dry himself with his own towels and things." Sometimes the band traveled by rail, as it had in 1931, but most of the time Armstrong's men rode the bus, and he rode it with them. "He was a hard worker and a hard-workin' man," Holmes added, "and he didn't ask you to do *nothin'* that he wouldn't do."

Few survivors of the big-band era romanticized it. Charlie Barnet summed up life on the road in six blunt words: "You stay tired, dirty and drunk." Mike Zwerin was more expansive: "You skim more than read, pass out rather than fall asleep. You work when everybody else is off, breakfast in the evening, dinner at dawn. Disorder is the order, physical alienation is so powerful, so omnipresent, that no treatment seems too extreme. . . . You've got to find a familiar internal place to hang on to, it's a matter of survival. And there is one place, a warm corner called stoned." Armstrong curled up in that corner most nights, though experience had taught him to be more disciplined in his use of marijuana. Gone were the carefree days when he got the whole band high before a recording session, though he encouraged his musicians to smoke pot and is said to have preferred hiring those who did. "He never worked with it," said one sideman. "He'd wait until he got off [the bandstand] and get with his typewriter and hunt and peck jokes. When he'd write someone a letter, that would be his letter. He'd send them a joke. . . . Write jokes every night. Get off of work, put some salve on his lips, handkerchief on his head." It was no way to live, but he knew no other, and everyone agreed that he seemed to thrive on it. His playing, according to Charlie Holmes, was better than ever:

> Other trumpet players would hit them [high] notes, just like they do nowadays. They'd be hitting high, but they sound like a flute up there or something. But Louis wasn't playing them like that. Louis was hittin' them notes right on the head, and *expanding*. They would be notes. He was hittin' *notes*. He wasn't squeakin'. They wasn't no squeaks. They were notes. Big, broad notes. . . . The higher he went, the *broader* his tone got — and it was beautiful!

But even Armstrong had his limits, and Glaser, unlike Johnny Collins, acknowledged them. In 1937 he hired two key sidemen, J. C. Higginbotham and the trumpeter Henry "Red" Allen, both of whom had graced Luis Russell's group in the days when it was one of the best bands in Harlem. Higginbotham's punchy, gruff-toned trombone solos soon became a highlight of Armstrong's records and stage performances. Allen, a New Orleans expatriate who had worked with Fate Marable, Joe Oliver, and Fletcher Henderson, was an even more imaginative player with a knack for making harmonically "wrong" notes sound right. The two men had split a chorus on Armstrong's 1930 recording of "I Ain't Got Nobody," interweaving their styles so seamlessly that few could tell them apart. Now Glaser hired Allen to serve as Armstrong's relief man, a role he played so well that he would soon be billed as "SATCHMO'S UNDERSTUDY." "Louis gave Red an hour's time on his own, to play his own numbers. . . . Red could do anything he wanted to play," Charlie Holmes said. In the studio he stuck to ensemble parts—he would record only a single short solo with the Armstrong band—but that didn't bother him. "It was no fault of Louis', and I played plenty with the band," Allen said. "It was a happy feeling. I don't care whose band it was, I'd have been happy about it if Louis was there, because I enjoy being in his company so much, on and off the bandstand." Armstrong was glad to have Allen there, too. At the age of thirty-six, he had learned at last to burn the bright candle of his talent at only one end, and from then on he would take care to travel with musicians who helped to carry the load without stealing the show.

Luis Russell and his men were now playing extremely well for Armstrong, though their commercial recordings do not always display them to good advantage. Airchecks of Armstrong's *Harlem* series show that the band sounded much more exciting in front of live audiences. The clarinetist Albert Nicholas, a New Orleans old-timer disinclined by nature to exaggeration, remembered years later how "that band could play. . . . [Y]ou had fifteen men swinging like a small band." Five or six times a year the group paused in New York or Los Angeles to cut a few sides with Armstrong for Decca, and once each year or two its leader left his musicians behind and flew to Hollywood to make a movie. The rest of the time he stayed on the move, usually accompanied by Alpha, who rode in a chauffeured Packard with two bulldogs and a maid, and a personal valet who took care of his clothes and ironed the two hundred cotton handkerchiefs that he carried with him. Joe Evans, a saxophonist who joined the band a few years later, was fascinated by the latter ritual: "Every night, when Louis Armstrong started to play, the valet put out a stack. Louis held his horn with the handkerchief around it or wiped his face one time and put the handkerchief into a bag." The valet doubled as a spy who checked in each day with the ever-cautious Glaser, telling him what Armstrong was doing and whom he was seeing.

It was a hard life for a young woman, especially one who liked to live well, and Alpha, who had taken to calling herself "Alpha Armstrong," decided that she deserved a marriage license to go with her new last name. Armstrong, however, was starting to have his doubts about their relationship: "Alpha was all right but her mind was on furs, diamonds, and other flashy luxuries and not enough on me and my happiness. I gave her all the diamonds she *thought* she wanted but still she wanted other things. . . . We had some real spats. She'd get to drinking and grab that big pocketbook of hers and hit me in my chops with it. Then I'd want to go after her and beat on her awhile, but some of the cats would grab me and say, 'Don't hit her, Pops.'" He may also have come to feel that she was intellectually underendowed, for his scrapbooks contain a cartoon called "What's Wrong Here" in which a woman is shown saying, "Betty has drank two glasses of milk." The caption reads "Right: Betty has DRUNK two glasses of milk." In the margin is a handwritten notation: "LOUIE WON THIS BATTLE AFTER ALMOST FIVE YEARS WITH ALPHA." For years he had hidden behind the fact that he was still legally married to Lil, but in 1938 his long-estranged second wife pulled the rug out. "Louis didn't really want to marry Alpha," Lil told Chris Albertson, "but she was threatening him with a breach of promise suit, and he was afraid of all the publicity, so he asked me not to give him a divorce, because that would be the only way he could really get out of it. I gave him the divorce just to spite him, I guess." The decree became final in September of 1938, and Louis and Alpha were married in Houston eleven days later. But it was too late, for a few weeks after that, Armstrong returned to New York and met the woman who would become his next wife.

Born in Queens in 1914, Lucille Wilson was a smart, shapely middle-class Catholic whose father had lost his business, a small taxicab fleet, in the Depression. Forced to go to work to help support her family, the seminary-educated Lucille got a job as a chorus girl. A few years later she was dancing in the chorus line at the Cotton Club, where she caught Armstrong's eye while the band was playing an extended engagement at the club, which had moved downtown to the theater district. Armstrong, whose preference for dark-skinned women was so marked that he wrote a piece for *Ebony* about it, was struck not only by "the glow of her deep brown skin" (he liked to call her "Brown Sugar") but also by the fact that she had gotten into the Cotton Club's chorus line in spite of it. "Lucille was the first girl to crack the high-yellow color standard used to pick girls for the famous Cotton Club chorus line," he wrote in *Ebony*. "I think she was a distinguished pioneer." He noticed that she helped support her family out of her modest salary, selling homemade cookies on the side to bring in extra money. He bought all of them and from then on paid "strict attention" to her: "One night when Lucille came into my Dressing Room to deliver her Cookies, I just couldn't hold back the deep feeling and the warmth that I had Accumulated for her ever since I first layed eyes on her in the front line of the Cotton Club floor. . . . I said Lucille, I might as well tell you Right Now— I have *Eyes* for you. And has been having them for a *long* time. And if any of these *cats* in the show Shooting at you—I want to be in the Running."

Though she was a member in good standing of the black bourgeoisie, Lucille knew all about the ways of the rougher world in which she worked. "She spoke in a very proper English unless she'd had a few drinks," Jack Bradley said. "Then she'd start with the *motherfuckers*." She also knew that her new suitor already had a wife, and at first she kept him at arm's length. But he was determined to win her over: "You keep running from me, so whoever you're going out with, man, woman or child, I'm going too." Before long they were going to movies between shows and taking long rides in Armstrong's Packard, and when the job was over and he had to return to the road, he promised to stay in touch. Lucille had the sense to take his assurances with a grain of salt. He was freshly married, fairly famous, and disinclined to be faithful, none of which made him a good risk. He dated Lucille whenever he was in New York, but four years went by before he and his third wife came to a final parting of the ways — and when they did so, it would be Alpha's doing, not his.

9

"THE PEOPLE WHO CRITICIZE"

Losing Touch, 1938–1947

IN THE EARLY THIRTIES jazz had no history save for what was engraved in the memories of the men who made it and the grooves of the records they cut. Buddy Bolden and Bix Beiderbecke were dead, and Joe Oliver, Bunk Johnson, Jelly Roll Morton, and Sidney Bechet had dropped out of sight. The only music that mattered was the music of the moment. Then Benny Goodman, who had listened to the Creole Jazz Band at Lincoln Gardens when he was in knee pants, recorded a Fletcher Henderson–arranged version of Morton's "King Porter Stomp" in July of 1935 that became a surprise hit and an anthem of the era of big-band swing that was around the corner. It was "King Porter Stomp" that drove the crowd wild at the Palomar Ballroom in Los Angeles a few weeks later. "That number started off with Bunny Berigan playing a trumpet solo, the saxophones and rhythm behind him," Goodman recalled. "Before he'd played four bars, there was such a yelling and stomping and carrying on in that hall that I thought a riot had broken out. When I went into my solo, the noise was even louder. Finally the truth got through to me: *We* were causing the riot." In that same year Bob Crosby, Bing's brother, started fronting a band whose members, many of whom were from

New Orleans, cut a series of swinging instrumentals for Decca based on 78s by Oliver, Beiderbecke, and Louis Armstrong, most of which were then out of print.

The surviving members of the Original Dixieland Jazz Band reorganized the following year and began playing in public for the first time since 1925, an event that caught the ear of *Time:* "Hot jazz cultists who have learned to treasure the Dixieland's out of print phonograph records as classics and museum pieces never believed they might actually hear them together again." A few months earlier *Time* had published an article on the swing craze that made prominent mention of Oliver, Beiderbecke, and Armstrong ("His trumpet solos . . . are as important to many lovers of American syncopation as Beethoven's 9th Symphony is to subscribers of the New York Philharmonic"). Hugues Panassié's *Le jazz hot,* mentioned in a footnote, was translated into English and rushed into print as *Hot Jazz: A Guide to Swing Music* around the same time that Otis Ferguson, one of America's first important jazz critics, began contributing essays about Beiderbecke, Goodman, and other musicians to the *New Republic.*

By 1938 interest in the early days of jazz was picking up speed. On January 16 the Goodman band gave a concert at Carnegie Hall that included musical impressions of Armstrong and Beiderbecke played by Harry James and Bobby Hackett. The next day Eddie Condon took Jess Stacy, Goodman's pianist, and a group of like-minded players into a New York studio and cut the first 78 sides to be released by Commodore, an independent record label founded by Milt Gabler that was devoted to small-group jazz. The launch of Commodore Records inspired a piece in *Life* called "Swing: The Hottest and Best Kind of Jazz Reaches Its Golden Age." In May Jelly Roll Morton emerged from the shadows to make the first in a series of autobiographical recordings for the Library of Congress in which he told the story of New Orleans jazz from his solipsistic point of view. Three months later he went public, sending an irate letter to *Down Beat* in which he proclaimed himself to be the "creator" of jazz: "For many years I was Number One man with the Victor Recording Company. *Tiger Rag* was transformed into *jazz* by me . . .

I may be the only perfect specimen today in *jazz* that's living." Later that year Panassié came to America and produced a series of sessions for Victor that featured Sidney Bechet and the New Orleans–born trumpeter Tommy Ladnier, who had previously been running the Southern Tailor Shop in Harlem.

The only piece missing from the puzzle was a factually reliable account of the music's early years, and in 1939 two young enthusiasts, Frederic Ramsey and Charles Edward Smith, supplied it with an anthology of historical and biographical essays called *Jazzmen*. The book's subtitle, *The Story of Hot Jazz Told in the Lives of the Men Who Created It*, pointed to what made it unique. Though *Jazzmen* contained a not-inconsiderable amount of romanticized misinformation about the founding fathers of jazz, it was still the first book of its kind to be based on primary source material, including interviews with Armstrong and Bunk Johnson and a cache of letters written by Joe Oliver shortly before his death in 1938, when he was living in poverty in Georgia, too sick to play the horn that had briefly made him the king of Chicago jazz: "I'm still out of work. Since the road house close I haven't hit a note. But I've got a lot to thank God for. Because I eat and sleep. . . . I've started a little dime bank saving. Got $1.60 in it and won't touch it. I am going to try to save myself a ticket to New York."

With the publication of *Jazzmen*, which Armstrong called "absolutely perfect" in a letter to one of the book's contributors, the revival of interest in New Orleans jazz took wing. It came too late to help Oliver, but Morton, who had been unceremoniously dropped from Victor's roster of artists in 1930, was now invited back to record "High Society," "I Thought I Heard Buddy Bolden Say," and "Oh, Didn't He Ramble" with an all-star band whose members included Sidney Bechet and Zutty Singleton. *Down Beat* had already run a story about Johnson (it was later included in *Jazzmen*) that quoted from a letter in which he claimed to have played with Bolden and taught Armstrong: "Louis would steal off from home and follow me. During that time, Louis started after me to show him how to blow my cornet. . . . [H]e liked the blues the best."

Armstrong, to whom the editors of *Jazzmen* devoted a whole chapter, was aware of the growing excitement over the music of his youth, for which he was partly responsible. In *Swing That Music* he had written about Bolden, Oliver, "The Old [i.e., Original] Dixieland Jazz Band," and "a young genius named Sydney Bachet" who by 1936 was so little known that no one bothered to correct the trumpeter's phonetic spelling of his name. In January of 1938 Armstrong cut "Struttin' with Some Barbecue" for Decca, followed in May by the first jazz recording of "When the Saints Go Marching In," the spiritual that he had learned as a member of the Colored Waif's Home Brass Band. It started off with one of the mock sermons that he loved to preach: "Sisters and brothers, this is Reverend Satchmo gettin' ready to beat out this mellow sermon for ya. My text this evenin' is 'When the Saints Go Marchin' In.' Here come Brother Higginbotham down the aisle with his *tram*-bone. Blow it, boy!" It was Armstrong's recording that turned the comparatively little-known song into a jazz standard. He had wanted to record it as early as 1931, but an OKeh executive who heard a run-through of his interpretation warned him that "you're a little ahead of your time . . . [T]he masses are not too much aware of the Holy Rollers."

In 1939 Armstrong waded into the early-jazz revival with both feet, recording big-band remakes of "Hear Me Talkin' to Ya," "A Monday Date," "Save It, Pretty Mama," "Savoy Blues," and "West End Blues" that were enlivened by the presence of a new drummer who was to become one of his closest friends. Big Sid Catlett (he stood well over six feet tall) drove the Russell band with flawless taste and propulsive vigor. Armstrong later called him "the greatest drummer ever picked up a pair of sticks." Roy Porter, a younger drummer who heard the two men around that time, found Catlett to be more impressive than his boss, recalling him as "a big man with so much finesse, especially with brushes, so smooth and clean." A consummate showman, he strode into the spotlight whenever asked but never got between the trumpeter and his fans.

All of Armstrong's jazz-oriented records for Decca were worthy, and some were masterpieces. But there were a half-dozen ballads and novelties for every "Saints" or "Struttin' with Some Barbecue," and certain of his critics thought he had no business recording such fare, no matter how well he played it. In 1938 John Hammond produced "From Spirituals to Swing," the first in a pair of Carnegie Hall concerts whose purpose was to present interested listeners with a cross section of what he believed to be the very best jazz and black popular music, untainted by commercialism. The musicians who played on his programs included Bechet, Count Basie, Benny Goodman, James P. Johnson, and Tommy Ladnier — but not Armstrong. In a *New York Times* article announcing the first concert, Hammond assured his readers that they would hear none of the "men of the highly publicized Negro jazz bands" who had "made serious concessions to white tastes by adding spurious showmanship to their wares and imitating the habits and tricks of the more commercially successful white orchestras." Anyone who had been reading his reviews of Armstrong's Decca releases in *Rhythm* would have known exactly whom he had in mind. He had disposed of "I'm in the Mood for Love" and "You Are My Lucky Star" in one irritable paragraph: "It isn't that Louis is playing bad trumpet nowadays. Far from it. But that magnificent originality and infectious enthusiasm that used to be the dominant factor in his work have now disappeared entirely . . . now he is a one-man show: comedian, jivester, and, lastly, musician." From then on nothing Armstrong did met with his approval. "If I may say so," he wrote, "a civilisation really stinks when it can permit and encourage the corruption of a great artist like the real Louis Armstrong."*

Hammond's was still a minority view. Even the highbrows were listening to Armstrong now, and liking what they heard. The classi-

---

*Hammond, a man of the left, took an equally dim view of Armstrong's less-than-correct politics. In 1940 Armstrong and the Mills Brothers recorded "W.P.A.," a novelty song by the black songwriter Jesse Stone, whose lyrics poked fun at the controversial relief programs sponsored by Franklin Roosevelt's Works Progress Administration: *Sleep while you work, while you rest, while you play, / Lean on your shovel to pass time away.* The song's sardonic portrayal of make-work welfare was consistent with the trumpeter's lifelong belief in self-help, but it enraged Hammond, who launched a successful campaign to have all recordings of "W.P.A.," Armstrong's included, taken off the market.

cal composer-critic Virgil Thomson, writing in *Modern Music* in 1938, called him "a master of musical art . . . His style of improvisation would seem to have combined the highest reaches of instrumental virtuosity with the most tensely disciplined melodic structure and the most spontaneous emotional expression, all of which in one man you must admit to be pretty rare." Arthur Dove, the first American abstract artist, painted a canvas that same year called *Swing Music (Louis Armstrong)*. Inspired by "Public Melody Number One," the painting, which now hangs in the Art Institute of Chicago, is an explosion of jagged red and silver shapes amid a fathomlessly dark landscape — a precise visual evocation of the effect of an Armstrong solo.

Among younger fans of swing, however, Armstrong was coming to be seen as a back number. Bunny Berigan and Harry James consistently outpolled him in the readers' surveys published each year by *Down Beat* and *Metronome* magazines. "How can they possibly vote for me when Louis is in the same contest?" asked a bewildered James, whose 1938 Carnegie Hall performance of "Shine" showed how he felt about Armstrong. Berigan was at least as ardent a fan. When asked what a dance-band musician needed to bring with him on the road, he was said to have replied, "A toothbrush and a photograph of Louis Armstrong." He practiced what he preached: in 1937 he recorded a version of "Mahogany Hall Stomp" that recalls the master with wondrous exactitude. But Berigan and James were playing hot music with the swing bands that were all the rage, while their older mentor was barnstorming the boondocks with a dance band whose recordings, his own singing and playing excepted, typically had less to offer the jazz fan. For his part Armstrong always spoke warmly of both men. Asked by *Down Beat* to list his favorite trumpeters, he replied, "First, I'll name my boy Bunny Berigan. Now there's a boy whom I've always admired for his tone, soul, technique, his sense of 'phrasing' and all. To me Bunny can't do no wrong in music." On another occasion he paid Berigan the ultimate compliment: "Theres two trumpet players — moved me any time they picked up one. . . . They are King Oliver and Bunny Berrigan [*sic*]."

Harry James ranked high on the same list. "That white boy—he plays like a jig!" he told Lionel Hampton. Yet he knew that many of their admirers thought him passé, and though he insisted that "most of the people who criticize don't know one note from another," he must have feared that time was passing him by.

In 1940 Jack Kapp unbent so far as to allow Armstrong to cut a small-group date for Decca, his first of any importance since 1929. He did so in the company of Sidney Bechet, with whom he had made some of his best recordings in the twenties. The session, which also featured Luis Russell and Zutty Singleton, was a deliberate attempt to evoke the good old days. The tunes included "2:19 Blues," a traditional New Orleans lament that Jelly Roll Morton had recorded in 1939, and "Coal Cart Blues," a song by Armstrong in which he sang about selling coal on the streets of Storyville. It was touching to hear Armstrong and Bechet playing together again, but the results were not entirely satisfying, and Bechet, for one, thought he knew why: "Louis, it seemed like he was wanting to make it a kind of thing where we were supposed to be bucking each other, competing instead of working together for that real feeling that would let the music come new and strong . . . it was like he was a little hungrier."

It didn't help that Decca's engineers buried Bechet in the mix (he is barely audible behind Armstrong's vocals). Just as important, though, the trumpeter was competing against the memory of himself when young, and his younger self had been given an unfair advantage by one of Jack Kapp's competitors. *Life*'s 1938 article about the history of swing inspired Ted Wallerstein, a Columbia Records executive, to hire George Avakian, a Yale undergraduate who was producing small-group jazz records on the side, to troll through the company's vaults and put together a series of reissue albums of "the original recordings that made jazz history." The resulting "Hot Jazz Classics" line was launched in 1940 with *King Louis*, which contained eight sides by the Hot Five and Seven, two of them previously unreleased. Next came sets devoted to Beiderbecke, Fletcher Henderson, and Bessie Smith, plus a second album of Hot Fives and Sevens whose notes, written by Avakian, proclaimed "Armstrong's early

OKeh records" to be "perhaps the most important he ever made —
and the best."

They were certainly better than the four new sides he had
recorded with Bechet, an experiment that would not be repeated.
Armstrong may have longed to play small-group jazz again, but he
knew that the big money was still in big bands. He had watched Joe
Oliver hesitate over leaving Chicago: "The agents and everybody . . .
had wanted to bring him in someplace, *any* night club, with his band.
But Joe wouldn't leave. 'I'm doing all right here, man,' he'd tell
them. He had good jobs with good tips. So time ran out on him. He
looked around, and when he came to New York — too late." Worse
was to come: "In 1937 my band went to Savannah, Ga. one day —
and there's Joe. He's got so bad off and broke, he's got himself a little
vegetable stand selling tomatoes and potatoes. . . . I gave him about
$150 I had in my pocket, and Luis Russell and Red Allen, Pops Fos-
ter, Albert Nicholas, Paul Barbarin — all used to be his boys — they
gave him what they had."

A year later Papa Joe was dead. Not long after that Armstrong received a piteous letter from Bunk Johnson, who had given up music,
was driving a sugarcane wagon in rural Louisiana, and needed money
for the most urgent of reasons: "Your old boy is down and in real
deep need for an upper plate and also a bottom plate and cannot
make money enough to have my mouth fixed. . . . Let your friend
Bunk hear from you as I cannot blow any more." That settled it, if
there had ever been anything to settle. Armstrong may not have
cared to die rich, but neither did he mean to live poor, and if that
meant that he would have to continue playing one-nighters with Luis
Russell's band until hell froze over, then that was what he would
do — so long as Joe Glaser told him to do it.

❧

In 1939 Armstrong made an abortive attempt to consolidate his
second career as an actor by starring in *Swingin' the Dream*, a musical based on *A Midsummer Night's Dream* and set in turn-of-the-
century New Orleans. He played Bottom, a piece of casting reminis-

cent of Max Reinhardt's decision to cast Jimmy Cagney in the same role in his 1935 film of Shakespeare's play, and enjoyed the task enormously. "Man, if Old Shakespeare could see me now!" he told Leonard Feather during the intermission of one performance. (To another friend he confided that he had learned his lines "on the toilet.") The other members of the 150-person cast included Maxine Sullivan as Titania, Butterfly McQueen as Puck, and Moms Mabley as Quince. The score was by Jimmy Van Heusen, one of the most artful songwriters of the day, and Eddie de Lange, who had penned lyrics for "Moonglow" and Duke Ellington's "Solitude." Agnes de Mille staged the dances, Walt Disney designed the sets, and the production featured three different bands, with Benny Goodman's sextet in a box to the left of the stage, Bud Freeman's Chicago-style Summa Cum Laude group on the other side of the house, and a full orchestra in the pit.

In theory *Swingin' the Dream* should have run forever, but the critics begged to differ, evidently with good reason. Brooks Atkinson dropped the blade in his *New York Times* review, calling it "an uneven show that represents a good idea indifferently exploited. . . . Although Louis Armstrong carries his golden horn whenever he appears, he hardly has a chance to warm it up until the show is well over." *Time*'s critic was even sharper: "As a show, it falls flat as a pancake. It is overcrowded, overelaborate, too much of a good thing . . . Louis Armstrong should stick to his blast, not try to play Bottom." Some of their colleagues were kinder, but even if the show had been better, the competition would have been too formidable, for *Swingin' the Dream* was playing opposite the original productions of *Life with Father*, *The Little Foxes*, *The Man Who Came to Dinner*, and *The Philadelphia Story*, and Bert Lahr and Ethel Merman opened the following week in Cole Porter's *Du Barry Was a Lady*. Unable to fill the 3,700-seat Center Theatre on the strength of reviews that were mostly tepid or worse, the producers shuttered the show after thirteen performances, losing a hundred thousand dollars in the process. All that remains is a fragment of the script, a pair of Al Hirschfeld caricatures, several production photos in which Armstrong looks as

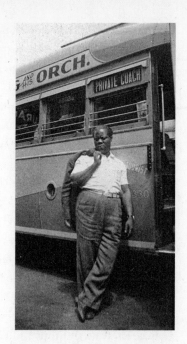

"A hard-workin' man": A previously unpublished snapshot of Louis Armstrong traveling with his big band in the thirties. Playing one-nighters on the road was brutally hard for dance-band musicians, and worse still for blacks who performed in the segregated South, where even a celebrity like Armstrong was treated like an inferior.

though he is having the time of his life, and one lovely song, "Darn That Dream," that he never played again, not caring to remind himself that he had once been part of a costly flop.

Chastened by the failure of *Swingin' the Dream*, Armstrong went back to his band, where nothing had changed, and resumed the life of a traveling musician. But change came soon enough: John Hammond lured Red Allen back to New York in 1940 to lead the house band at Barney Josephson's Café Society Downtown, and Allen and Hammond persuaded J. C. Higginbotham to join the group as well. Glaser struck back by planting an item in *Down Beat* claiming that the trombonist was "hard to get along with and was always griping about salary money." The other members of the band agreed with Higginbotham. "Hitting the road, you start coming back with 2 dollars and fifty cents after being out there for five weeks," Charlie Holmes said. Glaser had already installed the saxophonist-arranger Joe Garland as musical director in place of Russell, who stayed on as pianist. Another *Down Beat* story suggested that "when Joe Glaser took over as Louis' personal manager he wanted someone with more disciplinary talent than Russell evidenced to head up the overall operation." Pops Foster, who got the ax outright, later claimed that "Glaser fired the whole band to get a cheaper band. . . . The reason they told me was I was too old." True or not, there were plenty of new faces in the band by 1941, and Garland, who is now mainly remembered for composing "In the Mood," welded them into a tight-knit ensemble, though Armstrong had his doubts about the professionalism of some of his younger sidemen: "I used to have a lot of youngsters in the band during the Second [World] War. Musicians were pretty hard to get, good ones. And I'd say, 'Well, come on, boys, hit that A,' and they'd [say] 'I'm straight,' and they'd play sharp all night. Now what you gonna do about that?"

By then Armstrong had achieved his twin goals of becoming a broadly popular entertainer and winning acceptance in the white world — but at a price. While blacks still flocked to his public performances, they now bought fewer of his records. In 1941 an Alan Lomax–led team of Library of Congress researchers drew up an inventory of the records found on the jukeboxes of five juke joints in Clarksdale, the Mississippi town that later became famous as the home of the electric bluesmen John Lee Hooker and Muddy Waters. The local favorites, the researchers found, included Count Basie, Walter Davis, Earl Hines, Louis Jordan, Artie Shaw, Sister Rosetta Tharpe, and Fats Waller. Armstrong was represented by just two Decca sides, "2:19 Blues" and the gospel-flavored "Bye and Bye." He does not appear to have been any more popular among the younger musicians of the region, especially those who were interested in musical styles other than jazz. He is mentioned only in passing in the autobiography of B. B. King, born in 1925, and Ray Charles, born in 1930, speaks of Armstrong in his own book just long enough to say that he "did more to entertain me than to really influence my playing."

A year later the American Federation of Musicians banned its members from making commercial recordings, charging that they were being cheated by radio stations that played their releases without paying royalties. Armstrong played his last session for Decca in April of 1942, and from then until the summer of 1944 he could be heard only in person, on the radio, in movie houses, or on the "V-Discs" that he and other jazz musicians recorded for distribution to members of the armed forces. Airchecks show that he was continuing to play at a high level and that Garland had succeeded in turning his group into something resembling a modern swing band. But the AFM recording ban had the same effect on Armstrong as it did on all the other major bandleaders: it shut off one of his major sources of income and most effective engines of publicity. Though no one knew it, the ban also pulled the plug on the big-band era. After the AFM declared victory in 1944, the recording industry was dominated by the balladeers who had found favor during World War II, not the bandleaders who kept America dancing between the wars. Armstrong and Glaser hung on for as long as they dared, but sooner or later they would have to find a new basis for the trumpeter's musical career.

Armstrong had already found a new basis for his personal life. On October 2, 1942, he divorced Alpha, and ten days later he married Lucille Wilson. Neither event had seemed likely when his band passed through New Orleans in the fall of 1941, pausing long enough for him to visit black Storyville, which had changed beyond recognition since he left it for good in 1921. That was when he bragged in a letter to Leonard Feather that Alpha was now doing his laundry on the road. "She has that routine down to the last frazzle," he wrote. "She even learned my routine of how to keep plenty of handkerchiefs." But she was also having an affair with Cliff Leeman, Charlie Barnet's drummer, and one day she got tipsy and told her husband that they were through. Even though he had his eye on Lucille, the news took him by surprise and hit him hard. In November he recorded an unexpectedly sober instrumental version of a 1920 tune called "I Used to Love You (But It's All Over Now)" that he turned into a lament for his failed marriage. When Walter Winchell blew the whistle on Alpha in his newspaper column two months later, the trumpeter sent "Brother Winch" an angry letter in which he told his side of the story of his relationship with the "no good woman" on whom he had lavished "THOUSANDS and THOUSANDS of dol-

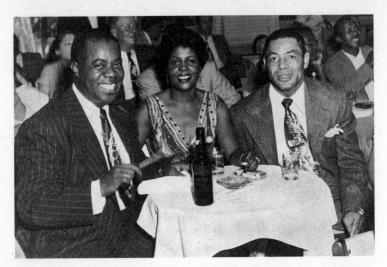

"The ideal girl for me": A previously unpublished photograph of Armstrong, his fourth wife, Lucille, and his adopted son, Clarence, at a nightclub, ca. 1940. After a string of troubled marriages, Armstrong found happiness with his beloved "Brown Sugar."

lars" worth of diamonds and furs: "Well, all I can say is maybe with all of that that I gave to that Gal — just wasn't enough . . . He [Lee-man] certainly must have given her Just the Amount of Everything that she wanted." *Down Beat* confirmed the bad news a month later in a story called "Louis, Wife Out of Tune." He was still smarting in 1944: "To believe that Alpha turned out in later years to be a no good 'Bitch' Why — I am Still *'Flabbergasted' (Surprised as Ol Hell)."*

Despite the damage that Alpha had done to his pride, Armstrong was able to see that the levelheaded Lucille was the sort of woman he needed as he entered middle age: "In fact it dawned on me — it seemed to me that Lucille was the ideal girl for me. In fact our lives were practically the same. Good Common Sense — great observers (not for any particular reason) but were not particular about phony people, etc. — what we *didn't* have we *did* without." The next time the band bus pulled into New York, he went straight to the Cotton Club and popped the question. Lucille replied that she was concerned about the difference in their ages and the fact that he was a famous man who had been married three times, while she was "just a little small Chorus Girl." His answer, which took her aback, makes us smile today:

> That's when I stopped her from Talking by slowly reaching for her *Cute* little *Beautifully Manicured* hand And said to her, "Can you Cook Red Beans and Rice?" Which Amused her very much. Then it dawned on her that I was very serious. *She* — being a *Northern* girl and *Me* a *Southern* Boy from N.O. She could see why I asked her *that* question. So She said: "I've never cooked that kind of food before. But — Just give me a little time and I think that I can fix it for you." That's All that I wanted to hear, and right away I said "How about Inviting me to your house for dinner tomorrow night?"

Two nights later Armstrong knocked on her door, decked out in his sharpest suit. He met her family for the first time, and they struck him as "the kind of Relatives that I could be at ease being around for the rest of my life." He sampled her red beans and rice and found them to be "just what the Doctor ordered. Very much delicious and I Ate Just like a *dog*." Then he repeated his proposal, and this time she accepted.

Armstrong went to Hollywood at the end of August to shoot *Cabin in the Sky*, in which he played one of a team of demonic "idea men" (complete with horns) whose job it is to help Satan concoct new ways to tempt unsuspecting mortals. Once his scenes were in the can, he headed for Chicago and his divorce hearing. Not knowing that Lucille had decided to join him there, he threw a bachelor party the night before and showed up at the courthouse with a raging hangover that left him even more hoarse than usual. Just before the hearing got under way, he looked back at the spectators and saw his fiancée sitting a few rows behind him. The judge, who knew nothing of jazz, was taken aback by his growly voice and asked if he had a cold. "*No* Judge it's Just this *Saw Mill* voice that All of my Fans said that I have," he replied. Amused by his nerve, the judge granted the divorce, and Louis and Lucille left for St. Louis, the next stop on the tour and the hometown of Velma Middleton, Armstrong's new singer. He was determined to marry Lucille as soon as possible, but she was Catholic, he nominally Baptist (so far as he knew) and thrice divorced, causing all the priests they approached to balk at tying the knot: "Lucille + Myself were getting desperate and so distraught until it wasn't even funny." In the end the couple was married in Middleton's home by her minister, a Baptist preacher, after which they returned to the road.

Lucille had no inkling of what it would be like to live out of a suitcase. "My honeymoon was eight months of one-nighters and I thought I was going to give up the whole marriage," she said later. "I'd never been away from home and I just couldn't take it." As for Armstrong, he soon saw that his new bride had some of the same hoity-toity ways that had driven him out of Lil's bed and into Alpha's arms. "As nice + sweet + wonderful as she is, she still has a sense of 'Aires' that I've never particularly cared for," he told Joe Glaser in a 1955 letter. But that, Armstrong realized, was a small price to pay this time around: "We get along real well and as I have said before, understand each other. We can stay at home for hours and days without any friction. She doesn't bother me until I want to be bothered. . . . The Average woman would have 'Quit' my ol ass — long long ago. The Woman understands me and there's no, ifs and ans about it." He also found her wonderfully attractive and never changed his high opinion of her good looks. Phoebe Jacobs, a publicist who met the Armstrongs a few years later and became close to both of them, remembered how he would "eye Lucille up . . . and say she was a thoroughbred. 'Look at those ankles. She looks like a good little filly.' I mean, he loved everything about Lucille. He treated her like she was a little doll." Above all he appreciated the way in which she grasped, as her predecessors had not, the single-mindedness with which he had dedicated himself to the life of art: "That trumpet comes first, before everything, even my wife. Got to be that way. I love Lucille, man, but she understands about me and my music."

Lucille did what she could to make the anonymous hotel rooms in which they lived more inviting. That Christmas Eve she bought a small tree, set it up in their room, and trimmed it, not knowing that her new husband, who had spent his childhood rummaging through garbage cans for food to sell, had never had a Christmas tree of his own. He came back to the room that night and was transfixed by the colored lights. "We finally went to bed," Lucille remembered. "And Louis was still laying up in the bed watching the tree, his eyes just like a baby's eyes would watch something. . . . So finally I asked him — I said, 'Well, I'll turn the lights out now on the tree.' He said, 'No, don't turn them out. I have to just keep looking at it.'" They carted the tree from town to town until it dried up and had to be thrown out.

Such gestures meant more to Armstrong than Lucille could have imagined, as did the house that they bought together in 1943. He had come to the reluctant conclusion that "I must *set* Lucille down. Not just to be a *Housewife* or anything like that. I figured if we want the Comfortable Happiness that I seek with that girl, She must stay home. And Keep our *Citadel* (I *call's* it) with that *wall* to *wall* Bed *Fresh* 'n' *Ready* to *go* at *all* times." So he sent her back to New York to look for a home, and she found one in a mostly white section of Corona, the Queens neighborhood where she had grown up. The price tag on the "*high* powered and *distinctive* looking" house that Lucille chose was sixteen thousand dollars, almost too high for them to swing — Armstrong was far from wealthy in the early forties — but she had squirreled away enough money out of her allowance to make a down payment, so she struck a deal with the owners, moved in, and started decorating. At tour's end Armstrong returned to Manhattan on the band bus, then hailed a cab to take him to the house at 34–56 107th Street, which he had not yet seen:

> *One* look at that big *fine* house, and *right* away I said to the *driver* "*Aw man quit Kidding* and *take* me to the address that I'm looking for." It was in the *wee* hours in the *morning* and I was *real beat* . . . I get up enough courage to get out of the Cab, and Ring the Bell. And sure enough the door opened and who stood in the doorway with a real thin silk Night Gown — *hair* in *Curlers*. To *me* she looked *just* like my *favorite flower* a Red Rose. The *more* Lucille *showed* me *around* the *house* the *more thrilled* I got. . . . *Yea you hear?* — *I got* (tee hee). Right then and I felt very grand over it all.

Not until the end of his life would Armstrong spend much more than two months out of each year in the Corona house, but he loved it all the same, both for the comfort it provided him and for what it symbolized. After three failed marriages and years of wandering, he had found a home that he loved and a wife whom he trusted. Armstrong himself was not the most trustworthy of companions, and Lucille learned in due course that her new spouse, like many other traveling musicians, had a roving eye. But though she hated his philandering, she learned to live with it and was careful not to make needless scenes: "I have partial vision on purpose . . . I call Louis when I am going to join him while he is on tour." For all his flaws, the fourth and last Mrs. Armstrong loved her Louis deeply and was determined to make a life with him come what may.

Alpha settled for $250 a month in alimony and her new romance, neither of which lasted for long. She died in 1943, and four years later Armstrong wrote a wistful song called "Someday You'll Be Sorry" that undoubtedly refers to their ill-fated marriage. He claimed that the song came to him in a dream, and that all he had had to do was write it down: "It wasn't just that song, man. It was like a whole opera. There must have been a dozen songs there complete with words and music. But 'Someday' was the only one I was able to write down." It became a permanent part of his repertoire, and he recorded it several times. Eventually he was able to speak of Alpha with fondness. "Of all his wives, I think it was Alpha that he had the most fun with," said Joe Muranyi, who joined Armstrong's band in 1967. "He always talked about her in a pleasant way." And he forgave Cliff Leeman, who in return kept quiet about the role he had played in breaking up Armstrong's marriage. Leeman said nothing about his affair with Alpha in the oral-history interview he gave many years later, preferring to talk about his friendship with the man he had cuckolded.

❧

Armstrong's domestic happiness compensated him for the fact that his career had taken a downward turn. The mid-forties were not without their high spots, one of which was a 1944 "All-American Jazz Concert" at the Metropolitan Opera House in which he shared a bill with the other winners of *Esquire*'s first critics' poll, including Sid Catlett, Roy Eldridge, Lionel Hampton, Coleman Hawkins, Billie Holiday, Red Norvo, Art Tatum, Jack Teagarden, and Teddy Wilson. But such starry nights were rare, for he was now traveling with a band of unknowns, none of whom is remembered today save for a young tenor saxophonist named Dexter Gordon, who went on to become a leading exponent of the rhythmically jagged, harmonically complex new style of jazz that bore the mysterious name of "bebop." It was, Gordon said, "a mediocre band. They were just playing Luis Russell arrangements from the thirties. Plus 'Ain't Misbehavin',' some new pops of the day; things like that. . . . All those big bands he had seemed to be almost like that." Nor was the band making much money: another Armstrong sideman claimed that its members pulled down no more than eleven dollars a night during World War II. But Gordon had nothing but praise for Armstrong. "Working with Louis? Oh, great," he said. "Love, love, love . . . that was what it was all about. All love. He was just beautiful — always beautiful. It was just a gas being with him. He let me play all the time. He really dug me." He dug Gordon so much, in fact, that he departed from his lifelong practice and hired the saxophonist himself, then told Glaser to give him a raise in order to keep him aboard. (One reason why they got along so well was that Gordon was a well-connected viper who shared his high-quality stash with his boss.)

Armstrong's admiration for Gordon sits awkwardly alongside his later statements about bebop, for which he claimed to have little but disdain. He was not the only older musician with mixed feelings about the new style. Benny Goodman flirted briefly with bop at the end of the forties, then put it behind him and spent the rest of his life playing variations on the big-band swing that had made him famous. Others took it more seriously: Charlie Parker and Dizzy Gillespie played in Earl Hines's wartime band, and Coleman Hawkins put together a quartet whose pianist was Thelonious Monk, the most radical of the younger players involved in the creation of bop. But all these men seem to have concluded that swing had run its course, and there are signs that Armstrong may have felt the same way. In January of 1945, a few months after the AFM recording ban came to an end, he went into Decca's New York studios and cut a pair of sides with a large studio band, both of which pointed in unexpected — and unexpectedly different — musical directions. "Jodie Man," a wartime novelty about draft dodgers who poach the girlfriends of servicemen, shows that he was paying attention to the new sounds in the air, for his succinct playing fits neatly into the open spaces in Bob Haggart's modern-sounding chart. "I Wonder," by contrast, is a smooth cover version of Cecil Gant's rhythm-and-blues hit in which Armstrong's suavely funky vocal suggests that he might also have opted for a style not far removed from the one that was later to make Ray Charles famous.

Even more provocative is "Snafu," recorded at an all-star session put together by *Esquire* for Victor to show off the winners of its 1946 critics' poll. The tune, written by Leonard Feather, is a boppish unison line, and the band that backs Armstrong is a Billy Strayhorn–led octet that contained four players — Don Byas, Neal Hefti, Chubby Jackson, and Remo Palmieri — who were experimenting with bebop. "Louis read his part with ease," Feather recalled, but "the notes came out staccato and self-conscious." Unwilling to put the trumpeter on the spot, Feather fumbled for a solution. Then he noticed that Hefti, who had come to the session with Chubby Jackson, had brought along his trumpet:

> "Louis," I said, "we want to get more of your own feeling into this. Why don't we just let Neal read the part, while you ad lib in the open spots, and then go into your own chorus?"
>
> The idea worked just as I had hoped. Neal, a fluent reader, handled the buoyant phrases of the tune while Louis tossed in a few perfectly spotted ad libs, then blew a masterfully improvised thirty-two-bar solo. The myth that he was set in his ways and had forgotten how to play spontaneously was immediately dispelled.

What is most striking about "Snafu" and "Jodie Man" is the way in which they give us a glimpse of what Max Harrison calls Armstrong's "ability, not much reflected by his recordings, to respond to a disciplined, imaginative and well-played setting, to fit into a tightly patterned sequence of musical events." He had responded much the same way in "Beau Koo Jack," but since then there had been precious few opportunities for him to show what he could do in the context of a sophisticated arrangement. Those who, like John Hammond, attacked Armstrong for playing pop tunes with a second-rate big band missed the point: many of the ballads he recorded in the thirties and forties were of the highest quality, and the Russell band often played them quite well. The problem was that Armstrong, who left the musical direction of his bands to other men, never pushed his arrangers to develop a distinctive style that would complement his own uniquely individual playing. Unlike Count Basie, Benny Goodman, or Woody Herman, all of whom succeeded in putting a personal stamp on their bands even though they wrote none of their own arrangements, he settled for less — and got it. That he was willing to do so is the great failing and impenetrable enigma of Louis Armstrong's career as a Swing Era bandleader.

The presence of Neal Hefti on "Snafu" points to another missed opportunity, for it was Hefti who wrote the new book of up-to-date charts that pulled Basie out of the Swing Era and established his postwar band as one of the most successful jazz groups of the fifties. Armstrong's fresh-sounding playing on "Snafu" and "Jodie Man" shows that he, too, could have moved forward without compromising his style. But he was afraid to walk away from the now-dated big-band sound that had swept him to fame, as well as reluctant to deprive his sidemen of their jobs: "I had eighteen men and they were a nice bunch of cats. I didn't want to see them all out of work."

It would have been easy for him to change his musical course. Bebop, after all, was not the sole alternative available to Armstrong in 1946. The revival of New Orleans jazz that he had helped to stimulate by writing *Swing That Music* a decade earlier was in full flower.

Sidney Bechet was making a living (though not much of one) playing small-group jazz, while a band of white Dixieland revivalists led by the San Francisco trumpeter Lu Watters was starting to attract attention by playing in a style based on the records that Armstrong had made with Joe Oliver in 1923. Bunk Johnson, who a few years earlier had been laboring in the rice fields of Louisiana, now appeared nightly in a Manhattan dancehall, cut records for Decca and Victor, and got written up in *Time:* "Their tunes were old; their playing was steady beat, banjo-plunking, authentic New Orleans — and meant to dance to. . . . Mostly the audience was in its thirties: they didn't swoon and scream, like bobby-soxers; they talked about the art of it." Johnson's recordings, most of them made in the company of Baby Dodds, Armstrong's old bandmate, and the veteran New Orleans clarinetist George Lewis, are ill tuned and a bit stiff in the rhythmic joints but full of life and excitement. Feather later played one of them for Armstrong in a "blindfold test" for *Metronome*, and though he failed to spot the players, his enthusiasm for their music was palpable: "You can hear from the first note that this has *soul*. . . . That clarinet is trying to tell a story — you can *follow* him. You can give that four stars right off. You can dance to it!" Yet he made no move to play it himself.

Armstrong was not resentful of Johnson's unexpected success, in which he had played a key role. In 1939 he told William Russell that Johnson was still alive, thus opening the way for Russell to track him down in Louisiana, interview him for *Jazzmen*, and make the first recordings of his playing three years later. Armstrong even helped to buy Johnson a new horn, and though it irritated him that the older man claimed to have given him lessons, he remained discreetly silent, saying only that he had always admired Bunk's playing: "He could play funeral marches that made me cry." But he must have been troubled by the fact that his own career, unlike Johnson's, seemed to be stalled. His appearance in *Cabin in the Sky* had been whittled down to a walk-on that *Variety* accurately summed up as "a few moments on the trumpet and a couple of lines," and his next three pictures, *Jam Session*, *Atlantic City*, and *Pillow to Post*, were all forgettable. The beboppers thought him ancient, and the traditional-jazz purists whom Feather called "moldy figs" thought him a sellout. In 1946 Rudi Blesh published *Shining Trumpets*, a moldy-fig history of jazz that dismissed everything Armstrong had done since "West End Blues" as a departure from the true faith. "Louis Armstrong could conceivably return to jazz tomorrow," Blesh wrote, explaining that the big-band recordings he made after 1928 were "foreign to Louis' nature."

By "jazz" Blesh had in mind a style that Armstrong had left behind long ago. Asked in 1945 about the New Orleans musicians of his youth, Armstrong replied, "Most of 'em couldn't stand the gaff—the pace is too fast for them today. They wouldn't hold your interest the way they did. Take me back thirty years—I could play that stuff with one finger!" He had no wish to turn back the clock that far, but he also knew that his music was growing stale. So did the critics. When he brought his band to New York, *Time* ran a review that gave with one hand and took away with the other: "The greatest jazzman of them all, Louis ('Satchmo') Armstrong, was back on Broadway. The word spread, the devotees gathered. But jazz purists who went prospecting for his golden trumpet notes had to pan out a lot of wet gravel. Satchmo arrived with one of the biggest (19 pieces), brassiest, and worst bands he ever had—a kind of unintentional satire on everything wrong with big bands." The review ended with a reference to Johnson whose point could not have been clearer if John Hammond had been making it: "Bunk now plays in Manhattan's Stuyvesant Casino dance hall, with the kind of small New Orleans jazz band that Louis abandoned years ago. Bunk still reveres his pupil. Says he: 'Don't expect me to play like my boy Louis, 'cause when Louis does up I does down.'" High Cs and pretty ballads, it seemed, were no longer enough to please the paying customers. Something had to give.

❧

Louis Armstrong's roundabout return to small-group jazz began in 1941, when Orson Welles, a man of violent but short-lived passions, decided to make a movie about jazz. Welles had seen *Jump for Joy*, Duke Ellington's ill-fated stage musical, in Los Angeles and fallen in love with the score, the band, the composer, and jazz in general. He summoned Ellington to his office and told him, "I want to do the history of jazz as a picture, and we'll call it *It's All True*. I want it to be written by Duke Ellington and Orson Welles, directed by Duke Ellington and Orson Welles, music written by Duke Ellington. . . ." Visions of sugarplums danced in Ellington's head, and when Welles offered to put him on salary at a thousand dollars a week, the bedazzled composer accepted on the spot. RKO, the studio that had brought Welles to Hollywood, did everything that he wanted until its cost-conscious managers realized that the creator of *Citizen Kane* couldn't be trusted to stay within a budget, so Ellington was put on the payroll and went to work.

The word soon got out that the Duke and the Boy Wonder of Hollywood were collaborating. *Down Beat* ran a story in August claiming that Armstrong would star in their movie, and the *New York Times* followed it up with a lengthy tribute to Armstrong by Leonard Feather which described "the forthcoming Orson Welles documentary picture" as "a general survey of swing music" that would be "based largely on the life stories of Louis Armstrong and his musical mentor, the late Joe 'King' Oliver. . . . [I]t will be a treat to see Louis in a part worthy of him, directed by a man with a sincere understanding of the subject." None of this was idle talk: Elliot Paul, an expatriate novelist and part-time jazz pianist who had returned to America to write screenplays, was working with Welles on a script called "The Story of Jazz" that was loosely based on *Swing That Music*. Armstrong was placed on a retainer by RKO, and in the spring of 1942 he played a month-long engagement at Casa Mañana, the Culver City nightspot that had previously done business as the Cotton Club, while waiting to be called for work on *It's All True*.

The call never came. *It's All True* was to be a multipart fictionalized quasi documentary, and when Welles flew to Brazil in February to immerse himself in one of the film's other subjects, Rio de

Janeiro's annual carnival, jazz got pushed to the back burner. *Citizen Kane* had flopped at the box office, and after RKO previewed Welles's next film, *The Magnificent Ambersons,* for an unsympathetic audience, the bosses came to the reasonable conclusion that it would likely do the same. At that point Welles was spending money hand over fist in Rio with little to show but miles of raw footage, so the studio pulled the plug and sent him packing. *Down Beat* told its readers that "Welles Jazz Film May Be Shelved, Louie May Never Be Immortalized in Great Movie." By then Ellington had written twenty-eight bars of music, for which he was paid $12,500. Armstrong went back on the road, not knowing that the law of unintended consequences was to lead him from *It's All True* to a six-piece combo with whose unpretentious music the world would fall in love.

Even after RKO washed its hands of Orson Welles, the idea of making a movie about the birth of jazz retained some of its commercial appeal. Welles himself had not lost interest in the project, or in jazz. In 1944 he hosted a radio variety show called *The Orson Welles Almanac* that featured a New Orleans–style jazz band whose members included Kid Ory and Zutty Singleton, and he spoke to Armstrong around that time about starring in a biographical film, to which the trumpeter responded with a six-page letter outlining the story of his life. But Welles made *The Stranger* instead, and Elliot Paul shopped "The Story of Jazz" elsewhere. At some point in 1946, it metamorphosed into a starless B movie called *New Orleans,* a humdrum melodrama in which a genteel young soprano sneaks into a Storyville cabaret, discovers jazz, and falls in love with the club's debonair owner. The producers of *New Orleans* were not wholly devoid of good intentions, however, and so they commissioned Joe Glaser to assemble an Armstrong-led combo to supply the music heard in the fictional "Orpheum Cabaret." The group featured Ory, Singleton, and two other New Orleans émigrés with distinguished pedigrees. The guitarist Bud Scott, Bill Johnson's successor in the Creole Jazz Band, had played banjo on several of its 1923 recordings; Barney Bigard had been summoned in 1924 by Oliver to replace

Johnny Dodds, then spent the next decade and a half playing for Duke Ellington, after which he and Scott joined Ory's *Orson Welles Almanac* band.

Glaser also talked the producers into hiring another of his clients, Billie Holiday, to make her feature-film debut — as a maid. In public she put the best possible face on the assignment, assuring Leonard Feather that "I'll be playing a maid, but she's really a cute maid." Later on she was more frank: "I didn't feel this damn part. . . . You just tell me one Negro girl who's made movies who didn't play a maid or a whore." Bigard recalled her as being "ornery" on the set, and her performance is listless save when she is singing. Armstrong, by contrast, played himself and did it well. His part was now a supporting role — he squired Holiday and led the band at the Orpheum Cabaret — but it was still bigger than his usual cameo, and when *New Orleans* wrapped in November, he was excited about it: "I finally finished making the film called *New Orleans*. And let me tell you, I think it's going to be a pretty good lecture on this music called jazz. . . . Billy and I are doing quite a bit of acting (ahem); she's also my sweetheart in the picture . . . Ump Ump Ump. Now isn't that something? The great Billy Holiday, my sweetheart?"

The film didn't live up to his expectations, but the jazz was good, at least by Hollywood standards. Once the credits are out of the way, the first music heard on the soundtrack is the cadenza to "West End Blues," and the rest of the film is sprinkled with handsomely played bits and pieces of such tunes as "Basin Street Blues," "Dipper Mouth Blues," and "I Thought I Heard Buddy Bolden Say." None of them, however, is performed in a manner much like that of the bands that played in Storyville, and the studio recordings cut by the *New Orleans* band for Victor while the film was being shot do not sound any more authentic. Instead they pointed to the possibility of a new stylistic path for Armstrong, for despite the presence of Ory, Scott, and Singleton, they are not moldy-fig jazz but small-group swing with a touch of down-home seasoning. That was just what Leonard Feather, who produced the sessions, had hoped for, and their "more cohesive and less traditionalist sound" (as he described it) was one to which Armstrong would soon return, just in the nick of time.

The bottom fell out of big-band jazz in the winter of 1946. *Time* ran an obituary for the era: "The big brassy jazz bands had become a luxury that people were unwilling to pay for. . . . In the past eight weeks, Benny Goodman, Tommy Dorsey, Harry James, Les Brown and Jack Teagarden decided to disband. Gene Krupa and Jimmy Dorsey cut salaries. This week Woody Herman gave up too." Joe Glaser needed no journalist to read him the writing on the wall. "Promoters all over are going broke — bookings are being cancelled at the last minute — I can name at least half a dozen Colored bands that will disband in the next 30 days and at least 30 white bands that will disband," he had written to Joe Garland that summer. Eleven years earlier Glaser had told one of Armstrong's sidemen that "I'm going to control everything in black show business before I'm through," and a few years after that his one-man show metamorphosed into the Associated Booking Corporation, whose other clients included Holiday and Lionel Hampton. Armstrong was still the jewel in the ABC crown, but his price was falling fast. One music-business insider was told that "the fee for the 16-piece band had fallen to $350 for a week night or $600 for a Saturday." Glaser knew that it was time to shake things up, but he didn't know how. "My boss (Mr Glaser) so anxious that I make good he will send someone from his office — someone who doesn't even know how we play — or what we play — there he will suggest that we play this tune or that tune because he thinks we can do a better job, or some kind of Jive," Armstrong told the readers of the *Melody Maker.*

Feather responded by offering to produce the trumpeter's long-overdue Carnegie Hall debut, suggesting that he appear with a combo similar to the one heard in *New Orleans.* Armstrong was too loyal to leave his big band behind, but he did agree to open the program with a set accompanied by Edmond Hall's swing sextet. The resulting concert, held on February 8, 1947, gave Ernie Anderson, Eddie Condon's press agent, the idea to present Armstrong "playing with his peers in a programme of his classics." Working with Bobby Hackett, who played in the lyrical manner of Bix Beiderbecke but admired Armstrong unreservedly, Anderson drew up a list of musicians and songs and showed it to the trumpeter. "Don't change a thing," he replied. "But you do have a problem. I can't do this unless Joe Glaser wants me to." So Anderson went to his bank and got a cashier's check for $1,500 made out to Glaser. He then visited the manager's office, handed the check to the receptionist, and told her to give it to her boss. Seconds later Glaser burst out of his private office. "He threw a hostile glare at me and shouted, 'What are you trying to do, you jerk?'" Anderson recalled. "I was deeply offended by this but I remained calm and said, 'That's for Louis for one night without the band.' After all I knew Joe Glaser well enough to know that he was never going to give up that check." Glaser cooled down enough to hear Anderson's pitch: he would present Armstrong at Town Hall, accompanied by an all-star combo. "If this works as I think it will, instead of $350 a night for Louis, you'll be getting $2,500 a night," he added. Glaser agreed, and the stage was set for what would be, after his debut with Joe Oliver at Lincoln Gardens, the most consequential performance of Louis Armstrong's life.

In 1947 America closed the books on World War II and plunged headlong into an era in which fear and promise were inseparably commingled. It was the year of the first transistor and the first supersonic flight — and the year in which the Cold War got under way. Jackson Pollock started work on his first drip painting in January, and Clement Greenberg dubbed him "the most powerful painter in contemporary America" in a widely discussed essay published that fall.* In Hollywood the style of moviemaking that a French critic had dubbed *film noir* reached its peak with the release of *Out of the*

---

*Like most of his fellow abstract expressionists, Pollock loved jazz and believed (in the words of his wife, Lee Krasner) that it was "the only other really creative thing happening in this country." He was also a Louis Armstrong fan whose record collection contained such Armstrong 78s as "Lazy River," "Mahogany Hall Stomp," and "St. James Infirmary."

Past, in which Robert Mitchum tells Jane Greer to "build my gallows high, baby," then escorts her to a rendezvous with death. Martha Graham might well have been thinking of a similar rendezvous when she gave titles to the two dances that she choreographed in 1947, *Errand into the Maze* and *Night Journey*.

All these works of art reflected the state of the American mind to which W. H. Auden gave a name in July when he published a book-length poem called *The Age of Anxiety*. So did many of the jazz recordings released that year. Though bebop was not yet widely known, Charlie Parker and Dizzy Gillespie were putting out one classic record after another, all of them jarringly up to date by comparison with the big-band swing that had come before them. The big hits of the moment, however, were not Gillespie's apocalyptic "Things to Come" or Parker's "Relaxin' at Camarillo" (named after the mental hospital in which the heroin-addicted saxophonist had been incarcerated for much of the preceding year) but such novelties as Perry Como's "Chi-Baba, Chi-Baba (My Bambino Go to Sleep)" and Tex Williams's "Smoke! Smoke! Smoke! (That Cigarette)." For all its interest in avant-garde art, Cold War America also longed for musical comfort food.

Those who picked up a copy of the *New Yorker* on May 17 and opened it to the "Goings On About Town" section would have found plenty of ways to amuse themselves that weekend. On Broadway Ingrid Bergman was starring in Maxwell Anderson's *Joan of Lorraine*, John Gielgud in *The Importance of Being Earnest*, Judy Holliday in *Born Yesterday*, and Ethel Merman in *Annie Get Your Gun*. Those with more adventurous tastes could also have caught *The Medium*, Gian Carlo Menotti's new opera, which had just opened at the Ethel Barrymore Theatre, where it ran for 212 performances, twice as long as the original production of *Porgy and Bess*. Gallerygoers interested in abstraction were free to choose between exhibitions by Robert Motherwell and Aaron Siskind. Ballet Theatre was dancing a mixed bill of works by Frederick Ashton, Agnes de Mille, and Antony Tudor at City Center, and Norman Granz was presenting Coleman Hawkins and Buddy Rich in a "Jazz at the Philharmonic" concert at

Carnegie Hall. It was, in other words, a typical Saturday night in New York City, which had emerged by default as the cultural capital of the West after the cities of Europe were bombed into rubble. But "Goings On About Town" inexplicably overlooked another concert, one in which Louis Armstrong appeared not with his big band but with seven top jazzmen. Of all the performances given in New York that night, it was the one that would be remembered longest.

Town Hall was (and is) a 1,500-seat auditorium in the theater district whose elegant proportions and near-perfect acoustics made it an attractive venue for classical musicians. Marian Anderson made her New York recital debut there in 1935, and Béla Bartók, Feodor Chaliapin, Kirsten Flagstad, and Sergei Rachmaninoff were among the many other noted artists to be heard from its stage. (Andrés Segovia played there the night before Armstrong.) In 1942 Ernie Anderson persuaded Eddie Condon to hire the hall and put on what *Time* called "a bimonthly series of jive concerts cooked to the epicure's taste." The series attracted the attention of Virgil Thomson, now the chief music critic of the *Herald Tribune*, who declared it to be "a full and noble expression of the musical faculties." From then on jazz would be a regular part of Town Hall's musical offerings, and though Condon and his colleagues did most of the playing, Parker and Gillespie made a memorable joint appearance there in 1945, joined by Sid Catlett, who had quit Armstrong's big band in 1942 to lead a quartet that became a fixture of the smoky nightclubs that lined New York's 52nd Street.

A traditionalist who had no liking for bebop, Anderson knew how and with whom he wanted to present Armstrong. The program that he and Bobby Hackett drew up was a survey of the trumpeter's landmark recordings that ranged from "A Monday Date" and "Tiger Rag" to "Do You Know What It Means to Miss New Orleans?" and "Back o' Town Blues," a down-and-dirty Armstrong-penned lament about a pair of unfaithful lovers that he had recorded with his big band a year earlier. The first name on their list of sidemen was Jack Teagarden, whose bluesy playing and soft-spoken singing Armstrong had admired ever since they recorded "Knockin' a Jug" in 1929.

Since then the two men had performed together on only a few scattered occasions, and Armstrong was glad to welcome him aboard. Sid Catlett shared the drummer's throne with George Wettling, who had first heard Armstrong with Joe Oliver at Lincoln Gardens a quarter century earlier; Bob Haggart, who arranged Armstrong's music for Bob Crosby and later scored some of the trumpeter's Decca big-band sessions, agreed to play bass. On clarinet was Peanuts Hucko, a veteran of Glenn Miller's Army Air Force Band who played swing and Dixieland with equal flair. Dick Cary, a young pianist who knew Armstrong's repertoire inside out, helped Hackett rehearse the band. Hackett played second cornet, the same role that Armstrong had filled for Joe Oliver in Chicago. "I tell you I was scared to death," he said. "It's like playing in front of God."

What these men had in common was that none was a New Orleans revivalist. Though they were intimately familiar with the music of the Hot Five and Seven, all but Cary had spent the thirties and forties in swing bands. Hackett and Wettling were also part of Eddie Condon's first-string team of Chicago-style jazzmen, and Catlett, the only one of the group who had worked regularly with Armstrong, could play any kind of music, bebop included. He was the drummer on the legendary 1945 session at which Parker and Gillespie recorded the bop anthems "Hot House," "Salt Peanuts," and "Shaw 'Nuff." Musicians such as these could be counted on to put a fresh spin on the good ol' good ones — and to spur their leader to the heights of inspiration.

Unable to make the afternoon rehearsal, Armstrong showed up backstage well before the festivities were set to begin. "We don't have to rehearse," he assured his musicians. "We'll just hit at eleven-thirty and play the show!" Sidney Bechet, whom Anderson had invited to sit in, called in sick earlier in the day, though it turned out that he wasn't really sick, just jealous: he showed up at Jimmy Ryan's later on to play his regular Saturday-night gig. Otherwise all was in readiness. Teagarden was a self-destructively hard drinker and Hackett a recovering alcoholic who had just joined AA, but both men, like their colleagues, were sober as judges and eager to blow. Fred Robbins, whose frenzied hipster patter ("Hiya cat, wipe ya feet on the mat, let's slap on the fat and dish out some scat!") had made him New York's most popular jazz disc jockey, was the master of ceremonies. Come eleven thirty he launched the proceedings with a few pointed words: "Louie opens tonight with some of the golden things from his early OKeh days. And in another respect this concert is unique, that is, we've surrounded Louie with the best jazz musicians obtainable." Then Armstrong strode onto the stage of Town Hall and stomped off "Cornet Chop Suey." All at once the years of split lips and one-night stands slipped from his shoulders. Buoyed up by his superlative sidemen and relieved at long last of the need to tow a seventeen-piece band of nobodies behind him, he played not like a forty-five-year-old trumpeter whose career was in trouble but like the flying cat of the Sunset Café, young and strong and ready for anything. By evening's end he was a star once more. . . .

Such, at any rate, is the legend of the Town Hall concert. The reality, as is so often the case, was somewhat different, if not greatly so. To begin with, Armstrong already had several recent small-group appearances under his belt. He had cut eight sides for Victor with the *New Orleans* band, fronted Edmond Hall's sextet at Carnegie Hall, and performed with small bands on two radio shows in the past nine months. The trumpet solos on his last few big-band sides for Victor showed no signs of wear and tear. And though his price had dropped precipitously in the past year, he was still more than popular enough to sell out a 1,500-seat hall on a Saturday night. It says much about his enduring fame that his name is nowhere to be seen on the posters for the concert — only his picture.

All this notwithstanding, the Town Hall concert was a watershed in Armstrong's professional life. It was, for one thing, the first time that he had ever given a full-evening concert with a combo, and it appears to have been the first time since 1926 that he had appeared in public as the leader of a small group of his own. Not that he needed a good band to play well. "I work with two bands, the one on stage and the one in my head," he would later tell Ruby Braff. "If they sound good on stage, O.K., I'll play with them. If not, I just

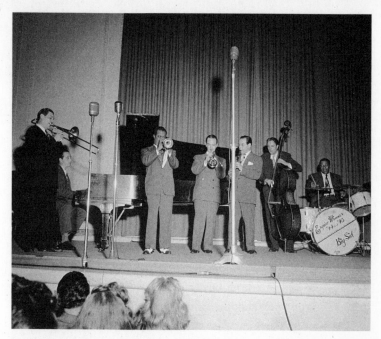

"It's like playing in front of God": Town Hall, 1947. This concert, the first time since 1926 that Armstrong had appeared in public as the leader of a small group of his own, changed his life. He and Joe Glaser subsequently scrapped his big band and put together the All Stars, the combo with which he performed until his death in 1971. The picture is by Bill Gottlieb, the most noted jazz photographer of the forties. From left: Jack Teagarden, Dick Cary, Armstrong, Bobby Hackett, Peanuts Hucko, Bob Haggart, and Sid Catlett.

turn up the volume of the band in my head." But the band with which he was playing at Town Hall that night sounded very good indeed, and its presence made a difference. Cary, Haggart, Hucko, and Wettling gave him solid, trustworthy support; Catlett, something more. His flashing cymbal work and get-a-move-on backbeats had always been a tonic to Armstrong, and on this occasion he glowed with a life-enhancing fire that recalls Whitney Balliett's words of praise for his playing: "He reined in the obstreperous, pushed the laggardly, and celebrated the inspired." Hackett's contributions were more discreet — he was out to make his Pops look good — but no less essential to the evening's effect. The delicate obbligato he wove behind Armstrong's firm-toned lead on the first eight bars of "Rockin' Chair" was worth the price of the ticket all by itself.

As for Jack Teagarden, he and Armstrong had been born to sing Hoagy Carmichael's vaudevillian duet about a drunken old man and his gin-fetching son. Their voices — Teagarden's rumpled and lazy, Armstrong's sly and amused — wound round one another like two old friends embracing after a long separation. Teagarden made no secret of his pleasure. The greatest of all jazz trombonists had fallen on hard times, having twice made the costly mistake of trying to lead a big band of his own. In 1947 he was deeply in debt and treading water, and the Town Hall concert was a welcome opportunity for him to forget his troubles and blow alongside the musician he admired above all others. "I've been waiting a long, long time, 'bout twenty-three years, for this opportunity, because I'm really in heaven tonight," he said in a brief onstage interview with Robbins. "*Good*, Jackson," Armstrong happily replied.

The concert was somewhat uneven in quality, mainly because of its impromptu nature. From time to time Armstrong squeezed out an attention-snatching high note that sounded inappropriate in so friendly a setting. But he was never one to let his own mistakes, much less anyone else's, get in the way of making great music, and on "Back o' Town Blues," played much more slowly than on the good-humored big-band version he had recorded a year earlier for Victor, he cut loose with a solo whose opulent tone and irreducible economy showed that he was still at the top of his game. A year later Humphrey Lyttelton, after hearing Armstrong play live for the first time since before the war, described the experience in language that can be applied equally well to his solo on "Back o' Town Blues": "I was particularly struck by the almost puritanical simplicity of his playing; all the old trappings and ornaments which were such familiar characteristics of his earlier phases have been swept away . . . and there was left a music which, with its purity and serenity, brought us perhaps nearer to the fountain-head of his genius than we have ever been before."

Anderson had arranged to have the concert recorded on acetate discs, and "Ain't Misbehavin'," "Back o' Town Blues," "Pennies from Heaven," "Save It, Pretty Mama," and "St. James Infirmary" were released by Victor the following February to general acclaim. At the time, though, comparatively little fuss was made over the event, which went unmentioned in the *New York Times*, *Time*, and the *New Yorker*. Only the jazz press took note of the occasion: *Down Beat*'s review was headed "Satchmo's Genius Still Lives," and the *Melody Maker* ran a piece by a correspondent who reported that Armstrong's playing "had all the freshness and vigour of the early Hot Five and Seven days. He never strove for effects, never played to the gallery." But one person in the audience was listening with the closest possible attention. Joe Glaser, who was sitting in a box seat, knew at once that his troubles were over. Not only had Armstrong proved himself capable of thrilling a crowd without the support of a big band, but in Jack Teagarden he had found the foil of a lifetime. Like the businessman he was, Glaser struck while the iron was smoking hot: he signed Teagarden to a long-term contract on Monday morning, then gave the members of the big band two months' notice.

On May 28 Glaser planted an article in *Variety* announcing that Armstrong would be appearing that fall in a "series of concert appearances, using a handful of established star soloists." Two weeks later the trumpeter reported to Victor's New York studios with Hackett, Hucko, and Teagarden in tow to record "Rockin' Chair," "Someday You'll Be Sorry," and a pair of Armstrong-Teagarden blues duets, accompanied by a Basie-style rhythm section led by the big-band pianist Johnny Guarnieri. Nine days after that, the full Town Hall band, with Jack Lesberg replacing Haggart and Ernie Caceres added on baritone saxophone, reassembled at the Winter Garden Theatre to plug the opening of *New Orleans*. Unlike the Town Hall performance, this one was broadcast by NBC, and an aircheck shows that the Armstrong-Teagarden Mutual Appreciation Society was in full swing. "Come in, Mr. Louie," Teagarden says after singing a mellow chorus of "Basin Street Blues." "I got it, Pops,

I'm goin' on in," Armstrong replies, then scats a chorus of his own, winding up with a heartfelt "Take it, Brother T."

New Orleans, to no one's surprise, was a flop. James Agee called it "a crime" in his film column for the *Nation.* "Put it down as a fizzle in every respect but one," Bosley Crowther wrote in the *New York Times.* "That is the frequent tooting of Louis Armstrong on his horn." But Armstrong barely had time to think about the failure of the film, much less lose any sleep over it. His big band played its last gig in July, and a few days later he was headed for sunny California, where he and Brother T had an appointment with posterity.

10

"KEEP THE HORN PERCOLATING"

Renewal, 1947–1954

BILLY BERG'S VINE STREET jazz club was the hippest room in Hollywood. A savvy local musician described it as "the first really cosmopolitan club [in California] with a good deal of publicity behind it where negro and white people mixed without any pressure. It was a groovy atmosphere, an atmosphere that embraced people from all walks of life." It also embraced all kinds of music. Billy Berg's was where Charlie Parker and Dizzy Gillespie had made their West Coast debut in 1945, and the pop singer Frankie Laine was discovered there the following year. In January of 1947 Louis Jordan's Tympany Five, a popular black combo that mixed jazz with rhythm and blues, settled in for a residency that was cut short when Jordan's wife went after her unfaithful husband with a carving knife. Seven months later Joe Glaser booked Louis Armstrong's as-yet-unnamed sextet into the club, asking for and getting $2,500 a night, $26,000 in today's dollars — the exact amount that Ernie Anderson had predicted.

Glaser picked Hollywood for the group's debut because Armstrong had just finished shooting Howard Hawks's *A Song Is Born*, a leaden remake of *Ball of Fire*, the 1941 screwball comedy in which Gary Cooper plays an unworldly scholar at work on an entry on slang who learns the language of jive from Barbara Stanwyck. In the new version, Danny Kaye and Virginia Mayo replaced Cooper and Stanwyck, and the subject of their inquiries was changed from slang to swing, thus allowing Hawks to hire Armstrong, Tommy Dorsey, Benny Goodman, Lionel Hampton, and the Golden Gate Quartet, all of whose talents were wasted. The only good that came of the film was that it broke Armstrong's cinematic losing streak, performing well at the box office and reminding producers that he knew what to do in front of a camera.

Once *A Song Is Born* was out of the way, Glaser got down to the more important business of putting together a full-time version of the all-star lineup that had backed Armstrong at Town Hall. In addition to Teagarden, Sid Catlett and Dick Cary were held over, but Peanuts Hucko was replaced by Barney Bigard, who had appeared onscreen in *New Orleans*, and Velma Middleton, who had been singing with Armstrong since 1942, was brought aboard as well. Morty Corb, a local studio bassist, rounded out the group. While Glaser was still playing it close to the vest — he had yet to announce a permanent change of musical format for Armstrong — everyone seems to have taken for granted that what had worked in New York would work in Hollywood. Armstrong and company opened at Billy Berg's on August 13, and Bing Crosby led what Anderson called "a show-business invasion that packed the place." The band had gone through the motions of rehearsing two days earlier, but it was mostly for fun. "I don't need no rehearsals," Armstrong told a reporter. "I don't go through that and never will. All these cats I'm playing with can blow. We don't need no arrangements. . . . I say follow me, and you got the best arrangement you ever heard."

The rest, as *Time* reported in a review called "Satchmo Comes Back," was history:

Louis Armstrong had forsaken the ways of Mammon and come back to jazz. Shorn of his big (19-piece), brassy, ear-splitting commercial band, he was as happy as a five-year-old with his curls cut off. . . .

Hoagy Carmichael led the cheering when Old Satchelmouth, his steak-thick lips parted in a grin, stepped on the stand with some of the greatest names in jazz behind him — Clarinetist Barney Bigard, Trombonist Jack Teagarden and Drummer Sid Catlett. Out in the smoke, waiting for the first golden notes, were half the big noises of U.S. sweet & swing — Johnny Mercer, Woody Herman, Abe Lyman, Benny Goodman.

Louis didn't let them down. When he swung into *I Gotta Right to Sing the Blues*, they heard the old, pure, easy phrasing and big, clear, ranging tone that had made Louis King of Jazz.

Patronizing though it was, Armstrong never got a better notice, or a more profitable one. Until then Glaser had hedged his bets, warning Bigard that the gig was only a trial run: "At first it was going to be two weeks at Billy Berg's to see if the band would take off after the movie publicity [for *New Orleans*]." But the new band did so well that Berg booked it for two more weeks, plus an additional two-month run in December. As soon as the *Time* story hit, Glaser was inundated with offers from clubs across the country. Corb was afraid to fly, so Arvell Shaw, the bassist from Armstrong's big band, replaced him, and the group worked its way east by playing back-to-back gigs in Chicago, St. Louis, Cedar Rapids, Davenport, Indianapolis, Milwaukee, Cleveland, New York, and Boston, where it gave a concert at Symphony Hall that was recorded by Ernie Anderson and later released by Decca. Satisfied that Town Hall was no fluke, Glaser made it official: the big band would be replaced by what he dubbed "Louis Armstrong and His All Stars." "Joe makes it sound like a basketball team," Eddie Condon quipped, but the title was accurate enough, and it became even more so when Cary was replaced by Earl Hines, with whom Armstrong had not performed since 1928. Like Teagarden, Fatha Hines had gotten himself deeply into debt — he dropped thirty thousand dollars running a Chicago nightclub — so when Glaser made him an offer, he closed the club with relief and flew to France to play with his old friend at the Nice Jazz Festival. After twenty years of wandering, Castor and Pollux were reunited at last.

Once the band became a going proposition, Armstrong's losing streak was over for good. But Glaser never took his success for granted and worked the band hard: the All Stars crisscrossed the United States ten times and went to Europe twice between 1947 and 1951. "I resented Joe Glaser's attitude," said Barrett Deems, who played drums with the All Stars from 1954 to 1958. "He treated us like we were his money machine. He just would not let us stop. It was all work and no play." Armstrong was as much to blame as Glaser, for he had come to feel that nonstop work was the best way to keep his chops in shape: "Them days off are bad — your lip gets soft and slack, and when you go to work next day you're scufflin'." No one felt the strain more than the trumpeter himself. "We don't have no days off — feel like I spent nine thousand hours on buses, get off a bus, hop a plane, get in town just in time to play a gig, chops are cold, come off that stage too tired to raise an eyelash," he said. Yet it was still easier than the big-band days, for a combo could play long runs in nightclubs instead of jumping constantly from one town to the next, thus allowing him to spend more time with Lucille. "That's when Louie needed me, coming in from work to hotel with no one to talk to, that's when you really need a companion," she said.

It helped that Glaser spent a sizable chunk of the take on creature comforts. The All Stars traveled with a road manager and two valets, one for Armstrong and the other for the rest of the band. "Doc" Pugh, Armstrong's personal valet, became a permanent part of his entourage. He was, Ernie Anderson said, "Louis' most trusted companion . . . He knew secrets that no one else would ever know." But everyone else in the band was treated generously as well. According to Arvell Shaw, "When we were doing one-nighters, we had a very large bus. . . . Other than that we would fly or take the train — all first class." The bassist Jack Lesberg, who toured with the All Stars in 1956, marveled at the pains that Glaser took to keep things running smoothly and comfortably: "Each member of the band had five suits and one was always ready and pressed for you to wear in plenty of time before you went on. There was always a car to take you to wherever you had to play, and the same to take you back to your hotel. A meal was always ready at whatever time." As for the money, the original All Stars received weekly salaries ranging from $150 for Cary to $500 for Teagarden, with raises every six months or so — more than enough in 1947 to ease the bite of the band's unrelenting schedule.

At first Glaser traveled with Armstrong's new band, as he had in 1935, but after a few weeks he left the job in the hands of a road manager, Pierre "Frenchy" Tallerie, whom Barney Bigard succinctly described as "a real ass-hole." Milt Hinton, who served a brief tour of duty with the All Stars in 1953, agreed: "He didn't like anyone and you couldn't believe a word he said. Everyone knew he hated Louis and Louis couldn't stand him. In fact, some people said that's why Joe made him road manager. He knew if Louis did something wrong, Frenchy would report him, and if Frenchy tried to steal, Louis would do exactly the same thing." As well as being a spy and a misanthrope, Tallerie was also a racist. One day the band bus drove past a field in Kansas that was full of black and white cows. "Gee, I hate to see that," he said to no one in particular. "A black and a white cow, just like a white man and a colored woman." It must have galled him that the All Stars were integrated, not by chance but as a matter of policy. In 1947 and for years afterward, it was still uncommon for a working jazz group to be racially mixed, especially one whose leader was black. That Sid Catlett was the only black sideman in Armstrong's Town Hall band had not gone unnoticed by critics, one of whom wrote that "it was perhaps a pity that Louis could not have been backed by a coloured group, for political reasons." The truth was that Anderson and Bobby Hackett had picked the players who they thought would show Armstrong off to best advantage, but Glaser evidently felt that a mixed band would appeal to middle-class white audiences, and Armstrong was glad to go along with him.

After Dick Cary quit at the end of 1947, Teagarden was the only white All Star, and it made him uncomfortable to stay in separate hotels and eat in segregated restaurants when the band toured the South. The ever-optimistic Armstrong claimed that the band's southern tours were "wonderful, everywhere but Memphis. I couldn't have Jack on the stand there, so we don't play there at all." Later on the proportions varied, but Glaser always took care to keep the All Stars racially mixed. The band was also as drug-free as he could make it, though Armstrong's devotion to marijuana kept Glaser in constant fear that he would run afoul of the law again.* Some of their most heated arguments arose from his refusal to give it up. According to one of Armstrong's friends, "Glaser would scream and Louis would say, 'Fuck you.'" That was why Cary quit: he was taking prescription sedatives, and when he went to ask for his six-month raise, Tallerie told Glaser that he was "a drug addict," a barefaced lie that caused the pianist to resign in disgust. In 1967 Kenny Davern was offered the clarinet chair, and Glaser's assistants made him roll up his sleeves so that they could check for needle tracks. "We don't want junkies with the star," they said.

Armstrong held himself aloof from such matters. "I never pick my own bands — too many good musicians around, makes bad friends," he explained to an interviewer a few years later. Instead he left it to his manager to hire, fire, and negotiate with his sidemen, though he would speak privately to Glaser from time to time about musicians who he thought might be suitable. It was a good cop/bad cop arrangement: Glaser played the heavy, letting Armstrong be one of the boys. "He didn't have a big ego," Hinton said, "so he never wanted special treatment. He'd travel right along with us, in buses or planes — it didn't matter to him." His modesty was no pose, but at least one of his later sidemen saw that it was facilitated by Glaser's willingness to make the decisions and take the heat. According to the clarinetist Joe Darensbourg, who joined the All Stars in 1961, the band was "like a family affair. One thing that helped to seal this was the deal between Louis and Joe." That was what Armstrong had had

---

*He came close to doing so in 1954, when customs inspectors in Honolulu found a joint in an eyeglass case tucked into Lucille's overnight bag. "Charged with trying to smuggle marijuana, Lucille contended that the whole case was crazy because she doesn't even wear glasses," *Time* reported. (Armstrong did.) Everyone in the band was searched, but no charges were filed.

in mind when he told Glaser in 1935 that all he wanted to do was "blow my gig." By signing away responsibility for his professional life, he was freed to devote himself to the thing that mattered most: his music.

Of the charter members of the All Stars family, it was Catlett to whom Armstrong was closest — they spent hour after hour swapping dirty jokes on the band bus — but everyone who worked with the drummer liked him as well. "Sid's personality reflected his playing," said Mel Powell, who had gotten to know him during his brief stay with Benny Goodman's band. "He was lovable and loving. He was gentle. He was compassionate and concerned." He was also a carouser who seemed never to go to bed, and his rowdy ways were catching up with him by the time he joined the All Stars. Ill health forced him out of the band a year and a half after it made its debut at Billy Berg's, and he died of a heart attack two years later at the untimely age of forty-one. Catlett cut only four studio sides with the band, but airchecks and concert recordings show that he and Armstrong were as compatible on stage as off, though the ever-professional trumpeter had started to lose patience with Catlett's growing irresponsibility by the time he left the band:

> He got so he played everythin' except the drums. He played the chicks, he ran with the cats, he played the horses, played the numbers an' when he should have been concentrating on 'proving up his drumming, he just wasn't there. I talked to him 'cause I was very fond of Sid, but he'd come late for rehearsal time after time. He'd arrive just as we was in the middle of our opening number "Sleepy Time Down South" an' he'd start to tighten up his drums — scrunch, scronch, scraanch — just as we was playin' real pretty.

Jack Teagarden's tombstone bears the inscription WHERE THERE IS HATRED, LET ME SOW LOVE. His colleagues agreed that the trombonist did just that. "He never got angry about anything, either on the stand or off it," Barney Bigard said. He was never happier than when playing alongside Armstrong: "Louis can't do anything wrong. The sound is there — and the beat. There's never a doubt in his mind as to what he's going to do, and no matter what everybody else is doing, Pops just goes right ahead." Armstrong felt the same way about Teagarden. In 1966 he said that it had been "like a holiday" when the trombonist joined the All Stars, adding that "we understood each other so wonderful." Their rapport can be seen in a 1957 TV performance of "Rockin' Chair" in which the broad-shouldered Teagarden puts an arm around the shorter Armstrong and looks affectionately at him as they amble through their well-worn routine: "Fetch me some water, son!" "You *know* you don't drink water, father." More than a friend, Teagarden was also Armstrong's peer, both as an instrumentalist and as a singer, and his presence not only stimulated the trumpeter but ensured that he would never have to wear himself out on the bandstand, an important consideration now that his youth was behind him. Glaser's instinct had been right: Teagarden's easygoing way with a song complemented Armstrong instead of threatening him. If his chops were down, he could step aside and let Brother T drawl his way through "Stars Fell on Alabama" or fire off an up-tempo "Lover," then come roaring back with one of his own specialties.

Off stage Teagarden was a cordial, unforthcoming man who drank ceaselessly, sometimes spiking his whiskey with Benzedrine, though he never showed any sign of drunkenness. Instead of smoking pot with Armstrong or raising hell with Catlett, he would retire to his room and tinker with small engines that he built himself. "If we played a long engagement someplace and you went into Jack's hotel room, you'd see nothing but all kinds of wires, little whistles and steam engine things," Bigard recalled. Kenny Davern, who played with Teagarden after the trombonist left the All Stars, found him "warm but distant. There, but not there. Emotionally closed off. Sometimes it seemed that his idea of spending an afternoon was to come into a place where we'd be playing and tune the piano. . . . I got the idea sometimes that all that tinkering was his way of putting something between him and the world, so he wouldn't have to deal with it." Some of those who knew him best — nobody knew him well — thought that his reserve was a mark of disillusion. His great gifts never brought him great rewards, not even after he joined the All Stars: four-fifths of his paycheck went directly to his creditors and ex-wives. "If I don't have enough to buy a pint of Four Roses every day," he told Dick Cary, "I'm going to quit playing." But he never did, perhaps because playing with Louis Armstrong was its own reward.

Unlike Teagarden, Velma Middleton was easy to know. Earl Hines described her as "a happy-go-lucky girl who worshipped Louis. She was just another boy so far as we were concerned, and she fitted right in with the band." Middleton was a fat woman with a mountainous bosom, and the film of "Swingin' on Nothing" that she made with Armstrong's big band in 1942 shows that she was also an agile, uninhibited dancer capable of doing splits. Virtually everything written about her in the forties and fifties made snide mention of these facts. *Time* described her as "a 250-lb. lady named — by the Gagwriters Association — Miss Petite of 1946. She waddled through 'Shoo Fly Pie and Apple Pan Dowdy' and then did a split which almost literally brought down the house." Jazz purists turned up their noses at her mildly racy blues duets with a mock-lascivious Armstrong, but audiences loved her onstage antics, and so did her boss. "Wait'll you see Velma's split," Armstrong told a pair of fans. "She sings and dances and makes a split just like tearing a piece of paper." Middleton's bandmates had no difficulty seeing what he saw in her. "Velma wasn't a great singer," said Trummy Young, who joined the All Stars in 1952 and played alongside her for nine years, but he immediately added that she and Armstrong were "a fantastic team. . . . I would have hated to follow them on stage, man."

Barney Bigard was less companionable. George Avakian remembered him as "always a little bit distant, a little bit cold," and at least one of his colleagues concurred. "He would complain a lot, but he didn't like going to the boss and telling *him* — he'd just tell us, all of us, about the things he didn't like," Earl Hines said. But Bigard was a master musician whose liquid New Orleans–style clarinet sound

Duke Ellington had used to incomparable effect. "He had that woody tone which I love on the instrument," Ellington wrote in his autobiography. "He was invaluable for putting the filigree work into an arrangement, and sometimes it could remind you of all that delicate wrought iron you see in his hometown." He was also an alumnus of Joe Oliver's band, which he had joined shortly after Armstrong moved to New York to play with Fletcher Henderson, and his stint with Kid Ory had reintroduced him to the New Orleans style after a decade of big-band work with Ellington. Unlike so many of his fellow New Orleans musicians, Armstrong was never parochial, but it pleased him to have a hometown boy on board, and Bigard appears to have enjoyed his stay with the All Stars at least as much as Armstrong enjoyed having him there.

Not so Hines. "The one thing was that they never really hit it off too well . . . you could feel the animosity between them," Bigard said. Part of the problem was that his accompanying was flashy and self-centered: "Sometimes Louis would get after Earl because he put too much show into it all and wasn't giving the soloists the support he should have." But the real problem, the clarinetist thought, went further back. Had the two old friends fallen out at some point in the preceding twenty years? Or was it that they had both been fronting bands of their own for too long to ease into a relaxed leader-sideman relationship? No one knew for sure, but it was evident to the other All Stars that things weren't what they used to be in the days of the Hot Five.

Yet no matter how he may have now felt about Hines, Armstrong gave the pianist and his other sidemen ample opportunity to shine on the bandstand.* "Everybody in the All Stars got a chance, your spot

---

*Ample — but not infinite. The pianist Marty Napoleon, who briefly replaced Hines in 1951, recalled that during his first performance with the band, Armstrong featured him on a showy vocal version of "Darktown Strutters' Ball" that "tore down the house." The trumpeter called a rehearsal after the show, astonishing the other members of the band: "They'd never had a rehearsal before. At the rehearsal, Louis played a tape of their show when Hines was with the band. 'Listen, Pops,' he told me. 'This was what Earl used to do.' It was his piano solo [on] 'Boogie Woogie on the St. Louis Blues.' I took the hint. Next day, I started practicing piano solos. I never sang with the band again."

where you went out and did your thing, your solo spot," Arvell Shaw said. "He wanted you to go out there and get a standing ovation if you could, stand on your eyelashes and get a standing ovation — he loved that. . . . [H]e realized the better you were the better it made his band." That was the point of having an all-star band: it allowed Armstrong to pace himself. So, too, did the All Stars' repertoire, which consisted for the most part of a retrospective of his hits, augmented by the featured numbers played by his sidemen, the newer songs he was recording for Decca and performing in his films, and "Indiana," a tune recorded by the Original Dixieland Jazz Band in 1917 that Armstrong played for the first time in 1951, subsequently using it to open all of his shows ("It sits good on the chops, you need something comfortable, and from then on I'm set for the night"). At dances the fare ranged more widely, but in clubs and on the concert stage, his programs came to be centered on a dozen or so staples, "Back o' Town Blues," "Basin Street Blues," "High Society," "Muskrat Ramble," "My Bucket's Got a Hole in It," "On the Sunny Side of the Street," "Rockin' Chair," "Royal Garden Blues," "Struttin' with Some Barbecue," "Tiger Rag," and "When the Saints" recurring time and again.

The All Stars rarely played any of the numbers that Armstrong had recorded with the Hot Five, a fact for which he saw no reason to apologize: "I say, people got all those records and let them play 'em. Haven't heard 'em by now, shame on them." It mattered no more to him that many (though by no means all) of his solos had hardened into set pieces. That had always been his way, and he saw no reason to change. "Well, y'know it's a real consolation always getting that same note — just hittin' it right," he explained. "The public can get to know you better by them old tunes than by anything new. So, like Heifetz and Marian Anderson, we play the same tunes; every time they play the same solo they get the applause — so do we."* Most of

---

*One of Armstrong's bones of contention with Hines was the pianist's unwillingness to reproduce his solo from the 1928 recording of "West End Blues" when the All Stars played the song on stage. "Earl would play something else every night and it never would match this, and I couldn't figure that out," the trumpeter recalled in 1956.

his fans were similarly consoled by his constancy, dismissing his critics as wrong-headed. "It's like calling Tchaikovsky a bum because his
piano concerto sounds the same way each time you hear it," said Max
Kaminsky.

Just as Armstrong continued to play the solos of yesteryear with
renewing force, so did his band take care to perform their familiar
repertoire in a way that bore no more than a superficial resemblance
to funny-hat Dixieland-style jazz. "What we played with Louis
wasn't Dixieland," Earl Hines said. Arvell Shaw made a related point
when he said that the All Stars were not "a New Orleans type of
band." They infused the good ol' good ones with the same swing-
based sophistication heard in the studio recordings cut in 1946 by
Armstrong's *New Orleans* band, playing in a style that had more in
common with Eddie Condon's Chicago-style small-band sides of the
late thirties than with the rougher-hewn style of Bunk Johnson. In
1965 Leonard Feather recalled how the members of the *New Orleans*
band had responded when asked to emulate Johnson and his fellow
revivalists:

> Louis had been instructed to familiarize himself with music
> parts that had been taken off recordings of "When the Saints Go
> Marchin' In," "Maryland, My Maryland," "Hot Time in the
> Old Town Tonight," etc. Some of them had been transcribed
> from primitive New Orleans music recorded by a research crew
> sent to Louisiana by the producer; others were regular records
> by Bunk Johnson. So the men listened to some of them records
> they were supposed to "learn" from. As Armstrong, Bigard and
> the others were gathered around the machine, they erupted in
> roars of laughter at the welter of wrong notes, out-of-tune
> horns, and generally unspeakable non-music.

Even after making allowances for Feather's anti–New Orleans
bias, this account rings true. "I wouldn't call them Dixieland — to
me that's only just a little better than bop," Armstrong said of the All
Stars. "*Jazz* music — that's the way we express ourselves." Anyone
who sought to divert him from his chosen form of expression soon
discovered that he had a will of iron when it came to musical matters.

Few outsiders suspected how adamant he could be, especially when they heard him talking about his debt to Joe Glaser: "The film called *New Orleans* didn't have anything to do with the change to small combo. . . . Anything that I have done musically since I signed up with Joe Glaser at the Sunset, it was his suggestions. Or orders, whatever you may call it." Such statements led many to suppose that he was his manager's puppet. They were half-right—but only half. Armstrong played where Glaser told him to play, but once he got there, he played what he wanted to play. "I should know what I'm doing musically by now after thirty some odd years—and from the master-King Oliver School," he had told the editors of the *Melody Maker* in 1946. He was even surer of himself now that the All Stars were selling out clubs and concert halls across America. "You couldn't tell him what to do on the stage . . . the one thing he fought for," one of Glaser's assistants said. "He wanted to do his show."

In addition to having a crystal-clear idea of what he wanted the All Stars to play, Armstrong knew how he wanted it played. One of the reasons why he had gotten along so well with Joe Garland in the days when the younger man was running his big band was that "he disliked bad notes the same as me. . . . That's why I try to make all my records with good notes at least and that's the way they all came out. I wouldn't let it pass. 'Oh, that's all right, let it go.' Bullshit! It had to be O.K. by me as long as the notes were right, whatever I attempted to do, high or low." He had tolerated second-rate playing in those days—he had had little choice—but now that he was leading a small group of handpicked musicians, he expected them to work as hard as he did, and when they failed to do so, he made his displeasure known, then and later. "Don't fuck with my hustle!" he once growled at an imprudent sideman who'd had too much to drink before a show.

It wasn't often, though, that Armstrong had occasion to rake a colleague over the coals. Except for Hines, who never figured out how to be an effective sideman, the members of the All Stars knew what their leader wanted and gave it to him, and he reveled in the results:

Did you ever hear that story about that rabbit in the briar patch? And they caught him and some shit what he was doing wrong. They said, "We'll fix you — we're going to throw you in the briar patch." And the rabbit, "Oh, mister, please, please don't throw me in there." Yes! They threw him in there and he said, "You can all kiss my ass. That's where I wanted to be all the time!" Then he cut out, ya know. Well, that's the way it is. Forming a small band from the big band, hell, that's just like a rabbit in the briar patch for me because that's where I started. Ya dig?

Now that he had found a winning formula, it was understandable that he chose not to vary it. It is, however, less easy to understand why a man who throughout his life had been receptive to an exceptionally wide variety of music should have turned his back on bebop. Not long after the All Stars took their first bow at Billy Berg's, Armstrong told a columnist for *Metronome* that bop "doesn't come from the heart the way real music should. . . . You won't find many of them cats who can blow a straight lead. They never learned right. It's all just flash." A month later he doubled down in a *Down Beat* story provocatively titled "Bop Will Kill Business Unless It Kills Itself First," declaring that he preferred the music of Buddy Bolden, Bunk Johnson, and Joe Oliver to "that out-of-the-world music, that pipe-dream music, that whole modern malice. . . . So you get all them weird chords which don't mean nothing, and first people get curious about it just because it's new, but soon they get tired of it because it's really no good and you got no melody to remember and no beat to dance to."

Armstrong was not alone in disliking bop. Two years earlier a reviewer for *Down Beat* had dismissed Charlie Parker's "Now's the Time" with similar incomprehension: "This is the sort of stuff that has thrown innumerable impressionable young musicians out of stride, that has harmed many of them irreparably." And on occasion Armstrong, who always acknowledged that Dizzy Gillespie was a first-class musician, admitted that the fault might be his: "Very personally, I don't care for most bop, except maybe for Parker, some Miles Davis, some Thelonious Monk. But some people who I'd swear to be of sound mind are very high on it, and I suspect that if I understand it, which I largely don't, I'd be in a better position to make up my mind about bop." But such statements were few and far between. More often he seemed to go out of his way to look for chances to attack the boppers, even going so far as to use Guy Lombardo, of all people, as a stick with which to beat them: "Give this son of a gun *eight* stars! Lombardo! These people are keeping music alive — helping to fight them damn beboppers. . . . They're my inspirators!"

What was it about bebop that irked him? Up to a point the answer was obvious enough. Except for Gillespie, whose jokey demeanor on the bandstand was more like Armstrong's than either man cared to admit, the boppers disdained the showmanship that was his trademark. More than a few of them were heroin addicts (that was what he had had in mind when he spoke of their "pipe-dream music") whose habits made it impossible for them to conduct themselves with the professionalism that was his byword. Above all, though, their music was uncompromising in a way that he saw as threatening to the public's acceptance of jazz. Instead of "overdoing the jazz situation" by playing "stiff arrangements that the ear can't understand," Armstrong chose to offer his listeners music that they could enjoy without exertion. Joe Oliver had taught him to "play the lead so people can know what you're doing," a lesson that he thought the boppers needed to learn. "I guess musicians would dig this more than the untrained ear," he said of Woody Herman's 1949 big-band recording of "Keeper of the Flame," whose boppish ensemble passages strike postmodern ears as scarcely less traditional-sounding than Armstrong's own recorded solos of the twenties. Yet the creator of such revolutionary utterances as "West End Blues" and "Weather Bird" claimed to find them shocking: "This thing looks like everybody is trying to kill themselves. That kind of music is liable to start a fight!"

He was, in short, a middlebrow, albeit one of genius, and in due course he received the ultimate middlebrow accolade: on February 21, 1949, he became the first jazz musician to appear on the cover of *Time*. The same magazine that once had called him "a black rascal raised in a waifs' home . . . with a jail sentence in his past for using drugs" now lauded his artistry: "Louis says: 'Jazz and I grew up side by side when we were poor.' The wonder is that both jazz and Louis emerged from streets of brutal poverty and professional vice — jazz to become an exciting art, Louis to be hailed almost without dissent as its greatest creator-practitioner."

This time no mention was made of his 1930 marijuana arrest, which might have made him appear disreputable to the magazine's middle-class readers. Instead the story ran through all the soon-to-be-familiar anecdotes — Storyville, the Waif's Home, Fate Marable, Joe Oliver, the Hot Five, "Heebie Jeebies," stardom, the triumphant return to small-band jazz — helping to set in stone what was to become the Armstrong legend. It was the *Time* cover story that made his teasing "definition" of jazz part of the music's folklore: "Man, when you got to ask what is it, you'll never get to know." It quoted Gene Krupa: "No band musician today on any instrument, jazz, sweet, or bebop, can get through 32 bars without musically admitting his debt to Armstrong. Louis did it all, and he did it first." It also pointed out that the leader of the All Stars was no longer part of the avant-garde: "Louis gives the back of his hand to the latest variety of jazz, bebop (or bop). The boppers, who know the way he feels, tend to speak of him in the past tense." Elsewhere the piece was at once accurate and condescending:

> A simple man whose main life is his music, he has occasional fits of sullenness and sometimes falls into a temperamental rage, but usually he is gay, good-humored and gabby about small things. . . . Money doesn't worry Louis any more than his taste in music. He leaves all that to his manager and friend — a man Louis, with a kind of plantation politeness, still calls "Mister" Glaser.

A *Time* cover carried far more weight in the forties than it does today, when most Americans get their news from TV or the Internet. Only seven other popular musicians had been so honored in the first quarter century of the magazine's existence, and one of them, Bing

Crosby, invited Armstrong onto *Philco Radio Time*, his new network radio show, to celebrate. Crosby was as famous in 1949 as when the two men had costarred thirteen years earlier in *Pennies from Heaven*, and the warmth of his introduction of Armstrong, like the *Time* cover itself, showed that the trumpeter had become a mass-culture celebrity in his own right: "I got a big charge out of seeing a bright satchel-mouthed face beaming at the world from the cover of *Time* magazine — the face of one of my best friends. . . . Tonight I'm just poppin' with pride to give a friendly five to the most sensational horn of them all, Louis 'Satchmo' Armstrong!"

The same broad-gauge appeal that landed Armstrong on the cover of *Time* also attracted the attention of a brand-new medium. Radio was still big in 1949, but television was growing bigger by the week, and Armstrong had already gotten in on the ground floor. On November 21, 1948, two months after Milton Berle was installed as the host of *Texaco Star Theater* and became the first star of network television, the All Stars made their TV debut on *Toast of the Town*, a Sunday-night variety show hosted by Ed Sullivan, a Broadway columnist turned tastemaker for the electronic age. The program, renamed *The Ed Sullivan Show* in 1955, ran without a break until a month before Armstrong's death, and throughout much of that time he would be a frequent guest, sharing the stage with everyone from Van Cliburn to the Rolling Stones. Nor was Sullivan his only broadcast outlet. Armstrong turned up at one time or another on virtually every variety show that aired on network TV in his lifetime, and it was these appearances that did more than anything else to establish him as an indelible presence in postwar American pop culture. Unlike his movies, television presented him as a star, not a stooge, usually playing and singing in front of an audience, a setting in which he was completely at home. Not a few of his TV appearances, to be sure, were pro forma, but even when the All Stars were dishing up yet another version of "When the Saints Go Marching In," Armstrong came across so clearly and compellingly that the music mattered less than the man who was making it. In movies he played a part; on TV he played himself.

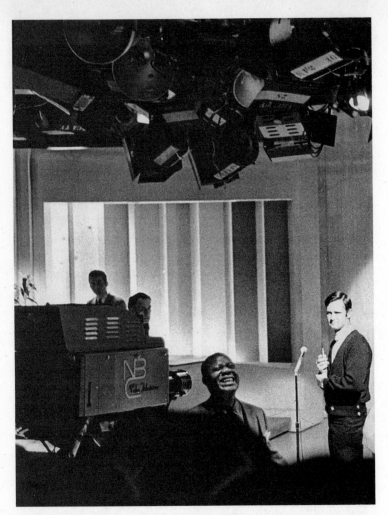

A previously unpublished photograph of Armstrong rehearsing for a 1960 appearance on *The Bell Telephone Hour*. He was one of the first jazz musicians to perform on network television, and his guest spots on such popular programs as *The Ed Sullivan Show* were in large part responsible for his emergence as an icon of postwar pop culture.

He did the same thing in the recording studio, though most of the records he was cutting for Decca showed off a different side of his artistic personality than did his live performances. Milt Gabler, Armstrong's producer at Decca, was himself something of a split personality. Commodore Records, the independent jazz label he had launched in 1938, specialized in Chicago-style jazz, a music in which he was the most devout of believers. But Gabler also had a day job: he had gone to work for Decca's artists-and-repertoire department in 1941, and in that capacity he stuck to the middle of the road, turning out such chart-topping hits as the Andrews Sisters' "Rum and Coca-Cola" and the Weavers' "Goodnight Irene." Though Gabler knew as well as Bing Crosby that Armstrong was a giant of jazz, his job was to sell records, and like Jack Kapp before him, he knew how to do it. Most of the Armstrong singles that Gabler produced for Decca were pop ballads and cover versions of hit songs previously recorded by other artists: "That Lucky Old Sun" in 1949, "La Vie en Rose" in 1950, "Because of You" and "A Kiss to Build a Dream On" in 1951, "Your Cheatin' Heart" in 1953. "We'd use Louis to cover the hits," Gabler explained, "because he'd do it in his own way. . . . [A]s soon as Louis would make a pop tune, his record would go on all the [jukeboxes] immediately. And get air play." Gabler picked three-quarters of the songs that Armstrong recorded for Decca, and Armstrong himself chose the rest. It was the trumpeter, for instance, who brought in "Blueberry Hill," a Gene Autry song based on an Appalachian folk ballad called "The Little Mohee" (the tune is better known as "On Top of Old Smoky") that was to become one of his most requested numbers after he recorded it for Decca in 1949.

These pop sides are not to be sneered at—not all of them, anyway. "Your Cheatin' Heart," for instance, becomes a thoroughly good-humored romp whose rocking two-beat accompaniment would have made perfect sense to Hank Williams, while Armstrong's glowing tone turns his medley of "Tenderly" and "You'll Never Walk Alone," recorded in 1954, into a comforting near-aria. "Blueberry Hill" and "A Kiss to Build a Dream On" are unassumingly friendly ballads sung with a charm that only a critic could resist. And on one memorable occasion Gabler teamed Armstrong with Louis Jordan's Tympany Five for a hard-swinging duet version of "You Rascal You" in which he ad-libs with colossal gusto, then tosses off three trumpet choruses full of the old-time fireworks.* Yet for all their virtues, most of Armstrong's Decca singles were far removed in tone from the jazz he was playing in public every night, if only because on most of them he is accompanied not by his own band but by faceless studio orchestras. The All Stars made no studio recordings between the fall of 1947 and the spring of 1950, and only a handful of isolated sides for Decca from then to the end of 1956. The Symphony Hall concert didn't make it onto LP until 1951, and the Teagarden-Bigard-Catlett-Hines version of the All Stars was never recorded commercially.

Only once did Gabler record the All Stars in a representative sample of their live repertoire. In April of 1950 Armstrong and his sidemen taped studio versions of ten numbers from their stage show, the best remembered of which is "New Orleans Function," the medley of "Flee as a Bird" and "Oh, Didn't He Ramble" in which the members of the band re-create an old-time jazz funeral. Armstrong supplies the narration: "And now, folks, we gonna take you down to New Or-*leans*, Loosiana. Tell you the story about 'Didn't He Ramble.' 'Course you know there was a funeral march in front of 'Didn't He Ramble,' where they take the body to the cemetery and they lower ol' Brother Gate in the ground. And, uh . . . dig it!" Even more affecting is "That's for Me," written by Richard Rodgers and Oscar Hammerstein for *State Fair*, their 1945 film musical. Armstrong recorded the ballad, which he sings with unselfconscious sweetness, in tribute to his "Madame Lucille":

> Can't call her "Mademoiselle" now . . . I changed that when we was playing at the Cotton Club in New York, when she was "Mademoiselle" dancing in that chorus, and I'm blowing that trumpet right at them buns! I mean, you know, she was in the front line there. That was it. Every time I look at Lucille danc-

---

*Armstrong's solo is all the more impressive considering that his lip was in bad shape that day. "Louis came in town and his lip had busted on him — had busted all the way down . . . Finally he says, 'Let's go,' and we went and played it," Jordan recalled. "He even played those high Cs and things with his lip busted."

ing, she had that little step where they'd raise their hand and hit about three steps in front and everything, that tune that I loved so well dawned on me.

The rest of the session is full of similar gems, and one wonders why Gabler never repeated the experiment. It wasn't as though Armstrong the jazzman lacked an audience, or that his fans were unwilling to buy records that featured him in a small-group setting. The following year George Avakian transferred the Armstrong anthologies originally released on 78s by Columbia to the new long-playing format in an expanded four-disc version called *The Louis Armstrong Story* that remained in print for years. But Decca was uninterested in following suit, perhaps because Joe Glaser had different ideas about what Armstrong should be doing in the studio. "He used to say, 'Give him a Top Ten hit!'" Milt Gabler remembered. "That's what he wanted." So "New Orleans Function" and "That's for Me" gave way to "C'est Si Bon" and "Cold Cold Heart," and Glaser got what he wanted: if none of Armstrong's Decca singles cracked the Top Ten, they still sold more than well enough to keep the pot boiling. As for Armstrong, he was as happy to sing pop tunes in front of big studio bands as he was to play the blues with Jack Teagarden. "I don't know if they told Louis that they were gonna use that large a band, but when Pops walked in, and he saw that great big orchestra with a choir and everything, his eyes flew out of his head!" recalled Johnny Blowers, who played drums on the "Blueberry Hill" session. "He said, 'Looka there, man! There's a symphony!'"

By then Sid Catlett had been replaced by Cozy Cole, a much-admired alumnus of Cab Calloway's big band. Cole joined the group cold, with no rehearsal. After a couple of nervous nights on the bandstand, the drummer asked Barney Bigard when Armstrong would finally get around to walking him through the band's book. "Man, don't pay Louie any mind, because Louie ain't going to tell you nothing," Bigard replied. Cole went to his new boss and asked him what to do. "Cozy, man, we don't have time to just say a lot of things up there, just cock your ear and straight ahead," Armstrong said. While Cole was no Catlett, he knew how to hold his own and was soon swept up into the routine, acquitting himself more than adequately on the "New Orleans Function" sessions and for the rest of his four years with the All Stars, though Armstrong, who liked his playing, would later admit to a reporter that he wasn't "a real New Orleans drummer."

Cole's baptism of fire came in the fall of 1949 with a five-week European tour that took the All Stars to Basel, Bordeaux, Brussels, Copenhagen, Geneva, Helsinki, Lyon, Marseille, Milan, Naples, Paris, Rome, Rotterdam, and Stockholm, where forty thousand fans met them at the airport. It was on this trip that Louis and Lucille were invited to a private audience with Pope Pius XII. Ernie Anderson claimed that Armstrong had mixed feelings about the invitation: "He explained that when he had married Lucille in St. Louis, [a] black Catholic priest had refused to perform the ceremony in the church because Louis had been divorced. . . . 'I'll never forget that,' Louis said gloomily." But Lucille persuaded him to change his mind, and what followed became one of the highlights of his anecdotal repertoire: "The pope was such a fine little old fellow, you know, oh, he welcomes you so nice. . . . So the pope say, 'Have you any children?' And I say, 'No, Daddy, but we're workin' on it!'"

Three months after recording "New Orleans Function," Armstrong celebrated what he believed to be his fiftieth birthday. The *New York Times* had already published a tribute by Howard Taubman, the paper's chief classical music critic: "He approaches his work with thought and pride. . . . No matter how much traveling he has done, no matter how little sleep he has had, he sees to it that he has two hours to bathe, dress, eat and get ready for an engagement. On top of that, he takes pains to arrive at a hall or theatre two hours before starting time."

Taubman didn't know the half of it. Armstrong had settled into the elaborate self-protective ritual of a middle-aged man who thinks he knows what's good for him. His pre-show routine invariably omitted dinner. Instead he holed up in his dressing room, dosing himself with the home remedies by which he swore:

> I take a little swig of glycerine and honey every so often to wash out the pipes. And that gas is the way most of the boys have passed out. They call it heart attack, but it ain't nothing but gas. I get a little pain in the stomach — run right to that Maalox. Maybe the only reason I still got my lip is a salve I keep with me — made by a trombone player in Germany. It draws the tiredness out, keeps my lips strong.

When the show was over, he retreated again to his dressing room, this time to greet his friends and fans. "He didn't care who or how many came either," Milt Hinton said. "He'd just sit there in his undershirt with a handkerchief tied around his head, talking and fooling with his horn for hours." The word had long since gotten around that he was a soft touch, so there was always somebody backstage looking for a handout. As Barney Bigard told it, "These musicians, old friends from New Orleans, even bums, would come to him and say, 'Oh, Louis, I don't have nothing to eat with in the morning,' and he would peel off some dollars. He would tell me sometimes, 'Pops, I know they are just taking me. But what can I do? . . . Let 'em go. Poor bastards. They think they're fooling me. But it's all right.'" Afterward he sometimes went out for a late supper. One such meal, according to *Time*, consisted of "ham & eggs, with potatoes, hot biscuits, hominy grits and coffee on the side. When complimented on his appetite, Satchmo replies: 'Man, that's just a synopsis.'" Or he might visit a friend's home, though even then he was careful to conserve his energy. "If he came to your house, you had a party for him, Louie found a chair and he wouldn't move from that chair until it's time to leave," Lucille said. He could be cajoled into singing, but he never played his horn: "If someone pushed into the end of the trumpet, that could mess your lip up good."

More often he went back to his hotel room, where he ordered a room-service dinner or sent out for Chinese food, his favorite cuisine

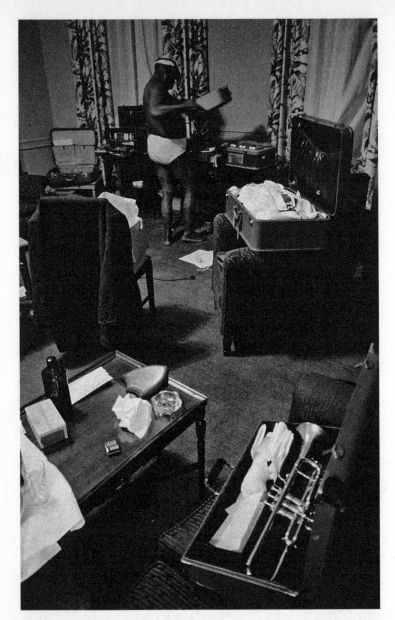

On the road in 1958. Armstrong did what he could to brighten the hotel rooms in which he spent the greater part of his adult life, but they were rarely more than faceless, functional quarters in which he rested from the exhausting workload that often left him "too tired to raise an eyelash."

after red beans and rice. Sometimes he called Joe Glaser to fill him in on the day's events. Then he unwound by smoking a joint, catching up on his correspondence, and listening to music on the two reel-to-reel tape recorders that he carried with him wherever he went. Armstrong was one of the first Americans to purchase commercially manufactured tape recorders (Bing Crosby was another) when they became available after World War II. In the beginning he used them to document his live performances and refine his stage act, but before long he transferred his record collection to tape so that he could listen to music on the road, and he also started taping after-hours conversations with his friends and family, a practice that continued until he died, by which time he had accumulated 650 reels of tape. Most of them are full of music: "I have all my records on tape, interviews, and every classical number that you can think of. . . . And I index them — why, that's my hobby." His collection was an eclectic mishmash that comprises, among other things, Walter Gieseking playing Debussy, Helen Traubel singing the "Liebestod," Debussy's *Prélude à l'après-midi d'un faune* and Shostakovich's First Symphony, the original-cast albums of *The King and I* and *South Pacific*, recordings of *Julius Caesar* and *Don Juan in Hell*, and jazz and pop in profusion: Bix Beiderbecke, Bunny Berigan, Bing Crosby, Fats Waller, Bert Williams, and a surprising amount of modern jazz, including albums by Stan Kenton, the Modern Jazz Quartet, Thelonious Monk, Gerry Mulligan, and George Shearing. A chronic insomniac, Armstrong listened to music not only for pleasure but also to lull himself to sleep. According to Milt Hinton, "One of his two valets would load [the recorders] and, as soon as Pops got into bed, the first one would be turned on. The music was always the same — his own or Guy Lombardo's — and within a couple of minutes he'd usually be snoring." He liked his lullabies loud, so much so that his sidemen learned to request rooms on other floors of the hotels where the All Stars stayed.

Along with the music he loved, Armstrong's tapes preserve the flotsam and jetsam of a life lived on the road, a farrago of nightclub gigs, TV appearances, radio interviews with long-forgotten disc jockeys, and — best of all — hours and hours of casual chat. Armstrong taped himself telling jokes, getting high with friends, reminiscing about days gone by, reading the Gettysburg Address, playing along with his old records, dining with his wife in Corona, and fighting with her in hotel rooms. On one reel we can hear him trying to lure Madame Lucille into bed at five A.M. for a little hanky-panky. When she declines without thanks, he plays his trump card: "It's up to you to keep the horn percolating. That's your happiness and mine. . . . You know the horn comes first. Then you and Joe Glaser." A little later she notices that the recorder is running and commands him to "turn your tape off. In fact, erase off some of that shit." He refuses, explaining to her that the tape is for "posterity," little knowing that it would eventually make its way into an archive, there to be played by scholars yet unborn.

Lucille's is not the only female voice heard on Armstrong's tapes. When she left the road and went back to Corona, he sought comfort in the arms of other women, including one whom he described in a 1955 letter to Glaser as "my Sweetheart + secretary . . . I gave her a real beautiful 'Fleetwood Cadillac' for a Christmas Present." In the same letter he informed Glaser that he had impregnated yet another woman, referred to in the letter as "Sweets," and that he wanted to send her one hundred dollars a week in child support. He passed on Black Benny's advice to "always have another woman for a Sweetheart," adding that the news that he had fathered a child had taken Lucille down a peg: "Sweets having that baby for me, gave Lucille one of the best *ass* whippings in her life." It wasn't that he loved her less, but she had been putting on "'*Aires*'" and needed to be taught a lesson, and Sweets was at hand: "Some how, it *dawned on us* that we both hadn't had Any *Ass* in ages. With Lucille riding around in her big and beautiful Cadillac, and would only travel if persuaded by you, period. . . . I just *Kept On* laying those hot Kisses up on her fine 'Chops.' When two people are in a room by themselves, Kissing will lead to fucking every time." But he wasn't in love with Sweets: "You know deep down in your heart, that I love my wife Lucille + She love's Me. Or else we wouldn't been together this long. Especially doing the Crazy things that I usually do for *Kicks*."

Armstrong wrote few letters more revealing than this one, though it omits the rest of the story of Sweets, which Barney Bigard confided to an oral-history interviewer:

> Oh, he was walking around like a peacock. . . . He said, "Lucille, how'd you feel if you adopt my kid?" She said, "What kid?" He said, "My kid. I got a baby by Sweetie." She said, "Who told you you got a baby by Sweetie? You better not bring no baby around here." She says, "You couldn't make a baby with a pencil. Now you're talking about your kid. She done fool you and she's got a boyfriend. He must have did it and he's telling her to tell you that you're the father." She said, "You sure are stupid."

Whatever else he had done that day, there was always one last chore before bedtime: "I wouldn't dare to go to bed without taking my physic, Swiss Kriss. Got to get all those impurities out every day." Like many other stocky men, Armstrong was a food faddist who longed for a surefire way to lose weight that didn't require him to cut back on red beans and rice. Lucille introduced him to Swiss Kriss, an herbal laxative invented by the nutritionist-huckster Gayelord Hauser. A potpourri of anise, calendula, caraway, hibiscus flowers, lemon verbena, parsley, senna, and dandelion, papaya, peach-tree, and peppermint leaves, it reminded Armstrong of the greens that his mother had "picked down by the tracks in New Orleans" and boiled down into a homemade laxative that she gave her children to counteract the effects of the greasy food they ate. He tried it, liked it, stuck by it, and encouraged his friends and colleagues to do the same. Most declined, especially after they saw how potent it was. Joe Evans told in his autobiography of a night on the road when Armstrong miscalculated the timing of his daily dose: "When it was time to come back onstage, Louis wasn't in place. He yelled to Joe Garland from the toilet, 'Hey, Joe, play another number. I'm talking with Swiss Kriss right now. I'm just sittin' on the rocking chair. I'll be out there later, somebody announce the act.'" The mishap did nothing to diminish his belief in its curative powers, which was so strong that he printed up cards with a snapshot of

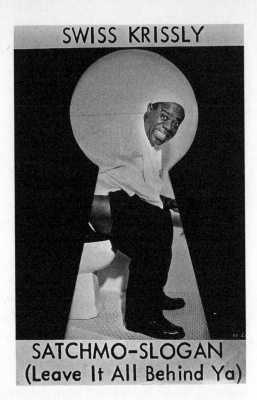

SWISS KRISSLY

"I'm talking with Swiss Kriss": Armstrong was a devoted user of the potent herbal laxative that he took each night before retiring. He believed so strongly in its health-giving powers that he had this card printed up to send to his friends.

SATCHMO-SLOGAN
(Leave It All Behind Ya)

himself sitting on a toilet. The caption was "SATCHMO-SLOGAN (Leave It All Behind Ya)."

Armstrong's homegrown routine puzzled his friends and horrified his doctors, but it kept him going strong. "I'd say Louie played about 80 percent of the time, really played," said Cozy Cole. "Twenty percent of the time, sometimes, you know, his chops would be down or it's all according to how long the jump was. . . . Some nights, man, it used to be incredible the way that Louie would play up there." Once in a while the mask would slip and he would admit his weariness: "All hotels are alike — bed, bureau, two pillows. Maybe after a show, you try to make one or two joints, have a ball, get stoned, and that's it for the night. That's my life." But Bing Crosby's son Gary, who shared a bill with Armstrong in 1955, said that he "put out the same amount of energy and enthusiasm whether two people were sitting there or the joint was packed to the rafters."

From time to time he went home to Corona for a rest. "Sometimes when he had a few days off — and Lucille would accept this — he'd go up to Harlem for two or three days," Jack Bradley recalled. "Shoot crap in the gutter with the boys, probably see all his old girlfriends." More often, though, he stuck close to the house, for his face (and voice) had become so familiar that he could no longer walk the streets of New York without being mobbed: "Sometimes them big crowds can spook you. Get to pressing you and grabbing your clothes. You get a funny feeling they might trample on you." Instead of going out, he lapped up Lucille's cooking and made love to her in their giant bed, visited the dentist to keep his chops in order, fussed with his tape recorders, and wrote stacks of letters: "Don't like to keep my friends waiting too long for answers. Being busier than a cat on a tin roof ain't no excuse." Corona suited him, and when Lucille suggested that they move to a bigger place on Long Island, he put his foot down. "I absolutely forbid it," he said. "I've just gotten to know my neighbors here. I don't want to move." The neighborhood, one of the few outside Harlem where black New Yorkers could buy homes in the forties and fifties, had become an enclave for entertainers — Cannonball Adderley, Harry Belafonte, Ella Fitzgerald, Dizzy Gillespie, Billie Holiday, Willie Mays, Sidney Poitier, and Clark Terry all lived there at one time or another — and on occasion Armstrong would hold court. But his real home, he knew, was on the road, and as much as he loved Lucille, he was always relieved to return to his natural element, where the music never stopped playing and the fans never stopped clapping:

I can make it in New York without trouble. But I don't mind traveling and that's where the audiences are — in the towns and cities — and that's what I want, the audience. I want to hear that applause. . . . I figure why should I go out on a vacation, some woods, some place there with a whole lot of people don't even speak my language? I mean, if I go out there they gonna call on me to play now, so I just play every night and stay in shape and make a little loot to boot, and I'm happier.

And so his middle years passed by, a nonstop parade of nightclub gigs and concerts, recording sessions, forgettable movies, guest shots on TV, and indistinguishable hotel rooms. It was, as he said, a rough life, but he was well paid for it, especially for the movies. Certainly there was no other reason why he should have made them, since none of them, whether big- or small-budget, was any good. The silliest of the lot was Raoul Walsh's *Glory Alley*, a B-minus Bourbon Street *film noir* about a neurotic boxer in which Armstrong, playing opposite Ralph Meeker and Leslie Caron, is relegated to the minor supporting role of a trainer-manservant who plays trumpet on the side for no apparent reason. The only thing the movie shows is that he could read lines, and one comes away from it suspecting that Armstrong, like Frank Sinatra, could have had a second career as an actor had he been willing — and white.

All that changed from year to year were the faces on the bandstand. In 1951 Earl Hines and Jack Teagarden both gave notice, Teagarden to start a group of his own and Hines because he was unsatisfied with the publicity he was getting as a member of the All Stars. "I had had a contract with 75 per cent publicity and a good salary," the pianist told Stanley Dance, "but [Glaser] wanted to list me merely as a sideman. . . . [T]hat was my reason for leaving." Armstrong was unimpressed: "Earl Hines and his big ideas. Well, we can get along without Mr. Earl Hines. What really bothers me, Pops, is losing Jack. That Teagarden, man, he's like my brother." In due course Glaser worked his usual magic, bringing Billy Kyle and Trummy Young aboard as replacements. Kyle was a fine soloist whose crisp, clean playing had come to the attention of nightclub audiences during his prewar tenure as the pianist of John Kirby's chamber-jazz sextet, and Young, a veteran of the big bands of Hines and Jimmie Lunceford, was one of the most admired trombonists of the Swing Era. Both men stayed with the All Stars for a decade, and their presence gave the group a continuity that helped to make up for its loss of star power. The band's performances became more consistent in quality, and in Young Armstrong found a friend who over time became as close to him as Teagarden and Catlett had been.

At one point Glaser offered the piano chair to Mary Lou Williams, but she turned it down when he warned her that she would not be able to play in the bop-influenced style that she had embraced after World War II: "I am sure you know the group plays a certain type of music and it would be necessary for you to conform, and if you are willing to do this let me hear from you immediately." She wasn't, and Young also bridled for a time at the band's conservatism: "We had a big repertoire, but [Armstrong] just stuck with things he felt had won over audiences for him." But the longer he played with the All Stars, the more he came to appreciate Armstrong's virtues, not only as a musician but also as a showman. "When I got with Louis, I found out I knew nothing about the stage," he said. "He was a master of that stage. You had a hard time following Louis on that stage. I don't care who you were."

↦

Like most stars, Armstrong had his temperamental moments, but few of them made it into print, his angry response to Hines's resignation being a rare exception to the rule. It was only in private that any of his sidemen would speak of his short fuse: "He can raise hell with you. Now in two seconds he's forgotten all about it and even what it was all about." So said Barney Bigard—but not until after he had quit the All Stars. Once in a while, though, a journalist would mention Armstrong's darker side. Upon meeting him for the first time in Nice in 1948, Humphrey Lyttelton was struck by "his implacable, ruthless hostility toward anyone who he feels has done him wrong." He also noted "the ferocity with which he directed the band. If Sid Catlett's drums started to intrude too heavily upon a solo, Louis would turn and hiss at him like a snake. And more than once Earl Hines's exuberance was curbed by a sharp, 'Cut it, Boy!'"

Benny Goodman, himself no slouch in the temperament department, saw Armstrong at his most ruthless when the two men worked together in 1953. The clarinetist had reassembled most of the members of his original big band for a reunion tour, then hired the All Stars as his opening act, offering Glaser 50 percent of the gross. John Hammond, who was Goodman's brother-in-law, served as tour manager, and he recounted in his autobiography what happened when Armstrong and his sidemen met with Goodman to rehearse their joint appearance in the finale of the show:

> Louis was, of course, a gregarious man, so everybody greeted him and there was bedlam for some twenty minutes. Benny stood it as long as he could, then asked Louis if he would mind sending his entourage out so the rehearsal could continue. Louis took offense. He considered himself a co-star in the show, although actually Goodman was the boss. After a brief conversation with Benny, Louis left. The next day, when he was supposed to show up for another rehearsal, he didn't appear.

That was Hammond's version, and he was a biased witness, so it is worth comparing his account of the rehearsal with that of Steve Jordan, Goodman's guitarist. According to Jordan, Goodman kept Armstrong and the All Stars "waiting around for two or two and a half hours" while he ran through his own numbers. Finally Armstrong asked him to "go through this thing, so we can get back to our hotels and get some sleep," but the clarinetist ignored him and kept on rehearsing. "Louis's feelings were so hurt he actually started to cry," Jordan said. "Georgie Auld went over and patted him on the back, and Louis said, 'That son of a bitch! When he was a little boy in short pants, I used to let him sit in with my band to learn how to play, and now he lets me hang around and wait like I'm nobody.'"

What happened next took place not in a rehearsal hall but on stage for all to see. It was the first night of the tour, a concert in New Haven. As Hammond told it, "Louis decided that his part of the show was going to be just as long as Benny's, so Louis went on and did his regular vaudeville act. He was on for an hour and twenty minutes. He was supposed to be on for forty." Goodman summoned

Armstrong from the wings at evening's end for the grand finale, but he refused to come on stage. The next stop was Newark, where Armstrong showed up late for the show, forcing Goodman to open for him. After the show the trumpeter called Joe Glaser to tell him what was going on, and Glaser promptly called up Goodman and administered a tongue-lashing: "Who the fuck do you think you are? When this man lands in Europe there are 35,000 people waiting for him. Can you do that? How dare you tell him what to do! He's a legend! He's bigger than you!"

From Newark the musicians headed for Carnegie Hall, where Goodman, normally the soul of temperance, started drinking when things got out of hand. "He sounded terrible," said Bobby Hackett, who came to the concert. "He just couldn't do anything. It was embarrassing. Jesus, if I'd been able to do so I'd have stopped the show." A few days later Goodman collapsed and was carted off to a hospital, claiming to have suffered a heart attack. The doctors were unable to find anything in particular that was wrong with him, but he canceled out of the rest of the tour anyway, and Armstrong took over as headliner. Even John Hammond acknowledged his magnanimity in victory: "Louis could well have asked for a larger percentage of the grosses, because he was [now] the star attraction. It wasn't in him to take advantage of the situation. He never said a word about money." A few weeks later Hackett ran into him at a recording session. "How's the TKO artist today?" he asked. Armstrong just smiled.

That story didn't make it into Armstrong's second book, which came out a few months after the Goodman tour, but there were plenty of other eye-opening tales in *Satchmo: My Life in New Orleans* for his fans to mull over. Unlike *Swing That Music*, *Satchmo* offered an unvarnished recounting of his young years, one in which he acknowledged the sordidness of life in black Storyville. The book was written with the same freshness of style that marked Armstrong's speech and correspondence, a quality that Tallulah Bankhead, one of his most ardent admirers, had praised two years earlier in the pages of *Ebony*. "I love to talk to him," Bankhead wrote, "because of his basic sincerity and his very original gift of expression. He uses words like he strings notes together — artistically and vividly."

While it is not known precisely when or why Armstrong started writing *Satchmo*, it is likely that he began work on the book not long after the publication in 1947 of *Horn of Plenty*, a biography of the trumpeter by his old friend Robert Goffin. In 1939 Goffin had fled to America to escape Hitler's wrath, after which he did what he could to set himself up as a jazz journalist, contributing articles to *Esquire* and writing a book called *Jazz: From the Congo to the Metropolitan*. But his English wasn't good enough for him to find much work, so in 1944 Armstrong agreed to collaborate with him on a biography, sending him cash and a manuscript memoir that Goffin used as the basis of his own book: "There may be several spots that you might want to straighten out — or change around . . . What ever you do about it is alright with me . . . I am only doing as you told me . . . To make it real — and write it just as it happened."

Goffin was surprised by how adept a writer Armstrong proved to be. "I was astonished by the high quality of the style and by the way [the manuscript] was written," he said. "Where and when was Armstrong, who never went to school, able to learn writing with such a faultless and fluent art? . . . Armstrong's text was so authentic and sincere that I did not dare to use it all for my book. My friendly pen decided to ignore many crude details." Unfortunately for Armstrong, Goffin's pen turned his down-to-earth narrative into an unreadable mélange of pseudo-southern dialect and floridly descriptive prose: "Louis's hand grasped hers and held it tight. The walk home in Lil's company was sheer delight. Already the first struggling rays of dawn were dispelling the shadows." Published in May of 1947, just before the Town Hall concert, *Horn of Plenty* was dismissed by jazz critics as sentimental blather (the headline on *Metronome*'s review was "Goffin's Horn Fluffs Aplenty"). The only review to appear in a mainstream publication, a five-paragraph notice in the *New York Times*, unconvincingly praised it as "a detailed, colorful picture of Perdido Street. The book illustrates tragically, without any preaching, but by effective exposition (which is always the best kind of sermon if the right kind of people are listening) the incredible odds stacked against all Negroes." Tommy Rockwell had already threatened to sue Goffin for suggesting that he had had a hand in Armstrong's difficulties with the mob, which must have caused other editors to steer clear of *Horn of Plenty*. It sank from sight and is now unknown save to scholars.

The failure of *Horn of Plenty* may have inspired Armstrong to do more writing himself, if only to set the record straight. Three years later *Time* announced that he was "cashing in on his gift of gab by putting it onto paper. With three Armstrong articles due for publication in the U.S., he [is] also pecking away at an autobiography." The first article, "Stomping Piano Man," was a review of *Mister Jelly Roll*, the book that Alan Lomax stitched together from Jelly Roll Morton's oral-history recordings. The editors of the *New York Times Book Review* had the good sense to run his piece the way he wrote it: "I think [*Mister Jelly Roll*] is one of the finest stories ever written on early New Orleans Jazz, and I, being a personal friend of Jelly Roll, you know that story thrills me, of his life. . . . [H]e was talkin' with some musicians one day, about his ability on the piano, and some little guy comes up and asks him — he said 'Jelly, you must be the best piano player in town.' And Jelly answered by saying, 'In town???? In the world!' Heh heh." Next Armstrong cleared up the matter of his relationship with Bunk Johnson, who had died a year earlier, in a piece published in the *Record Changer:* "Bunk didn't actually teach me anything; he didn't show me *one* thing. . . . I mean, there could be similarity of tone, but that's all."

By 1952 he was telling his correspondents that he was well advanced on a book: "I have my tape recorder right here by my right side, which I have, pretty near all of my recordings, on reels . . . So, when I listen to my records, I can get food for thoughts, since I'm writing my life's story." Not long after that the finished product was published in French and German translations, and the first English-language edition of *Satchmo: My Life in New Orleans* appeared in America two years later. Unlike *Horn of Plenty*, it was received enthusiastically. Cleveland Amory's *Times Book Review* notice summed up the critical response:

> [I]n a fall when we are going to have to get hep to all sorts of slick, obviously ghosted autobiographies, usually with an equally obvious axe to grind, it is refreshing indeed to dig at least one unpretentious, rough-hewn, honest-to-badness memoir. . . . [T]here is an extraordinary quality in this book which makes one wish that its publishers had not taken it from Louis' hands so abruptly but had induced him to continue and write his whole story.

Amory was referring to the fact that *Satchmo* ends on the night in 1922 when Armstrong made his debut with Joe Oliver's band in Chicago. His instincts were sound: the words *End of Vol. 1* appear at the end of the French edition of *Ma vie, ma Nouvelle-Orléans*, and such manuscript material as has survived suggests that he had indeed written a longer book, possibly much longer. It was rumored that Glaser made him end *Satchmo* in 1922 for fear of the consequences were he to speak candidly of his marijuana arrest and his difficulties with the Chicago mob. "Joe . . . and all them people don't like for me to talk about the olden days," he said in 1967. "All the prosty-*toots* and the fine gage and the bad-ass racketeers. But hell, man, I got to tell it like it was! I can't go around changing *history!*" Later he told Dan Morgenstern that he was writing a sequel: "I've been writing all down, and I mean *all*." But none of this latter book is known to exist, only a fragmentary continuation of *Satchmo* and a separate manuscript that may or may not be part of the sequel he had in mind. In 1974 Lucille said that "Louis gave his writings to Joe Glaser, and I never saw them again."

That *Satchmo* was heavily copyedited prior to publication can be seen by examining the surviving typescript, but the purpose of the editing was to regularize Armstrong's grammar, spelling, and punctuation, not to censor him. While the published version is less idiosyncratic in style than the letters and unpublished manuscripts that have surfaced since his death, *Satchmo* is, unlike *Swing That Music*, a fully authentic document, and there is no reason to suppose that he disapproved of any of the changes made by his editors. He had no reason to do so, for they had served him well, preserving most of the distinctive features of his prose style while making it more accessible to a general audience. The result is an excitingly written, scrupulously honest account of the early life of a great artist, one that adds immeasurably to our understanding of his life and work. No major jazz musician has produced a better book.

Becoming an autobiographer, however, did not make Armstrong self-important. A few weeks before *Satchmo* came out, he appeared on *Stage Show*, a TV series hosted by Tommy and Jimmy Dorsey on which the three musicians played "South Rampart Street Parade." "I think we should get together on the tempos there, right?" Armstrong told the brothers on camera. "I'll tell ya whatcha do now. Not too slow, not too fast—just half-fast." The studio audience roared with delight. That was Satchmo: he took his music seriously, but never himself.

11

"THE NICE TASTE WE LEAVE"

Ambassador Satch, 1954–1963

BY 1954 LOUIS ARMSTRONG had settled comfortably into middle-aged renown. He commanded top fees and worked as often as he liked, meaning most nights that he wasn't en route from one gig to the next. His latest movie role was a bandstand cameo opposite Jimmy Stewart in *The Glenn Miller Story*, a predictable biopic that did predictably well at the box office. In March he plugged the film by appearing as the mystery guest on the popular prime-time TV game show *What's My Line?* Panelist Bennett Cerf spotted his voice in a minute and a half, further proof of his fame. Yet it was growing harder to find anyone who admitted to taking an interest in the music he was now making, for jazz was undergoing yet another sea change, and Armstrong was looking old-fashioned once again. Coleman Hawkins, who prided himself on keeping up with the times, told Leonard Feather that Armstrong was "playing just like he did when he was twenty years old; he isn't going any place musically." He came in sixth among trumpeters in the 1954 *Down Beat* readers' poll, behind Chet Baker, Dizzy Gillespie, Harry James, Roy Eldridge, and Shorty Rogers. Bebop was no longer "out-of-the-world music" for hipsters but the new lingua franca of jazz in the fifties, and the trumpeter who placed ninth that year, a twenty-eight-year-old heroin addict from St. Louis with the resoundingly upper-middle-class name of Miles Dewey Davis III, would soon shoulder aside everyone else on the list, Armstrong included, to become the best-known figure in postwar jazz.

"Miles changed the tone of the trumpet for the first time after Louis — the basic tone," said Gil Evans, Davis's friend and collaborator. "Everybody up to him had come through Louis Armstrong." Not only did he play his horn differently, but he played it with an attitude that could scarcely have been further removed from Armstrong's desire to give uncomplicated pleasure to the paying customers who came to hear him. "That sonofabitch is bad for jazz," a booking agent told Nat Hentoff. "He doesn't give a damn for audiences, and he lets them know it by paying no attention to them. I mean you don't have to wave a handkerchief or show your teeth like Louis Armstrong to let the audience feel you care what they think about your music. But not him." Yet Davis's style was a pared-down, more overtly lyrical version of bop whose simplicity and directness appealed to listeners ill at ease with Charlie Parker's electric frenzy, and his fragile, shiveringly poignant abstractions of such familiar ballads as "My Funny Valentine" and "When I Fall in Love" spoke to the young people of the fifties in the same way that Armstrong's "Star Dust" and "I Gotta Right to Sing the Blues" had spoken to their parents.

The tradition-minded Davis both respected and admired his great predecessor: "I love his approach to the trumpet; he never sounds bad. He plays on the beat and you can't miss when you play on the beat — with feeling. . . . A long time ago, I was at Bop City, and he came in and told me he liked my playing. I don't know if he would even remember it, but I remember how good I felt to have him say it." But he had no wish to emulate Armstrong's platform manner, and he felt the same way about Dizzy Gillespie's bandstand comedy:

> I always hated the way they used to laugh and grin for the audiences. I know why they did it — to make money and because

they were entertainers as well as trumpet players. They had families to feed. Plus they both liked acting the clown; it's just the way Dizzy and Satch were. I don't have nothing against them doing it if they want to. But *I* didn't like it and didn't *have* to like it. I come from a different social and class background than both of them, and I'm from the Midwest, while both of them are from the South. So we look at white people a little differently. . . . I felt that I could be about just playing my horn — the only thing I wanted to do. I didn't look at myself as an entertainer like they both did.

Instead of playing to his crowds, Davis turned his back on them — and they ate it up. Their response exemplified the transformation that jazz had undergone in the half century since Little Louis Armstrong stood outside Funky Butt Hall, listening through a crack in the wall as Buddy Bolden played for a roomful of dark-skinned working-class blacks. Not only had it evolved into a middle-class music, but the men and women who made it now thought of themselves as artists, self-aware and proud. Armstrong was proud, too, but his was the unself-conscious pride of the artisan, and it stung him to the quick when Gillespie told *Time* that the difference between Armstrong's generation of jazzmen and the boppers was that "we study." He was still fuming over that crack in 1966: "These cool cats that say my music's old fashioned. They say they *study* music. Funny they got to and I didn't have to go into no rudimentals."

Yet it was understandable that Gillespie, Davis, and their contemporaries claimed for themselves the prerogatives of the artist, that critics who believed in the cultural significance of jazz responded to that claim, and that Armstrong's old-fashioned way of mixing high art with low comedy made both groups ill at ease. Even a Swing Era journalist like George T. Simon was now capable of writing with lofty disapproval about his backward-looking antics: "There is no need for a man as great as Louis to have to resort to such behavior. . . . [H]e was mugging like mad, putting on the personality, bowing, scraping and generally lowering himself as a human being in the eyes of his worshippers." It didn't help, either, that so many of the records that he was now making for Decca were so far removed in tone (if not in spirit) from the music he was playing with the All Stars. It was the old, old story: many jazz fans of the fifties believed, however mistakenly, that Louis Armstrong was too popular to be good.

At that moment George Avakian stepped into Armstrong's life with a timely proposal. Avakian, whose musical taste was as catholic as Armstrong's, was eager to record him for Columbia, of whose pop album division he was now in charge. The only stumbling block was that Joe Glaser, who had no interest in presenting Armstrong as anything other than an entertainer, was content to stick with Decca. It was Jim Conkling, the president of Columbia, who came up with the solution: Avakian's *Louis Armstrong Story* albums had been selling well, but the trumpeter, who had recorded the original OKeh 78s on which they were based for flat one-time cash payments, wasn't making a dime off them. Why not offer him a 1 percent royalty on Columbia's OKeh reissues in return for signing an exclusive contract? That was the kind of talk Glaser understood. In short order the deal was done, and on July 12, 1954, Armstrong and the All Stars began taping *Louis Armstrong Plays W. C. Handy*, the best album they ever made.

The project was Avakian's idea. "For years I had planned that one day, when possible, I would make a series of albums with Pops," he said later. "He was an artist who should have been represented in unified packages, complete with explanatory notes." The music of the "Father of the Blues" (as Handy billed himself) was a logical starting point, and Armstrong, who had been identified with "St. Louis Blues" ever since he recorded it with Bessie Smith in 1925, was agreeable. "You choose the tunes," he said. "You know me, you know what I like." Avakian picked eleven of Handy's best-known songs and sent the music to Armstrong, who worked the tunes up on the road. A few weeks later he called the producer at home. "I'm laying over in Chicago next month for a few days," he said. "Line up the studio and I'll be ready." Avakian booked three afternoon sessions in a Chicago

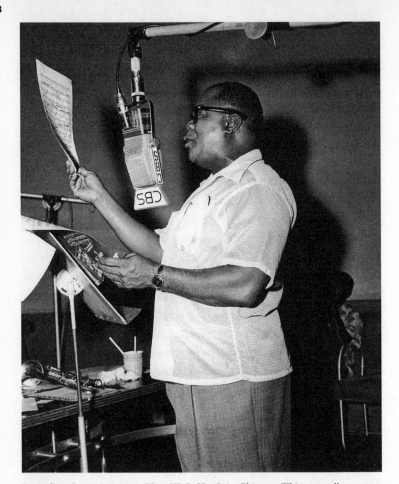

Recording *Louis Armstrong Plays W. C. Handy* in Chicago. This 1954 album, produced by George Avakian, captured the trumpeter at the peak of his middle-aged
powers. "I can't remember when I felt this good about making a record," he said
afterward.

studio. "Louie came in with no music beyond the sheet music I'd
given him and a few sketches that Billy Kyle had made," he recalled.
"'We can work out these longer performances any way you want,' he
said, 'but why don't you choose the order of the solos? I don't want
to do these things the way we'd do them in a club. It'll be fresh for
us that way.'"

That was what Avakian wanted to hear. Except for the "New Orleans Function" session, virtually all of Armstrong's studio recordings for Decca had conformed to the three-minute, three-chorus mold of his old 78s. Avakian, by contrast, proposed to lead him into the age of the long-playing record. Not only was *Louis Armstrong Plays W. C. Handy* a thematically unified, meticulously sequenced single-composer album, but most of the songs on it ran well past the three-minute mark, including an album-opening version of "St. Louis Blues" that played for nearly nine minutes. It was, in short, a concept album *avant la lettre*, recorded seven months before Frank Sinatra and Nelson Riddle "invented" the genre with *In the Wee Small Hours*. Armstrong responded enthusiastically to his producer's musical suggestions, and the brilliance of his playing reflects his excitement. Rehearsal tapes made at the sessions show that he played a dominant role in structuring and polishing the arrangements, but it was Avakian who gave to *Louis Armstrong Plays W. C. Handy* its shape and conceptual unity, and it says much about Armstrong that he was not only willing to accept the younger man's tactful guidance, but capable of recognizing and acknowledging the quality of the results. "I can't remember when I felt this good about making a record," he told Avakian after the album was edited.

The release of *Louis Armstrong Plays W. C. Handy*, coming as it did in the wake of the American publication of *Satchmo*, should by all rights have had an immediate effect on Armstrong's critical reception. Instead it went unremarked (though it sold gratifyingly well). Joe Glaser, Jack Kapp, Milt Gabler, and Ed Sullivan had done their work too efficiently: for better or worse, Armstrong was entrenched in the middlebrow camp at a time when jazz and pop were moving in opposite directions. A month after *Satchmo* came out, *Time* put the cerebral pianist Dave Brubeck on its cover, praising his "intense, quiet" quartet albums as "some of the strangest and loveliest music ever played since jazz was born." A week after Avakian started recording the Handy album in Chicago, Elvis Presley strolled into a Memphis studio and cut a rockabilly-style cover version of an old rhythm-and-blues tune called "That's All Right," the first stage of the musical rocket that he would ride all the way to superstardom. Was there a place for Armstrong between these two extremes? Or was his long run in the limelight coming at last to an end?

Gabler and Avakian each responded to his dilemma in character-istic ways. In 1955 the trumpeter wound up his Decca contract with a string of irredeemably trivial singles, including a cover version of the Platters' "Only You" and a ludicrous doo-wop arrangement of a rock-and-roll novelty called "Ko Ko Mo." In between these exer-cises in pandering, Columbia released *Satch Plays Fats*, another con-cept album in which Armstrong and the All Stars served up tightly routined, snappily played versions of nine of Fats Waller's best songs. Then, as if to prove to Gabler that virtue could be its own reward, Avakian recorded a straight-down-the-center jazz single that put the All Stars on the pop charts.

Lotte Lenya had recently opened in an off-Broadway revival of the Brecht-Weill *Threepenny Opera* that became a sleeper hit, run-ning for 2,611 performances. Avakian saw the show and came home convinced that "Mack the Knife," Marc Blitzstein's English-language version of "Moritat," had the makings of a hit — but he was unable to persuade any of Columbia's artists to play his hunch. Turk Mur-phy, a San Francisco trombonist and early-jazz revivalist who had won modest fame as a member of Lu Watters's band, suggested that the song might suit Armstrong. Murphy wrote and recorded a small-band arrangement that Avakian brought to the trumpeter, who lis-tened and laughed out loud. "Oh, I'm going to *love* doing this!" he said. "I *knew* cats like this in New Orleans. Every one of them, they'd stick a knife into you without blinking an eye! 'Mack the Knife'! Let's go!"

Murphy's arrangement, which the All Stars recorded in Septem-ber of 1955, was a spare sketch well suited to the talents of the All Stars. "Dig, man, there goes Mack the Knife!" Armstrong rasps gen-ially by way of introduction. Arvell Shaw and Barrett Deems, who had joined the group the preceding May, lay down a springy, pulsing two-beat accompaniment over which Billy Kyle strews Basie-like twinkles. A muted Armstrong plays the penny-plain melody with

Barney Bigard and Trummy Young riffing softly behind him. Then he puts down his horn and tells the tale of the bloodthirsty Macheath with a glee that has nothing whatsoever to do with the grim lyric: *Oh, the shark has pretty teeth, dear / And he shows them a-poi-ly white.* At the end he pulls out his mute, says, "*Take* it, Satch," and leads the band through a rocking-out chorus. The results were irresistible, and no one tried to resist them, least of all *Time*'s record reviewer: "Satchmo plays a lilting chorus and growls some free variations on the fine Marc Blitzstein lyrics . . . Then he hears a shouted 'Take it, Satch,' and the Armstrong trumpet takes it high." Released as fast as Avakian could slap it onto a 45, "Mack the Knife" rose to number 20 on *Billboard*'s pop chart, and though Bobby Darin's hard-swinging cover version, cut three years later, sold even better, it was Armstrong who turned "Mack the Knife" into a standard.*

The All Stars headed back to Europe after putting "Mack the Knife" in the can, this time for a Continent-wide tour jointly devised by Avakian, Glaser, Edward R. Murrow, and Fred Friendly, whose camera crew filmed Armstrong and the band on stage and off for an episode of *See It Now*, the TV documentary series hosted by Murrow and produced by Friendly, that aired in mid-December. A few weeks earlier, while the tour was still under way, the *New York Times* had run a front-page story called "United States Has Secret Sonic Weapon — Jazz" in which the house organ of the liberal establishment claimed that Armstrong's European concert tours had made him the "most effective ambassador" for the American way of life and offered a pointed suggestion: "What many thoughtful Europeans cannot understand is why the United States Government, with all the money it spends for so-called propaganda to promote democracy, does not use more of it to subsidize the continental travels of jazz bands . . . With a small Government subsidy, [Armstrong] might play the smaller intermediate towns and his tour [be] stretched to six months by train instead of six weeks by bus." The story had bureau-

---

*Armstrong's recording also inspired Ella Fitzgerald to add the song to her repertoire in a version that featured her pitch-perfect imitation of his gravelly voice.

cratic fingerprints all over it: "Somewhere in the official files of one of Washington's myriad agencies all this has been spelled out. Because nothing has been done about it, more than one observant American traveling the Continent has remarked: 'We don't know our own strength.'" Two weeks later the *Times* ran a follow-up piece announcing that the State Department had decided to sponsor foreign tours by American jazzmen, and on December 15 the White House earmarked $92,500 to send Dizzy Gillespie's band to the Middle East for the first in a long series of government-sponsored jazz tours intended to demonstrate to Third World countries that American capitalism was better than Soviet Communism.

Avakian rushed to capitalize on the free publicity by taping an album by the All Stars to which he gave the ideal title of *Ambassador Satch*. The cover showed Armstrong dressed in a cutaway, holding a dispatch case in one hand and his trumpet in the other. The broad smile on his face, he told Ernie Anderson, was one of anticipatory pleasure: "It was the same morning I had already made a date with my connection to pick up half a pound of fine mutah. So when you see that picture of Ambassador Satch you know he's got half a pound of fine jive right there in his satchel." John Foster Dulles's State Department, which may or may not have known about Armstrong's fondness for mutah, had already approved him for a government-sponsored tour, though at the moment it wasn't necessary, since he was playing to sold-out houses across Europe, including a performance in West Berlin. "A lot of them Russian cats jumped the Iron Fence to hear Satchmo, which goes to prove that music is stronger than nations," he told a *Newsweek* reporter.

Once the tour was over, the All Stars (minus Velma Middleton) flew to California to start work on their next film. Like *A Song Is Born* before it, *High Society* was a musical remake of a Hollywood classic, *The Philadelphia Story*, and it had a cast comparable in star power to that of the original, with Bing Crosby, Frank Sinatra, and Grace Kelly standing in for Cary Grant, Jimmy Stewart, and Katharine Hepburn. The new version turned C. K. Dexter-Haven, the glamorous playboy-socialite of George Cukor's 1940 film, into a wealthy music lover who sponsors the first Newport Jazz Festival, thereby supplying a pretext for Crosby and Armstrong to team up on a Cole Porter–penned tune called "Now You Has Jazz" in which Crosby introduces the members of the All Stars one by one. It was to be their first joint screen appearance since *Pennies from Heaven*, though the two men had sung together on radio many times in the past decade and had even cut a hit single for Decca, a paean to summertime laziness called "Gone Fishin'" in which "Mr. Satch and Mr. Cros" tell of how they've *gone fishin' / Instead of just a-wishin'*.

To rework a film as fine as *The Philadelphia Story* was, of course, a losing proposition, though the results could have been a good deal worse. Armstrong serves as the modern-day equivalent of a Greek chorus, poking his head into the action at odd intervals and singing a prefatory mock-calypso song in which he tells the backstory: *Brother Dexter, just trust your Satch / To stop that weddin' and kill that match*. His part is undeveloped, however, and it is interesting to learn that Charles Walters, the director, had had something more ambitious in mind for him: "The only thing I regret about my film *High Society* is that they didn't let me develop the Cupid side of the Louis Armstrong character. . . . I wanted to make more of that idea, and the character, but 'they' refused, saying it wasn't worth it." But Armstrong made the most of it — he always did — and his charisma is everywhere evident, especially in "Now You Has Jazz," in which he and Crosby swing so hard that Porter's arthritic hep-cat lingo (*Now you take some skins / Jazz begins*) sounds almost hip. By the time Armstrong leans into the camera and growls "End of story!" as the credits roll, you realize that he has stolen the picture out from under the noses of his illustrious collaborators.

Armstrong enjoyed himself on the set. "Well, we had a lot of fun, and everybody was so wonderful," he told a friend. "You wouldn't think they was acting. You'd think they was really, you know, living their parts." (Two of them were: Crosby had just concluded a torrid affair with Kelly.) Once he finished work on the film, he hit the road

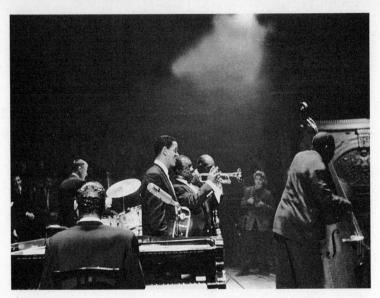

"The best of 'em all": A previously unpublished photograph by Joel Elkins of Armstrong and his band on stage at the Amsterdam Concertgebouw, 1955. Though critics of the fifties had little use for their music, Armstrong never led a better or more consistent group than this insufficiently appreciated edition of the All Stars. From left: Barrett Deems, Billy Kyle, Trummy Young, Armstrong, Edmond Hall, and Arvell Shaw.

again, flying to England on May 3 for two and a half weeks of non-stop music-hall performances in London and the provinces, his first shows there since 1933, when the British musicians' union had clamped down on foreign visitors. Then he paid his first visit to Africa, flying to Ghana for a *See It Now*–sponsored junket during which he lunched with Kwame Nkrumah, the country's controversial prime minister, and played for a mammoth crowd that made no attempt to contain its collective excitement. "I have never seen a reception like that in my life," Barrett Deems remembered. "You talk about the Beatles today—you should have seen Louie...You would have thought he was a god. People just swept him off his feet."

Upon returning to America, the All Stars played a string of what

Deems remembered as "ninety-seven straight one-nighters," then repaired to Rhode Island for the real-life Newport Jazz Festival. A week later, on July 14, came Armstrong's New York Philharmonic debut, which was to be the climactic scene of *Satchmo the Great*, the documentary that Murrow and Friendly were stitching together out of their *See It Now* segment and the additional footage they had shot in Europe and Africa. Three weeks later *High Society* was released, and the reviews were no more enthusiastic than the ones Armstrong received for the Lewisohn Stadium concert, though that didn't stop anyone from going to see it. *Time* called the film "simply not top-drawer," and Bosley Crowther's *New York Times* notice bore the headline "No 'Philadelphia Story,' This; 'High Society' Lacks Hepburn Sparkle." Armstrong's performance at Newport fared no better with the critics. "He demonstrated with finality that it takes more than rolling eyes, handkerchief on head and chops, and the same old Paramount theater act to warrant using an hour's time at an American festival of jazz," Jack Tracy wrote in *Down Beat*, complaining that he was playing "the same old tunes and fronting the same indifferent band he's been working with for too long."

The critics were right about *High Society*, but dead wrong about the All Stars. With the addition of the Louisiana-born clarinetist Edmond Hall to the front line in September of 1955, the band had entered what would come to be recognized as its peak years, though Armstrong himself knew it perfectly well at the time:

> Oh yeah, that first group of All Stars was a good one all right, but I think the group I have now is the best of 'em all. It seems to me this band gets more appreciation now than the other All Stars. Some of the other Stars got so they was prima donnas and didn't want to play with the other fellows. They wouldn't play as a team but was like a basket ball side with everybody trying to make the basket. They was great musicians, but after a while they played as if their heart ain't in what they was doin'. A fella would take a solo but no-one would pay him no attention — just gaze here, look around there. And the audience would see things like that — I don't praise that kind of work y' know. . . .

The All Stars now ain't like that and the audience appreciate the spirit in the band. As musicians they ain't any better, but a lot of people say these boys seem like they're real glad to be up there swingin' with me.

Edmond Hall's playing surely had much to do with his leader's renewed enthusiasm. "I don't listen to fanatics that try to tell me how to blow my horn. . . . If they just listen to that horn now, they get the best trumpet that I ever had in me," Armstrong said at the time that *High Society* was released. It was close to the truth: the clarinetist's edgy, cutting tone galvanized him in the same way that Sid Catlett's buoyant drumming had goaded him to outdo himself, as can be seen on a *Timex All Star Jazz Show* kinescope that preserves a televised performance of "On the Sunny Side of the Street" in which Satchmo, Hall, and Trummy Young scrub the dust off that oft-played chestnut. Blunt and succinct, it is the finest performance that Armstrong ever gave in front of a TV camera, and he gave it at a time when America's top jazz magazine had written him off as a handkerchief-headed relic.

━━◆

The paying customers knew better, and so did George Avakian. Even though the producer was busy recording *'Round About Midnight*, Miles Davis's debut album for Columbia, he had lost none of his excitement at the prospect of making more albums with the jazzman he loved best. "We had all kinds of plans, and Louie was so enthused," he said. "Louie loved Milt Gabler — he said so — but Milt was geared to the dollar, as Decca always was, and Louie made it clear to me that he appreciated getting the opportunity to do something other than cover versions of 'La Vie en Rose.'" The next item on his to-do list was a collaboration between Armstrong and Duke Ellington. Both men were up for it, and Avakian started making plans. Then Joe Glaser stepped in. Armstrong's contract with Columbia had expired, so Avakian asked Glaser for an extension in order to record an Armstrong-Ellington big-band album. Glaser didn't need to be told that "Mack the Knife" and the Handy and Waller albums had sold far better than expected, and that the release of *High Society* was bound to push Armstrong's price up still higher. So he made his move:

> Joe told me, "No more term contracts for Louie. From now on, everything that you want to do, you tell me what you want, how much you want to pay, and I'll get back to you and tell you if it's O.K." I decided that I didn't want to go into it like that — I didn't trust Joe not to take my ideas to another label for more money than Columbia was offering. The next time Louie was in town, he asked me out to the house, and I told him what had happened. He said, "George, I've got to do whatever Joe says. He saved me from the gangsters in Chicago, he saved me from the gangsters in New York. My whole life has just been so much easier and everything has worked out so well, and so I have to go along with anything Joe says." And he actually had tears in his eyes as he said it.

Instead of recording with Ellington for Columbia, Armstrong briefly took up with Norman Granz, who had parlayed the commercial success of his "Jazz at the Philharmonic" concert tours into a parallel career as the owner of an equally successful record label. Because Verve Records specialized in the audience-friendly blending of small-group swing and bebop known as "mainstream" jazz, Granz elected not to record Armstrong with the All Stars. Instead he teamed the trumpeter with Ella Fitzgerald, the biggest name in the Verve stable, for a duet album accompanied by the Oscar Peterson Trio, with Buddy Rich sitting in on drums. Fitzgerald, with whom Armstrong had previously cut a half-dozen undistinguished duet sides for Decca, was a longtime fan, and she went out of her way to make him feel at home when they recorded *Ella and Louis* together that August. "When she made the album with Louis," Granz recalled, "she insisted that he select the tunes, and she sang them all in his keys even if they were the wrong keys for her."

Armstrong must have enjoyed working with Peterson's trio, by far the most polished rhythm section with which he would ever perform, for he went on to tape five more albums for Verve during the following year, all of them variously treasurable. Granz was more a promoter than a producer, and so these albums, except for the jazz version of *Porgy and Bess* that Armstrong and Fitzgerald recorded together in 1957, lacked the strong conceptual unity that had been the hallmark of the trumpeter's collaborations with Avakian. Moreover, Granz was unable to persuade Glaser to take the making of records seriously: "I always got [Armstrong] under the worst conditions. We'd work for months to set everything up and then . . . at the last minute we'd find he'd have a concert somewhere that evening. Everything would have to be rushed." It stands to reason that Armstrong's lip sometimes sounded tired on his Verve albums, most of which emphasize his singing over his playing and many of which are further marred by the unsuitably glossy orchestral arrangements of Russ Garcia. Yet they still have a distinctive musical identity, for which Granz was primarily responsible. Not only was he the first (and only) producer to record the trumpeter in a mainstream jazz setting, but the songs he picked were very different from the ones Armstrong had been recording for the past couple of decades. Except for "Mack the Knife," "You'll Never Walk Alone," a 1950 recording of Frank Loesser's "Sit Down, You're Rockin' the Boat," and a duet version with Velma Middleton of Irving Berlin's "You're Just in Love" taped in 1951, Armstrong had not recorded any show tunes since the late thirties. Gabler was interested only in pop songs, while Avakian opted for explicitly jazz-oriented material. Granz, on the other hand, presented him in the same way that he presented Fitzgerald, singing show tunes and blue-chip standards in front of a modern rhythm section. While he had recorded many such songs in his OKeh days, the combination of his home-style singing with the urbane backing of Peterson's trio gave them a special quality all their own. Never before had Armstrong sung anything like the slower-than-slow version of "How Long Has This Been Going On?" that he recorded for Verve in 1957, tiptoeing through the fey internal rhymes of Ira Gershwin's verse in his gumbo-ya-ya New Orleans accent: *As a tot, when I trotted in little velvet panties, / I was kissed by my sisters, my cousins and my* ahn-*ties.*

Perhaps in response to the more ambitious recordings that Armstrong was making for Granz and Avakian, Milt Gabler departed from his chart-conscious ways for the trumpeter's next Decca project. The popularity of *The Glenn Miller Story* and *The Benny Goodman Story,* which had been released in February of 1956, had caused Gabler to wonder if a similar picture about Armstrong might do equally well at the box office. Since both films had been produced by Universal Pictures, which was owned by Decca, the thought occurred to him that he would do well to plan ahead for a possible soundtrack album featuring the All Stars: "We would need all the great tunes Louis had made for OKeh, and I could redo them from the early days on up and they would own their own masters of that material and have it on tape so it'd make a good transfer to film." The label had just released a four-LP retrospective boxed set of Bing Crosby's recordings narrated by the singer himself, so Gabler decided to kill two birds with one stone by producing another set devoted to Armstrong. "I chose all the tunes, and I had Bob Haggart do the arrangements for the small group stuff and Sy Oliver for the sax section things," he later explained to Dan Morgenstern. "I told them to copy [Armstrong's solos] from the original records and just jot the notes down so it would come back to Louis' mind. He wasn't asked to stick to it, but it would be like the original with variations." Then he ensured that Armstrong and the All Stars would be fresh for the recording sessions by paying the trumpeter (and Glaser) extra to book the band into Decca's New York studios as if they were playing at a club:

> I told Joe Glaser that I wanted him to book Louis in New York exclusively for the sessions . . . I wanted the All Stars off in the evening, not from 2 to 5 in the afternoon, as customary, with them having to work at night. This way I could book them from 7 to 10, when it was a natural thing, giving the guys time enough to have had dinner and get to the studio and be relaxed and not have to think about going to work later.

All that remained was to write the script. Gabler asked Armstrong to "try to recollect something about each tune, or the composers, or how he came to record it, and I wrote it all out on a yellow pad and gave it to Leonard Feather to put it together . . . just as a reminder to Louis; he could read the relevant paragraph, and then go to the mike and tell his story." Then the All Stars began recording the album that Gabler called *Satchmo: A Musical Autobiography.* The sessions proceeded smoothly, and by the end of January of 1957 Gabler had taped high-fidelity remakes of most of Armstrong's best-known recordings of the twenties and thirties, including such classics as "Dipper Mouth Blues," "Gut Bucket Blues," "Cornet Chop Suey," "Heebie Jeebies," "Knockin' a Jug," "Mahogany Hall Stomp," "Lazy River," "I Surrender, Dear," and "That's My Home." The only thing that went wrong during the sessions was that Armstrong read most of Feather's text straight off the page instead of using it as a springboard for his own impromptu reminiscences, which explains why the spoken parts of the album sound so flat.

"Folks, if you're ready to join me, I'd like to do a little reminiscin'," Armstrong said at the beginning of the first side, with Billy Kyle noodling away at "Sleepy Time Down South" in the background. "I wanna take you back to some of the places where my kind of music really began. And I'll talk a while about some of the people that made the music. But most of all, I wanna bring back the music just the way it was played in those good old days." He did nothing of the sort. The performances on *A Musical Autobiography* are free impressions of the OKeh 78s that had made him famous, played in the manner of the All Stars circa 1956. Those who expected otherwise were sorely disappointed, and the critics who knew better were mostly unwilling to accept the new performances on their own terms. John S. Wilson, who had already proclaimed his unalterable opposition to the All Stars in his *New York Times* review of Armstrong's Lewisohn Stadium concert, returned to the charge the following September: "There is an unquenchable fire about Mr. Armstrong's trumpet that from time to time bursts through these efforts to relive the past, but he can never completely escape his plodding accompaniment . . . by the rather spavined little band that [he] has been working with for the past few years." Even *Time*, which was usually in Armstrong's corner, sounded a note of skepticism: "The album . . . should give latter-day jazz fans, who know him only as the aging vaudevillian, an idea of what the shouting was about."

A more balanced appraisal came from Whitney Balliett, who launched the *New Yorker*'s first jazz column in April of 1957. Balliett had frequent occasion to write about Armstrong during his long tenure as that magazine's jazz critic, starting with his review of the 1957 Newport Jazz Festival, in which he spoke with undisguised distaste of an All Stars performance "which delivered, in a manner that was close to unintentional self-caricature, a program that has become as unalterable as the calendar." But Balliett was more receptive to traditional jazz than most critics of the day, and he was all but alone in thinking that the trumpeter's showmanship was a legitimate aspect of his art: "Armstrong's stage presence — a heady and steadily revolving mixture of thousand-watt teeth, marbling eyes, rumbling asides, infectious laughter, and barreling gait — is as endearing a spectacle as we have had on the American stage." Though he believed most of the remakes of the small-group sides included on *Satchmo* to be "inferior" to the originals, he also felt that the album also contained "some of his most durable work. . . . Armstrong plays and sings with a lift and ease that at times remind one of his greatest period."

Balliett was on the mark. *Satchmo: A Musical Autobiography*, like *High Society*, is better than its reputation, in spite of the fact that Armstrong and Gabler too often made the mistake of trying to improve on perfection. Not always — they steered clear of "West End Blues" — but the trumpeter's second try at "Hotter than That" served only to show that the middle-aged Armstrong could no longer play with the darting brilliance of his younger self. Hearing him attempt "Potato Head Blues" in 1957 is like seeing a well-preserved fifty-six-year-old ballerina dance one of the variations with which she brought down the house three decades ago. When, on the other hand, he summoned up remembrance of lyricism past, it was with a richness and depth of tone that equaled and sometimes, as in "I Can't Give You Anything but Love" and "When You're Smiling," surpassed the playing of his youth.*

That was what struck Martin Williams when he reviewed *Satchmo*. "Armstrong is astonishing," he wrote, "and astonishing because he plays what he plays with such great power, authority, sureness, firmness, and commanding presence as to be beyond style, beyond category, almost (as they say of Beethoven's last quartets) beyond music." It was true: at fifty-six he remained capable of astonishing even the most seasoned of listeners. David Halberstam made the same discovery after spending a day watching him at work. "I had gone . . . to write a twilight-of-career piece about him," Halberstam wrote. "It's perfectly true that he paces himself carefully but the essence of the trumpet is all there, still able to touch a man in almost any mood; and the voice, deep and gravelly, is still expressive, light and flirtatious or deep and sentimental." Yet there were those who still persisted in supposing that the innocent delight he took in pleasing crowds somehow compromised the truth of his art. As usual the man himself knew better. "Man, you don't pose, never!" he had told Humphrey Lyttelton in 1948. And mere days before the release of *A Musical Autobiography*, he had proved to the whole world that he didn't — not ever.

❧

When W. C. Handy first heard Armstrong at the Vendome Theater in 1926, he was struck by the fervor with which the all-black audience responded to his singing. "There was something in that voice that they appreciated, the pride of race," Handy said. Others noted the same quality. In speaking of the "insouciant challenge" of Armstrong's mid-twenties demeanor, Rex Stewart had in mind the same frank masculinity that can be seen in his early film appearances, es-

---

*Armstrong was especially pleased with his remake of "When You're Smiling." According to Dan Morgenstern, "Whenever the band bus left from Louis's house, usually the case since they'd pick him up last, the *Autobiography* version of 'When You're Smiling' would be playing — house door open, volume pretty high."

pecially the "Public Melody Number One" sequence of *Artists and Models*, in which he wields his trumpet like a machine gun — or an erect phallus. In those days he was still the "bad cat" of Stewart's admiring recollection, and it never occurred to anyone that a time might come when his exuberance would embarrass younger listeners who saw it not as showmanly but as submissive.

That time came with a vengeance when *Time* published its 1949 cover story on Armstrong. The occasion for the story was his appearance as "King of the Zulus" in that year's Mardi Gras celebrations. The all-black Zulu Social Aid and Pleasure Club, founded in 1909, crowns a carnival king who marches in the group's annual parade, dressed in a grass skirt and made up in minstrel-style blackface. As a boy Armstrong had watched the Zulus march through the streets of New Orleans and dreamed of being their king: "All of the members of the Zulus are people, for generations, — most of them — brought up right there around, Perdido *and* Liberty — Franklin Streets . . . So finally, I grew into manhood — ahem — and the life long ambition, never did cease . . . I have traveled all over the world . . . And no place that I've ever been, could remove the thought, that was in my head, — that, someday, I will be the King of the Zulus." In 1926 the Hot Five recorded a Lil Armstrong–penned vaudeville number called "The King of the Zulu's (At a Chit' Lin' Rag)," and Armstrong remade it for *Satchmo: A Musical Autobiography* in a version whose sternly proclamatory minor-key trumpet solo has long been recognized as one of the supreme musical statements of his middle age. When the Zulus tapped him to be their king in 1949, he was thrilled to the marrow. "There's a thing I've dreamed of all my life," he told *Time*, "and I'll be damned if it don't look like it's about to come true — to be King of the Zulus' Parade. After that I'll be ready to die."

Armstrong's dream was not unusual for a black man born in New Orleans at the turn of the twentieth century. Sidney Bechet, who would have liked nothing better than to receive the same honor, wrote in his autobiography that "it is the ambition of every big guy in New Orleans to be the King of the Zulus." But younger blacks now looked askance at the Zulu Social Aid and Pleasure Club, and *Time* took note of their displeasure: "Among Negro intellectuals, the Zulus and all their doings are considered offensive vestiges of the minstrel-show, Sambo-type Negro." That was not the only mention made of the extent to which black attitudes toward "easygoing, non-intellectual Louis" had changed. It was in *Time* that Dizzy Gillespie spoke dismissively of how "all [Armstrong] did was play strictly from the soul — just strictly from his heart." And it was *Time*, not Gillespie, that mentioned the "plantation politeness" with which Armstrong referred to "*Mister* Glaser." The implication was clear: Armstrong may have been an artist, but he was also an old-time accommodationist who went along to get along.

Gillespie kept on taking potshots at Armstrong. A few months later he called him a "plantation character" in a *Down Beat* interview, and in 1952 he recorded a parody called "Pops' Confessin'" that skewered the older man's vocal and instrumental mannerisms in a way that struck some listeners as less affectionate than malicious. Gillespie's target fired back at him two years later with a parody of "The Whiffenpoof Song" that made equally malicious mention of the drug use of the boppers: *All the boppers were assembled / And when they really high / They constitute a weird personnel.* But Gillespie and the other boppers were not the only "Negro intellectuals" who found Armstrong's behavior embarrassing. James Baldwin, whose novels and essays had made him one of the black community's most prominent cultural figures, was openly nasty about it in "Sonny's Blues," a short story published in *Partisan Review* in 1957. The story contains this exchange between the narrator and his younger brother, who wants to become a jazz musician: "I suggested helpfully: 'You mean — like Louis Armstrong?' His face closed as though I'd struck him. 'No. I'm not talking about none of that old-time, down home crap.'" From pride of race to down-home crap: the world's greatest trumpeter had traveled a long way since 1926.

Those who defended Armstrong often did so awkwardly. "God bless Louis Armstrong! He Toms from the heart," Billie Holiday said. Though she meant well, the allusion must have hurt, for Armstrong did not see how anyone could think of him as an Uncle Tom:

> I think that I have always done *great* things about *uplifting* my race. . . . Some folks, even some of my own people, have felt that I've been "soft" on the race issue. Some have even accused me of being an Uncle Tom, of not being "aggressive." How can they say that? I've pioneered in breaking the color line in many Southern states . . . I've taken a lot of abuse, put up with a lot of jazz, even been in some pretty dangerous spots through no fault of my own for almost forty years.

He was not the only black entertainer of the fifties whose younger colleagues criticized his onstage clowning, musically unchallenging repertoire, and willingness to play before segregated audiences. Louis Jordan, whose group was then at the height of its popularity, heard the same kind of criticism and brushed it off: "I wanted to give my whole life to making people enjoy my music. Make them laugh and smile. So I didn't stick to what you'd call jazz. I have always stuck to entertainment. . . . I made a whole lot of money in the South, and the white people helped me make more money. So, who's the fool?"

Armstrong felt much the same way. He saw his contribution to the cause of racial justice in a different light:

> I have my own ideas about racial segregation and have spent half of my life breaking down barriers through positive action and not a lot of words. . . . I don't socialize with the top dogs of society after a dance or concert. Even though I'm invited, I don't go. These same society people may go around the corner and lynch a Negro. But while they're listening to our music, they don't think about trouble. What's more, they're watching Negro and white musicians play side by side. And we bring contentment and pleasure. I always say, "Look at the nice taste we leave. It's bound to mean something."

Even when he sang "Black and Blue," he made a point of blunting its confrontational edge: "I don't want to do nothing that would ask people to look at the song and be depressed and thinking about marching and equal rights."

One reason why he soft-pedaled such matters was his awareness that he had become "a greater attraction among whites than my own people, a thing which has always disturbed me." Though he made that remark to a reporter for a black newspaper, it was more than mere racial diplomacy that made him say so: he was genuinely distressed by the fact that he seemed to be losing touch with blacks. "One time he did a gig in Texas," Jack Bradley recalled. "He told me, 'Down the street Louis Jordan was playing, and there was only a couple dozen people at my place, and his place was *turnin' away niggers!*' And that really hurt him." In fact he still had a considerable black following, especially among older listeners, but Joe Glaser's success at marketing his music to mainstream audiences inevitably meant that most of the people who now came to see him were white, and he changed his act accordingly. On stage he mentioned the color of his skin only to get laughs, wiping sweat from his brow and declaring that "My makeup's comin' off" or introducing Trummy Young as "Bing Crosby in Technicolor" when the trombonist shared a vocal chorus with him on "Now You Has Jazz." Political correctness meant nothing to him. In 1951 he made a new recording of his theme song, "Sleepy Time Down South." On the first take he sang the lyrics as written, complete with the word *darkies*. On the second take he was prompted to change it to *people*. Then he eyed Gordon Jenkins, the conductor on the date, and growled, "What do you want me to call those black sons-of-bitches this morning?" Five years later he played his 1931 recording of "Shine" on a Voice of America broadcast. "See, now, what's wrong with 'Shine'?" he said afterward. "I mean, people so narrow-minded they worryin' about the title, they forgot to listen to all that good music!"

Yet in private he spoke with open-eyed sharpness of race relations in America: "The majority of white people, two-thirds of 'em [don't like] niggers, but they always got one nigger that they just crazy about, goddamn it. Every white man in the world got one nigger at least that they just love his dirty drawers." And he needed no reminding that things were hard for his people, for fame did not always insulate him from the realities of life in a country where segregation was still permitted. Even in Hollywood he was sometimes treated less as a star than as a servant. On one of his private tapes he describes an encounter on the set of *Glory Alley:* "This ofay, he wasn't nothing but a call boy. He'll come to the stars' dressing rooms and let them know when they want them. He'll say, 'Mr. Gilbert Roland, Mr. Meeker, Miss Caron . . .' Then he'll come to me, 'Satchmo, you better come on out there . . .' I said, 'Listen, you tell MGM to shove that picture up their ass. Why are you on me with that shit? 'Cause I'm colored?'"

For the most part Armstrong suffered such slights in silence. As always, he preferred to look on the bright side. "As time went on and I made a reputation I had it put in my contracts that I wouldn't play no place I couldn't stay," he told a journalist in 1967. "I was the first Negro in the business to crack them big white hotels." But southern hotels were harder to crack, and Barrett Deems later recalled what he had had to go through in order to tour in the South in the fifties. It was scarcely different from what he had gone through in the thirties:

> The [road] manager and I were the only two white guys in the organization, and here's Louis with five or ten grand in his pocket, his wife with a twenty thousand dollar mink coat, and they both had to sleep in a gymnasium in North Carolina because they couldn't find any accommodations. That was a killer. It takes the heart out of a man. I used to ask Joe Glaser why he booked us down South. He never answered, but I knew the answer: he wanted the money, and Louie Armstrong never complained.

That was part of why the State Department wanted to send the All Stars on a tour of the Soviet Union. Not only was Armstrong the world's best-known jazzman, but government officials planning the tour felt confident that he would not complain in public about the plight of his people. They didn't know that his patience, like that of his people, was wearing thin. In the three years since the U.S. Supreme Court had ordered the desegregation of America's public schools to take place "with all deliberate speed," the civil-rights movement had started moving faster than anyone in the White House had anticipated. In 1955 Emmett Till was murdered in Mississippi for the capital crime of being black, and the white men who bragged of killing him were acquitted by an all-white jury. Four months later Rosa Parks refused to give her bus seat to a white passenger in Montgomery, Alabama, and when she was arrested, a local Baptist minister named Martin Luther King Jr. led a boycott of the city's bus system, which was officially desegregated in December of 1956. Change was in the wind.

A month after that Armstrong went on *The Ed Sullivan Show* and sang "Nobody Knows the Trouble I've Seen," his face a mask of seriousness and inward involvement. He said nothing about the Montgomery boycott. He didn't have to. His music said all that needed saying, as it would when he played for a segregated audience of blacks in Georgia. "When we hit Savannah we played 'You'll Never Walk Alone' and the whole house — all Negroes — started singing with us on their own," he recalled. "We ran through two choruses and they kept with us and later they asked for it again. Most touching damn thing I ever saw. I almost started crying right there on stage. We really hit something inside each person there." In between these two appearances the All Stars played in Knoxville. This time the audience was separate but equal: two thousand whites sat on one side of the auditorium, a thousand blacks on the other side. Even that was too much integration for the unknown man in a passing car who threw a stick of dynamite at the auditorium, then drove off into the night. It exploded while Armstrong was singing "Back o' Town Blues." "That's all right," he told the terrified audience. "It's just the phone."

Five months later the band played at the fourth Newport Jazz Festival. George Wein, who ran the festival, had been reading reviews of Armstrong's recent appearances and decided that it was time for the trumpeter to spruce up his act. He came up with the idea of a "birthday tribute" at which Armstrong would be serenaded by some of the artists with whom he had worked in the past, including Red Allen, Ella Fitzgerald, J. C. Higginbotham, Kid Ory, and Jack Teagarden. Johnny Mercer agreed to sing "Happy Birthday" and present him with a cake. Joe Glaser liked the idea so much that he agreed to travel to Newport to make sure it came off without a hitch. He and Wein further agreed that since Fitzgerald was to be on the bill, there would be no need for Velma Middleton to perform, a decision that might help to mollify the critics, none of whom cared for her singing. But neither man had reckoned with Middleton — or her boss. It was not until the day of the performance that they sprang their surprise on Armstrong. He listened in silence as the two men explained what they had in mind. "We don't need Velma since Ella will join you for the second half with the All Stars," Glaser said. Middleton, who was eavesdropping nearby, burst into tears, and Armstrong exploded. "Everybody out!" he shouted. "We do our show, period! Nobody rides on my coattails! Velma sings!" Later on Wein heard him telling her, "Who's your daddy? Haven't I been your daddy all these years? I'll take care of you." And so he did: he played his regular nightclub set that night, leaving his mystified guest stars waiting vainly in the wings.

Such scenes, as Armstrong's friends and colleagues knew, were far from uncommon. He had always been given to inexplicable explosions of anger that came and went like summer storms. As Joe Muranyi put it:

> He could be the greatest, most generous guy in the world. He loved poor people, crippled people, plain folks. Yet if he wanted to, and knew you, he could tear you to pieces verbally. He knew where to put the knife and make you cry. He had that other side. And it was a very big factor. The anger. The unreasonable, monumental rages. He'd have a temper tantrum — and the next day it'd be like nothing ever happened. But you never knew what would set him off. It was almost irrational.

Sometimes, though, his anger was wholly rational. At Newport he had been furious with Joe Glaser for meddling with his act, the sole aspect of his professional life over which he refused to cede control to his manager. And on September 17, 1957, he blew up in front of Larry Lubenow, a journalism student from the University of North Dakota who was interviewing him for the *Grand Forks Herald,* for an even more compelling reason: he was mad at the president of the United States.

Armstrong was staying at the Dakota Hotel in Grand Forks, whose bell captain tipped off Lubenow that the trumpeter was the first black who had ever been allowed to stay there. Lubenow begged his editor to let him talk to Armstrong. The editor agreed but warned the young reporter not to ask any questions about "politics." It happened, though, that the politics of race were in the news that week. In Little Rock, Arkansas, nine black children whose parents believed that *Brown v. Board of Education* meant what it said were seeking without success to enroll in the city's Central High School. Governor Orval Faubus, seeing an opportunity to enhance his political standing in Arkansas, ordered the state's National Guard to "maintain the peace and order of the community" by surrounding the school. The guardsmen were joined by a mob of white segregationists determined to keep the Little Rock Nine out of Central High. "I tried to see a friendly face somewhere in the mob — someone who maybe would help," one of the children said. "I looked into the face of an old woman and it seemed a kind face, but when I looked at her again, she spat on me." President Eisenhower met with Faubus on September 14 but so far had taken no steps to ensure that the children would be allowed to enroll in school. Instead they stayed home as the rest of the country looked on in anguish.

Three days later Lubenow snuck into Armstrong's suite, having persuaded the bell captain to let him bring the trumpeter his dinner. Lubenow immediately admitted what he had done, and the two men started chatting about music. Armstrong volunteered that Bing Crosby was his favorite musician. But when Lubenow brought up Little Rock, a pleasant conversation abruptly turned into a one-sided harangue. "It's getting almost so bad a colored man hasn't got any country," Armstrong said, adding that the president was "two-faced" and had "no guts" and that Faubus was a "no-good motherfucker." As Lubenow scribbled away frantically in his notebook, the trumpeter started singing an impromptu parody of the national anthem: *Oh, say can you motherfucking see / By the motherfucking dawn's early light.* Then he went even further, saying that he had no intention of touring the Soviet Union for the State Department. "The way they are treating my people in the South, the government can go to hell," he said, calling Secretary of State Dulles "another motherfucker." How, he asked, could a black man possibly represent the United States abroad when it was treating black people so shabbily at home? "The people over there [would] ask me what's wrong with my country. What am I supposed to say?"

Knowing that Armstrong had just handed him the story of a lifetime but that it was unprintable as it stood, Lubenow urged him to come up with a euphemism for "no-good motherfucker." The two men settled on "uneducated plowboy," and Lubenow went straight back to the *Herald* to write up the interview. But it was too late to get the story into the next day's paper, and the Associated Press's Minnesota editor refused to touch it without ironclad proof that Armstrong had really called Dwight Eisenhower gutless. Lubenow returned to the Dakota Hotel the following morning, this time accompanied by a *Herald* photographer who snapped a picture of the two men together. Lubenow showed Armstrong the typescript. "Don't take nothing out of that story," the trumpeter said approvingly. "That's just what I said, and still say." Then he scrawled "solid" on the typescript and signed it.

That was solid enough for the Associated Press, which put the story on the wires: "Trumpet player Louis Armstrong said last night he had given up plans for a Government-sponsored trip to the Soviet Union . . . Mr. Armstrong said President Eisenhower had 'no guts' and described Gov. Orval E. Faubus of Arkansas as an 'uneducated plow boy.'" The AP's Washington desk called Foggy Bottom for comment and tacked on a paragraph: "In Washington the State Department declined to comment on Mr. Armstrong's statements. Officials made no attempt, however, to hide the concern they caused.

Mr. Armstrong was regarded by the State Department as perhaps the most effective unofficial goodwill ambassador this country had. They said Soviet propagandists undoubtedly would seize on Mr. Armstrong's words." Every major newspaper in America ran the story the next day, and it was picked up by CBS and NBC on their nightly newscasts.

Frenchy Tallerie tried to smooth things over by "quoting" Armstrong as saying that Lubenow had "hounded me so much I said the hell with everyone, including the president." Armstrong wasn't having any of it. "I ain't gonna say no more," he told another reporter the next day. "I done said it. He [Tallerie] is speaking for himself. I don't have to go by what he says." Other black celebrities rushed to identify themselves with his words. Jackie Robinson lauded him for his candor, adding that President Eisenhower was "lacking in leadership." Eartha Kitt called Ike a "man without a soul. . . . How can he possibly sit and not have any emotion for what is happening right under his nose? He is not even two-faced. He has not even shown us one side of his face." And a State Department spokesman, this time speaking on the record, confirmed that the White House had approached Armstrong about touring behind the Iron Curtain: "Mr. Armstrong has made a tremendous hit wherever he has gone and we've always been pleased when he has gone abroad."

The only person of note who attacked Armstrong publicly in the weeks that followed was Sammy Davis Jr., who called him a hypocrite for speaking out against Eisenhower while playing for segregated audiences in the South: "For years Louis Armstrong has been important in the newspapers. They have always been ready to give space if he had anything to say that really was important, and he never has. Now this happens. I don't think it's honest. If it is, why didn't he say it two years ago? He doesn't need a segregated audience." Asked if Armstrong cared to comment on Davis's statement, Joe Glaser replied, "If Sammy Davis, Jr., wants to talk about Louis Armstrong and get some publicity, let him. But Louis is not interested in getting into any argument with him. Who cares about

Sammy Davis, Jr.?" Glaser was more interested in the publicity that Armstrong was reaping as a result of his outburst. "Now the people who've been calling him an Uncle Tom can see that he's a real, real man," he said.

By that time President Eisenhower had changed his mind. Though he claimed to regard racial segregation as "criminally stupid," his immediate reaction to *Brown v. Board of Education* had been to assure Earl Warren that its white opponents only wanted to make sure that "their sweet little girls are not required to sit in school alongside some big, overgrown Negroes." But he had no intention of being defied by a mere governor, and so on September 24 he ordered that the Little Rock Nine be admitted to Central High, declaring that "law cannot be flouted with impunity by any individual or any mob of extremists." He backed up his words by federalizing the ten-thousand-member Arkansas National Guard and sending the army's 101st Airborne Division to Little Rock, the first time that military troops had been sent into a southern city since Reconstruction. The crisis was over.

Armstrong sent Eisenhower a congratulatory telegram:

> DADDY IF AND WHEN YOU DECIDE TO TAKE THOSE LITTLE
> NEGRO CHILDREN PERSONALLY INTO CENTRAL HIGH
> SCHOOL ALONG WITH YOUR MARVELOUS TROOPS PLEASE
> TAKE ME ALONG O GOD IT WOULD BE SUCH A GREAT
> PLEASURE I ASSURE YOU. . . . MAY GOD BLESS YOU
> PRESIDENT YOU HAVE A GOOD HEART.

Was it possible that his harsh words had swayed the president? It isn't likely — Eisenhower's mind didn't work that way — but the State Department's response to his statement showed that it had been noticed by the administration, and there were some who thought that it must have made a difference. "I think it was what Louis said that got Ike up off his rear over this Little Rock business," Max Kaminsky told the *Melody Maker*. "That episode is one hell of a smear over America, and it takes a hell of a lot of guts for Louis to stand up and say the things he said. Louis is not an Uncle Tom. He's a great man, apart from the fact that he's the greatest jazz trumpet player that ever lived."

Armstrong was unrepentant. "I wouldn't take back a thing I've said," he told the *Pittsburgh Courier,* one of the country's most widely read black newspapers. "I've had a beautiful life over 40 years in music, but I feel the downtrodden situation the same as any other Negro. My parents and family suffered through all of that old South . . . [and] when I see on television and read about a crowd spitting on and cursing at a little colored girl . . . I think I have a right to get sore and say something about it." He stayed sore for a long time. In 1956 Louisiana legislators had passed a law that forbade black and white musicians to play together in bars and clubs. A newly emboldened Armstrong spoke out against it: "They treat me better all over the world than they do in my hometown — that even includes Mississippi. I ain't going back to New Orleans and let them white folks in my own hometown be whipping on my head and killing me for my hustle. I don't care if I never see New Orleans again." The racially integrated All Stars stayed well away from New Orleans until 1965, after the Civil Rights Act was passed.

Now that celebrities are accustomed to sounding off about political matters, it is possible to underestimate the significance of Armstrong's statements on race. Sammy Davis, after all, had had a point: the All Stars *did* play for segregated audiences, and Armstrong never complained to Glaser about it. "I never question owners of dance halls or my manager about the racial pattern of places I am contracted to play. . . . I have been with Joe Glaser too many years to worry about where I play and for whom," he had told a reporter for the *Courier* in 1956. Nor would he ever take part in civil-rights demonstrations. "My life is music," he explained to a reporter. "They would beat me on the mouth if I marched, and without my mouth I wouldn't be able to blow my horn. . . . [T]hey would beat Jesus if he was black and marched." But to judge him by the standards of today is to disregard the realities of 1957. It was no small thing for a black man, even Louis Armstrong, to go up against one of the most beloved public figures of the century. Everybody liked Ike, a soldier-politician whose nickname and grin were as famous as Armstrong's own. "When he smiled, it was just like the sun came out," Norman Rockwell said. It would have been far easier for Armstrong to stick to blowing his gig. Instead he took on the man in the Rockwell painting — and won.

Even more remarkably, he was promptly forgiven by the public. An attempt by the Ford Motor Company to boot him off *The Edsel Show*, the upcoming TV extravaganza with which Ford planned to launch its ill-fated new line of automobiles, was aborted when CBS executives declined to cooperate. The All Stars appeared as scheduled, performing alongside Bing Crosby, Rosemary Clooney, Bob Hope, and Frank Sinatra less than a month after Armstrong's outburst had put him on the front pages, and no one is known to have uttered a word of complaint. It was a crystal-clear sign of how white audiences had come to feel about him: they had been welcoming Satchmo into their homes via TV for the better part of a decade and in so doing had come to love him. That love may well have been his foremost contribution to the cause of racial justice, a contribution that no other black man in America, not even Martin Luther King, was capable of making in 1957.

Two months later the All Stars were featured still more prominently in the first of a series of four *Timex All Star Jazz Show* prime-time TV specials that would team Armstrong with Hoagy Carmichael, Bob Crosby, Roy Eldridge, Bobby Hackett, Coleman Hawkins, Gene Krupa, Carmen McRae, Anita O'Day, Jack Teagarden, the Dave Brubeck and Gerry Mulligan quartets, the Dizzy Gillespie, Chico Hamilton, and George Shearing quintets, and the big bands of Duke Ellington, Lionel Hampton, and Woody Herman. The following April the *New Yorker* ran a cartoon by Mischa Richter that showed a group of soberly suited Washingtonians seated around a conference table discussing an urgent matter of state: "This is a diplomatic mission of the utmost delicacy. The question is, who's the best man for it — John Foster Dulles or Satchmo?" Secretary Dulles never did get around to sending Satchmo abroad, but his successor, Christian Herter, invited the All Stars to tour Africa on behalf of the State Department in 1960. This time Armstrong said yes, taking care to dodge political questions throughout the twenty-seven-city tour: "The reason I don't bother with politics is the words is so big. By the time they break them down to my size, the joke is over."

By then Armstrong had made it up with Dizzy Gillespie, burying the hatchet by sitting in with his group on a Timex telecast. Years later Gillespie got around to publicly admitting his mistake. "Hell, I had my own way of 'Tomming,'" he wrote in *To Be or Not to Bop*, his 1979 autobiography, going on to say that "I began to recognize what I had considered Pops' grinning in the face of racism as his absolute refusal to let anything, even anger about racism, steal the joy from his life and erase his fantastic smile. Coming from a younger generation, I misjudged him."

The Glaser-Armstrong moneymaking machine continued to purr along smoothly as the fifties gave way to the sixties. Armstrong grew so popular that Glaser used him to blackjack hapless nightclub bookers, letting them know that anyone who wanted to hire the All Stars would be expected, as Ernie Anderson put it, "to take two or three others of ABC's attractions that weren't doing so well." Nor was Glaser above knifing the competition, signing up-and-coming trumpet stars to exclusive management contracts, then relegating them to the boondocks. "Glaser signed both me and Hot Lips Page, but I swear he did it to keep us under wraps and away from Louis, who was having a little lip trouble then," Roy Eldridge claimed. Bobby Hackett confirmed it: "He'd make believe he's representing you, any trumpet player, but it's strictly to keep you out of Pops' way. You'd never get any place." Lucille was certain that Glaser was robbing her husband under the cover of their fifty-fifty deal and tried to persuade him to switch to a percentage agreement. But Armstrong, Anderson said, was content to leave things as they were: "When he felt Glaser was getting ahead of him, he simply called him up and asked for 'a little taste,' and Glaser would wire him $2,500."

The crowds that flocked to see him in person ignored the fact that his playing was showing signs of wear and tear. The fragility of his lip had been audible on some of the sessions he had recorded for Norman Granz in 1956 and 1957, if not so much so as to justify Gunther Schuller's later description of his playing on *Ella and Louis* as "infirm and short-breathed, no longer in tune." The problem was that Armstrong was working too hard for a man in his late fifties, racing from gig to gig in a way that would have taxed the endurance of a younger man. At one point in 1958 he played sixty-one college concerts in a row, afterward telling a reporter that "I've got more alma maters than anybody." A Monterey Jazz Festival concert filmed that year shows what he sounded like on an off night: he sang more songs and played fewer solos, and when he did play, much of his upper-register work was effortful. On occasion, Dan Morgenstern recalled, his lip would give out completely:

> Louis was on *The Tonight Show* with Steve Allen one night. He'd been in the hospital and hadn't been playing for a while. It was a nightmare, because he was unable to play properly. I'd never heard him playing clams and muffing notes like that. I was afraid he'd had a mild stroke — but his singing was perfect. He never showed any sign of distress, and the next time I saw him, he was perfectly fine.

The condition of Armstrong's chops, however, was the least of his health-related worries. Trummy Young had already noticed that he had "a bad congestion problem. . . . He coughed hard all the time." Glaser and Lucille noticed, too, and insisted that a doctor, Alexander Schiff, be added to the All Stars entourage whenever the band went abroad. It was Schiff who found a frightened Armstrong kneeling beside his bed in an Italian hotel room early in the morning of June 22, 1959. The band had flown into Spoleto the day before to play a concert at Gian Carlo Menotti's Festival of Two Worlds that was to be taped for *The Ed Sullivan Show*. Armstrong's valet woke Schiff and took him to the trumpeter's room, where the doctor, seeing that his ankles were swollen and fearing the worst, administered digitalis and called an ambulance. "I don't know why they're taking me to the hospital," Armstrong said. "I'm fine." But he wasn't: the All Stars performed without him that night, and newspapers around the world reported that he was "seriously ill" and that his condition was "grave." Schiff said that he had pneumonia but carefully hedged his bets, adding that "the musician's heart was weak from years of blowing on a trumpet."

Like so many other middle-aged men who are unexpectedly forced to confront their mortality, Armstrong reacted at first by denying it. He checked himself out of the hospital on June 29 and returned home a few days later. "I have never felt better," he told a reporter who met his plane, joking that "Bix tried to get me up there to play first horn." He had already written to Dizzy Gillespie with similar bravado: "Ole Doc Schiff put some kind of jive into me, that's making everything stand up better than before — Wow. . . . [T]here's one thing that you should always remember — you can't kill a nigger. Ha Ha Ha." And Schiff's cover story held water: it was not until after Armstrong's death that his doctors acknowledged that he had indeed suffered a heart attack. Armstrong himself may not have fully understood what he was up against. "The Italian doctors said it was a heart attack, but Dr. Schiff who travels with me kept telling them I had pneumonia," he later said. "When they changed the medicine around I got OK." But he knew that something had gone badly wrong, as did his bandmates, and so he grudgingly began to change his ways. His homemade diets grew more rigorous, if never austere. At one point he and Lucille printed up a leaflet called "Lose Weight the 'Satchmo' Way" in which they described his eating regime, which relied heavily on Swiss Kriss, orange juice, and salad: "You can eat from soup to nuts, eat as much as you want to." He even started working a bit less. "When I first went with Louis, we didn't have many nights off because he was strong then, you know, and he was very strong," Trummy Young said. "And he played hard, and he didn't want to relax. But later on he got a little weaker, then we started having nights off."

He was past his prime now, and though there were to be many more great nights on the bandstand, *Satchmo: A Musical Autobiography* had marked the end of the major phase of his recording career, in part because he never again worked with a producer who was prepared to challenge him rather than simply rolling the tape and hoping for the best. On occasion, though, he did rather more than suggest what he had sounded like in the old days, and one of those occasions was the first session on which he played after his heart attack. The Dukes of Dixieland were an all-white banjo-and-tuba combo from New Orleans whose early-stereo Audio Fidelity albums were selling by the carload to moldy figs who wished with all their hearts that Dizzy Gillespie and Miles Davis had never been born. Armstrong, who appeared with them on the second Timex special, liked their music: "They're home boys. Whenever we're playing in the same town, I go and sit in. We have a ball." He agreed to record with them, and the two albums they cut together are full of happy surprises, including a version of "Avalon" in which Armstrong cuts loose with a pair of high, wide, and handsome solos that sound nothing like the playing of an old man.

Even better was the Bob Thiele–produced *Louis Armstrong and Duke Ellington*, recorded in 1961, though it is far from what George Avakian had had in mind five years earlier when he envisioned teaming Armstrong with the Ellington band. Instead Ellington sat in on piano with the All Stars for a program of his own compositions. Armstrong was inspired both by Ellington's playing and by the program, whose highlight is a version of "Black and Tan Fantasy" in which he dug deep into his memory and dredged up the same funky riff that he had lifted from Joe Oliver's "Jazzin' Babies Blues" solo to serve as the climax of "Muggles." Not all of the tracks are as memorable as "Black and Tan Fantasy" or "Azalea," a subtly harmonized Ellington song inspired by a passage from *Swing That Music* in which Armstrong recalled the "hundreds of different kinds of flowers" that had bloomed in the New Orleans of his boyhood: *I've got to go back there / And find that blossom fair.* But the album still holds together splendidly well, better than anything else that Armstrong recorded after 1957.

Most of his later sessions were less interesting. *Bing & Satchmo*, the long-awaited duet album that he recorded with Bing Crosby in 1960, was an overblown big-band date that would have been twice as satisfying had Billy May, the conductor-arranger, hired half as many musicians. And *The Real Ambassadors*, a Dave Brubeck–penned musical about race relations in America that featured the All Stars, Carmen McRae, Lambert, Hendricks, and Ross, and the rhythm section of the Brubeck Quartet, is sometimes too earnest for its own good, though it does contain one of Armstrong's most haunting vocal performances, a ballad called "Summer Song" in which he makes magic out of Iola Brubeck's nostalgic lyric. Nor did his later movies improve noticeably in quality. In 1961, for instance, he shared the screen with Paul Newman and Sidney Poitier in Martin Ritt's *Paris Blues*, a film about two expatriate American musicians and the tourists who sleep with them. It says everything about Walter Bernstein's pretentious script that Newman's character is called "Ram Bowen," an elephantine reference to Arthur Rimbaud. Only the Ellington-Strayhorn score and the eye-catchingly down-to-earth performance of Armstrong, who plays (what else?) a jazz trumpeter named Wild Man Moore, saves *Paris Blues* from total unwatchability.

As ever, he was at his best not on the big screen but in his TV appearances. Mostly it is the showman we see on his *Ed Sullivan Show* spots, recycling such overexposed items from his repertoire as "Indiana," "Tiger Rag," and "When the Saints." But he never shed his poise and dignity, and whenever it suited him to play for real, as it did in the 1961 versions of "C Jam Blues" and "In a Mellotone" performed on a Sullivan telecast that united him with Ellington for the first and only time on TV, he was pithy and direct, blowing like a crafty old pro as Ellington smiled his world-weary smile. Around that time an interviewer asked Armstrong about his reputation as a clown, and his reply was unexpectedly sober: "We get just as big a hand standin' up playin' anything we want. . . . It's nice, but you don't get no more hands than you would if you hit that note right."

To watch him playing "In a Mellotone" with Ellington is to see and hear what he meant.

The All Stars had undergone extensive remodeling prior to that telecast. Bigard, the last remaining charter member, left for good after his third tour of duty, handing in his notice six months after Velma Middleton suffered a fatal stroke backstage in Sierra Leone, midway through the group's State Department–sponsored African tour. Billy Kyle and Trummy Young were still holding down the piano and trombone chairs, and Danny Barcelona, who replaced Barrett Deems in 1958, stayed on board all the way to the end, but the band was no longer as fresh-sounding as it had been during Edmond Hall's tenure, and sometimes it sounded as though it were playing by rote. Armstrong was part of the problem, for his own playing now fluctuated unpredictably in quality. "When I joined the band Louis was going strong, still playing well," said Joe Darensbourg, who replaced Bigard in 1962. "It seemed to me after I had been there a couple of years his lip would get sore. He had quite a problem there." It wasn't his only problem. By now Armstrong had played too many "Blueberry Hill"s to be taken seriously by young listeners. Like the vaudeville comedians who would book a night in Pough-keepsie to break in a new joke, he had perfected his act and preferred not to tinker with it. "Everybody was forever trying to change the tunes played," Darensbourg said. "For that matter, Joe Glaser wanted them changed, but all of them was afraid to tell Louis."

Once again *Time* summed up the conventional wisdom in a story about "jazz snobs": "Today, one good word spoken for Louis Armstrong spells cultural death. John Coltrane, Ornette Coleman and Thelonious Monk are the musicians to admire — it doesn't really matter that they are also the best." But Armstrong had one last surprise left in him, and it was a humdinger. Eleven months after *Time* declared him to be yesterday's news, his next record soared to the very top of the charts.

12

"I DON'T SIGH FOR NOTHING"

At the Top, 1963–1971

S IX DAYS AFTER John Kennedy was buried, Louis Armstrong and the All Stars played a college concert in Massachusetts. Instead of ending the show with "Sleepy Time Down South," Armstrong stepped to the microphone and played an unaccompanied chorus of "God Bless America." When he was done, he looked out at the audience and said, "That was for President Kennedy. Good night." Then he disappeared into the wings. Two days later, on December 3, 1963, the band showed up at a New York recording studio for its first session in two years. It isn't likely that their sorrowful leader was in the mood to cut a pair of show tunes, but such was the task before him, and it was important that he do his best. Not since 1961 and *The Real Ambassadors* had anyone shown any interest in recording the most famous jazz musician in the world. It was taken for granted that he had nothing new to say, and in the year of *The Freewheelin' Bob Dylan*, *Getz/Gilberto*, Johnny Cash's "Ring of Fire," Miles Davis's *Seven Steps to Heaven*, and the Beatles' "She Loves You," nobody wanted to hear anything that wasn't new.

While Armstrong must have felt grateful to be making a record after so long a layoff, this one didn't look like much. Instead of an album-length project like *The Real Ambassadors* or *Louis Armstrong and Duke Ellington*, the All Stars were cutting a single for Kapp Records, an independent label run by Dave Kapp, Jack's brother. The session was produced by Dave's son Mickey, and the A side was a cheery ditty called "Hello, Dolly!" that came from a new musical by a Broadway songsmith named Jerry Herman who had only one previous show under his belt. Herman's second musical was still in previews, and no one, least of all Armstrong, had any idea how it would do. For the flip side, the All Stars quickly knocked together a lightly swinging version of "A Lot of Livin' to Do," a song from *Bye Bye Birdie*, which had closed two years earlier. It was, in short, a job of work, a one-shot affair that had been arranged by Jack Lee, a song plugger for E. H. "Buddy" Morris, Herman's publisher. As Mickey Kapp told it, "Jack came to see my dad with the song. My dad didn't want to record it, so Jack went in my office and played it, and I liked it. Joe Glaser permitted Armstrong to record it as a favor to Jack, Buddy, and my dad, but he only let us do the two songs."

The All Stars embarked on the task before them with their usual professionalism but no great enthusiasm. Jack Bradley, who photographed the session, said that Armstrong "shook his head in dismay" when he looked at the lead sheet for "Hello, Dolly!" He preferred "A Lot of Livin' to Do," and so did everyone else. Herman's tune was naggingly repetitive, his lyrics simple to the point of vapidity. Even Kapp thought that the song needed a little something to pep it up:

> I'm in the booth, Louis is in the studio, and he says to me, "How would you like me to sing this?" And I'm sitting there thinking, "God, what am *I* going to tell *him* — Louis Armstrong?" So of course I said, "Any way you feel it." But then I asked him to change the first line from "Hello, Dolly, well, hello, Dolly" to "Hello, Dolly, this is Louie, Dolly!" And from the studio he said, "It's not Louie, it's *Louis!*"

After the song was recorded, Kapp decided that it needed "a heavier rhythm sound," so he brought in a seventh musician, a veteran session guitarist named Tony Gottuso who doubled on banjo and lived near the studio, to overdub a banjo part. Except for his sessions with the Dukes of Dixieland, Armstrong hadn't recorded with a banjo player since the early thirties, and the twangy instrument was now so completely identified with Dixieland and bluegrass that the thought of using one must have struck him as quaint. Not that it would have mattered: Joe Glaser wanted him to record "Hello, Dolly!" for the Kapps, and that was all he needed to know. No sooner was the session over than he forgot about it and went about his business, flying off to Puerto Rico three weeks later for a holiday engagement at the Hotel San Juan.

In Armstrong's absence Kapp sent an acetate of the single to Joe Glaser's office. Cork O'Keefe, an old colleague in the band-booking business, dropped in for a visit shortly afterward, and Glaser played the A side for him. "Listen to that, Cork, it's a fucking hit," he shouted. He was right: "Hello, Dolly!" is at least as catchy as "Mack the Knife" and very nearly as well played. Like all great pop records, it is concise (two and a half minutes) and wholly to the point. An upward glissando by Gottuso leads into an eight-bar introduction by the rhythm section, at the end of which Armstrong enters with a straight-from-the-shoulder vocal in which he frees up the squared-off rhythms of Herman's melody, putting an even more personal spin on the lyric by stressing the *s* at the end of his first name: *Hello, Dolly / This is* LEW-*issss, Dolly.* Next comes a rocking ensemble chorus in the band's best New Orleans style, after which Armstrong comes back to sing another half chorus, wrapping it up with a jazzy tag that sells the title of the song one more time: *Dolly, never go away / Promise you'll* ne-*ver* go *a*-way / *Dolly, never go away again!* In addition to adding Gottuso's banjo, Kapp discreetly sweetened the mix with a touch of overdubbed strings, but otherwise "Hello, Dolly!" was a pure product of Louis Armstrong and the All Stars, as plain and tasty as a plateful of red beans and rice.

A decade earlier it would have been a surefire hit, but pop music had turned inside out since Armstrong recorded "Blueberry Hill" for Milt Gabler. The Beatles now owned the *Billboard* charts — they recorded five of the top twenty songs of 1964—and most of the year's other hits were either rock or Motown-style black pop. Glaser was sure that Herman's song would be the exception that proved the rule, but no one agreed, least of all Armstrong. In January he spent a week cohosting Mike Douglas's TV talk show, performing twenty-two songs with the All Stars. "Hello, Dolly!" was not among them. Only Herman's publisher suspected that Glaser was on to something. Before opening on Broadway, *Hello, Dolly!* was previewed in Detroit, where the show was still known as *Dolly: A Damned Exasperating Woman*, a title that nobody liked. Then, as Herman remembered it, a representative from E. H. Morris

> showed up at my hotel room in Detroit clutching a 45 RPM record. I had no equipment for playing recordings in my room so I took him to the Fisher Theatre, where the company was rehearsing, and waited until Gower [Champion, the show's director] called a break. Then we let all the company hear it.... Armstrong had made it New Orleans Dixieland. He had taken the parochialism out of the number and substituted a universality. Everyone in the room could tell that this record had "hit" written over it. The music publisher was the first to speak after Armstrong's growl faded away. "There's the title of your show," he announced. "This record's going to sell a million copies."

Hello, Dolly! opened at Broadway's St. James Theatre on January 16, 1964. The reviews ran in the New York papers on the morning of the last day of Armstrong's stint on *The Mike Douglas Show*. They were positive, if not extravagantly so: Howard Taubman called the show "the best musical of the season thus far" in the *New York Times* but criticized the production for "lapses of taste" on the part of Gower Champion. No one else in the audience seemed to notice them. *Hello, Dolly!* became the hottest ticket on Broadway, making a name-above-the-title star out of Carol Channing and doing almost as well by Ginger Rogers, Martha Raye, Betty Grable, Pearl Bailey, Dorothy Lamour, Phyllis Diller, and Ethel Merman, all of whom followed her into the title role. Merman closed the show in 1970, by which time it had run for 2,844 performances.

As for Armstrong's record of what was now the title song, it started getting airplay as soon as it came out. Glaser called him on the road and urged him to add "Hello, Dolly!" to his act. No one in the band remembered how it went, and none of the local stores had a copy of the record on their shelves. "Couldn't find it, so they had to fly one out of New York to us and we listened to it," Joe Darensbourg said. "Then we started playing it and the very first time Louis did it on stage . . . he had to take about eight curtain calls, so he knew right then he had a hit." From then on he sang it every night. Unlike his earlier singles, it kept on selling, and disc jockeys played it ceaselessly. Soon it was clear that the song was not just a hit but a phenomenon, and Glaser negotiated a sizable fee for Armstrong to sing it for the first time on TV on *The Hollywood Palace*, ABC's popular Saturday-night variety series. In the meantime *What's My Line?* invited him to make his second appearance as mystery guest. The show paid only a standard five-hundred-dollar fee to all its celebrity guests, but the mystery-guest slot was a prestigious booking, so Glaser said yes, then called up the producers of *The Hollywood Palace* to assure them that his client would not be singing "Hello, Dolly!" on *What's My Line?*

On March 22 Glaser escorted Armstrong to the Manhattan theater from which *What's My Line?* was telecast each Sunday night, stashed him backstage out of sight of the panel, then went into the house to watch the show. The studio audience cheered lustily as Armstrong made his entrance, signed in, and started fielding questions from Bennett Cerf, Arlene Francis, Dorothy Kilgallen, and Hollywood producer Ross Hunter, the guest panelist. This time around he answered in a girlish squeak, throwing his blindfolded questioners off the trail for several minutes. "It's not Van Cliburn, is it?" a befuddled Francis asked. Kilgallen, a veteran Broadway columnist who was also a jazz buff, called for a conference. "What about Satchmo?" she asked. "He's got a hit single." Armstrong burst out laughing, and the panelists pulled off their blindfolds. Then Arlene Francis made an unexpected request: "I'm tired of playing it on the Victrola, on the hi-fi. Sing me 'Hello, Dolly!'" Armstrong sang her a whole chorus, grinning like a fox and stopping the show cold as Glaser looked on in horror, watching his deal with *The Hollywood Palace* go up in smoke.

Armstrong's impromptu performance helped fuel the song's slow but sure climb to the top of *Billboard*'s Hot 100 chart. A month later Mickey Kapp rushed the All Stars into a New York studio to cut ten more sides that would make up an album called, naturally enough, *Louis Armstrong's Hello, Dolly!* In addition to the title track and "A Lot of Livin' to Do," the album contained a mixture of show tunes, standard ballads, and new versions of such staples as "A Kiss to Build a Dream On" and "Someday You'll Be Sorry." Armstrong played and sang them the same way he always had, but this time the critics were paying attention. Even John S. Wilson of the *New York Times*, who had savaged the All Stars in 1956 when they were at their peak, changed his tune when the album came out: "Incredible though it may seem, Mr. Armstrong sings with greater vigor and zest than ever on this set. . . . Between vocal chores, [he] shows that he still has his customary authority on trumpet."

At last, on May 9, "Hello, Dolly!" became the most popular song in America, just ahead of the Beatles' "Do You Want to Know a Secret" and "Can't Buy Me Love." A week later Mary Wells's "My Guy" pushed it aside, but Armstrong had already made pop-music history. At sixty-three he was the oldest person ever to record a number-one song, and "Hello, Dolly!" was the next-to-last show tune to reach the top of the pop charts. (It was followed five years later by "Aquarius/Let the Sunshine In," a medley from *Hair* recorded by the Fifth Dimension.) Within two years the single version had sold three million copies. Its unprecedented success was the final step in Louis Armstrong's transformation from jazz star to pop-culture icon. Now more than ever, he belonged to the people.

After "Hello, Dolly!" Armstrong became ubiquitous on TV. In addition to *The Hollywood Palace, The Ed Sullivan Show,* and *I've Got a Secret,* on which he played "When the Saints Go Marching In" with

Peter Davis, his teacher from the Colored Waif's Home, he turned up on the programs of Jackie Gleason, Danny Kaye, and Dean Martin, asking for five-figure fees and getting them. Even after variety shows started to disappear from the airwaves, he remained a fixture of the small screen, for talk-show hosts discovered that he chatted as well as he played, and he became a regular guest on *The Tonight Show* and *The Dick Cavett Show*, trotting out his stock anecdotes as though they were newly minted.

Only the know-nothing neanderthals of the Deep South resisted him. Seven months after "Hello, Dolly!" topped the charts, the University of Alabama canceled an All Stars appearance at the school's Festival of Arts Week. The school's president swore that the color of Armstrong's skin had nothing to do with it, saying only that "at this time it would not serve the best interest of the program to bring Louis Armstrong." No one believed him for a moment. While racial attitudes were still in flux in the sixties — a restaurant owner in Connecticut had refused to let Armstrong use his men's room as late as 1960 — fewer and fewer Americans were willing to look the other way when their beloved Satchmo was treated with anything less than the respect he deserved. The climax of his eminence came when *Life* put him on its cover in 1966, photographed to glamorous effect by Philippe Halsman. Inside was a fourteen-page interview with Richard Meryman in which Armstrong spoke for himself at unprecedented length (it was later published as a short book). In it he looked back with the contentment of an old man who had seen all there was to see: "I don't sigh for nothing. Sixty years is a long time and there ain't going to be no more cats in the game that long."

Yet he was not quite ready to retire to Corona and count his blessings. "Pops loved to play the horn," Danny Barcelona said. "That's what kept him going. If we had two or three days off, he'd get restless and was ready to play again." One year his doctor ordered him to take some time off, and Joe Glaser duly informed the members of the band that they would be given eight weeks of paid vacation while Louis and Lucille took a Caribbean cruise. Three weeks later, Joe Darensbourg said, everyone got a call to return to New York: "Louis was itching to go back to work. He wasn't having any fun . . . The guys once told me that Louis had the feeling that, if he ever had a long lay off, he was afraid he wouldn't be able to come back." So he kept on riding the bus from show to show, mostly sticking to the good ol' good ones, though Mercury, his new label, sought to vary his repertoire after a fashion, pushing him to record more banjo-accompanied show tunes. First came "So Long, Dearie," another song from *Hello, Dolly!* After that he tried his hand at "Mame" and "Cabaret," both of which flickered onto the airwaves, then vanished again. "Hello, Dolly!" ensured that he would never want for work, and he gladly sang it every night for the rest of his life. "So now I do Dolly how many times? Six jillion? How ever many you want to say," he told a journalist in 1967. "Do it every show. And you got to admit, Pops, it gets the biggest hand of any number I do." It also brought in vast amounts of money. Joe Glaser went so far as to admit to a reporter for *Ebony* that the All Stars were now charging club owners between $3,500 and $5,000 a night: "Hell, Pops hasn't made less than a half-million bucks in any given year during the past 20 years. It's between us and Uncle Sam how much he actually takes in, but I can tell you this, for tax reasons we won't let it go over a million a year . . . Pops actually gives away—I mean gives away—$500 to $1,000 every damn week." But in spite of the song's lasting success, Armstrong was no longer the apple of the media's eye. Rock was here to stay.

"Hello, Dolly!" and the singles that followed were fresh in the mind of Gunther Schuller when he published *Early Jazz: Its Roots and Musical Development* in 1968. A brass player and classical composer turned academic, Schuller knew far more about jazz than most classical musicians. He had played French horn on Miles Davis's influential "Birth of the Cool" records in 1950 while doubling as principal horn of the Metropolitan Opera's pit orchestra, later composing a series of works in which he sought to fuse jazz and classical music into a new idiom that he called "Third Stream music." His book was the first scholarly study of early jazz, and it took Armstrong seriously: "By whatever definition of art—be it abstract, sophisticated, virtuosic, emotionally expressive, structurally perfect — Armstrong's music qualified." But Schuller's view of Armstrong, while sympathetic, was that of a high modernist, and after the trumpeter abandoned small-group recording in 1929, Schuller's opinion of his work turned sour and disapproving. It was the gospel according to John Hammond — Armstrong was a great artist who had sold out at the tender age of twenty-eight — reinforced by a scholar's certitude:

> For the rest there is a wasteland of whimpering Lombardo-style saxophones, vibraphones and Hawaiian guitars, saccharine violins, dated Tin Pan Alley tunes and hackneyed arrangements. . . . Occasionally, the accompanying band swings, as in "Shine" or "Ding Dong Daddy," but these are the exceptions. Armstrong had made his contribution, he had "paid his dues," and, as one of his friends put it to me once, he now wanted to enjoy the returns. It is a choice not unknown in the annals of the arts.

Early Jazz was praised as a major contribution to the then-new field of academic jazz scholarship, and after 1968 few critics would dare to dissent from its dismissal of Armstrong's post-1929 career. Some, like Murray Kempton, put it more gently, comparing him to "the River Mississippi, pure like its source, flecked and choked with jetsam like its middle, broad and triumphant like its end." Schuller himself would later temper his view of Armstrong's big-band records. Yet he never succeeded in coming to terms with Armstrong's populism, and when he came to write about the trumpeter's last years, it was with a ferocity that bordered on spite: "The end was not what it should have been. . . . [O]ur memories are beclouded by recordings of a sixty-three-year-old Louis singing 'Hello, Dolly!' against a cheap brassy Dixieland sextet (over a soggy string section yet), and straining for one more quivery high C."

Certain critics, however, felt differently, and one of them now emerged as an eloquent advocate for the music of Armstrong's middle years. "Musicians and dyed-in-the-wool Armstrong devotees . . . more often than not will cite examples of Louis' big band work when asked about their favorites," Dan Morgenstern wrote in his liner notes for *Louis Armstrong: Rare Items*, a 1967 Decca reissue devoted to Armstrong's big-band sides. He went on to praise "Ev'ntide," "Jubilee," "Skeleton in the Closet," the first version of "Swing That Music," and the 1938 remake of "Struttin' with Some Barbecue" as "miniature concerti for trumpet (and sometimes also voice) and orchestra, but miniature only in size; the conception is grand." Morgenstern's essay would come to be seen as prescient, but for the moment Schuller had prevailed, and those who believed that there was more to Louis Armstrong than "West End Blues" found it hard to get a hearing.

Armstrong himself believed, unlike the majority of his critics, that "I did my [most] interesting work as I have gotten up into the older age bracket." But even he was wearying of the formula that had briefly made him bigger than the Beatles, and in 1967 he jumped at the chance to record a new ballad brought to him by Bob Thiele, the producer of *Louis Armstrong and Duke Ellington*. "What a Wonderful World," Thiele said, was written "during the deepening national traumas of the Kennedy assassination, Vietnam, racial strife, and turmoil everywhere." Thiele, by contrast, wanted to reassure the world that it was "full of the love and sharing people make possible for themselves and each other every day" and decided that a recording by Satchmo would be the ideal vehicle for his rosy-colored message of hope. He cut a demo, took it to Joe Glaser, and got his approval to meet the trumpeter on the road in Washington, DC, and play it for him. "Pops, I dig it," Armstrong said before the record had finished playing. "Let's do it!"

Ever the optimist, Armstrong responded to the song's sentiments, set to an expansive tune that made them sound almost plausible. "The real meaning of the tune to Pops was that he was getting old, had a heart condition and was facing death," one of his sidemen later explained. "When death is in the room with you, it's perfectly natural to think about the 'wonderful world' you have in life." He even agreed to record it for scale, $250, in part because he liked the idea of getting away from the rigid repetition of the "Hello, Dolly!" formula. So did Glaser. But Larry Newton, the president of ABC

Records, Thiele's label, visited the studio while Armstrong and a studio orchestra were recording "What a Wonderful World," loathed the song and arrangement, and went so far as to threaten to halt the session before being brought to his senses. Newton was in a position to quash the promotion of the single once it was released, and did so: "What a Wonderful World" sank without trace in the United States, though it did unexpectedly well in England, where it stayed on the charts for thirteen weeks and sold six hundred thousand copies.

Not only were there no more hit records, but Armstrong's checkered film career was drawing to a close as well. It was, ironically, his next-to-last screen appearance in a feature film that gave him the best chance he ever had to display his natural gifts as an actor. Sammy Davis Jr., the star of *A Man Called Adam*, had long since recanted his criticisms of Armstrong's civil-rights record, and now he cast the trumpeter in what he would later describe as "a wonderful cameo" by "a great old jazzman." It was something more than that. Armstrong played "Sweet Daddy" Ferguson, an over-the-hill trumpeter whose granddaughter (played by Cicely Tyson) has fallen for Davis's character, a guilt-ridden bopper reminiscent of Miles Davis whose drinking is wrecking his career. The part was small, but Armstrong invested it with authority, and though he also played trumpet in a nightclub scene, it was his acting that stood out. The rest of the film, alas, was overwrought and overcooked, a steamy melodrama that *Time* described with curt exactitude as "a specialty act salted with social protest . . . There is a semifinal glimpse of the doomed genius staggering through city streets, climaxed by a moment of bitter glory when he blows his heart through a horn and dies. His ailment is never precisely named, though he coughs a lot whenever prejudice crowds him." *A Man Called Adam* died at the box office, and Armstrong's Hollywood career died with it, save for a final star turn in the film version of *Hello, Dolly!*

He was dying, too, by inches. A bout with pneumonia sidelined him for two months, and though he returned to the road as soon as he could, his energy was flagging. It was then that Joe Muranyi, a young clarinetist who, unlike most musicians of his generation, preferred traditional jazz to bebop, got a call from Joe Glaser inviting him to join the All Stars "if Louis goes back to work." When he did, Muranyi went with him, becoming the ninth and last clarinetist of the All Stars in June of 1967. The band had lately gone through a trying string of personnel changes. Tyree Glenn and Marty Napoleon (who had already put in a short stint with Armstrong a decade and a half earlier) replaced Trummy Young and Billy Kyle, leaving Danny Barcelona, who had been playing drums for Armstrong since 1958, as the only familiar face. Once Muranyi joined, though, the lineup became stable and stayed that way to the end.

For Muranyi, joining the All Stars was "almost like a religious experience. When Louis would talk about joining Joe Oliver, I'd think, 'That's what it was like for me to join Louis Armstrong.'" He was modest enough to know that the opportunity of a lifetime had come to him by default: "The older guys were dying, but Louis kept going, and that's how I got in there. It had been a style that just naturally happened, and these guys started to disappear, so Joe Glaser started buying what was on the market, and some of the players that came into the band later on didn't come from the roots. I did — I was a moldy fig. Humphrey Lyttelton told me, 'Joe, you're the only All Star who ever knew any of Armstrong's songs!'"

Muranyi respected Armstrong's privacy. "Louis knows you're around, and when he wants you, he'll let you know," Barcelona had warned him. But when Armstrong saw that his new sideman was a full-fledged moldy fig, he took a shine to the younger man, nicknaming him "Josephus," and they became friendly. Muranyi soon grew comfortable enough with Armstrong to "corner him and ask him questions. He'd get letters from people about old jazz happenings, and his valet would bring them to me and say, 'Pops wants you to read this.' One of them was about all the places that had music in New Orleans when he was a boy — and the names of all the hookers." Like Armstrong, he was a keen-eyed observer who remembered everything he saw. Much of it was unsurprising, for the trumpeter's habits, like his character, had hardened long ago. He still spent "hours and hours and hours and hours" writing letters to fans. He still exploded into fiery rages, then forgot all about them the next day. He was still smoking marijuana, too, if more cautiously than in the old days.* He still held a grudge against Zutty Singleton, telling Muranyi that "he's not good enough to play with us," though the clarinetist managed to bring the two men together for a long-deferred reunion. And he was still playing the same songs: "We basically played the same show every night. The inevitable 'Indiana.' 'Hello, Dolly!' and 'A Kiss to Build a Dream On.' Sometimes we'd do 'Mame.' Even the lines were canned." But he always played them with love, and at times, Muranyi said, he still managed to sound like a flying cat:

> I remember a gig in Chicago at the Sheraton O'Hare not long after I joined the band. We came out and played, and it was one of the best nights he had during the time I played with him. He was really knocking 'em over the fence. I didn't realize until later how exceptional a night it was. His playing was pretty consistent — except when it wasn't. He was having trouble with his chops, they weren't responding the way they used to, and so he had good nights and nights that weren't so good. Then he'd mostly sing.

He was still working hard, too, and putting his life at risk by doing so. When the All Stars flew to England in the summer of 1968, Glaser booked them into a nightclub that same evening. "We arrived in the morning, stayed up and played that night, the same fucking night that we traveled to Europe!" Muranyi remembered, his voice quivering with retrospective fury. "That's cruel. There was no need for it — but in a way, Louis invited it. He was such a mule, such a workhorse, and he didn't want to make adjustments to his lifestyle because it would have meant admitting his mortality." Once in a while he spoke of giving up one-nighters and retiring to Corona to

---

*Jewel Brown, who joined the All Stars after Velma Middleton's death and sang with the band until 1968, recalled an occasion shortly after the release of "Hello, Dolly!" when one of Armstrong's sidemen lit up a joint. "No, man, we can't do that shit no more," the trumpeter told him. "We done got too big!"

play in "some little spot . . . where you just come in and sit down and listen to all the music you want, you don't have to pay no admission, nothin.'" But everyone in the band knew that he hoped to die not in bed but on stage, if possible while blowing a chorus of "When the Saints Go Marching In." That was his life, and if he couldn't go on living it the way he always had, he saw no reason to go on at all.

The record dates had mostly dried up by the time Muranyi joined the All Stars, though Armstrong had one more goodish album in him, a collection of children's songs with the unlikely title of *Disney Songs the Satchmo Way*. Recorded for Walt Disney's Buena Vista label, this incongruous project contains slickly arranged but listenable performances of ten songs from the Disney studio's animated features, all of which the trumpeter sang and played with unflagging spirit. The best one, Muranyi thought, was "When You Wish upon a Star," the ballad from *Pinocchio* that the clarinetist called "his last great record." Armstrong sweetens Ned Washington's lyric with an affirming touch of tenderness: *If your heart is in your dream / No request is too extreme.* It was as though he were singing his own epitaph.

More and more he was preoccupied with the past. On his 1968 trip to England, he appeared on *Desert Island Discs*, the BBC radio series that invites its guests to choose eight records to take with them to an imaginary island. He picked three of his own sides, "Blueberry Hill," "Mack the Knife," and "What a Wonderful World," plus the version of "Bess, You Is My Woman Now" that he had recorded with Ella Fitzgerald in 1957 and a trio of 78s by Guy Lombardo, Jack Teagarden, and "my man Bobby Hackett." Yet he also made room for Barbra Streisand's "People," praising her as "Madame Streisand . . . she's tryin' to outsing everybody this year!" At sixty-seven his ears were still wide open. He even claimed to like the Beatles, remarking in another interview that their music came "right outa the old spirituals and soul and country music and jazz."

In May he flew to Hollywood to tape *Disney Songs the Satchmo Way* and shoot his appearance in *Hello, Dolly!* with Madame Streisand, who had been cast in Carol Channing's role. Their duet was pasted into the film in order to capitalize on the continuing popularity of his recording of the title song, and there wasn't much to it: Streisand sashays over to the Harmonia Gardens bandstand, and the baton-waving conductor of the all-black orchestra turns around, revealing himself to be none other than Satchmo. He and Streisand sing a chorus of "Hello, Dolly!" together, and his plainspoken directness cuts through her preening self-regard like a hot knife through a snowball. Then she pulls away and he waves goodbye, partly to her and partly to the audience, and is gone. The scene was shot in a half day, reportedly in one take.

Armstrong looks disturbingly thin in *Hello, Dolly!* A month later he bragged to a journalist that he had dropped sixty pounds: "Two meals a day is all you need. It's all I have and I never felt better." He was sure that his homemade diet was the reason why he had outlived so many of his less fortunate sidemen: Johnny Dodds had died in 1940, Sid Catlett in 1951, Baby Dodds in 1959, Velma Middleton in 1961, Luis Russell in 1963, Jack Teagarden in 1964, Billy Kyle in 1966, Red Allen in 1967. "Some of 'em needn't have gone," he told Max Jones. "They didn't take proper care of their insides." He did not see — or refused to admit — that he was in the same boat, and that it was sinking.

In September Armstrong went to the office of Gary Zucker, an internist at Beth Israel Medical Center who had taken charge of his case. He was wheezing and bloated, and Zucker, diagnosing congestive heart failure on the spot, ordered him to check into the hospital at once. "He practically ran out of my office," the doctor said. Two weeks later he returned, having spent the intervening period carousing. This time he was put in intensive care, and he stayed put. "Mr. Louis Armstrong decided he wanted to stay up all night as if he were a 21-year-old kid," Joe Glaser told Leonard Feather. "And Mr. Armstrong is now back in the hospital. . . . Louis'll be out soon. He's taking care of himself this time." As Zucker recalled it, Armstrong became "a very attached, devoted patient," though he made it clear to the doctor that "life wasn't worth anything" if he was unable to go on playing, and Zucker in turn tacitly agreed to "do everything, including compromise, to make it possible for him to entertain."

For the moment, though, there were no compromises. Armstrong was in and out of Beth Israel until the following April, and instead of going back on the road once he was out for good, he stayed home with Lucille. According to Phoebe Jacobs, he spoke of his illness as an "intermission," but he knew better: Armstrong had finally recognized the gravity of his condition, and it shook him to the core. "Now all I got to do is scan my life back and see what I was doing wrong," he says on a 1969 tape, sounding part puzzled and part scared. "Like I didn't get enough rest. I was always afraid I was going to miss something." The bleakness of his mood was atypical, though he had long been subject to fits of dark introspection that passed as quickly as his rages. "For all his popularity, Louis could be sitting in his dressing room and he looked like the saddest guy in the world," Joe Darensbourg said. "That always amazed me. He'd be sitting with his horn in his hand, just looking at it, turning it over, looking at the bell, picking it up and blowing a little, that's all." Now he could do nothing but look, for Zucker had ordered him to stop playing until further notice. He even persuaded Armstrong to stop smoking pot, a concession that Joe Glaser himself had never been able to extract. One day Jack Bradley paid him a visit. "Hey, man, I gotta tell you something — Mr. Glaser and the doctors finally convinced me to stop smoking shit," Armstrong said. Then he added in a stage whisper, "But *don't tell anyone!*"

Not long after Armstrong went into Beth Israel, Joe Glaser told Cork O'Keefe that it was time for him to call it quits, or at least cut back drastically on his touring. He asked O'Keefe to go to the hospital with him to talk to Armstrong. "Cork, if I go to Louie with this I'll start yelling and screaming and he'll start yelling and screaming," he said. O'Keefe had to leave for California but promised to do what he could as soon as he returned to New York. Glaser had a stroke that same night and was rushed to Beth Israel. Lucille and Gary Zucker tried to keep the news of his illness from Armstrong, who found out by accident when Tyree Glenn and Dizzy Gillespie came

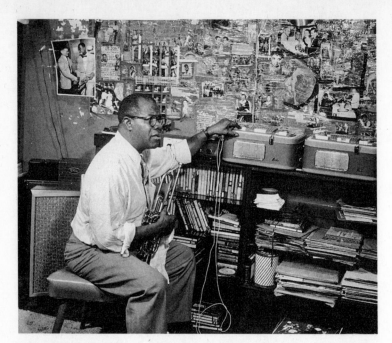

A rare photograph of Louis Armstrong at home in the early sixties, making a tape. The 650 surviving reels of private recordings that he made during the last quarter century of his life provide priceless glimpses of the offstage Armstrong, expansive and candid. They also document the wide range of his musical interests — he listened to everything from Bix Beiderbecke to Béla Bartók. Visible above the tape decks is one of the homemade collages (it no longer exists) with which he covered the walls and ceiling of his den.

to the hospital to donate blood for Glaser. They stopped by Armstrong's room to say hello and told him why they were there. He insisted on being wheeled to Glaser's room. When he returned, he told Lucille, "I went down to see him and he didn't know me." Glaser never emerged from his coma, dying the following June. He was seventy-two years old. Armstrong, who had returned home to Queens to convalesce, was shocked by the loss of the man who had looked out for him for so long. He went to the funeral, and Muranyi, who saw him there, said that he was "obviously ill and very heavily sedated. He had to be helped in by two people. It was clearly emotional for him. I went up to him afterward, figuring he wouldn't recognize me, he's so out of it, and I say, 'Hey, Pops! How you doin', Pops?' He peered at me, then put his hand out and said, 'My man!' And I cried."

Shortly after the funeral Armstrong wrote to Feather to assure him that "I am just waiting — resting — blowing just enough to Eulagize the Chops . . . I'm about to feel like my Old Self Again. I Never Sq[u]awk About Anything. I feel like this — As long as a person is Still Breathing, he's got a Chance, Right?" He gingerly resumed his career in October, flying to London to record an innocuous ballad called "We Have All the Time in the World" that was featured on the soundtrack of *On Her Majesty's Secret Service*, the new James Bond movie. *Hello, Dolly!* was released in December, and though the film was a $24 million dud — Vincent Canby called it "reverential to the point of idiocy" in his *New York Times* notice — Armstrong's cameo appearance put him back in the public eye. In January he started appearing on TV again, playing erratic, tentative-sounding trumpet solos that showed how much damage his illness had wrought. For the most part, though, he stayed home and puttered. Never before had he spent so long a stretch of time at the Corona house, proud though he was of it. George Avakian, who visited him there often, felt that Armstrong had not put his mark on the house: "I could tell it was Lucille's, not Pops's, except for one room — his den. It had piles of stuff everywhere. Papers, letters, stacks of records on the shelves and floor. Photographs everywhere, even taped on the ceiling." But now he began to feel at home, so much so that he wrote an essay called "Our Neighborhood" in which he told how he felt about the place where he lived:

> When my wife Lucille + I moved into this neighborhood there
> were mostly white people. A few Colored *families*. Just think —
> through the (29) years that we've been living in this house we
> have seen just about (3) generations come up on this particular
> block . . . Lots of them have grown up — Married had Children.
> Their Children + they still come and visit — Aunt Lucille +

Uncle Louis. And when there's *Death* in our block Lucille Always Bake a Turkey — Ham, *etc.*, put it in a big basket and take it over to the house . . . We don't think that we could be more relaxed and have better neighbors any place else. So we stay put.

While the Armstrong house didn't look fancy on the outside, he said, those who passed through the door saw "a whole lot of comfort, happiness + the nicest things. Such as *that Wall to Wall Bed* — a Bath Room with Mirrors *Everywhere* . . . A *Garage* with a magic up + down Gate to it. And of course our Birthmark *Car* a Cadillac (Yea). The Kids in our Block just thrill when they see our garage gate up, and our fine Cadillac *ooze* on out." Like the house itself, the Cadillac behind the magic gate was a visible symbol of what a half century of ceaseless work had brought him, and it thrilled him at least as much as it did the kids on the block.

"Our Neighborhood" was one of a series of autobiographical manuscripts that Armstrong wrote in the last two years of his life. In the longest of them, written while he and Joe Glaser were in Beth Israel, he described his relationship with the Karnofskys, the Jewish peddlers for whom he had worked as a child, contrasting their industry with the chronic laziness of the "Soul Brothers" who, like his father, chose not to live up to their responsibilities as husbands and parents. Though Armstrong had hinted at such feelings in *Satchmo* and various interviews, he had never expressed them so forthrightly. He hoped to publish "Louis Armstrong + the Jewish Family in New Orleans, La., the Year of 1907," which he called a "book," but it was buried among his personal papers after his death and did not surface until 1999.

Armstrong wrote not only to speak his mind but to fill his days. Instead of racing off to the next gig, he would pass an idle hour with Trumpet and Trinket, the two schnauzers that Joe Glaser had given him as presents, or get his hair cut at the neighborhood barbershop. "He didn't like me to put him ahead of anybody," said Joe Gibson, the proprietor of Joe's Artistic Barber Shop. "He would ask me how many customers I had, but he was never in a hurry." Once in a while

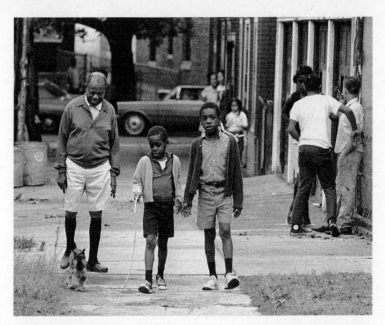

On the streets of Queens, 1970. Armstrong played with the children in the neighborhood whenever he returned home for a few days off. The dog is one of a pair of schnauzers given to him and Lucille by Joe Glaser.

he and Lucille would eat Chinese food at a local restaurant, even though "the whole neighborhood of kids . . . make a bee line in the Restaurant to my table for Autographs." More often he entertained friends at home and played on the stoop with his neighbors' children, asking whether they'd done their homework and buying them popsicles from the Good Humor man when they gave the right answer. "In the wintertime he'd have grab bags for the kids and he and Lucille would have a party and have the neighborhood kids in," Phoebe Jacobs recalled. He also continued to look after Clarence Armstrong, for whose welfare he had selflessly made himself responsible a half century earlier.* He rarely read books, preferring to write letters, lis-

---

*Though Clarence adored his adoptive father, Lucille was unwilling to supervise his day-to-day care, so instead of living with the Armstrongs, he was cared for by an older woman named Evelyn Hadfield, with whom he lived in a marriage-like relationship that Armstrong arranged so that Clarence would not be institutionalized.

ten to music, and catalog the tapes in his library, whose boxes he decorated with collages made out of Scotch tape and cut-up newspaper and magazine clippings: "My hobbie is to pick out the different things during what I read and piece them together and making a little story of my own." Unknown in his lifetime save to his friends, these colorful boxes, like the pages of clippings pasted into his scrapbooks and the giant-sized collages that covered the walls and ceiling of his den, have a freely associational quality that recalls the "visionary art" of untrained painters.

For all the pleasure that Armstrong took in his enforced vacation, he longed to be back in the saddle and feared that the death of his protector might keep him from returning there. Associated Booking renewed his contract in September of 1969, changing the old fifty-fifty split to the percentage deal that Lucille had always wanted, but Armstrong was unsure of the goodwill of Oscar Cohen, Glaser's longtime assistant and heir apparent, who now ran the agency. In January he sent Cohen a long letter full of praise as obsequious as anything that he had ever ladled over his predecessor: "*God Bless you* for looking out for my *interest* . . . it's 'Just like you *Daddy*' I felt it all of these 'years' even when you were UNDER Mr *Joe* Glaser's (*instructions*) every *move* that you made since the *first* day in that *office*, I could see an[d] felt the *feel* and *admirations* that you had for me." It is the saddest letter that Armstrong ever wrote, for it shows that forty years of success had failed to make him confident of his ability to maneuver in the world of music without the help of a white manager who "can + will put his Hand on your shoulder and say — '*This is* "My" Nigger.' "

Since he could not yet perform regularly, Armstrong had disbanded the All Stars, and he told Cohen that he intended to work as a single once he was well again:

> *Believe me* when I *tell* you, *most* of the *musicians*, whom I "*JAMMED*" with from a *lot* OF THE parts of the world, were *BY* far much better than my own *All Stars* Musicians. That's when I *realized* that my *personal* Musicians *we*[re] *all Bull shit* — from the *olden* days up in *Harlem*. All they wanted to do, is to

hang around the Bar — BULL SHIT the Chorus Girls — and waste a lot of time doing *nothing*! . . . *No* more of those *Primadonas* MUSICIANS as Mr *Glaser* used to *call* the musicians that I had in my *All Star* Band — HE WAS RIGHT. Wasting all of those UN *Necessary Salaries, etc.*

Not for years had Armstrong spoken ill of his sidemen. Did he mean it? Or was he simply trying to persuade his new manager that he could run a tighter, cheaper ship? It was clear that he had his doubts about Cohen, perhaps in part because Joe Glaser's will had unexpectedly left him high and dry. Glaser's estate was valued at more than two million dollars, but the only thing he bequeathed to his star client was his stake in International Music, Inc., the trumpeter's music publishing company. At first Armstrong had been devastated by Glaser's death, describing him in a letter to a friend as "the greatest for me and all the spades that he handled." Now, though, he was surprised and angry, so much so that he broke another precedent and complained to George Wein: "When we started, we both had nothing. We were friends — we hung out together, ate together, we went to restaurants together. But the minute we started to make money, Joe Glaser was no longer my friend. In all those years, he never invited me to his house. I was just a passport for him. . . . I built Associated Booking. There wouldn't have been an agency if it wasn't for me. And he didn't even leave me a percentage of it." According to Wein, Armstrong even claimed that when he visited the comatose Glaser in Beth Israel, he whispered in his ear, "I'll bury you, you motherfucker." What he did not know was that Glaser could not have left any part of Associated Booking to him, for it was no longer his to give.

Armstrong's business arrangement with Glaser had long been the subject of not-so-discreet talk in the jazz world. In *Beneath the Underdog*, his 1971 autobiography, Charles Mingus put the following words into the mouth of the real-life jazz trumpeter Fats Navarro: "*King Spook* don't even own fifty per cent of himself! His agent gets fifty-one, forty-nine goes to a corporation set up in his name that he don't control and he draws five hundred a week and don't say *nothing*." Mingus probably had Lionel Hampton in mind, but it was widely thought that the passage referred to Armstrong and Glaser. What was far less widely known, however, was that Glaser didn't own 50 percent of himself, either. At some point in the early sixties, a Broadway press agent asked Ernie Anderson, "Did you hear what happened to Joe? A guy from Chicago came into his office. 'I'm your new partner,' he told him. Joe recognized this character from the old days on the South Side. He knew instantly that either he did what he was told or he died."

Anderson was not always a reliable source, but this particular tale was more than gossip. Five years after Armstrong's death, the *New York Times* published a three-part investigative report about Sidney Korshak, the powerful Beverly Hills labor lawyer who was widely believed to be a fixer for the Chicago mob. A memo in Korshak's FBI file succinctly describes him as "a well-known hoodlum lawyer and associate of racketeers." According to the crime reporter Sandy Smith, "Sidney functioned as a gangster. He was their straight man. He would go into the corporations and those places that the gangsters couldn't get into, simply because they were such slobs." It was said that Korshak had gotten his start as a mouthpiece for Al Capone. The *Times* saw that rumor and raised it: "In 1962, according to court documents, Joseph Glaser, the head of Associated Booking Company, the nation's third largest theatrical agency, assigned all of the voting rights, dominion and control of his majority stock in the concern to Mr. Korshak and himself. The agreement meant that Mr. Korshak was able to assume complete control of the company upon Mr. Glaser's death in 1969." The news of the takeover came as a surprise to Armstrong's friends and colleagues, and the *Times* story, written by Seymour Hersh, stressed that there was "no evidence" that any of ABC's clients knew that Korshak controlled the agency, though some had suspected as much. "Sid and Joe were very close," said Freddie Bell, a Las Vegas lounge singer and Glaser client. "But I thought Sid was the power behind the throne, mostly involved in the money end. Joe was a loud-talking tough guy from Chicago, and Sid was just the opposite." That was the way Korshak wanted it. Jerry Heller, an ABC employee who later went on to manage such well-known rappers as Eazy-E, had been warned that the lawyer co-owned the agency with Glaser and that it was "a mob company," but months went by before he first became "aware of Sidney Korshak's presence" at ABC's West Coast offices in Beverly Hills. Then he was told that Korshak wanted to see him:

> I never really noticed it, but there was a gold drape hanging next to the switchboard at Associated as you exited the elevator on the second floor. . . . I fought my way through the heavily-woven folds of velvet drapery and found myself facing the door to a private elevator. I got in the elevator and saw there weren't any buttons to push. The doors merely closed and the elevator whisked me upward to a kind of bomb shelter on the roof. I know that's a strange sort of oxymoron, a bomb shelter on a roof, but that's exactly how Sidney Korshak's office [at ABC] struck me.

How did Korshak wrest control of Associated Booking from Glaser? No one will ever know for sure, but a few suggestive details are part of the public record. Jules Stein, the Chicago ophthalmologist turned band booker who founded the Music Corporation of America and turned it into the country's most powerful booking agency, loaned Glaser one hundred thousand dollars to launch ABC, and Glaser in turn introduced Stein to Korshak. Though Glaser paid back the loan six years later, it was whispered that the payment was notional. "Everyone knew that Stein worked for Al Capone in Chicago," Robert Mitchum said. "That's how MCA got into the band business." All this points to the possibility that Glaser may have "settled" Armstrong's problems with the Chicago mob by promising them a piece of the action. Judging by what Armstrong said to George Wein, he never knew that after 1962 Glaser was no longer in control of his own destiny — if he ever had been.

⟡

In 1970 Armstrong returned to the studio to tape a final pair of albums that added nothing to his reputation. *Louis Armstrong and His Friends*, recorded in May, is a bland all-star tribute on which he sings

"Mood Indigo," "Give Peace a Chance," an inferior remake of "What a Wonderful World," and a version of "We Shall Overcome" accompanied by a motley-sounding chorus made up of (among others) Tony Bennett, Ornette Coleman, Eddie Condon, Miles Davis, and Bobby Hackett. He left his trumpet at home, explaining to a reporter covering the sessions that "I'm waitin' for some word from the doctor about when I can play my horn again. But I play it anyway. Every night before supper." Three months later came *Louis "Country & Western" Armstrong*, a nondescript set of country tunes for which he dubbed his vocals on top of instrumental tracks taped by a Nashville rhythm section. In between were his "seventieth" birthday and a series of tributes that included concerts in Hollywood and Newport, a *New York Times* profile, a children's book by E. B. White called *The Trumpet of the Swan* whose hero is a trumpeter swan named Louis, and a feature in *Down Beat* in which scores of leading jazz musicians sang his praises. Miles Davis struck the only sour note, observing that "his personality was developed by white people wanting black people to entertain by smiling and jumping around." Dizzy Gillespie, by contrast, spoke of Armstrong with the utmost respect at the Newport Jazz Festival tribute. "If it weren't for Louis, there wouldn't be any of us," he said. "I'd like to thank Mr. Louis Armstrong for my livelihood."

Armstrong had the last word in the *New York Times*, in which he spoke pridefully of his own playing:

> Ain't nobody played nothing like it since, and can't nobody play nothing like it now. My oldest record, can't nobody touch it. And if they say, "Which record do you like the best?" I like them all, because I didn't hit no bad notes on any of them. . . . I'm indexing my reels, which will take me another year — I've so many. I still done but one shelf, but I've got five or six shelves with nothing but reels, and I'm in all of them. I want to hear me, that's what keeps me up to the time.

His rambling days were done, he said, and he claimed to be glad that it was so: "Now I have time to be at home, which I never did have — traveling all day long, buses, and going to airports, waiting all day for a plane, gets you there just in time to do the concert, no supper, no anything. Fifty-four years traveled — I started when I was 14. Well, I ain't going to do that no more." And he predicted that his funeral would be a grand occasion: "In New Orleans I played at as many funerals as I could get, and cats died like flies, so I got a lot of nice little gigs out of that. It's business. They going to enjoy blowing over me, ain't they? Cats will be coming from California and everywhere else just to play."

Come fall, though, he threw caution to the winds and started performing again. In October he played at a charity concert in London, and Humphrey Lyttelton was taken aback by how noticeably he had aged: "The always jaunty, stiff-limbed walk had a frail jerkiness about it and in repose his face wore a crumpled, defeated look. . . . [I]t seemed as if the head of a fifty-year-old was perched on the body of a man of ninety." He had already reconvened the All Stars for a job at the International Hotel in Las Vegas, having previously appeared on *The Johnny Cash Show* to plug *Louis "Country & Western" Armstrong* by joining the host in a duet version of "Blue Yodel No. 9," the song he had recorded with Jimmie Rodgers in 1930. Two weeks later he sang a half-dozen numbers on *The Flip Wilson Show*, then went to Washington to perform at the National Press Club, followed by a string of appearances on the talk shows of Johnny Carson, Dick Cavett, and David Frost. "You know, Louie's been quite sick," Lucille confessed anxiously to Jack Barry, Cavett's announcer. "I'm so happy to see him back there. All he was worried about, would he ever blow that horn again."

He was right to be worried. Gary Zucker tried to talk him into canceling a two-week stint with the All Stars at the Waldorf-Astoria's Empire Room in March, warning him that he might "drop dead" on the bandstand if he went through with it. But Armstrong was unfazed. "Doc, that's all right, I don't care," he replied. "My whole life, my whole soul, my whole spirit is to blooow that hooorn." Conceding defeat, Zucker struck a deal with his stubborn patient: he allowed Armstrong to perform on condition that the trumpeter would check

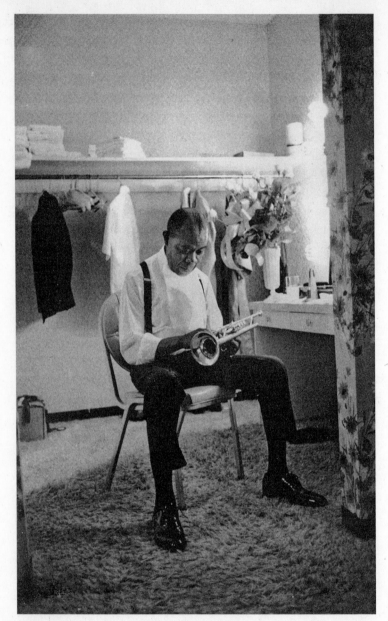

"The saddest guy in the world": A sickly-looking Armstrong in his dressing room in Las Vegas, nine months before his death. This Eddie Adams portrait shows the moody, introspective man whom the public never saw.

into a suite in the hotel, emerging only to go downstairs and play, then retiring to husband his strength for the next night's work, with the doctor dropping by each day to monitor his condition. After the first show Armstrong went back to his suite, turned on the television, and saw an unfavorable review of his performance by a TV critic. Joe Sully, who was representing Associated Booking at the Waldorf that night, was present as Armstrong watched the critic "pan the shit out of him." When the segment was over, he turned to Sully and asked, "But you'll still book me, huh, Joe?" John S. Wilson was more tactful in his *New York Times* review, saying that Armstrong "blows his trumpet sparingly but with enough emphasis to let it be known that he is back at the old stand." So he took heart and soldiered on to the end of the run, though it was clear to all who saw him backstage that his time was short. He soiled himself on the elevator before one show and had to return to his suite and change clothes. Yet on the last night he told Joe Muranyi to get ready to hit the road again: "While Tyree was soloing, Louis reaches over and grabs my hand and says, 'Josephus, don't worry. After this job I'm checking into the hospital. I have to have some things done, but don't worry — we're going to go around the world one more time. We've got plenty of work.'"

Three days later he was back in Beth Israel's intensive care unit, where a tracheotomy was performed to help him breathe. The headlines told the tale: "Armstrong in Hospital." "Armstrong Has Setback." "Armstrong Has Relapse." "Armstrong Gains Slightly." On May 7 he came home to Corona for the last time. He gave one more interview, saying that his legs were weak but that he would go back to work "as soon as my treaders get in as good shape as my chops," adding that he was "an old cat you can't lose." The last tape box he decorated bore a newspaper headline he had clipped from the *Miami Herald* on June 25: "Satchmo, Bouncing Back, Eager to Work Again." His spirits were high when Barney Bigard called on July 4 to wish him a happy birthday: "Lucille told us that she hadn't given him anything for his birthday yet and Louis said, 'Pops, Lucille's gonna give me some of that Jelly-Roll for my birthday.'" Two days later she awoke early in the morning and found him dead of a heart attack.

He lay in state at the Seventh Regiment Armory on Park Avenue, dressed in a navy-blue suit, a pink shirt, and a pink and silver tie. Lucille and Lil, who had come from Chicago for the funeral, viewed the body privately, and Lucille put a white handkerchief in his left hand. "He didn't look right without it," she said. Twenty-five thousand people — black and white, friends and strangers, stars and civilians — filed past the coffin. Dan Morgenstern stood in line with "a couple of middle-aged black guys who'd come in from Cleveland to pay their respects." The funeral, which was televised, took place at Corona Congregational Church. Five hundred mourners packed the sweltering sanctuary, and another two thousand looked on from behind police barricades. No jazz was played. Instead Peggy Lee sang "The Lord's Prayer" in a near-whisper, and Al Hibbler ended the service with "Nobody Knows the Trouble I've Seen" and "When the Saints Go Marching In." Many suspected that the ever-proper Lucille was responsible for the omission, but Ira Mangel of Associated Booking told the press that the trumpeter himself had wanted it that way: "He said if he had one band, he would have to have all of them." (A jazz funeral was held in New Orleans the next day.) The honorary pallbearers — Pearl Bailey, Count Basie, Johnny Carson, Dick Cavett, Bing Crosby, Duke Ellington, Ella Fitzgerald, David Frost, Dizzy Gillespie, Merv Griffin, Bobby Hackett, Harry James, Alan King, John Lindsay, Guy Lombardo, Nelson Rockefeller, Frank Sinatra, Ed Sullivan, and Earl Wilson — were all celebrities of one kind or another. Many of them were present in the church, as were Harold Arlen, George Avakian, Ornette Coleman, Benny Goodman, Gene Krupa, Zutty Singleton, and George Wein. Billy Taylor and Fred Robbins gave the eulogies, and Robbins ended his on a fervent note: "Move over, Gabriel! Here comes Satchmo!" Then a hundred-car procession bore Satchmo's body to Flushing Cemetery, while mourners threw flowers at Lucille's limousine all along the way.

That night CBS aired an instant special anchored by Walter Cronkite that showed footage from the funeral, clips from Ed Murrow's 1955 *See It Now* interview, and performances of "I Can't Give You Anything but Love" and "Sleepy Time Down South" by Lee, Gillespie, Hackett, Tyree Glenn, Budd Johnson, Earl Hines, Milt Hinton, and Buddy Rich. Also heard from was a black woman who was filmed while standing in line outside the armory, where she told a reporter that Armstrong had been "a friend to all people, all colors, all nations. When they say that he was the ambassador, that's what he was — the ambassador of love."

The *New York Times* started his four-thousand-word obituary on its front page. Like much of what had been written about him in years past, it contained a fair amount of misinformation, including his age and name. The story identified him as "Daniel Louis Armstrong," a canard that by 1971 was firmly entrenched in the Armstrong literature. A State Department official told the *Times* that he had "traveled on [official] tours to almost every corner of the globe." (He hadn't.) "We were almost like brothers," Earl Hines was quoted as saying. (They weren't, at least not after 1928.) But a *Times* obituary writer had interviewed Armstrong in 1969, and so the piece also included his own words: "It's been hard goddam work, man. Feel like I spent 20,000 years on planes and railroads, like I blowed my chops off. . . . I never tried to prove nothing, just always wanted to give a good show. My life has been my music, it's always come first, but the music ain't worth nothing if you can't lay it on the public. The main thing is to live for that audience, 'cause what you're there for is to please the people."

A few other apt phrases glinted in the acres of stuffy verbiage that greeted the news of his death. An editorial writer for the *Washington Post* spoke more truly than he knew when he called Armstrong "the disciplined craftsman whose art worked because he worked at his art." *Time*, by contrast, made a point of telling its readers that Armstrong's "minstrel-show appearance and jolly-fat personality made him more popular with whites than with his own race." But most of the tributes were unambivalently admiring, though none was more to the point than that of Duke Ellington: "He was born poor, died rich, and never hurt anyone on the way."

Armstrong's net worth was valued at $530,775 ($2.8 million in today's dollars), and his estate was subsequently estimated at twice that amount after the value of his record royalties was added to the tally. Most of it went to Lucille, with bequests of $5,000 apiece for Clarence and Armstrong's sister, Mama Lucy. Many were surprised that he hadn't left more behind. A reporter who saw George Avakian at the armory asked him whether Armstrong resented the fact that Harry James made more money. Stunned by the question, Avakian replied, "He loved Harry, and it didn't bother him at all that anybody made more money than he did." Later on he told James of the exchange. "What a dumb question that guy asked you," James replied. "You didn't give him the right answer. You should have said, 'Harry James would have given anything to have had what Louis Armstrong had.'"

Mama Lucy outlived him by sixteen years, Clarence by a quarter century, Lil Hardin Armstrong by a month. Whatever spite Lil felt at the collapse of their marriage had long since dissipated, and in old age she gave at least one observer the impression that she carried a torch for the man to whose early career she had contributed so much: "She still wore the rings he had given her; she preserved with the devotion of a museum curator his old cornet, letters, photographs, and earliest attempts at writing music; she spoke of him with an indifference belied by the spark in her eyes." In August Lil, who had continued to work as a musician after separating from Louis, performed at a memorial concert at Chicago's Civic Center Plaza. She played the last chord of "St. Louis Blues," then slid off the piano bench, stricken by a heart attack, dying on the spot. Lucille lived on in the Corona house until her own death in 1983. Armstrong had told her to "get yourself another man" after he died, but she never remarried. Lucille left her estate and assets to the Louis Armstrong Educational Foundation, which had been set up by the trumpeter in 1969, requesting that the house be given to the city of New York. Three years later the foundation arranged for it to be placed in the care of Queens College, which created an archive for Armstrong's papers, tapes, and personal effects, then began the slow process of raising enough money to restore the house and open it to the public as a museum.

—→

"Maybe in a hundred or two years from now they'll know how great he really was," Max Kaminsky said after Armstrong died. Philip Larkin was more optimistic. "It is already accepted — or if it isn't, it soon will be — that Louis Armstrong was an enormously important cultural figure in our century, more important than Picasso in my opinion, but certainly quite comparable," he wrote in a letter sent to a British publisher who had asked him about the wisdom of commissioning an Armstrong biography. A few months later he called Armstrong "an artist of Flaubertian purity, and a character of exceptional warmth and goodness." The occasion was a review of two new books about Armstrong, a longer version of Richard Meryman's *Life* interview and *Louis: The Louis Armstrong Story, 1900–1971*, a biography by Max Jones and John Chilton prepared with Armstrong's cooperation that included three extended autobiographical accounts. They were scrubbed up, but no more so than *Satchmo: My Life in New Orleans* had been, and Larkin spoke in his piece of the "compelling quality" of Armstrong's prose. He had already suggested that "before long there is bound to be a volume of his letters."

A quarter century passed before such a book was published. Though everyone knew that Armstrong was important, few felt the need to know much more than that. For many years after his death, his music was more admired than played, while the recordings of his later years were scarcely played at all, Gunther Schuller having declared them off-limits to persons of taste. All the important sites of his youth had long since been torn down: the Waif's Home, the honky-tonks where he played his first gigs, the shack on Jane Alley where he was born. Even Jane Alley itself was swallowed up by urban renewal in the mid-sixties. It was as if the man himself were slowly fading away, just as jazz was fading from the cultural tapestry. The success of "Hello, Dolly!" had been an end, not a beginning: it was never to be repeated, by Armstrong or anyone else. Rock was now the dominant mode of musical expression in America, and jazz musicians who wished to be heard by more than a handful of nostalgic fans changed their ways accordingly. Miles Davis had already plugged his trumpet into an amplifier and retrofitted himself as a rocker. Many young instrumentalists followed in his footsteps, while those musicians who disdained the path of fusion came to see themselves as makers of high art. The notion that a great artist might also be a popular entertainer was alien to both camps, and so Louis Armstrong's music remained alien to them as well.

Yet the music was there to be heard, and from time to time the larger world took note of its enduring significance. In 1977, for instance, NASA launched a pair of *Voyager* spacecraft bound for Jupiter, Saturn, Uranus, and Neptune. They carried copies of a golden phonograph record into which was engraved a collection of sounds and images meant to tell creatures from other worlds what life on this one was like. The record contained a wide-ranging selection of music, including Glenn Gould playing a Bach prelude and fugue, Otto Klemperer conducting the first movement of Beethoven's Fifth Symphony, Igor Stravinsky conducting the finale of *The Rite of Spring*, Blind Willie Johnson singing "Dark Was the Night," Chuck Berry's "Johnny B. Goode," and the Hot Seven's "Melancholy Blues."

In 1983 James Lincoln Collier published *Louis Armstrong: An American Genius*, the first independently written biography of the trumpeter to appear after his death. It was a psychobiography, a book with a thesis: Collier's Armstrong was at the same time "one of the most important figures in twentieth-century music" and a fatally flawed artist who had "failed his talent," an ill-educated black boy from New Orleans condemned by "a sense of his own worthlessness" to spend the bulk of his adult life gagging it up for white audiences instead of making the masterpieces that were in him. "This is all profoundly depressing, the depressingness of the half-truth," Philip Larkin wrote in testy reply. "What does Collier expect Armstrong to have done about it? Turn himself into Miles Davis?" *An American Genius* was valuable all the same, for it was based in part on interviews with several key figures in Armstrong's life, including Lucille, Milt Gabler, and Gary Zucker. But many critics savaged Collier for his factual errors and—just as important—his Schuller-like inability to appreciate Armstrong's populism.

The debate over Collier's book put Armstrong back in the news, and he stayed there. With the introduction of the compact disc in 1982, his recordings had begun to be systematically reissued, making it easier for scholars to study them at leisure. Many of his colleagues were interviewed for oral-history projects or published memoirs of their own. Academic monographs on his life and work started to appear, facilitated by the opening in 1994 of Queens College's Louis Armstrong Archives, directed by Michael Cogswell, which made copies of Armstrong's private tapes available to anyone willing to come and listen. Eleven years later Jack Bradley transferred the contents of his vast collection of Armstrong-related still photographs, films, sound recordings, letters, and other memorabilia to the Armstrong Archives, which now comprise the largest publicly held archival collection in the world devoted to a jazz musician. Not counting the uncataloged contents of Bradley's collection, they contain, among other things, 5,000 photographs, 1,600 commercial recordings, 270 sets of parts to the arrangements played by Armstrong's big band, 86 scrapbooks, 12 linear feet of personal papers, and 5 trumpets.

In 1987 "What a Wonderful World" was included on the soundtrack of Barry Levinson's *Good Morning, Vietnam* and reissued as a single, rising to number 33 on *Billboard*'s Hot 100 and subsequently becoming a pop perennial that is better known to younger listeners than "Hello, Dolly!" The next year Gary Giddins, the jazz critic of the *Village Voice*, brought out *Satchmo*, a brief life published in an illustrated coffee-table format. In addition to making the true date of Armstrong's birth known for the first time to the general public, Giddins upended the conventional critical wisdom, portraying Armstrong as "an artist who happened to be an entertainer, an entertainer who happened to be an artist—as much an original in one role as the other." *Satchmo* was the first book to make use of Armstrong's still-unpublished autobiographical manuscripts, and Giddins's insistence on taking his musical populism seriously helped persuade many younger critics and listeners to reconsider his big-band recordings. So did the advocacy of Wynton Marsalis, a hard-bop trumpeter from New Orleans who began to introduce Armstrong-derived stylistic elements into his playing and composing. "I had never really tried to learn any of his music," Marsalis confessed. "I was only dealing with the media image of Louis Armstrong. He was smiling. [But] then when you pick that trumpet up, that's when you really knew. It slaps that respect into you. . . . [M]ore than any other musician's, his sound carries the feeling and the meaning of jazz."

Marsalis made Armstrong's music the centerpiece of his programming when he became artistic director of Jazz at Lincoln Center in 1991. By then Armstrong had regained much of the cultural standing he enjoyed in his lifetime, thanks in part to the stewardship of the Armstrong Archives and the generosity of the Louis Armstrong Educational Foundation, which continues to support a wide range of musical, medical, and educational activities. New Orleans named a park and, later, the city's municipal airport after its native son, though guidebooks are careful to steer unwary tourists away from the crime-ridden Louis Armstrong Park ("Be very careful when wandering, and do not visit after dark"). A ten-foot-tall bronze statue of the trumpeter was erected there in 1980. Fifteen years later his smiling face, which had already been portrayed in Romare Bearden's collages and Jean-Michel Basquiat's paintings, appeared on a U.S. postage stamp. In 2000 David Ostwald, a tuba-playing lawyer and Armstrong enthusiast, put together the Gully Low Jazz Band, a combo that performs Armstrong's music once a week at Birdland, a nightclub in the theater district of Manhattan. The following year Ken Burns produced a ten-part TV documentary on jazz in which Armstrong was the key figure. His home in Corona was opened to the public in 2003, having been restored to something approaching the way it looked in its owner's lifetime. In that year the State Department distributed to countries around the world an essay in which his name headed a list of "all-American" modernists: "Louis Armstrong, Fred Astaire, Willa Cather, Aaron Copland, Stuart Davis, Duke Ellington, F. Scott Fitzgerald, Robert Frost, John Ford, George Gershwin, Howard Hawks, Edward Hopper, Flannery O'Connor, Jerome Robbins, Frank Lloyd Wright: surely these and others like them rank high among our exemplary figures, the ones whose work is indelibly stamped 'Made in U.S.A.'"

Armstrong's own unpublished and uncollected writings found their way into print with the publication in 1999 of Joshua Berrett's *Louis Armstrong Companion* and Thomas Brothers's *Louis Armstrong, in His Own Words: Selected Writings.* These books showed him as he was, not as others wished or imagined him to be, and the bluntness with which he spoke his mind from beyond the grave gave the lie to a half century of abuse that Ossie Davis, who acted opposite him in *A Man Called Adam,* summed up in a reminiscence of their brief acquaintance: "Most of the fellows I grew up with, myself included, we used to laugh at Louis Armstrong. We knew he was good, but that didn't save him from our malice and our ridicule. Everywhere we'd look, there'd be Louis — sweat popping, eyes bugging, mouth wide open, grinning, oh my Lord, from ear to ear. . . . mopping his brow, ducking his head, doing his thing for the white man." Davis changed his mind after meeting Armstrong, concluding that his horn was "where Louis kept his manhood hid all those years . . . enough for him . . . enough for all of us." But if he had ever felt the need to hide it, he did so in plain sight, and the admiring musicians who knew him best never doubted that he was not just a man but a miracle. Some, like Teddy Wilson, emphasized his artistry: "I don't think there has been a musician since Armstrong who had all the factors in balance, all the factors equally developed. Such a balance was the essential thing about Beethoven, I think, and Armstrong, like Beethoven, had this high development of balance. Lyricism. Delicacy. Emotional outburst. Rhythm. Complete mastery of his horn." Others spoke of his humanity. "As I watched him and talked with him, I felt he was the most natural man," the pianist Jaki Byard said. "Playing, talking, singing, he was so perfectly natural the tears came to my eyes." But all agreed on his greatness and marveled that such a being had walked the earth.

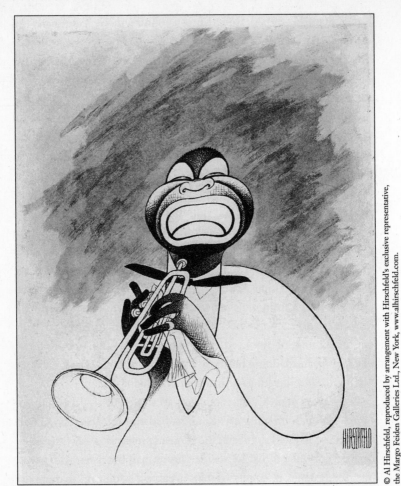

"Grinning, oh my Lord, from ear to ear": Many now feel ill at ease with the old-fashioned, crowd-pleasing entertainer portrayed in this 1990 caricature by Al Hirschfeld, but there was nothing false about Satchmo's unselfconscious smile.

Today we live in a time far removed from his, and it is harder than ever before to bridge the gap and see him clearly. Some now judge him by the standards of a world he never knew and find him wanting. "The relentlessly beaming smile, the handkerchief dabbing away the sweat, the reflexive bowing, the exaggerated humility and gracious-ness — all this signaled that he would not breach the manners of segregation, the propriety that required him to be both cheerful and less than fully human," one recent commentator has written. But that broad smile was no mere game face, donned to please the paying customers: it told the truth about the man who wore it. In return for his unswerving dedication to his art, he knew true happiness and shared it unstintingly with his fellow men, who responded in kind. Richard Brookhiser tells of how, when doing battle with cancer, he was unable to listen to any music other than the *Goldberg Variations* and Louis Armstrong: "Bach said everything is in its place; Armstrong said the sun comes shining through." It was a response that Armstrong would have appreciated. Not long before he died, he wrote to a friend that "my whole life has been happiness. Through all of the misfortunes, etc, I did not plan anything. Life was there for me and I accepted it. And life, what ever came out, has been beautiful to me, and I love everybody."

A few years earlier he had spoken to a journalist about a confrontation that burned itself into his memory:

> Years ago I was playing the little town of Lubbock, Texas, when this white cat grabs me at the end of the show — he's full of whiskey and trouble. He pokes on my chest and says, "I don't like *niggers!*" These two cats with me was gonna practice their Thanksgiving carving on that dude. But I say, "No, let the man talk. *Why* don't you like us, Pops?" And would you believe that cat couldn't *tell* us? So he apologizes — crying and carrying on. . . . And dig this: that fella and his whole family come to be my friends! When I'd go back through Lubbock, Texas, for many many years they would make ole Satchmo welcome and treat him like a king.

The whole story of Louis Armstrong's life is in that one encounter. Faced with the terrible realities of the time and place into which he had been born, he did not repine, but returned love for hatred and sought salvation in work. Therein lay the ultimate meaning of his epic journey from squalor to immortality: his sunlit, hopeful art, brought into being by the labor of a lifetime, spoke to all men in all conditions and helped make them whole.

AFTERWORD

KNOW OF NO MAN for whom I had more admiration and respect,"
Bing Crosby wrote to Lucille Armstrong after Louis Armstrong
died. One of the purposes of this book is to explain to a new generation why those words still ring true. To be sure, much has been
written about Armstrong's life and work, some of it penetrating and
perceptive. Yet this is, surprisingly, the first fully sourced biography
of Armstrong to be written by an author who is also a trained musician. It is not, however, a "scholarly" biography in the usual sense
of the word: *Pops* is less a work of scholarship than an exercise in syn-
thesis, a narrative biography based in large part on the research of
those academic scholars and other investigators who in recent years
have unearthed a wealth of hitherto unknown information about
Armstrong. They uncovered many of the facts I have sought to relate
and interpret. The interpretations are, of course, my own, but without these men and women, whose groundbreaking work is humbly
acknowledged in the source notes and bibliography, this book would
not exist.

I have also been privileged to draw on archival material unavail-
able to previous biographers, including the 650 reels of tape record-

ings privately made by Armstrong during the last quarter century of his life, which are now part of the Louis Armstrong Archives at Queens College/CUNY. These recordings are of great significance, and I have made extensive use of them, just as I have drawn heavily on Armstrong's own writings. He was one of a handful of jazz musicians, and the only major one, to leave behind a substantial body of prose writing in which his thoughts are presented in wholly or largely unmediated form, and it is in his own words that he comes across most clearly.

I cannot begin to list all the people who were of direct assistance to me in the writing of *Pops*. I am, however, especially grateful to Andrea Schulz, my ever-encouraging editor, who made sure that I made myself clear; Glen Hartley and Lynn Chu, my trusted and trustworthy agents; Barbara Wood, the copyeditor of my dreams; Victoria Hartman, who made *Pops* look as good as its subject; André Bernard, who brought me to Harcourt; Michael Cogswell and Dan Morgenstern, the all-knowing keepers of the keys at the Louis Armstrong Archives and the Institute of Jazz Studies, both of whom read the manuscript with painstaking care; Neal Kozodoy and Mark Gerson, whose timely intervention got me off to a much easier start; Susan and Roger Hertog, through whose Columbia University fellowship program I secured critical assistance in the early stages of my work; Patricia O'Toole, the omnicompetent overseer of the Hertog Fellows; Ariel Davis, Rose Newnham, and Stephanie Steward, who began as research assistants and ended as friends; George Avakian, Jack and Nancy Bradley, and Joe Muranyi, who brought me closer to Armstrong than I ever thought possible; Thomas Brothers, whose knowledge of his early years is unrivaled; Steven Lasker, the first scholar to provide accurate accounts of Armstrong's 1930 arrest for possession of marijuana and the origins of his relationship with Johnny Collins; Ricky Riccardi, whose forthcoming book on the All Stars will break important new ground; Peter Ecklund and Lucinda Lewis, who provided me with a professional perspective on Armstrong's lifelong lip problems; Philippe Baudoin, Joshua Berrett, Bob Brookmeyer, James Dapogny, Michael Fitzgerald, Krin Gabbard,

Ted Gioia, Mickey Kapp, Bill Kirchner, Elizabeth McLeod, Jeffrey Nussbaum, David Ostwald, Doug Ramsey, David Sager, Randy Sandke, and the late Richard M. Sudhalter, who generously shared their knowledge of the trumpeter and his times; Paul Doherty and Kevin Segura, who furnished me with copies of rare kinescopes and videotapes of his TV appearances; Alicia Noel, whose familiarity with the novels of Horatio Alger shed light on his youthful aspirations; the late Neil McCaffrey, who first played Armstrong's 1942 recording of "Sleepy Time Down South" for me; Michael Anderson and Fletcher Roberts, who commissioned the original *New York Times* articles that were the seeds from which *Pops* grew; and Walter Darby Bannard, who first suggested the title. I also thank the *Times*, *Commentary*, and Yale University Press, which published earlier versions of parts of the first and last chapters.

Above all I thank my mother, who called me into the living room of our Missouri home one Sunday night and sat me down in front of the TV, on which Louis Armstrong was singing "Hello, Dolly!" on *The Ed Sullivan Show.* "This man won't be around forever," she said. "Someday you'll be glad you saw him." That was back when the public schools in my hometown were still segregated, two decades after a black man had been dragged from our city jail, hauled through the streets at the end of a rope, and set afire. Yet even in a place where such a monstrous evil had been wrought, my mother came to love Armstrong — and, just as important, to respect him — not merely for the beauty of the music he made but also for the goodness of the man who made it. I wrote this book so that she, and others like her, might know more about the man they loved.

TERRY TEACHOUT
New York City
February 12, 2009

APPENDIX
Thirty Key Recordings by Louis Armstrong

SOURCE NOTES

SELECT BIBLIOGRAPHY

PHOTO CREDITS

INDEX

ABOUT THE AUTHOR

APPENDIX

Thirty Key Recordings by Louis Armstrong

1. "Chimes Blues" (Gennett, 1923, with King Oliver's Creole Jazz Band)
2. "Texas Moaner Blues" (OKeh, 1924, with Sidney Bechet and Clarence Williams's Blue Five)
3. "St. Louis Blues" (Columbia, 1925, with Bessie Smith)
4. "Heebie Jeebies" (OKeh, 1926, with the Hot Five)
5. "Cornet Chop Suey" (OKeh, 1926, with the Hot Five)
6. "Potato Head Blues" (OKeh, 1927, with the Hot Seven)
7. "Hotter than That" (OKeh, 1927, with Lonnie Johnson and the Hot Five)
8. "West End Blues" (OKeh, 1928, with Earl Hines and the Hot Five)
9. "Weather Bird" (OKeh, 1928, with Earl Hines)
10. "I Can't Give You Anything but Love" (OKeh, 1929)
11. "Ain't Misbehavin'" (OKeh, 1929)
12. "Sweethearts on Parade" (OKeh, 1930)
13. "Star Dust" (OKeh, 1931, first take)
14. "I Gotta Right to Sing the Blues" (Victor, 1933)
15. "Darling Nelly Gray" (Decca, 1937, with the Mills Brothers)

16. "Jubilee" (Decca, 1938)
17. "Struttin' with Some Barbecue" (Decca, 1938)
18. "Jeepers Creepers" (Decca, 1939, with Sid Catlett)
19. "Sleepy Time Down South" (Decca, 1941)
20. "Snafu" (Victor, 1946, with the Esquire All-American 1946 Award Winners)
21. "Back o' Town Blues" (Victor, 1947, with Jack Teagarden, Bobby Hackett, and Sid Catlett at Town Hall)
22. "Blueberry Hill" (Decca, 1949)
23. "New Orleans Function" (Decca, 1950, with Earl Hines, Jack Teagarden, and the All Stars)
24. "You Rascal You" (Decca, 1950, with Louis Jordan and His Tympany Five)
25. "Mack the Knife" (Columbia, 1955, with the All Stars)
26. "King of the Zulus" (Decca, 1957, with the All Stars, from *Satchmo: A Musical Autobiography*)
27. "How Long Has This Been Going On?" (Verve, 1957, with the Oscar Peterson Trio, from *Louis Armstrong Meets Oscar Peterson*)
28. "Black and Tan Fantasy" (Impulse, 1961, with Duke Ellington and the All Stars, from *Louis Armstrong and Duke Ellington*)
29. "Summer Song" (Columbia, 1961, with Dave Brubeck, from *The Real Ambassadors*)
30. "Hello, Dolly!" (Kapp, 1963, with the All Stars)

All of these recordings can be downloaded from iTunes.

Source Notes

ABBREVIATIONS

LA	Louis Armstrong
AA	Louis Armstrong Archives (Queens College)
IJS	Institute of Jazz Studies (Rutgers University)
IHOW	*Louis Armstrong, in His Own Words*
LAS	*Louis: The Louis Armstrong Story 1900–1971*
Satchmo	*Satchmo: My Life in New Orleans*
SP	*Louis Armstrong — a Self-Portrait*
STM	*Swing That Music*

All quotations from the sources listed above are by LA unless otherwise indicated.

LA's scrapbooks and privately recorded tapes (held by the Armstrong Archives) are cited as follows:

LA, scrapbooks, AA
LA, tape 1, AA

Prologue: "The Cause of Happiness"

SOURCES

DOCUMENTS

Lil Armstrong, *Satchmo and Me*, recorded interview (Riverside, hereafter cited as *Satchmo and Me*); George Avakian, interview, January 21, 2005; Jack Bradley, interview, July 7, 2008; Nat Hentoff, liner notes for *Satchmo the Great*, sound recording (Columbia); *Louis Armstrong: The Portrait Collection*, DVD (Multiprises); Gilbert Millstein, "The Most Un-Average Cat," liner notes for *Satchmo: A Musical Autobiography*, sound recording (Decca); Joe Muranyi, interview, September 1, 2007; *Satchmo the Great*, film (United Artists).

BOOKS

Bergreen, *Louis Armstrong*; Chilton, *Let the Good Times Roll*; Collier, *Louis Armstrong*; Le Corbusier, *When the Cathedrals Were White*; Davis, *Miles*; Foster, *Autobiography*; Giddins, *Satchmo*; Kaminsky, *Jazz Band*; Kempton, *America Comes of Middle Age*; Larkin, *All What Jazz*; Lyttelton, *Last Chorus*; Miller, *Louis Armstrong*; Osborne, *Herbert von Karajan*; Shapiro and Hentoff, *Hear Me Talkin' to Ya*; Stewart, *Jazz Masters of the Thirties*; Stratemann, *Louis Armstrong on the Screen*; Thomson, *A Virgil Thomson Reader*; Untermeyer and Williamson, *Mother Is Minnie*.

NOTES

LA's Philharmonic debut: This account is based on my interview with George Avakian. Because some members of the Philharmonic did not play at its summer concerts, the orchestra was billed as the "Lewisohn Stadium Symphony Orchestra."

"America's secret weapon": Felix Belair, "United States Has Secret Sonic Weapon — Jazz," *New York Times*, November 6, 1955. **"Two American Originals":** *See It Now*, December 13, 1955. **The two men chatted on camera:** *Satchmo the Great*. **"All White Folks call me Louie":** "The 'Goffin Notebooks,'" in *IHOW* (hereafter cited as "'Goffin Notebooks'"), 109. **At least one of his four wives:** Lil Armstrong pronounces LA's first name "Louie" on *Satchmo and Me*. Lucille, LA's fourth wife, usually called him "Lewis" (George Avakian, personal communication).

LA's CBS-sponsored visit to Ghana: "CBS shelled out some $25,000 to send Armstrong, his five-man All-Stars and a camera crew to the city of Accra, the Gold Coast, for a three-day junket" ("'Just Very,'" *Time*, June 4, 1956).

"At the conclusion of the scheduled program": "Bonus at Jazz Concert," *New York Times*, July 9, 1956.

LA's appearance had been a grudging concession: See Untermeyer and Williamson, 89–90, 110–11. The first concert of the season, a classical program featuring Marian Anderson, had drawn a crowd of only fifteen thousand.

"A wheelbarrow crunching up a gravel driveway": "Last Trumpet for the First Trumpeter," *Time*, July 19, 1971.

"Armstrong has recently begun offering": Whitney Balliett, "Jazz Records: The Three Louis," *New Yorker*, September 28, 1957.

"It's humor everywhere to me": Gilbert Millstein, "Africa Harks to Satch's Horn," *New York Times Magazine*, November 20, 1960. **"Uncle Tom-like subservience":** Dizzy Gillespie and Ralph Ginzburg, "Jazz Is Too Good for Americans," *Esquire*, June 1957. **"Nowadays, we try to work out different rhythms":** "Louis the First," *Time*, February 21, 1949.

"He say, 'Now, when you get to this cadenza'": Hentoff.

"Jazz of the thoroughly authentic kind": George Avakian, "Avakian Gives the Beat," *Stadium Concerts Review*, July 9, 1956. **"Many of the listeners":** "Louis Armstrong Storms Stadium," *New York Times*, July 15, 1956.

"Louie Armstrong has told me": *Satchmo the Great*. **"It is somewhat dis-**

turbing": John S. Wilson, "Music: Jazz Is Tested at Stadium," *New York Times*, July 16, 1956.

"I never read no writeups": *SP*, 55. **"The people expect all that"**: Ibid., 42. **"The note's what count"**: Undated TV interview, ca. 1961, in *Louis Armstrong: The Portrait Collection* (hereafter cited as "1961 interview"). **"I mean you don't just go around"**: *SP*, 58.

The fourth-highest-grossing film: Stratemann, 329.

"What you saw": Muranyi. **"Down-to-earth"**: Bradley. **He reacted by dropping his pants**: Millstein, "The Most Un-Average Cat." **"I don't care what company I'm in"**: Ibid. **"He was always happy"**: Chilton, 31–32.

"He be sittin' down in his underwear": Collier, 314–15.

"I tried to walk like him": Shapiro and Hentoff, 206. **"I stood silent"**: Robert Goffin, "Jazzmen's Greatest Kicks," *Esquire*, August 1944. **"The combination of Louis's dazzling virtuosity"**: Kaminsky, 40. **"Something inexhaustible"**: Larkin, 282. **"You can't play nothing on trumpet"**: Davis, 316.

"Imagine! Two hours of music": Osborne, 267.

"I like that deep stuff": Letter to Orson Welles, ca. 1945, Orson Welles Collection, Lilly Library, Indiana University. **"Most of my records"**: *SP*, 24. Enrico Caruso and John McCormack were at the peak of their worldwide popularity when Armstrong was a teenager. Amelita Galli-Curci and Luisa Tetrazzini were two of the most successful coloratura sopranos of the day. Henry Burr, a Canadian concert singer, recorded hundreds of ballads and popular songs between 1902 and 1929. See Joshua Berrett, "Louis Armstrong and Opera," *Musical Quarterly*, Summer 1992. **"Like when I play, maybe 'Back o' Town Blues'"**: *SP*, 56.

"I seen everythin' from a child, comin' up": Millstein, "Africa Harks to Satch's Horn." **"When I blow I think of times and things from outa the past"**: Larry L. King, "Everybody's Louie," *Harper's*, November 1967 (hereafter cited as "'Everybody's Louie'").

"I'm playin' a date in Florida years ago": Millstein, "Africa Harks to Satch's Horn."

"He is mathematics": Le Corbusier, 159. **"A master of musical art"**: Virgil Thomson, "Swing Music," *Modern Music*, May 1938, quoted in Thomson, 31. **"Model of greatness"**: "Every artist has models of greatness in the Arts which guide his development. Louis Armstrong has always been one of the most important for me" (quoted in Miller, 48).

"Disgustingly Segregated and Prejudiced": "Louis Armstrong + the Jewish Family in New Orleans, La., the Year of 1907," in *IHOW* (hereafter cited as "'Jewish Family'"), 33. **"Those people who make the restrictions"**: *LAS*, 244.

"To friend and foe": Lyttelton, 168. **"I got a simple rule about everybody"**: "Everybody's Louie." **A friend dropped in on him**: Erroll Garner, quoted in Giddins, 184. **"I can't go no place"**: *SP*, 34.

"Louis is real jealous": Foster, 189. **"I don't give a damn"**: Don Freeman, "We'll Get Along Without Hines' Ego, Says Armstrong," *Down Beat*, February 22, 1952.

"Louis bounced onto the opposite stage": Stewart, 47.

LA told a dumbfounded small-town newsman: "Louis Armstrong, Barring Soviet Tour, Denounces Eisenhower and Gov. Faubus," *New York Times*, September 19, 1957.

"Negroes *never* did stick together": "Jewish Family," 9.

Scholars cite them gingerly: The passage was carefully paraphrased in

Bergreen, and Giddins mentions it only in passing. **LA "doesn't pass judgment":** *Satchmo*, v–vi.

LA's "hobby": "Goffin Notebooks," 95. **"I was determined":** *Satchmo*, 107. **"The Lord will help the poor":** 1961 interview.

"I think I had a beautiful life": Israel Shenker, "'Just Plain Old Satchmo' Turns 70 Sweetly," *New York Times*, July 4, 1970. **"The *Negroes* always wanted *pity*":** "Jewish Family," 9, 8. **"You don't have to do a damn thing bad":** Millstein, "Africa Harks to Satch's Horn."

LA has been compared to Booker T. Washington: See, for instance, Brian Harker's review of Berrett's book *The Louis Armstrong Companion* and *IHOW* (*Notes*, June 2001). **"I never want to be":** *LAS*, 246.

"He endures": Kempton, 355. **"Showmanship does not mean":** Quoted in Howard Reich, "Jazz Giant's Private Views Show Anger Behind Smile," *Chicago Tribune*, July 29, 2001. **"When I pick up that horn":** Millstein, "Africa Harks to Satch's Horn."

1. "Bastards from the Start"

SOURCES

DOCUMENTS

Arthur Briggs, oral-history interview, IJS; *Eddie Condon's Floor Show*, TV show, June 11, 1949 (NBC); *I've Got a Secret*, TV show, December 27, 1965 (CBS); *Louis Armstrong: The Portrait Collection*, DVD (Multiprises); Jelly Roll Morton, oral-history interviews, Library of Congress, Washington, DC, cited by catalog number of original Circle 78 issue; Hilda Taylor, oral-history interview, Hogan Jazz Archive, Tulane University, New Orleans.

BOOKS

Anderson, *The Original Hot Five Recordings of Louis Armstrong*; Barker, *A Life in Jazz*; Bechet, *Treat It Gentle*; Bethell, *George Lewis*; Blassingame, *Black New Orleans 1860–1880*; Brothers, *Louis Armstrong's New Orleans*; Collier, *Louis Armstrong*; Darensbourg, *Jazz Odyssey*; Dodds, *The Baby Dodds Story*; Foster, *Autobiography*; Giddins, *Satchmo*; Gushee, *Pioneers of Jazz*; Liebling, *Liebling at Home*; Lomax, *Mister Jelly Roll*; Long, *The Great Southern Babylon*; Marquis, *In Search of Buddy Bolden*; Mezzrow and Wolfe, *Really the Blues*; Percy, *The Moviegoer*; Ramsey and Smith, *Jazzmen*; Rose, *Storyville, New Orleans*; Shapiro and Hentoff, *Hear Me Talkin' to Ya*; Walser, *Keeping Time*.

NOTES

"A culture that had ripened properly": A. J. Liebling, *The Earl of Louisiana*, in Liebling, 424. **"The ironwork on the balconies":** Percy, 14–15.

Musicians simply called it "the District": "Long after I left New Orleans guys would come around asking me about Storyville down there. . . . When I found out they were talking about the red-light district, I sure was surprised. We always called it the District" (Foster, 41). **"I am now in this great Southern Babylon":** Quoted in Long, 2. **"You can make prostitution illegal":** Ibid., 156.

"The earnest and general feeling": Barker, 71.

A measure of personal safety: See Blassingame, 1–22. **"Creoles of color":** See Brothers, 23–28. **"My folks was all Frenchmans":** Lomax, 4. **"The worst Jim Crow around New Orleans":** Foster, 73. **"He wasn't French":** Quoted in Brothers, 31. **"Wouldn't hire a man":** Bethell, 25.

"No matter how much his Diamond Sparkled": "Jewish Family," 24. **"At *ten* years old I could see":** Ibid., 17.

"I sure had a ball there": *SP*, 7.

At least one biographer found the date too pat: Collier, 18–21. **A researcher located an entry:** Giddins, 47–51. The researcher was Tad Jones, who also established the following additional facts about LA's ancestry: "On May 18, 1818, a slaveowner named Antoine Turcas purchased Daniel Walker, 32, from Richmond for about $600, a substantial price at the time. Walker . . . had a son, also named Daniel, who married Catherine Washington, born in 1837 and brought with her mother and sister from a plantation in Madison County, Miss., to New Orleans, where they were auctioned off together. Catherine and Daniel Walker had a daughter named Josephine who later married Ephraim Armstrong. They had a son named Willie, the father of Louis Armstrong. Catherine Walker, Louis's great-grandmother, attended the baby's baptism in 1901 as sponsor" (Ralph Blumenthal, "Digging for Satchmo's Roots in the City That Spawned Him," *New York Times*, August 15, 2000). **A fifteen-year-old country girl:** LA gives her age exactly in *STM*, 3, but an obituary notice preserved in his scrapbooks states that she was forty-four years old at the time of her death in 1927.

LA did not know the true year of his birth: The fact that LA believed himself to be thirteen months older than he really was must be kept in mind whenever he discusses the chronology of his life. **He registered for the draft in 1918:** A photograph of LA's draft registration card can be viewed online at www.doctorjazz .co.uk/draftcards2.html. **"The night I was born":** *Satchmo*, 2. **"A blasting fourth of July":** *LAS*, 43. **She misremembered the date:** According to Tad Jones, New Orleans police records showed that there was a gunfight near LA's birthplace on August 4, 1901 (Michael Cogswell, personal communication). **Surviving baptismal and census records:** The same records confirm that LA had no middle name, though *Time*'s 1949 cover story would identify him as "Daniel Louis Armstrong," an embellishment of unknown origin that soon became established as fact. "The Daniel . . . came out of clear skies, I guess, I don't remember Mayann (Mary Ann) ever calling me by Daniel" (*LAS*, 48). Gene H. Anderson speculates that LA might have been named after his paternal great-grandfather (Anderson, 22).

"A sharp man": *Satchmo*, 29. **"My father did not have time to teach me anything":** Ibid., 28–29.

"The man who May Ann told us was our father": "Jewish Family," 20.

723 Jane Alley: The house was torn down in 1964, and Jane Alley itself disappeared shortly thereafter to make room for the city's Traffic and Municipal Court building. (LA incorrectly referred to the street as "James Alley" in *Satchmo* and in various interviews.) None of the other buildings where LA lived in New Orleans prior to 1922 is still standing today. For a list of surviving Armstrong-related sites, see Bruce Eggler, "Lost Louis," *New Orleans Times-Picayune*, August 5, 2001. **"Whether my mother did any hustling":** *Satchmo*, 8. In the unedited typescript, LA canceled the coarser phrase *selling fish* and replaced it with the word *hustling* (IJS). **"Churchpeople, gamblers":** *Satchmo*, 8. **"That, I guess, is how I acquired my singing tactics":** Ibid., 11. **"The whole Congregation would be Wailing":** Letter to L/Cpl. Villec (1967), in *IHOW*, 170.

"I realize I have not done": *Satchmo*, 16.

"I couldn't keep track of the stepdaddies": Albin Krebs, "Louis Armstrong, Jazz Trumpeter and Singer, Dies," *New York Times*, July 7, 1971 (hereafter cited as *"Times* obituary"). All quotes from this story come from an interview conducted with LA in 1969 for posthumous use in his *Times* obituary. **"The urge to go out":** Ibid., 19.

"I had to work": "Jewish Family," 10.

A family of Jewish peddlers from Lithuania for whom he worked as a boy: In later life LA recalled having gone to work for the Karnofskys at the age of seven, but his earlier writings are inconsistent on the date. See *IHOW*, 192–93. **LA had little to say about them:** *Satchmo*, 94–95. **"Problems of their own":** "Jewish Family," 5, 8, 11. **Blues-blowing junkmen:** See *SP*, 11–12, and Brothers, 55–60.

"The Negroes always hated the Jewish people": "Jewish Family," 9.

LA wore a Star of David: *LAS*, 244. It is visible in many backstage photos (one of them is reproduced in Giddins, 186–87). **"So I can *Nibble* on them":** "Jewish Family," 11. **"The *Jewish* people":** Ibid., 18.

"It wasn't no classyfied place": *SP*, 8. **Buddy Bolden:** Bolden became insane and stopped playing in 1906. See also LA, tape 346, AA: "When I was five years old I used to hear Buddy Bolden. They used to play on the sidewalk before they go into the Funky Butt Hall on Saturday nights. So we couldn't go in there, we too young, but we could hear that half hour they played before they go in."

Sex could be bought for as little as ten cents: Foster, 43. See also Rose, 158–60, for excerpts from the transcript of an unexpurgated, astonishingly frank tape-recorded interview conducted in 1961 with "Carrie," an illiterate sixty-eight-year-old prostitute who grew up "in a poor neighborhood near Perdido Street . . . within a block of Louis Armstrong's birthplace." **Three-quarters of the arrests:** Marquis, 68. **"Many a time myself I went":** Morton, 1658-A. **A "bad boy":** *LAS*, 50–51. **"We'd go around to gamblers":** 1961 interview. **"I want you to go hear a little quartet":** Bechet, 91.

"Oh Mister, let me alone": *SP*, 15. **"Very few arrests of minors were made":** "Few Juveniles Arrested," *New Orleans Times-Democrat*, January 2, 1913, quoted in Brothers, 98. That the story gives his age as twelve suggests that LA already believed himself to have been born in 1900.

The Colored Waif's Home for Boys: LA spelled its name "Waif's Home" in *STM* and "Waifs' Home" in *Satchmo* and his correspondence. The former is correct.

LA may have already spent a brief stretch of time in the Colored Waif's Home: "Although records of the Waif's Home . . . were apparently destroyed, Capt. Jones recalled at the end of his life that Armstrong was in custody at least twice. According to Joseph L. Peyton, the clerk of court for Orleans Parish Juvenile Court since 1940 — and the successor in that job to his father, who had it from 1908 — Louis was in and out of the Waif's Home during his early teenage years" (Giddins, 65–66). In response to the similar recollection of Clay Watson, then head of the New Orleans Jazz Museum, LA told Max Jones, "Well, I went in January and I stayed all 1912, no, I stayed all of 1913, and I got out in June of 1914. So I stayed out there a year and a half. . . . I don't remember being taken to the Waifs' Home twice" (*LAS*, 51–52). In a 1960 radio interview in which he described his arrest, LA says that he "went back to the orphanage" on New Year's Day (LA, tape 564, AA). **"Since I had been raised in such bad company":** *Satchmo*, 39.

"He organized quartets": *I've Got a Secret*.

"I played all classical music": 1961 interview. This recollection cannot be literally true, since Mahler's music was all but unknown in the United States in 1913, but it does show that LA was first exposed to classical music at an earlier age than is generally supposed. **"Pops, it sure was the greatest thing":** *Times* obituary.

It was Davis who first taught him: *Satchmo*, 46. **"I did learn to play the cornet":** *LAS*, 55, 54. In his 1965 *I've Got a Secret* appearance, LA said that it was Davis who had given him his first lessons. **"I *kept* that *horn* for a *long* time":** "Jewish Family," 12. The cornet acquired by the Smithsonian Institution's National Museum of American History in 2001 and identified by the museum as "the instrument on which Louis Armstrong learned to play when he was just 12 years old" is a Sears, Roebuck model that the company did not list in its mail-order catalogs prior to 1920. See Jeffrey Nussbaum, Niles Eldredge, and Robb Stewart, "Louis Armstrong's First Cornet?" *Historic Brass Society Journal* 15 (2003). LA displayed this cornet on *I've Got a Secret*. When asked if it had been his first instrument, he replied, "Just about." **LA denied Bunk Johnson's claim:** "Bunk didn't show me nothing. He didn't even know me" ("Bunk Didn't Teach Me," *Record Changer*, July–August 1950, quoted in *IHOW*, 40–41). **"I showed him just how to hold [the cornet]":** William Russell, "Louis Armstrong," in Ramsey and Smith, 120–21. **"Of course, Louis was playing the cornet":** Bechet, 93. See also *IHOW*, 196–98.

LA's unorthodox technique: Arthur Briggs, who knew LA at the time of his first major embouchure-related crisis in 1934, described it in an oral-history interview: "You see, Louie did not have the tuition that we had. . . . He thought he — by using pressure that he would get the results that he wanted. By using pressure, though, he just smothered his lips." He also used mouthpieces with a narrow cushion, which interacted with his high-pressure technique to split his lip. In addition, LA suffered from chronic leukoplakia, which caused the formation of excessive scar tissue (*Times* obituary). He trimmed it away himself, thus causing further lip damage (Mezzrow and Wolfe, 257). Peter Ecklund, a jazz trumpeter who has studied LA's playing technique, says that his vibrato "was produced by shaking his hand rather than rocking his hand or using his jaw. He shook the horn, which may be an indication that he was using a great deal of pressure. You can see him [in films] swinging from side to side as he creates the vibrato. That's a clue to the amount of pressure he's using" (personal communication). According to Lucinda Lewis, the principal horn player of the New Jersey Symphony, who works with brass players suffering from embouchure problems, "It's not necessarily that Armstrong's playing mechanics were flawed as much as that they were not well enough developed at such an early age to withstand the kind and quantity of playing that eventually permanently injured them" (personal communication). **He split his upper lip:** *SP*, 39.

"And when that body's in the ground": Ibid., 10.

LA spent the night in Davis's home: LA, unedited typescript of *Satchmo*, 22 (IJS). **"My father had never paid me a single visit":** *Satchmo*, 53. **"That great big room":** LA, tape 426, AA.

"I feel as though although I am away": George W. Kay, "Louis Armstrong's Letter to His 'Daddy,'" *Second Line*, Summer 1976. **"I know lots of men":** *STM*, 5. He was no less grateful to the judge who had sent him to the Waif's Home: "Many years later, when I went back to New Orleans and had made good, old Judge Wilson . . . made a speech out at the home and told the boys they should use me 'as an example' and some day they might do something, too. I told Judge Wilson that he did the best thing for me he could have done" (ibid., 23–24). **"Me and**

my horn": Howard Taubman, "Satchmo Wears His Crown Gaily," *New York Times*, January 29, 1950.

"All you have to do": *Satchmo*, 58. **"I loved it"**: Ibid., 59.

"I, myself, happened to be creator": Jelly Roll Morton, "'I Created Jazz in 1902, Not W. C. Handy,' Declares Jelly Roll Morton," *Down Beat*, August 1938.

"You had bands that played ragtime": Foster, 51. **"If you played what he wrote"**: Ibid., 53.

"All of a sudden, Buddy stomps": Quoted in Gushee, 40.

Buddy Bolden "didn't play jazz": Morton, 1658-B. Bunk Johnson's 1947 recording of "The Entertainer," played "as written" but with tripletized dotted rhythms and interpolated "blue" sevenths, may give some hint of what Bolden's "ragtime" playing sounded like. **The distinction is a subtle one:** "At a dance every third number was a waltz. Now if you play a waltz, people look at you real funny and wonder what the hell you're doing. They don't know how waltzes was a very important part of ragtime" (Darensbourg, 15). **"A negro band . . . plays varied rags"**: Quoted in Gushee, 32.

The word *jazz* first appeared in print: Gushee, 299–300. **"Between you and me"**: *Satchmo*, 161.

"In the matter of the jass": "Jass and Jassism," *New Orleans Times-Picayune*, June 20, 1918, quoted in Walser, 8. **They drew a bright line:** "Canal Street was the dividing line and the people from the different sections didn't mix. The musicians mixed only if you were good enough. But at one time the Creole fellows thought the uptown musicians weren't good enough to play with them" (Dodds, 13). **"The only thing Louis could play then"**: Foster, 60.

"A hustle that was a little lighter": *Satchmo*, 94. **"Bad, strong women"**: Ibid., 64. **"I always felt inferior"**: Ibid., 199. **"I wouldn't think of staying away"**: Ibid., 87–88. **"Got religion and gave up men"**: *Times* obituary.

"A pretty decent salary": *Satchmo*, 81.

The role played by Storyville: "The musicianers would go to those houses just whenever they didn't have a regular engagement or some gig they was playing . . . All that what's been written about you got to play your instrument in a whorehouse, it's all wrong" (Bechet, 53). **"When all of us were playing the District"**: Foster, 40.

"I'm telling you it was a sad situation": LA, "Storyville—Where the Blues Were Born," *True*, November 1947. ("Cotch" was a card game played in New Orleans.)

"Half-spoiled chickens": *Satchmo*, 81–82.

He lost his virginity: Ibid., 101–2. **Landed a gig:** *SP*, 17. **Oliver tutored LA on an informal basis:** "He gave me lessons out of an exercise book—then we'd run down little duets together" (ibid.). **"I loved Joe because he'd take more time"**: 1961 interview. LA is also known to have taken lessons from Arnold Metoyer, a Creole cornet player and teacher. According to Metoyer's widow, he studied "music theory" from "a great big book," probably Jean B. Arban's *Complete Conservatory Method for Trumpet* (Taylor). LA referred to Arban's *Method* by name in *SP* (55).

"If he got himself a pair of long trousers": Kid Ory (as told to Nesuhi Ertegun), "Louis Was Just a Little Kid in Knee Pants; Ory," *Down Beat*, July 14, 1950. **"Several automobiles"**: *Satchmo*, 143–45.

LA met Daisy Parker at the Brick House: Ibid., 150–68. Except as indicated, all direct quotes from LA about Daisy in this chapter are from *Satchmo*.

They were married at City Hall the next day: LA stated in his ₁₂3 divorce hearing that he and Daisy were married on March 19, 1918.

"You black son-of-a-bitch": *LAS*, 59. "Give up her line of work": *Times* obituary. "We did love each other": *STM*, 38.

"Feeble-minded": Ibid., 162. **LA adopted the child:** He always spoke of Clarence as his "adopted son," but Lil Armstrong claimed that he never legally adopted the boy (Gary Giddins, "Satchuated," *Village Voice*, April 15, 2003). "A School where they teach the Backwards Boys": "Goffin Notebooks," 89. "As Clarence Grew older": Ibid. **Clarence spoke a few halting words:** *Eddie Condon's Floor Show.*

LA was in a receptive mood: "I wanted to get away from New Orleans for another reason and that was because I was not happy there just then" (*STM*, 37). **The S.S. *Sidney*:** Not *Sydney*, as LA spells it in *Satchmo*. **Marable had heard LA:** Tony Catalano, quoted in Shapiro and Hentoff, 76. **"When some musician would get a job":** Ibid.

LA knew how to read music: "Louis was the only one out of Ory's band who could read at all, and Louis couldn't read so good" (Foster, 126). **"Fate Marable had just as many jazz greats":** *Satchmo*, 182–83. **"Deadly serious":** "Everybody's Louie."

"We'd proved to them": *Satchmo*, 142–43. **"There ain't no one":** Bechet, 81. **"The chance to play the music":** *Satchmo*, 145.

"One big chance": Ibid., 185. **"We made good tips":** LA, unedited typescript of *Satchmo*, 89 (IJS). **"I'm just the same as one of those people":** LA, radio interview, 1960, in Brothers, 48. **"Big things":** LA, unedited typescript of *Satchmo*, 80 (IJS).

2. "All Those Tall Buildings"

SOURCES

DOCUMENTS

Lil Armstrong, *Satchmo and Me*; LA, undated series of five Voice of America radio broadcasts, recorded ca. July 1956 (original tapes held by IJS, hereafter cited as "VOA series"); *Louis Armstrong: The Portrait Collection*, DVD (Multiprises); James T. Maher, oral-history interview conducted by researchers for Ken Burns's *Jazz* (transcript available online at www.pbs.org/jazz/about/pdfs/Maher.pdf); David Sager, liner notes for *King Oliver off the Record: The Complete 1923 Jazz Band Recordings*, sound recording (Archeophone).

BOOKS

Albertson, *Louis Armstrong*; Allen and Rust, *King Joe Oliver*; Ernest Anderson, *Esquire's 1947 Jazz Book*; Gene H. Anderson, *The Original Hot Five Recordings of Louis Armstrong*; Bechet, *Treat It Gentle*; Bergreen, *Louis Armstrong*; Bernhardt, *I Remember*; Brooks, *The Young Louis Armstrong on Records*; Brothers, *Louis Armstrong's New Orleans*; Charters, *A Trumpet around the Corner*; Collier, *Louis Armstrong*; Condon, *We Called It Music*; Darensbourg, *Jazz Odyssey*; Dodds, *The Baby Dodds Story*; Foster, *Autobiography*; Freeman, *Crazeology*; Giddins, *Satchmo*; Hoffmann, *Jazz Advertised*, vol. 4; Kenney, *Chicago Jazz*; Kenney, *Jazz on the River*; Liebling, *Liebling at Home*; Mezzrow and Wolfe, *Really the Blues*; Ramsey and Smith,

Jazzmen; Russell, *New Orleans Style*; Schuller, *Early Jazz*; Shapiro and Hentoff, *Hear Me Talkin' to Ya*; Travis, *An Autobiography of Black Jazz*; Walser, *Keeping Time*; Williams, *Jazz Panorama*.

NOTES

Well-dressed black men: See Baby Dodds's description of the S.S. *Sidney*'s first visit to Hannibal, Missouri, Mark Twain's hometown: "They saw Negro roustabouts but had never seen a Negro with a tie and collar on, and a white shirt, playing music. They just didn't know what to make of it" (Dodds, 28).

Proud of his formal musical training: Marable was taught by his mother, a Paducah piano teacher, and in addition claimed to have studied music at New Orleans's all-black Straight University. **"One block long":** Quoted in Kenney, *Jazz on the River*, 19–20. **"We were playing":** Beulah Schacht, "Story of Fate Marable," *Jazz Record*, March 1946, quoted in Kenney, *Jazz on the River*, 45.

Streckfus supervised the music: "He went in for the finest in 'Jazz.' He understood it. And, whenever he was on the *mound* he'd pull up a chair at our rehearsals and *watch look* and listen, very carefully to every note which came out of our instruments. *And* Oh *Brother* if those notes weren't right, or those *Chords* etc. that's when you'd hear from him, and how" ("The Armstrong Story," in *IHOW*, 70, hereafter cited as "'LA Story'"). **The musicians "could not get the idea":** Interviews with Joseph Streckfus, March 18 and February 20, 1958, Hogan Jazz Archive, Tulane University, New Orleans, quoted in Kenney, *Jazz on the River*, 48.

The band then added rags to its repertoire: "The band played 'Skeleton Jangle,' 'Tiger Rag' and they played the big popular ballad of the day, 'Whispering'" (Jess Stacy, "Riverboat Shuffle: Cape Girardeau, Missouri," in Ernest Anderson, 44). **The band "started romping":** Foster, 122. **"Some semi-classics":** Dodds, 23n. **"We had loads of fun":** Ibid., 26. **A sharp-tongued, hard-drinking martinet:** LA refers to him as "that little Hatchet-Mouth Boy" in an unpublished 1936 letter, and Baby Dodds described him more euphemistically as "a pretty stern fellow who kept strict order" (Kenney, *Jazz on the River*, 55, and Dodds, 23). **"Our Waterloo":** *Satchmo*, 183–84. **Blacks-only dances:** Jack Bland, "That Was St. Louis: Reminiscences of a Mound City Blue Blower," in Ernest Anderson, 45.

"It was very hard for clarinet to do": Bechet, 92–93. LA left the obbligato part to his clarinet players when he performed "High Society" in later years, but he quotes from it in his 1930 recording of "Sweethearts on Parade." **Shields's demanding clarinet breaks:** Brian Harker, "Louis Armstrong and the Clarinet," *American Music*, Summer 2003. **"It wasn't blue anymore":** Russell, 20. **"What are all those tall buildings?":** *Satchmo*, 191. **"Louis was so shy":** Marge Creath, quoted in *LAS*, 60.

"You can't imagine such energy": Jess Stacy, "Riverboat Shuffle: Cape Girardeau, Missouri," in Ernest Anderson, 44. **"Now, Louis, you are a special trumpeter":** Quoted in Kenney, *Jazz on the River*, 58. **"A pair of fat man's trousers":** *Satchmo*, 193. **His five-foot-six frame:** LA gave his height as five-foot-six on his passports, all of which he kept (AA). **"It was on the riverboat":** Dodds, 24. LA's leukoplakia evidently contributed to the development of the nodular growths on his vocal cords that left him permanently hoarse (Collier, 310).

A "permanent, full-fledged member": *Satchmo*, 218–20. **Sousa's marches:** LA can be heard singing along with Serge Koussevitzky's recording of "Semper Fidelis" on one of his private tapes, after which he recalls playing the march with the

Tuxedo Band (LA, tape 258, AA). **LA's earliest surviving letter:** Letter to Isidore Barbarin, September 1, 1922, in *IHOW*, 43. **A "thrilling pleasure":** LA, "New Orleans," in Giddins, 215. **"This was before I even knew who he was":** Darensbourg, 16.

Dodds said that he and LA quit: Dodds, 31–32. **"Louis got fired":** Floyd Campbell, quoted in Travis, 239. **Marable claimed to have fired LA:** Kenney, *Jazz on the River*, 58.

"I could read music very well": *STM*, 68. **He could read written-out rags:** The clarinetist Albert Nicholas recalled in a 1972 interview that LA "could read through the Red Back Book [a popular collection of orchestrated rags] without missing a single note" (quoted in Brothers, 262). **LA "made so much money":** LA, "Storyville — Where the Blues Were Born," *True*, November 1947.

"An inferiority complex": LA, tape 426, AA.

Oliver was cockeyed: Accounts of what was wrong with his left eye vary, though all agree that he had "only one good eye" (Dodds, 40). See also Allen and Rust, 1. **"As rough as pig-iron":** Quoted in Collier, 67.

"Sometimes Oliver would come outside": Edmond Souchon, "King Oliver: A Very Personal Memoir," in Williams, 25 (hereafter cited as "Souchon").

"No trumpet player ever had the fire": "Joe Oliver Is Still King," *Record Changer*, July–August 1950, quoted in *IHOW*, 37, 38. **He was no longer at the peak of his powers:** "Joe wasn't in his prime, like he was before he sent for me" (*IHOW*, 39). **He had already broached to LA the possibility of joining the band:** *STM*, 35.

Fifty-two dollars a week: *SP*, 28.

"A sense of '*Aires*' ": Letter to Joe Glaser, August 2, 1955, in *IHOW*, 160. **"Now when I was a teenager":** 1961 interview.

A six-foot-six thug: Black Benny Williams figures prominently in other reminiscences of New Orleans. In 1968 LA included him on a list of "Bullies and Trouble Makers" from his New Orleans youth, but he also described him in the same document as "a great drummer and a good musician and our idol" (LA, "New Orleans," in Giddins, 221–22). **Sidney Bechet and Kid Ory:** See Bechet, 92, and Kid Ory (as told to Nesuhi Ertegun), "Louis Was Just a Little Kid in Knee Pants; Ory," *Down Beat*, July 14, 1950. **"He would not bother anyone":** *Satchmo*, 77. **"Not scared of anyone":** *LAS*, 232. **The great man asked LA to stand him to a drink:** *Satchmo*, 212–13.

"Joe Oliver is my idol": LA, "New Orleans," in Giddins, 215. **August 8, 1922:** This is the date given by LA in *Satchmo*. Other sources vary as to the exact date, and on another occasion LA recalled it as "July 8, 1922, I'll never forget it" ("Chicago, Chicago, That Toddlin' Town: How King and Ol' Satch Dug It in the Twenties," in Ernest Anderson, 40, hereafter cited as " 'Chicago, Chicago' "). See also Gene Anderson, "The Genesis of King Oliver's Creole Jazz Band," *American Music*, Autumn 1994. **"Glad rags":** Ibid., 227.

"You are the young man": Ibid., 231. On other occasions LA recalled that he was met by the porter, but *Satchmo* is specific on this point. **"I'd never seen a city that big":** *SP*, 28. **"It was a wonderful place":** Liebling, *Chicago: The Second City*, in Liebling, 166. **"I made it my business":** Lil Armstrong, "Lil Armstrong Reminisces about Early Chicago Days," *Down Beat*, June 1951.

"The big, black doorman": Freeman, 6.

"A hall with benches": Dodds, 35.

"The thing that hit your eye": Shapiro and Hentoff, 100. Eddie Condon claimed that young white musicians were not made welcome at Lincoln Gardens unless Oliver gave the high sign: "A nod or a wave of his hand was all that was necessary; then the customers knew that the kids were all right" (Condon, 111). According to other accounts, however, the club drew racially mixed crowds, and Oliver even let the white cornetist Muggsy Spanier sit in with the band. See Muggsy Spanier, "Louis My Idol and Inspiration; Spanier," *Down Beat*, July 14, 1950.

"Really jumpin' in fine fashion": "Chicago, Chicago," 40. **"Come on IN HEAH":** LA, "New Orleans," in Giddins, 216. **A huge dish of red beans and rice:** Satchmo, 234.

Musicians eager to hear the new kid in town: "Now when Louis joined Joe Oliver, the first ten rows at the Gardens was nothing but musicians" (Preston Jackson, quoted in *LAS*, 65). **"The news spread like wildfire":** Tommy Brookins, quoted in *LAS*, 72. **Lil Hardin met LA the next night:** According to *Satchmo and Me* and *STM* (70–71), Lil had yet to rejoin the Creole Jazz Band (with which she had already worked) and was then playing at the Dreamland Café, where Oliver took LA to meet her for the first time shortly after his arrival. In his subsequent accounts of their first meeting, however, LA states specifically that she was already playing with Oliver at Lincoln Gardens: "I particularly enjoyed Lil that night, with that four (4) beats to the bar — for a woman I thought she was really wonderful" ("LA Story," 50). **"Everything he had on was too small for him":** Quoted in Albertson, 13.

"I never tried to go over him": "LA Story," 50. **"My boyhood dream":** Satchmo, 240.

"Plenty of work": "LA Story," 74. **"Nobody took the job as work":** Dodds, 35–36.

"Perspiration as big as a thumb": Ibid., 69. **A single marathon session:** According to Gennett's records, the last four sides were recorded on April 6, meaning that the session must have run well past midnight. See Brooks, 1–26. **Overnight accommodations were not available for blacks:** Dodds, 69. In addition to the early recordings of Oliver, Jelly Roll Morton, Bix Beiderbecke, and the New Orleans Rhythm Kings, Gennett also recorded such Klan-inspired ditties as "The Bright Fiery Cross" and "The Jolly Old Klansman." When Jelly Roll Morton recorded with the New Orleans Rhythm Kings for Gennett in 1923, George Brunies told the hotel clerk that Morton was "not a Negro. I started to say he was from Puerto Rico, but some of them are black, so I said South American" (quoted in Charters, 214).

The records "miss conveying the way that Oliver was playing": Souchon, 30. **"As the door opened":** Condon, 111. **"Seven, eight, nine minutes of a gorgeous tune":** Maher. Bert Kelly, a Chicago musician who heard the band at Lincoln Gardens, later recalled that "Oliver had a book of several hundred stocks [i.e., commercially published "stock arrangements" of popular songs] and would play them for the dancers. It wasn't until after midnight, when the musicians getting off work would come in, that the band would begin to play the hot repertoire for which [it] would become famous" (Maher). Four of the band's 78 sides, "Sobbin' Blues," "Buddy's Habit," "Room Rent Blues," and "Riverside Blues," appear to be based on stock arrangements (Sager, 11). See also Bud Freeman: "The evening's music started with stock orchestrations, not with jazz or blues. The band would set up and play a number that might run ten or fifteen minutes" (Freeman, 7). The Original Dixieland Jazz Band's 1920 recording of "I'm Forever Blowing Bubbles," a waltz, may give some idea of what Oliver's band sounded like when playing such fare. **"Very much like the Oliver band":** Dodds, 70. **"Those other [jazz] records that had come before":** Shapiro and Hentoff, 68.

Digital transfers: The transfers heard on *King Oliver off the Record: The Complete 1923 Jazz Band Recordings* (Archeophone OTR-MM6-C2) are unusually clean and listenable. **Other recordings of jazz made around the same time:** Allen Lowe's *That Devilin' Tune: A Jazz History* (West Hill Radio Archives WHRA-6003) contains Kid Ory's 1922 sides, Fate Marable's "Frankie and Johnny," and recordings by Sidney Bechet, Jelly Roll Morton, Ethel Waters, and many other musicians active between 1895 and 1923. **The more polished dance music that Oliver was playing:** "By the time Oliver had reached Chicago and the peak of his popularity, his sound was not the same. It was a different band, a different and more polished Oliver" (Souchon, 29). **"Oh *what* a band *they* had":** "Jewish Family," 33.

"I don't know how they knew": Shapiro and Hentoff, 100. **"While the band was just swinging":** "Chicago, Chicago," 40. The breaks on the band's second version of "Snake Rag," cut for OKeh on June 22, are especially bold and well recorded.

LA was the only member of the band: "It is worth noting . . . that only in Armstrong's two choruses [in "Chimes Blues"] is the harmonic change in the sixth bar performed correctly. Louis moves to an F sharp diminished chord, where previously the ensemble had stubbornly tried an F minor chord, with pianist Lil Hardin blithely continuing in F *major!*" (Schuller, 83). **"The Oliver band played for the comfort of the people":** Dodds, 36. **"For years, King Oliver's Band has served up jazz":** Quoted in Frederic Ramsey Jr., "King Oliver and His Creole Jazz Band," in Ramsey and Smith, 74.

"This is a matter of business": Ibid., 68.

Jointly credited to Oliver and LA: Brian Harker has speculated that LA wrote the introduction to "Dipper Mouth Blues," a sequence of descending diminished-seventh arpeggios (Harker, "Louis Armstrong and the Clarinet"). **"Everything I did":** Will Jones, "It's the Bunk, but It Helped," *Minneapolis Tribune*, July 20, 1949. **LA spent a whole week:** William Russell, "Louis Armstrong," in Ramsey and Smith, 126. **"Lou~~i~~ ~~e~~ver could play that solo":** *Satchmo and Me.* **Oliver readily confessed to be~~i~~~~ng~~ a poor sight reader:** "I'm the slowest goddamned reader in the band" (Bernhardt, 94). That Oliver could read music, however, is not in doubt. On the 1924 duet recording of "King Porter" that he made with Jelly Roll Morton, he is reading from the written cornet part to the stock orchestration of Morton's most famous composition (Charters, 216).

"It was just a little light solo": VOA series. **A raggy arpeggiated figure:** "The solo's angular, arpeggiated melody—which he played twice—had so little of [LA's] unique style that the musicians around him described that some of his Chicago friends were surprised. In New Orleans, however, several musicians recognized the solo as one of the familiar choruses that [the trumpeter] Buddy Petit featured. The same solo turned up a few months later played by the trombonist on a recording by Charlie Creath's orchestra in St. Louis. Creath . . . was a gifted cornetist and a close friend of Armstrong's from the summers on the riverboats" (Charters, 175–76). **"To show you how much stronger I was":** "Joe Oliver Is Still King," in *IHOW,* 39. **"Looking so lonesome":** *Satchmo and Me.*

"My inspiration and my idol": "Joe Oliver Is Still King," in *IHOW,* 37. **"Joe Oliver tell me":** *SP,* 56. **"Any time you play straight lead":** 1961 interview. **"You can't find another band":** *SP,* 58. LA's liking for Lombardo was not so unusual at the time as it now seems. Mezz Mezzrow claimed that in Harlem, "Guy Lombardo was head man on the juke boxes—the girls liked him especially, because his sax section had such a lyrical quality and played the sentimental tunes so pretty" (Mezzrow and Wolfe, 210).

"As long as I keep him with me": *Satchmo and Me.* **"There's a kid down there":** Paul Mares, unpublished interview notes (n.d.), Williams Research Center, Historic New Orleans Collection, New Orleans, quoted in Brothers, 254. **"A green looking country boy":** Dave Peyton, "Creole Musicians," *Chicago Defender* (n.d.), LA, scrapbooks, AA. **"The little frog-mouthed boy":** *Talking Machine World,* August 15, 1923, quoted in Kenney, *Chicago Jazz,* 131.

"Knowin' that my tone was stronger": VOA series.

LA's name appears in none of OKeh's ads: See, for example, Hoffmann, 50, 63. "On [an] evening when he was sick": Quoted in Shapiro and Hentoff, 98. "Whether he'd let Louis play first or second": Dodds, 35.

"I never cared to become a band leader": *Satchmo,* 186.

"A ragtime pianist": John Hammond, "An Experience in Jazz History," in Walser, 90.

"Wuthless immoral music": Lil Hardin Armstrong, unpublished interview notes (n.d.), IJS, quoted in Collier, 111. Lil actually spent only a year at Fisk: Bergreen, 182.

"When I sat down to play": Lil Armstrong, "Lil Armstrong Reminisces about Early Chicago Days," *Down Beat,* June 1951.

"I liked the numbers we were playing": *Satchmo and Me.* "Read music—yes": "Jewish Family," 26. LA found Lil more formidable: "She was the best. She would give out with that good ol' New Orleans 4 Beat" ("LA Story," 65). "A Big High-powered Chick": "Goffin Notebooks," 109. "The master mind of the two": "LA Story," 61. "Lil with the better education": LA, tape 426, AA.

"Classical trumpet music": *STM,* 71. See also *Jazzmen:* "Lil bought a book of standard cornet solos and proceeded to drill them into Louis" (William Russell, "Louis Armstrong," in Ramsey and Smith, 125). LA took lessons: Ibid. They jointly registered "Cornet Chop Suey": The lead sheet is in LA's hand. All surviving Hot Five manuscript lead sheets on deposit at the Library of Congress, including "Cornet Chop Suey: A Jazz Fox Trot," are reproduced in Gene H. Anderson, 222–37.

"As long as he's with Joe": *Satchmo and Me.* "He's a fellow who didn't have much confidence": Shapiro and Hentoff, 101.

"Oliver was keeping Louis' money": *Satchmo and Me.*

LA v. Daisy Armstrong: The filings in LA's divorce case can be viewed online at http://198.173.15.34, the Web site of the Clerk of the Circuit Court of Cook County. LA said that Daisy came to Chicago to reconcile with him. He "showed her my Divorce Papers" and said that he was "a changed man since I came to Chicago and married Lil" ("Goffin Notebooks," 91). Daisy died in Gretna, Louisiana, on February 8, 1950. "Miss Lillian Hardin": "Miss Lillian Hardin Is Bride of Louis Armstrong," *Chicago Defender,* February 16, 1924, LA, scrapbooks, AA.

"Every other page in my story": LA, tape 219, AA. "Whenever Joe came to the house": Albertson, 15. Oliver had been skimming his sidemen's salaries: *Satchmo and Me.* Oliver refused to show the band the royalty checks: Dodds, 48. LA was more circumspect, saying only that the other players quit because they didn't want to go out on the road with Oliver, who toured the Midwest in 1924 ("Goffin Notebooks," 92, and "Chicago, Chicago," 42).

LA claimed not to have been troubled: "King Oliver's men were always talking about striking for something or other. I was a young member and didn't 'dig' their personal grievances much" (*LAS,* 19). "I listened very careful": LA, tape 426, AA. "You can't be married to Joe": *Satchmo and Me.* "You made me quit": Quoted in Albertson, 15.

"That's when Louis started playing": *Satchmo and Me.* **Fifty-five dollars a week:** Ibid.

"Our care-free optimism": W. J. Henderson, "Ragtime, Jazz, and High Art," *Scribner's Magazine,* February 1925.

3. "A Flying Cat"

SOURCES

DOCUMENTS

Lil Armstrong, *Satchmo and Me;* LA, VOA series; *Jazz,* auction catalog (Guernsey's, 2005); *Louis Armstrong: The Portrait Collection,* DVD (Multiprises); Jelly Roll Morton, oral-history interviews; Ralph Peer, oral-history interviews, UCLA; *Satchmo,* TV documentary (WNET).

BOOKS

Albertson, *Louis Armstrong;* Allen and Rust, *Hendersonia;* Anderson, *The Original Hot Five Recordings of Louis Armstrong;* Berrett, *Louis Armstrong and Paul Whiteman;* Brothers, *Louis Armstrong's New Orleans;* Chilton, *Let the Good Times Roll;* Collier, *Louis Armstrong;* Condon, *We Called It Music;* Dance, *The World of Earl Hines;* Dodds, *The Baby Dodds Story;* Freeman, *You Don't Look Like a Musician;* Giddins, *Crosby;* Goffin, *Horn of Plenty;* Gushee, *Pioneers of Jazz;* Hodes and Hansen, *Selections from the Gutter;* Hoffmann, *Jazz Advertised,* vols. 4, 7; Magee, *The Uncrowned King of Swing;* Manone and Vandervoort, *Trumpet on the Wing;* McCarthy, *Louis Armstrong;* McDonough, *Coleman Hawkins;* Mezzrow and Wolfe, *Really the Blues;* Milhaud, *My Happy Life;* Morgenstern, *Living with Jazz;* Ramsey and Smith, *Jazzmen;* Shapiro and Hentoff, *Hear Me Talkin' to Ya;* Stewart, *Boy Meets Horn;* Stewart, *Jazz Masters of the Thirties;* Sudhalter and Evans, *Bix: Man and Legend;* Waters, *His Eye Is on the Sparrow;* Wein, *Myself among Others;* Williams, *Jazz Panorama.*

NOTES

"Against the beat of the drums": Milhaud, 110.

"'The damn-it-to-hell bass'": Waters, 140. **Modeling it after Paul Whiteman:** Dave Peyton, writing in the *Chicago Defender,* would later describe Henderson's band — admiringly — as "not at all like the average Negro orchestra but in a class with the good white orchestras such as Paul Whiteman, Paul Ash and Ted Lewis" (quoted in McDonough, 11). **Broadway at 51st Street:** The building housing the original Roseland Ballroom was torn down in 1956, and the ballroom then moved to its current site on 52nd Street. **"Two high-grade Dance Orchestras":** *New York Clipper,* February 22, 1924, quoted in Allen and Rust, 113. **"Matinee tea dances":** Hoffmann, vol. 7, T-7.

"He was a pleasant man": Stewart, *Jazz Masters of the Thirties,* 21–22. **"He'd look at your hair":** Howard Scott, quoted in Magee, 29.

"I said to myself": "Chicago, Chicago," 42. **LA "had on big thick-soled shoes":** Kaiser Marshall, "When Armstrong Came to New York," in Hodes and Hansen, 83 (hereafter cited as "Marshall"). **"Long underwear down to his socks":** Quoted in Frank Driggs, "Don Redman: Jazz Composer-Arranger," in Williams, 96 (hereafter cited as "Driggs"). **"Used to playing in bands":** "Chicago, Chicago," 42. **"After he made one mistake":** Marshall, 83.

"One passage began triple fortissimo": Fletcher Henderson, "He Made the Band Swing," *Record Changer*, July–August 1950 (hereafter cited as "Henderson").

"Big-head motherfuckers": LA, tape 426, AA.

LA "*really* learned to read in my band": Henderson. "In that big town": *STM*, 80. "Gettin' a little lackin'": VOA series. "After a while the cats in Fletcher's band": *SP*, 33.

"Louis and I used to play": Shapiro and Hentoff, 275. "I could see all these musicians": 1961 interview.

"Harlem had heard a little bit about me": *STM*, 81. "What he carried with him": Stewart, *Jazz Masters of the Thirties*, 40. "I was always hitting them notes": LA, tape 426, AA. "Louis played that opening night": Quoted in Magee, 73. "I *Cut Loose*": "Goffin Notebooks," 93. "I think they made him play ten choruses": Robert Goffin, "Jazzmen's Greatest Kicks," *Esquire*, August 1944.

"RED HOT as written": Quoted in Magee, 80. LA probably never heard it: "Never heard him play till I got his record 'Singing [*sic*] the Blues'" (*SP*, 26). "Singin' the Blues" was recorded in 1927. "Louis' solo was *so* good": Shapiro and Hentoff, 206.

Oliver "didn't want to hear any one person": Quoted in Brothers, 121.

"A little book of manuscripts": Felix Manskleid, "Passing Notes on Fletcher Henderson," *Jazz Monthly*, December 1957, quoted in Allen and Rust, 134. "The record that made Fletcher Henderson": Ibid. "From the time Louis catapulted onto the New York scene": Stewart, *Jazz Masters of the Thirties*, 44. "Play like Louis": Stewart, *Boy Meets Horn*, 123. "Really swing-conscious": Henderson. LA "changed our whole idea about the band": Driggs, 96.

"In Fletcher's billing": *Satchmo and Me*. "There is considerable discussion": *Variety*, October 7, 1925, quoted in Allen and Rust, 139. "I want to put a band in": *Satchmo and Me*. "COME BY STARTING DATE": Albertson, 17.

"I had to choose": "Goffin Notebooks," 93. "Although I was a Singer": "LA Story," 63. "About three weeks after he joined us": Henderson. "The compliments Fletcher received": "LA Story," 64. "A million dollar talent": LA, radio interview (n.d.), quoted in Collier, 133. "I gathered that those two Big shot Boys": "LA Story," 64.

"He said to me": Letter to Joe Glaser, August 2, 1955, in *IHOW*, 160.

Fanny Cotton: She is mentioned several times in Goffin's *Horn of Plenty* (204–5, 236, 254–55, 296–97). It is not known how Goffin learned of her existence, however, since LA does not refer to her in the manuscript (published in *IHOW* as "The 'Goffin Notebooks'") that he prepared for Goffin to use in the writing of this heavily fictionalized biography.

"Fletcher only let me play": LA, tape 426, AA.

"I was there to make the records": *LAS*, 236.

"I WILL BE THERE": *Satchmo and Me*. "I said — 'Fletcher Thanks'": "Goffin Notebooks," 94.

Ralph Peer: See Richard Sudhalter's "Ralph S. Peer: A Life of Infinite Variety and Many Achievements," available online at the Web site of Peermusic (www .peermusic.com/aboutus/rsp01.cfm). "Hillbilly and nigger stuff": Peer.

"Whenever we needed a New York trumpet player": Ibid. Peer may have been exaggerating the role he played in organizing LA's Chicago recording sessions, most of which were produced by Richard M. Jones, OKeh's Race Division manager in Chicago. Kid Ory claimed that Jones put together the first Hot Five session, while LA and Johnny St. Cyr credited Elmer Fearn, another OKeh executive. For a discussion of these competing claims, see Anderson, 13–17.

The sign posted in front of the Dreamland Café: Contemporary newspaper ads for the club also bill LA as "THE WORLD'S GREATEST 'JAZZ CORNETIST'" (*Chicago Defender*, November 28, 1925, reprinted in Anderson, 12). "Girl, are you crazy?": *Satchmo and Me*.

LA introduces each one in turn: Kid Ory introduces LA on the record. Dodds was supposed to say a few words as well, but according to LA, he succumbed to stage fright: "We had a go at it, but when it was Johnny's turn he started stuttering out what he'd got to say. I laughed, and Johnny said 'Alright then you say the mother-fucking thing yourself' — then all of us laughed, Johnny as well" (*LAS*, 238).

"So we made a short rehearsal": Johnny St. Cyr, "The Original Hot Five," *Second Line*, September–October 1955 (hereafter cited as "St. Cyr"). St. Cyr was actually playing the "guitar-banjo," a larger instrument with six strings that he used on all of the Hot Five's recordings.

LA was allowed to pick his own sidemen: "Jazz on a High Note," *Esquire*, December 1951, quoted in *IHOW* (hereafter cited as "'Jazz on a High Note'"), 130. "When we went down to the Okeh Recording Company": Ibid.

"I dropped the paper": Ibid., 132. Johnny St. Cyr recalled that Elmer Fearn asked LA who was going to sing "Heebie Jeebies." "Louis said nobody because there were no lyrics to this song. So [Fearn] insists on singing, because vocals were starting to sell well at that time. So Louis sat down and scribbled out some lyrics" (St. Cyr). Presumably this was the sheet he dropped. The authenticity of this story has been widely questioned, but LA never deviated from it, and Kid Ory's account is substantially similar: "That was the record where Louis forgot the lyrics and started scattin'. We had all we could do to keep from laughing. Of course, Louis said he forgot the words, but I don't know if he intended it that way or not" (Edward "Kid" Ory [as told to Lester Koenig], "The Hot Five Sessions," *Record Changer*, July–August 1950). See also George Avakian: "The first version of the 'Heebie Jeebies' story I ever heard was from Richard M. Jones, who said he produced the session — he was probably Elmer Fearn's man on the firing line for black artists at OKeh. I didn't believe his statement that when Louis dropped the music, he pulled the microphone down with him as the two of them tried to retrieve the lead sheet, because I knew the recording had been made acoustically. But I printed the story in the first Armstrong reissue album, *King Louis*, because Louis's sole comment when I asked him about it was so wonderful — a sly 'Yeah, sump'n like that!'" (personal communication).

LA didn't invent scat singing: According to Jelly Roll Morton, "The first man that ever did a scat number in the history of this country was a man from Vicksburg, Mississippi, by the name of Joe Sims, an old comedian. And from that, Tony Jackson and myself, and several more grabbed it in New Orleans" (Morton, 1657-B). Cliff "Ukulele Ike" Edwards and Red McKenzie were the first singers to record scat solos (Giddins, 151). "Heebie Jeebies" is said to have sold some forty thousand copies: *STM*, 85. One of the reasons why it sold so well is that OKeh commissioned the theatrical choreographer Floyd Du Pont to create a special "Heebie Jeebies" dance, then cross-promoted the dance and the record ("How the 'Heebies Jeebies' Reached Apex of Popularity and Developed a New Dance," *Talking Machine World*, November 15, 1926, quoted in Anderson, 53–54). OKeh made no mention of his singing: "More wild jazz than you ever thought could be packed into one record is unpacked by Louis Armstrong and his Hot Five when they let loose with 'Heebie Jeebies'" (*Chicago Defender*, May 1, 1926, reprinted in Hoffmann, vol. 4, 124). "Louis Armstrong sure has the loop": LA, scrapbooks,

AA. **"You would hear cats greeting each other"**: Mezzrow and Wolfe, 120. **" 'Ha! Ha! Ha!' "**: Ibid., 122.

"You're crying in your horn": LA told this story to Carl-Erik Mossberg in Sweden in 1956. **"There's a world of amusement"**: OKeh ad (n.d.), LA, scrapbooks, AA.

LA's contract: Tommy Rockwell, letter to E. A. Fearn, January 7, 1927 (AA). **"Do you know who is singing"**: Albertson, 35. The record was either "Drop That Sack" or "Georgia Bo Bo," both of which were recorded for Vocalion on May 28, 1926, by the Hot Five, billed on the label as "Lil's Hot Shots." Unlike "Georgia Bo Bo," "Drop That Sack" is an instrumental, meaning that it would have been the performance to which LA referred in the version of the story that he told to George Avakian: "The president of OKeh . . . played the record for him and asked, 'Louis, who's the trumpet player on that record?' His answer, in ten magnificently unforgettable words, was, 'I don't know, boss — but I won't do it again' " (Avakian, personal communication). On yet another occasion LA told the story in such a way as to suggest that the record in question was Johnny Dodds's 1927 version of "Wild Man Blues," on which he plays but does not sing (LA, tape 96, AA).

"Our recording sessions": Edward "Kid" Ory (as told to Lester Koenig), "The Hot Five Sessions," *Record Changer*, July–August 1950. **Old friends who "knew each other's musical styles"**: Ibid. **"He would tell each of us"**: Dodds, 72.

"Cornet Chop Suey": A comparison of the Hot Five's recording of "Cornet Chop Suey" with the lead sheet that Louis and Lil registered for copyright in 1924 reveals that Armstrong follows the written-out melody closely, thus demonstrating that it was, unlike most of the other Hot Five sides, a composition rather than a collective improvisation on a preset framework. **"We used to sit on the back stairs"**: LA, tape 49, AA. Payment of $50 a side was then standard in the recording industry. According to George Avakian, LA's fee had been raised to $250 by 1927 (Avakian, personal communication).

"You couldn't buy his records": *Satchmo* (WNET). **"We had heard that if you buried things"**: Manone and Vandervoort, 69.

The original Hot Five performed together in public only once: Anderson, 80–82. **"The famous cornetist"**: Dave Peyton, "Louis Armstrong Coming Back," *Chicago Defender*, November 7, 1925, quoted in Allen and Rust, 140. **"The feature man in Lil's new band"**: *Chicago Defender*, November 21, 1925, quoted in Allen and Rust, 140.

LA joined the "Little Symphony": For a detailed description of the Vendome Theater, see the Web site "Jazz Age Chicago" (http://chicago.urbanhistory.org/ven/ths/vendome.shtml), hereafter cited as " 'Jazz Age Chicago.' " **"Playing Classic and Symphony Music"**: "Goffin Notebooks," 94. **The resplendent operatic interlude**: "Satchmo had warmed up, as usual, on a few bars from Mascagni's *Cavalleria Rusticana*" ("Satchmo Comes Back," *Time*, September 1, 1947). **"I was at home then"**: *LAS*, 106–7. **"Whenever Louis would play"**: *Satchmo* (WNET). **LA made the switch from cornet to trumpet**: *SP*, 33.

"The guys who called me 'Henpeck' ": LA, tape 426, AA. **Much to Lil's displeasure**: "Lil and her mother had some bad tempers. And it would make my Blood Boil when I'd see them Abuse, my son Clarence" ("Goffin Notebooks," 97). **"You're a magician!"**: *Satchmo and Me*. **"Whenever we'd break up"**: LA, "Why I Like Dark Women," *Ebony*, August 1954 (hereafter cited as " 'Dark Women' ").

A pretty teenager named Alpha Smith: All direct quotations from LA regarding his affair with Alpha are from the "Goffin Notebooks," 95–97. **"First

thing I look at is her general shape": LA, "Satchmo's Views on Women," *Ebony*, January 1950. **"Poor Louis never had a chance"**: Albertson, 25.

"Why don't you come on over": Dance, 45.

"Close those windows": Muggsy Spanier, "Louis My Idol and Inspiration; Spanier," *Down Beat*, July 14, 1950. **"125 choruses of Tiger Rag"**: Quoted in Collier, 162. **"Wasn't long before all Joe Oliver's crowds"**: Spanier, "Louis My Idol and Inspiration." **A passerby "could hold an instrument"**: Condon, 133.

"I couldn't help thinking I had travelled pretty far": STM, 84. LA was so impressed that he forgot it was Lil who had first gotten him that billing the year before. **"I always admired Mr. Glaser"**: "Goffin Notebooks," 99.

"A nice little cute fat boy": SP, 36.

"When one of Capone's Boys": Letter to Oscar Cohen, "Jan. 21/23," 1970 (reproduced in *Jazz*, 14–17).

A brothel upstairs: The building where the Sunset Café was located is still in existence (it now houses a hardware store). Visitors to the second floor can see the small partitioned cubicles once used by the prostitutes (Randy Sandke, personal communication). **"Twenty or more improvised choruses"**: Freeman, 15. **"Zutty . . . would dress up"**: Shapiro and Hentoff, 110–11.

"I was young and strong": SP, 35. **"Well, I tell you"**: Sudhalter and Evans, 192. **"He started out like a new book"**: Quoted in McCarthy, 41.

"Noisy, corrupt": Dave Peyton, "The Musical Bunch," *Chicago Defender*, May 19, 1926, quoted in Anderson, 134.

"I never had any time": STM, 85. **Specially made cylinder recordings of LA's playing**: According to Elmer Schoebel, who worked for Walter Melrose's publishing company, "Melrose said he was going to publish a set of Louis Armstrong breaks but there was a technical problem of getting the Armstrong 'hot' breaks down on paper. Finally, Melrose and I hit upon the idea of having Armstrong record his breaks. We bought a $15 Edison cylinder phonograph and 50 wax cylinders, gave them to Louis and told him to play. The cylinders were duly filled up by Armstrong and the breaks were copied in written form" (Schoebel, "The Elmer Schoebel Story," *Doctor Jazz*, October 1968). The cylinders have not survived. **"A cute little Hupmobile"**: SP, 38. **"Throughout the world"**: The title page is reproduced in *LAS*, 86. **"Louis Armstrong is a fine example"**: Dave Peyton, "The Musical Bunch," *Chicago Defender*, June 18, 1927, LA, scrapbooks, AA.

The young white musicians: LA, tape 96, AA. **"Nothin' doin', boys"**: Quoted in William Russell and Stephen W. Smith, "New Orleans Music," in Ramsey and Smith, 22. See also Gushee, 169–77.

"This particular recording really 'gassed me'": "Jazz on a High Note," 128. **LA worked out set-piece solos**: His solos on the two surviving takes of "Copenhagen," for instance, are almost identical (as opposed to the solos on the two takes of "Stomp Off, Let's Go," which are very different). This practice continued to the end of his career, especially in his later years, when he made a practice of recording and listening to his stage shows. One indication that "Potato Head Blues" was not improvised in the studio is that measures fifteen and sixteen of the stop-time chorus are identical to the third of the two-bar breaks LA played in the Creole Jazz Band's 1923 recording of "Tears." **"Don't play anything you can't play twice"**: Chilton, 140.

"Son — Carry on": "Goffin Notebooks," 90.

"I just played the way I sang": Wein, 292.

Lil sued LA: For her side of the story, see Max Jones, "Lil Armstrong, Royalties, and the Old Songs," *Melody Maker*, April 8, 1967. **LA said that he wrote it**

himself: "I used to sit out on the steps of my house I bought with Lil and write four or five tunes . . . Wrote 'Gut Bucket Blues,' 'Drop That Sack,' 'Old Man Mose,' 'Struttin with Some Barbecue'" (*SP,* 37). LA also claimed to have written two tunes subsequently copyrighted by other musicians, "Muskrat Ramble" (credited to Kid Ory) and "I Wish I Could Shimmy Like My Sister Kate" (variously credited to Clarence Williams and Armand J. Piron). These latter claims to authorship are generally believed to be true (Morgenstern, 61). According to LA, "We [i.e., the Hot Five] all just made ["Muskrat Ramble"] up, but Ory had nerve enough to claim it" (VOA series). See Anderson, 74–78, for a detailed discussion of the authorship of "Muskrat Ramble." **A harmonic twist of which he was fond:** Throughout his life LA was drawn to ballads like "When It's Sleepy Time Down South" and "Do You Know What It Means to Miss New Orleans?" whose melodies pivot on the major seventh of their underlying harmonies. **She had resumed her studies:** Berrett, 73–74.

"A little corporation": Dance, 54. **A South Side hall:** An ad announcing that "LOUIS ARMSTRONG WORLD'S GREATEST CORNETIST AND HIS STOMPERS" would be playing for dancing at the Warwick Hall ran in the *Defender* on December 10, 1927 (Anderson, 153). **"I don't know what happened":** Quoted in *LAS,* 117.

"Comes Intermission time": "Goffin Notebooks," 100.

4. "It's Got to Be Art"

SOURCES

DOCUMENTS

LA, VOA series; *Louis Armstrong: The Portrait Collection,* DVD (Multiprises); Artie Shaw, oral-history interview conducted by researchers for Ken Burns's *Jazz* (transcript available online at www.pbs.org/jazz/about/pdfs/Shaw.pdf); Zutty and Marge Singleton, oral-history interview, IJS.

BOOKS

Albertson, *Louis Armstrong;* Barker, *A Life in Jazz;* Carmichael, The Stardust Road; Clarke, *Wishing on the Moon;* Copland, *Reader;* Copland and Perlis, *Copland: 1900 Through 1942;* Dance, *Earl Hines;* Dance, *The World of Earl Hines;* Dodds, *The Baby Dodds Story;* Hammond, *John Hammond on Record;* Holiday, *Lady Sings the Blues;* Johnson, *Bix;* Lion, *Bix;* Miller, *Louis Armstrong;* Orenstein, *A Ravel Reader;* Pleasants, *The Great American Popular Singers;* Schuller, *Early Jazz;* Shapiro and Hentoff, *Hear Me Talkin' to Ya;* Sudhalter and Evans, *Bix: Man and Legend;* Wilson, *Teddy Wilson Talks Jazz;* Wyatt and Johnson, *The George Gershwin Reader.*

NOTES

The Savoy Ballroom: For a detailed description of the Savoy, see "Jazz Age Chicago." **The money was good:** LA received one hundred dollars a week (Charlie Carpenter, quoted in Dance, *The World of Earl Hines,* 146). **Possible for the two men to pay off the lease:** LA, quoted in Shapiro and Hentoff, 112.

"What are you doing to me?": Charlie Carpenter, quoted in Dance, *The World of Earl Hines,* 144–45.

"What future was there for a black classical pianist?": Dance, *Earl Hines*, 6.

"A lot of people have misinterpreted the whole thing": Dance, *The World of Earl Hines*, 52. One thing Hines admitted having taken from LA was the trumpeter's vibrato, which he adapted to the fixed-pitch piano: "I used tremolo to give an effect like his vibrato . . . I'd reduce the weight of the note and use the sustaining pedal as the sound of the note thinned out" (ibid.). "I'm too technical to play the blues": Dance, *Earl Hines*, 5. "I got sick of playing a lot of pretty things": Ibid., 12. "Eccentric": Wilson, 102. "I'd be sitting there playing and grinning": Dance, *Earl Hines*, 4.

"I always remember that first tune": Dance, *The World of Earl Hines*, 45.

"Louis was wild and I was wild": Ibid.

"Because Louis was up North making records": Henry "Kid" Rena, quoted in Barker, 59. "I was just like a clarinet player": BBC interview (n.d.), quoted in Pleasants, 101. **The solos of Herbert L. Clarke:** Ten of the cornetist's 78s, including "Bride of the Waves" and "The Debutante," were in LA's record library at the time of his death (AA). All were recorded prior to 1928, and most of the actual 78s owned by LA appear to have been released while he was still living in New Orleans. Turn-of-the-century brass soloists like Clarke and the trombonist Arthur Pryor (whom LA mentions by name in *Satchmo*) often played transcriptions of operatic arias. "I've heard trumpet solos from 1908": Leonard Feather, "Louis Still Lauds Guy, Digs Turk but Not Bird," *Down Beat*, August 25, 1954.

A "metric modulation": Most trumpeters who play LA's cadenza fail to observe the exact relationship of the two tempos, which is part of what gives the passage its rhythmic unity. Gunther Schuller was the first musician to notate it correctly in the transcription of "West End Blues" he published in 1968 (Schuller, 116).

"An impassioned, almost stammering repetitive phrase": Ibid., 119.

"I sat on a rug-covered bandstand": Shaw. **No alternate takes survive:** OKeh did not preserve alternate takes, only the versions selected for mastering. "S.O.L. Blues," recorded by the Hot Seven on May 13, 1927, is a preliminary version of "Gully Low Blues," recorded the following day. **Hines talked about it:** Albertson, 38–39.

"Earl Hines, he was surprised": VOA series. **Within days of its release:** Waters's performance of "West End Blues" was recorded on August 21, 1928. She does not refer to it (or to LA) in *His Eye Is on the Sparrow*, her 1951 autobiography, but the relationship of her scat chorus to the Hot Five recording is palpable. "I heard a record Louis Armstrong made": Holiday, radio interview with Willis Conover, 1956, quoted in Clarke, 48. "Sometimes the record would make me so sad": Holiday, 10–11.

LA was "flattered": VOA series.

"And always, once you got a certain solo": *SP*, 43.

"I don't even hear them": Singleton.

"Always remember—Louis Armstrong never bother": "Scanning the History of Jazz," *Jazz Review*, July 1960, in *IHOW*, 175.

"If I have to say it myself": "Goffin Notebooks," 101.

"He was a cute little boy": Sudhalter, 39. (See also *Satchmo*, 209; *SP*, 26; and Dodds, 24.) Beiderbecke told members of his family that he heard Fate Marable's band in Louisiana, Mo., in the summer of 1921, but he did not mention LA and the two men may well have been earlier (Jonson, 693).

"I had been diggin' Beiderbecke": Quoted in Shapiro, 158. **LA played "From Monday On":** VOA series. The other records played by LA on this broadcast were Sidney Bechet's "Summertime," Bing Crosby's "You Must Have Been a Beautiful Baby," Duke Ellington's "New East St. Louis Toodle-Oo," the Ella Fitzgerald–LA duet recording of "You Won't Be Satisfied," Dizzy Gillespie's "'Bout to Wail," Bunk Johnson's "When the Saints Go Marching In," Joe Oliver's 1929 recording of "West End Blues," and Jack Teagarden's 1940 recording of "St. James Infirmary."

"Now you talking about jam sessions": Ibid., 159. **"It wasn't a cutting session":** Sudhalter and Evans, 249. LA states in his *Hear Me Talkin' to Ya* reminiscence of Beiderbecke that he was playing at the Sunset Café, but he may have had in mind an earlier session, perhaps the one to which he referred in 1961: "He'd come up to the Sunset, which closed at four or five in the morning. Then we closed the doors and we played the things *we* wanted to play" (1961 interview).

"Tears rolled down Oliver's face": Lynn Harrell, quoted in Shapiro and Hentoff, 160. **"I was thrilled to death":** *SP*, 26. **"Bix had a way of expressing himself":** Sudhalter and Evans, 249. (In the book LA is made to say "want to make you go" instead of "make you want to go," which is clearly an incorrect rendering of what he said.) **"Half the time he didn't eat properly":** LA, radio interview, 1970, quoted in Lion, 289–90.

A series of radio broadcasts: *LAS*, 118. Advertisements for the broadcasts are preserved in LA's scrapbooks. **"Even then they were already writing overloaded arrangements":** Dance, *Earl Hines*, 35.

"I got a new cigarette": Charlie Carpenter, quoted in Dance, *The World of Earl Hines*, 146. The "white arranger" is thought to have been Mezz Mezzrow, but Carpenter does not name him. **"It makes you feel so good":** Hammond, 105.

"Our vir-tee-o-so number": VOA series. **"We had no music":** Dance, *Earl Hines*, 36. LA's account is similar: "When I went to Chicago at this time at this recording, they said, 'Well, what do we play?' I said, 'Well, come over here, Earl, and we'll dig this.' And I ran it down on the trumpet, see? And it sounded so good, [Elmer Fearn] said, 'Let's put it on right now'" (VOA series). **A multithemed rag composed by LA:** In 1956 LA described "Weather Bird" as "a tune Fate [Marable] had written and we had a big arrangement on it" (ibid.). Four years later, though, he specifically told a radio interviewer that he had written the song while playing with Marable, which suggests that Marable wrote the arrangement but not the song (LA, tape 564, AA). Oliver shares composer credit on the label of the 1923 Gennett recording of "Weather Bird Rag," but LA copyrighted the song in his own name that same year (Dan Morgenstern, "Louis Armstrong and the Development and Diffusion of Jazz," in Miller, 101). He re-registered the song in 1929, and his holograph lead sheet, now on deposit at the Library of Congress, is reproduced in Jeffrey Taylor, "Louis Armstrong, Earl Hines, and 'Weather Bird,'" *Musical Quarterly*, Spring 1998.

Hines "could swing a gang of keys": *STM*, 84. **"Of course, everybody knows":** "Jazz on a High Note," 129. **"He's good, sure":** Don Freeman, "We'll Get Along without Hines' Ego, Says Armstrong," *Down Beat*, February 22, 1952.

"I like to listen to him": Hawkins said this to Dan Morgenstern (Morgenstern, personal communication).

LA and Don Redman retired to the men's room: Dance, *Earl Hines*, 38.

"The only musical idiom in existence": George Gershwin, "Fifty Years of American Music," *American Hebrew*, November 22, 1929, in Wyatt and Johnson, 116–17. **"I am waiting to see more Americans":** Olin Downes, "Mr. Ravel Returns," *New York Times*, February 26, 1928, quoted in Orenstein, 340. **"The substance not only of the American composer's fox trots"**: Aaron Copland, "Jazz Structure and Influence," *Modern Music*, January–February 1927, in Copland, *Reader*, 87. **Jazz "might have its best treatment"**: Copland and Perlis, *Copland: 1900 Through 1942*, 134.

"'Why,' I moaned": Carmichael, 53. **"Obsessed with the idea"**: Shaw. **LA's "first record that really made any wide inroads"**: This statement comes from a deposition by Oberstein that is part of the court filings in the case of *Louis Armstrong, Plaintiff, against Thomas G. Rockwell, Joseph N. Weber, et al., Defendants*, filed in the U.S. District Court, Southern District of New York, in 1931 (AA, hereafter cited as *Louis Armstrong, Plaintiff*).

No more than a half dozen continue to be played: "Basin Street Blues," "Muskrat Ramble," "St. James Infirmary," "Squeeze Me," "Struttin' with Some Barbecue," and "Twelfth Street Rag" all became jazz standards, while "Big Butter and Egg Man," "Cornet Chop Suey," "Weary Blues," and "West End Blues" are still played by traditional jazz revivalists.

5. "The Way a Trumpet Should Play"

SOURCES

DOCUMENTS

LA, VOA series; Lawrence Brown, oral-history interview, IJS; *The Johnny Cash Show*, TV show, October 28, 1970 (ABC); Zutty and Marge Singleton, oral-history interview, IJS.

BOOKS

Amis, *Memoirs*; Barnet, *Those Swinging Years*; Berrett, *The Louis Armstrong Companion*; Bryant, *Central Avenue Sounds*; Chandler, *The Raymond Chandler Papers*; Chilton, *The Song of the Hawk*; Clayton, *Buck Clayton's Jazz World*; Collier, *Louis Armstrong*; Condon, *We Called It Music*; Bing Crosby, *Call Me Lucky*; Gary Crosby and Firestone, *Going My Own Way*; Dance, *The World of Swing*; Hadlock, *Jazz Masters of the Twenties*; Hampton, *Hamp*; Hoffmann, *Jazz Advertised*, vol. 7; Larkin, *All What Jazz*; Lees, *Portrait of Johnny*; Magee, *The Uncrowned King of Swing*; Marmorstein, *The Label*; Mezzrow and Wolfe, *Really the Blues*; Porterfield, *Jimmie Rodgers*; Ramsey and Smith, *Jazzmen*; Royal, *Marshal Royal*; Schuller, *The Swing Era*; Shapiro and Hentoff, *Hear Me Talkin' to Ya*; Singer, *Black and Blue*; Sudhalter, *Lost Chords*.

NOTES

A **"burly, rough-looking character"**: George Avakian, personal communication. **"He couldn't carry two notes"**: Cork O'Keefe, quoted in Collier, 179. O'Keefe and Rockwell later joined forces to found the Rockwell-O'Keefe Theatrical Agency, one of the most powerful musical booking agencies of the Swing Era. For more on Rockwell, see Marmorstein, 61–62, and Sudhalter, 774.

"Mr. Fagan the owner would come to us": "Goffin Notebooks," 103. **Rockwell asked LA to come to New York**: LA came to New York by himself in March to record for OKeh, then returned a few weeks later with the rest of the Dickerson band. The two trips are mistakenly conflated in many sources, including LA's account ("LA Story," 103–5). **"It's just as though they could see right through my back":** *STM,* 95.

"Long before [the] time of opening": *Chicago Defender,* March 13, 1929, quoted in Collier, 205.

"It's the last time": VOA series.

"You ought to make a record": Condon, 199–200.

Eddie Lang was admired by LA: He was one of the dedicatees of *STM.*

"After we recorded that number": Marshall, 85.

"The boat was still far off": Robert Goffin, "Jazzmen's Greatest Kicks," *Esquire,* August 1944. **"The first time I heard Jack Teagarden":** *Satchmo,* 188. According to LA, he met Teagarden "[m]y last week in New Orleans while we were getting ready to go up river to Saint Louis," meaning the summer of 1919. Teagarden gives 1921 as the date of their first meeting, but this is almost certainly not correct. In 1959 he told an interviewer that he first heard LA on Bessie Smith's 1924 recording of "Cold in Hand Blues" (*Down Beat,* August 20, 1959). **"He was from Texas":** *SP,* 27.

"Rockwell knew it had to be different": George Avakian, personal communication. **"Lulu White was a famous woman":** LA, "Storyville — Where the Blues Were Born," *True,* November 1947 (ellipses in original).

It was probably Tommy Rockwell's idea to team LA with Luis Russell: Rockwell was already booking dance bands in early 1929, while LA, who had been in Chicago since 1925, was no longer closely familiar with the New York jazz scene.

"I told them": "Goffin Notebooks," 104.

"We were popular all through the Towns we passed through": Ibid.

"He said 'Louie'": Ibid., 105.

"The pit band looked pretty surprised": Singleton, "Zutty First Saw Louis in Amateur Tent Show," *Down Beat,* July 14, 1950. **LA signed a one-year management contract:** Copies of the contract are included in the court filings in the case of *Louis Armstrong, Plaintiff.*

"Louis Armstrong was supposed to be the first cornetist": Quoted in *LAS,* 123. See also Chilton, 60, and Magee, 120–22.

"Almost as much work was put in": Robert Benchley, "The Theatre: Fall Openings," *New Yorker,* October 26, 1929.

"Immerman's is opened to Slummers": Quoted in Murray L. Pfeffer, "My Harlem Reverie" (available online at http://nfo.net/usa/harlem.html).

"In the audience, any old night": *STM,* 90.

"Among the better places for first visitors": "Goings On About Town," *New Yorker,* October 20, 1928. **Harlem's "most lowdown and amusing places":** "Goings On About Town," *New Yorker,* December 7, 1929.

Waller and Razaf wrote *Hot Feet*: Harry Brooks received credit as co-composer, but the extent of his contribution to the score is not known (Singer, 204). **"The first floor show of New York's exclusive night clubs":** *Pittsburgh Courier,* March 16, 1929, quoted in ibid., 205.

"The most jolliest musician": VOA series. **"We used to play for the films":** Quoted in Shapiro and Hentoff, 256. **"From the first time I heard it":** *STM,* 91. **Dutch Schultz had the idea for "Black and Blue":** Singer, 216–19.

"Everything a revue should have": Charles Brackett, "The Theatre: Statement," *New Yorker,* June 29, 1929. (This is the same Charles Brackett who later collaborated with Billy Wilder on *The Lost Weekend* and *Sunset Boulevard.*) **"Best tune: 'Ain't Misbehavin'":** "New Plays in Manhattan," *Time,* July 1, 1929. **"One song . . . stands out": "'Hot Chocolates' Is High Spirited," *New York Times*, June 21, 1929.

"Here it is": *Chicago Defender*, September 28, 1929, reprinted in Hoffmann, 239.

"Didn't exactly feel I had the world at my feet": *SP*, 40. "I believe that great song": *STM*, 91.

"Chicago's own Louis Armstrong": Dave Peyton, "In Old New York," *Chicago Defender*, July 1929, LA, scrapbooks, AA. "GOOD LUCK ALWAYS": "Goffin Notebooks," 106.

Issued both as race records and as part of OKeh's regular line: OKeh began this policy with "West End Blues."

"Compare a record by Crosby": Rudy Vallée, introduction to *STM*, xvii. "I'm proud to acknowledge my debt": Ken Murray, "Louis, Bix Had Most Influence on Der Bingle," *Down Beat*, July 14, 1950. "Bing's voice has a mellow quality": Gary Crosby and Firestone, *Going My Own Way*, 224.

"Louis never had a very good band": Bing Crosby, *Call Me Lucky*, 140–41. "It's ridiculous to think": George James, quoted in Dan Havens, "A Year with Satchmo, 1931–32: George James Talks to Dan Havens," *Jazz Journal International*, January 1992 (hereafter cited as "James").

"Vincent Lopez came in there": Hadlock, 16–17.

"I started blowin' all them high notes": George T. Simon, "Bebop's the Easy Way Out, Claims Louis," *Metronome*, March 1948, reprinted in Berrett, 144. "Louis Armstrong . . . is some cornet player now": Quoted in Frederic Ramsey Jr., "King Oliver and His Creole Jazz Band," in Ramsey and Smith, 84. (Oliver probably meant concert E-flat and F.)

"Well, right after intermission": Dance, 80.

"A dazzling lesson": Schuller, 168.

"Armstrong shouts a couple of blues choruses": Larkin, 200. "A kind of gurgle": Amis, 39.

"The impression is heart-rending": Quoted in Hugues Panassié, "Louis Armstrong at the Salle Pleyel," in Berrett, 73.

"Louis Armstrong, the hottest trumpet player in America": OKeh newspaper ad (n.d.), LA, scrapbooks, AA. "A very ingratiating manner": "Lewis [sic] Armstrong and Orchestra," *Variety*, January 29, 1930, LA, scrapbooks, AA.

"He had just come out of the hotel": Clayton, 36.

LA "looked at the humorous side of life": Mezzrow and Wolfe, 213. "Louis has everything about 100 per cent": "New York's 'Star' Musicians," *Melody Maker*, November 1929, LA, scrapbooks, AA.

"The Guys in the Band Commenced to making Late Time": "Goffin Notebooks," 106. "The boys, (the lushies) commenced to messin' up": "The Satchmo Story," in *IHOW*, 116 (hereafter cited as "'Satchmo Story'"). "I had to get in front of my own band": *SP*, 40. "He was a great artist himself": Mezzrow and Wolfe, 236–37. For Singleton's version of the break, see his oral-history interview. "There's two musicians": LA, tape 17, AA.

"Louis Armstrong, the most torrid of the horn-tooters": Walter Winchell, "On Broadway," *New York Mirror*, March 14, 1930, LA, scrapbooks, AA. "New conceptions": "Goings On About Town," *New Yorker*, February 8, 1930. Mills thought it might be profitable: Hampton, 35.

"I had a friend who ran on the [railroad]": "Satchmo Story," 117. A "welcoming, infectious smile": Royal, 43. "Majestic": Barnet, 25. "The big man in Culver City": Quoted in Bryant, 38–39. "Two policemen were always on duty": Chandler, 252. In *The Big Sleep* this real-life club almost certainly became the fictional Cypress Club, whose manager, the well-dressed Eddie Mars, may have been based on Frank Sebastian.

A local black newspaper: "Louie Armstrong Famed Record Artist in City," *California Eagle*, July 11, 1930. **LA and Lil met Jimmie Rodgers:** Porterfield, 258–60. Porterfield found this notation in Rodgers's hand on his lyric sheet for "Blue Yodel No. 9": "Recorded in Hollywood 7-16-30/Louis Armstrong Trumpet, Lillian on Piano." Rodgers can also be heard playing guitar on the record, but his strumming is barely audible. **"I'd been knowin' Jimmie":** *The Johnny Cash Show.*

One of his timeless tales of romantic mischance: Rodgers appears to have based the song on Nolan Welsh's 1926 recording of "The Bridwell Blues," on which Armstrong plays cornet. **"No change for me, daddy":** *LAS*, 268.

"King of the Trumpet": LA, scrapbooks, AA. **"Louis fell in love with us":** Hampton, 37. **"We were on the air one night":** Dance, 270. **"I had already heard some of the greatest men":** "Satchmo Story," 118–19. **"Lionel used to get so Enthused":** "Goffin Notebooks," 107.

"The only man that ever made me enjoy coming to work": Brown. **"The kind of musician you could sit there all night":** Quoted in *LAS*, 131. **"The most extraordinary trumpeter":** W. E. Oliver, *Los Angeles Evening Herald*, July 21, 1930, LA, scrapbooks, AA. **"The great Louis Armstrong":** Johnny Mercer to Ginger Meehan (n.d.), quoted in Lees, 70.

"Oh, that's a new instrument": Hampton, 37–38. **Hampton responded by picking up a pair of mallets and rattling off "Cornet Chop Suey":** "The name of the song that I played was 'Chinese [*sic*] Chop Suey'" (Sue Smallwood, "A Lifetime Filled with Good Vibes Jazz," [Hampton Roads] *Virginian-Pilot*, November 20, 1994).

LA canceled his contract: LA and Tommy Rockwell both attested in affidavits filed in 1931 that the contract had been unilaterally canceled by LA the preceding September (*Louis Armstrong, Plaintiff*). **Ex-Flame:** All surviving documentation of this film is reproduced or described in Stratemann. The *California Eagle* reported on July 11 that LA had come to Los Angeles not only to play at the Cotton Club but to "make a big picture at a leading studio" ("Louie Armstrong Famed Recording Artist in City"). No other evidence that LA came to Los Angeles specifically to appear in *Ex-Flame*, or any other film, is known to exist. **"Hottest of the hot trumpeters":** *Variety*, November 12, 1930, LA, scrapbooks, AA. **"For those who like hot jazz":** "December Records," *Time*, December 15, 1930.

6. "Don't Let 'Em Cool Off, Boys"

SOURCES

DOCUMENTS

Lil Armstrong, *Satchmo and Me*; Budd Johnson, oral-history interview, IJS; Zilner Randolph, oral-history interview, IJS.

BOOKS

Barnet, *Those Swinging Years*; Berton, *Remembering Bix*; Chilton, *The Song of the Hawk*; Clarke, *Wishing on the Moon*; Clayton, *Buck Clayton's Jazz World*; Collier, *Louis Armstrong*; Dance, *The World of Earl Hines*; Gleason, *Celebrating the Duke*;

Goffin, *Horn of Plenty;* Jones, *Jazz Talking;* Mezzrow and Wolfe, *Really the Blues;* Stratemann, *Louis Armstrong on the Screen;* Sudhalter, *Stardust Melody;* Wald, *Escaping the Delta.*

NOTES

"I felt at no time": "LA Story," 115.

"Pepper Grass, Dandelions, and lots of weeds": "Satchmo Story," 112. **"Fresh — neat and very much contented":** "Satchmo Story," 112. **"I never was born to be a Square":** Ibid., 113. **"An Assistant — a friend":** Ibid., 114. **In the age of bootleg liquor:** "Of course, the stuff that was around in those days was pure marijuana, not the kind today that is laced with all sorts of foreign substances. It doesn't even *smell* right. In the old days, there was nothing about it that would prevent your going about your business and performing properly" (Barnet, 20). **"Show a dope fiend a bucket of water":** LA, tape 426, AA.

LA's preference . . . was known to jazz musicians everywhere: "But whenever you went to different cities, soon enough a guy would knock on your hotel door with a phonograph and Louis's and [Billie Holiday's] records, and other records he thought you'd like, and a little thing of pot; and then if you'd like to buy some more pot from him, it was fine; if not, you were just as welcome to this. And this happened all over the country . . . It was connected with being in show business; practically nobody smoked pot except people that were in show business, or Mexicans or Indians" (Marie Bryant, quoted in Clarke, 203–4). **"King of the Vipers":** Budd Johnson, quoted in Dance, 211–12. **"The first person I ever saw smoke marijuana":** Barnet, 19–20. **"Oh God, now that I am a dope addict":** Clayton, 46.

"Every one of us that smoked the stuff": Mezzrow and Wolfe, 93. **"Man, they can say what they want":** Ibid., 213.

"Roll our cigarettes right out in the open": Ibid., 93. **"As dangerous as a coiled rattlesnake":** H. J. Anslinger with Courtney Ryley Cooper, "Marijuana: Assassin of Youth," *American Magazine,* July 1937. **"At first you was a mis-do-meanor":** LA, tape 426, AA.

November 14, 1930: Local newspaper radio listings show that "Sebastian's Dance Orchestra" was scheduled to broadcast over KFVD from eleven P.M. to midnight and that "Sebastian's orchestra" was scheduled to broadcast over KMIC from midnight to two thirty A.M. (Steven Lasker, personal communication).

"While Vic and I were blasting this joint": LA, tape 426, AA.

Another local bandleader had informed on LA: This may be a reference to Curtis Mosby, the owner of the Apex Nite Club, a black-and-tan nightspot that was in direct competition with the Cotton Club. A report published in a local black newspaper two weeks earlier described Frank Sebastian as "one of the prejudiced hateful men when colored citizens were in front" and claimed that he was "the chief influence in the effort to close Curtis Mosby's Apex Nite Club" ("Infamous Cotton Club Insults War Veterans," *California Eagle,* October 31, 1930). **The downtown [Los Angeles] city jail:** The Cotton Club's parking lot was so large that part of it was within the city limits of Los Angeles, thus making LA and Vic Berton subject to arrest by Los Angeles policemen. **"A felony punishable by not less than six months":** "Drug Charge against Jazz Band Musicians," *Variety,* November 19, 1930. **Black newspapers across the country took note of LA's arrest:** See, for instance, "Louis Armstrong Nabbed on Drug Felony Charge" (*Chicago Defender,*

November 29, 1930) and "Louis Armstrong, Famous Trumpeter, Sentenced on Dope Charges" (*California Eagle*, March 13, 1931). **"In California, Cornetist Louis Armstrong":** "Muggles," *Time*, September 7, 1931. Surviving court filings and transcripts in the case of *The People of the State of California, Plaintiff, v. Louis Armstrong, Defendant*, filed in the Superior Court of the State of California, in and for the County of Los Angeles, show that LA was charged with violating the State Poison Act, which made it illegal to possess marijuana. He was arraigned and pleaded not guilty on December 8. LA appeared in court again on January 23, then changed his plea to guilty on March 10, at which time he was sentenced. LA recalled that he spent a total of nine days in jail before being released, though his account, taped nearly four decades later, incorrectly suggests that he served this time immediately after his arrest in November of 1930 (LA, tape 426, AA). All subsequent accounts of the arrest are based on the transcript of this tape that was published in *LAS* (132–38) and repeat the error. *Variety*'s November 19 story, however, correctly reports that LA and Vic Berton "were released on bail within 24 hours," indicating that LA did not go to jail until March 10 and was there until March 19. His sentence was suspended that day, and he left Los Angeles for Chicago immediately afterward.

"No substantial legal precedent": Barnet, 20.

"Abe Lyman, Vic's leader": Berton, 389. Lyman actually led the Cocoanut Grove band from 1921 to 1925. In 1930 its leader was Gus Arnheim, who had been Lyman's pianist. Berton was sentenced to ninety nights in the county jail, from which he was released each morning so that he could fulfill his professional commitments. Court records show that Berton and LA were not tried together and that LA's case was not handled similarly.

Frank Sebastian made a point of coming: LA, tape 426, AA. **"So you leave [marijuana] alone":** *The People of the State of California, Plaintiff, v. Louis Armstrong, Defendant*.

"The vultures who surrounded Louis": *Saturday Review*, September 25, 1971, quoted in Collier, 223. **Little is known of Collins:** Contrary to previous published accounts, Collins was not sent to California by Tommy Rockwell in order to get LA out of jail. According to an item published on August 30, 1930, in *Hollywood Filmograph*, a local trade paper, he had been "the booker for the RKO Theatres in New York City" before coming to Hollywood to book musical acts at the Blossom Room of the Roosevelt Hotel. LA played for him there on at least one occasion in September, around the time that he canceled his management contract with Rockwell (Steven Lasker, personal communication). **"He was a gangster":** LA, tape 255, AA. **"Mr. Johnny Collins [became] my Manager":** "Goffin Notebooks," 108. **Budd Johnson believed:** Johnson.

"I was still married to Lil Armstrong": "Goffin Notebooks," 107. LA claimed on the same occasion that Alpha visited him briefly in Los Angeles.

"All glitter and glass": James. **Later on he hired Zilner Randolph:** Randolph later said that he joined the band on the road in May (Paige Van Vorst, "Z.T. & Old Man Mose," *Mississippi Rag*, April 1975). He does not play on the recordings made by LA in Chicago that April. **"Don't let 'em cool off, boys":** James. **"A Band that Really deserved a *whole lot* of *Credit*":** "Goffin Notebooks," 108. **"He didn't let much ruffle him":** James.

"There was never much fooling around": Ibid. **Most of the charts were stocks:** Randolph.

"That's my song, give me that copy": Jason Berry, article in *New Orleans*, April 1977, quoted in Collier, 245.

A **"big, bad-ass hood"**: "Everybody's Louie." **He stated unequivocally:** *Louis Armstrong, Plaintiff.*

"When are you gonna open here?": "Goffin Notebooks," 110.

"I knew it was [Rockwell] that did it": LA, tape 255, AA.

"Having a 'Feud'": "Goffin Notebooks," 109. **"Only trying to get him to change managers":** "Jail Musician for Blackmail of Armstrong," *Chicago Defender*, April 25, 1931. **LA claimed in a court filing:** *Louis Armstrong, Plaintiff.* **"The Gangsters started a fight":** "Goffin Notebooks," 109.

"We looked on Al Capone": Quoted in Gene Lees, "The Glenn Miller Years I," *Jazzletter*, June 2007. **A "bad 'sommitch'":** "Goffin Notebooks," 110. **"I felt that — as dirty as Connie Fired me":** Ibid., 109.

"Stop fooling around with other people's artists": This story was told to James Lincoln Collier by Cork O'Keefe, Rockwell's business partner (Collier, 225). Mezz Mezzrow claimed that an attempt was also made around this time to "rub Connie Immerman out," but he did not say whether it had anything to do with the battle over LA's contract (Mezzrow and Wolfe, 242). **"The incidents involving Frankie Foster":** "Rockwell May File Suit over Louis Biog," *Down Beat*, March 26, 1947. The offending language does not appear in the published version of *Horn of Plenty* or in the autobiographical manuscript prepared by LA to aid Goffin in writing the book. According to LA, he and Goffin agreed to leave Rockwell's name out of *Horn of Plenty* in order to avoid a lawsuit (LA, tape 255, AA).

Rockwell filed a grievance with the American Federation of Musicians: Copies of all documents related to the grievance are part of the court filings in *Louis Armstrong, Plaintiff.*

"It's no trouble at all": "Goffin Notebooks," 110. **On May 23:** *LAS*, 289. The chronology of the preceding sequence of events is problematic. LA left Los Angeles on March 19 and arrived in Chicago three days later (*Chicago Defender*, March 28, 1931). He later claimed in his *Louis Armstrong, Plaintiff* affidavit that Rockwell and his hoods had first threatened Collins "[o]n or about April 11th 1931" and that his own meeting with Frankie Foster took place "[o]n Tuesday of the week following" (i.e., April 14). According to the affidavit, LA played at the Showboat between April 1 and May 12, but in *LAS* he says that he played at the Showboat for only two weeks (138) and left town the morning after Foster threatened him (145). Preston Jackson, a member of the Randolph band, claimed that LA continued to play at the Showboat for an unspecified period of time: "But thereafter, a squad brought Louis to work each night and brought him home" (Jones, 135). The Associated Press sent out a wire story in which Collins claimed that LA "was being threatened and followed around by hoodlums" and that the Chicago police had "furnished Louis with an escort, to accompany him home in the early morning hours" ("Gang Threats Aid to Music," *Reno Evening Gazette*, April 17, 1931). LA and the Showboat band recorded for OKeh in Chicago on April 20, 28, and 29. *LAS* claims that LA left Chicago in "mid-May . . . and toured through Illinois, Kentucky, Ohio and West Virginia" before arriving at the Greystone Ballroom on May 23 (289). His next recording session took place in Chicago in November.

"I did not know whether they had forgotten about me": *STM*, 96.

"The best way to travel": James.

"When our train pulled into the old L. & N. Station": *STM*, 96–97.

"They had Canal Street all lit up": James. **"The train of automobiles":** "Armstrong's Visit Creates a Sensation," unidentified newspaper clipping, LA, scrapbooks, AA.

They "gathered outside right along the levee": *LAS*, 148. "I just haven't the heart to announce that nigger": Ibid., 148–49. "The first time a Negro spoke on the radio": Gleason, 36.

"'Your home is in Chicago now?'": "Armstrong, Wizard of the Cornet, Former Item Newsie; Used to Live at Waifs' Home," *New Orleans Item-Tribune* (n.d.), LA, scrapbooks, AA.

"I remember, too, when we was staying": Preston Jackson, quoted in Jones, 138. Reasons that remain unclear: "John Collins decided to give a dance with our band . . . Now he'd rented a big warehouse for this farewell dance and when the time came for it to start, the governor wouldn't let him in. The doors was locked" (Preston Jackson, quoted in Jones, 136).

"Dressed up in their party clothes": "Darktown Strutters Walk Away," clipping from otherwise unidentified San Antonio paper, September 8, 1931, LA, scrapbooks, AA. The scrapbooks also contain an ad published in the August 29 *Louisiana Weekly* announcing that LA "Will Play All Evening / Monday, August 31st / Dancing for Colored Only / Benefit of Hospitalization Work for Colored / The U.S. Army Supply Base / At Poland and Dauphine Streets."

LA had "recently aroused the ire": "Armstrong's Visit Creates a Sensation," unidentified and undated newspaper clipping, LA, scrapbooks, AA. Collins filed a suit on LA's behalf: *Louis Armstrong, Plaintiff.*

LA had brought Alpha: Goffin, 274–75. "You don't need me": *Satchmo and Me.*

Rockwell and LA settled out of court: The surviving filings in *Louis Armstrong, Plaintiff* do not record the final disposition of the case, presumably meaning that a settlement was reached at some point in 1932. Eli Oberstein's deposition (see below) was taken on January 11. "In consequence of the colored trumpeter's hair-raising experiences": Bryce Oliver, "Gang Mutes Trumpeter," *New York Daily Mirror,* December 30, 1931, LA, scrapbooks, AA. "There was so much happenin'": LA, tape 426, AA. "The highest paid colored band in the world": *Tulsa Sunday World,* September 13, 1931, reproduced in Stratemann, 16.

"Why, do you know I played ninety-nine million hotels": "Everybody's Louie." "Most of the time while touring the South": LA "as told to David Sachs," "Daddy, How the Country Has Changed!" *Ebony,* May 1961 (hereafter cited as "'Daddy, How the Country Has Changed!'").

"You're in Memphis now": Preston Jackson, quoted in Jones, 136–37. Mezz Mezzrow heard it in New York: "Halfway through the broadcast he announced that he wanted to dedicate his next number to the Chief of Police of Memphis, Tennessee. 'Dig this, Mezzeerola,' he warbled while the band played his intro. Then he started to sing *I'll Be Glad When You're Dead You Rascal You*" (Mezzrow and Wolfe, 234–35).

"The largest selling artist making records today": Eli Oberstein, deposition in *Louis Armstrong, Plaintiff,* January 11, 1932.

An equally coincidental resemblance: The descending arpeggio in "Star Dust" to which the words *night / Dreaming of a song* are set is identical to the climactic two-bar break in "Potato Head Blues." Though the song was composed around the same time that the recording was made, it was not published until 1930.

"A singular, and incomparable, event": Sudhalter, 142.

LA's sidemen counted the high Cs in "Shine": "Scoville Browne, who played with Armstrong during the 1930s, said that guitarist Mike McKendrick would count the notes out loud as Louis hit them" (Collier, 219). LA's first surviving film appearance: LA and his band can also be heard (and briefly seen) in a

Betty Boop cartoon called "I'll Be Glad When You're Dead You Rascal You" that was made around the same time. Here LA plays a cannibal, and his disembodied head pursues Bimbo and Koko through the jungle as he sings the title song.

"The white man's notion of Harlem jazz": Charles Edward Smith, "Class Content of Jazz Music," *Daily Worker*, October 21, 1933.

OKeh was paying LA $1,000 a side: George Avakian, personal communication. **One of the reasons why LA left OKeh:** "Columbia and OKeh were a bankrupt part of a bankrupt company, so there was no money for jazz at all" (John Hammond, quoted in Chilton, 77). **The company stopped placing ads in black newspapers:** OKeh's last *Chicago Defender* ad, for LA's "Star Dust," appeared on December 12, 1931 (Wald, 35).

"Ladies & Gentlemen, this is the Reverend Satchelmouth Armstrong": "Black Rascal," *Time*, June 13, 1932. **"Many years ago":** "Everybody's Louie."

Taft Jordan parroted LA's interpretation: Jordan recorded "On the Sunny Side of the Street" in 1933, a full year before LA cut his own version, further proof that he perfected many of his best-known set pieces on the bandstand well in advance of recording them.

"First we noticed a blister on his chop": James.

7. "I Didn't Blow the Horn"

SOURCES

DOCUMENTS

Arthur Briggs, oral-history interview, IJS; Gösta Hägglöf, liner notes for *Louis Armstrong in Scandinavia, vol. 1*, sound recording (Storyville); Budd Johnson, oral-history interview, IJS; Teddy Wilson, oral-history interview, IJS.

BOOKS

Berrett, *The Louis Armstrong Companion*; Brown, *Georgia on My Mind*; Chilton, *The Song of the Hawk*; Collier, *Louis Armstrong*; Cunard, *Negro*; Dance, *The World of Swing*; Delaunay, *Django Reinhardt*; Dregni, *Django*; Driggs and Lewine, *Black Beauty, White Heat*; Feather, *The Jazz Years*; Giddins, *Satchmo*; Goddard, *Jazz Away from Home*; Goffin, *Horn of Plenty*; Hammond, *John Hammond on Record*; Hughes, *Second Movement*; Jackson, *Making Jazz French*; Lambert, *Music Ho!*; Larkin, *All What Jazz*; Mezzrow and Wolfe, *Really the Blues*; Panassié, *Hot Jazz*; Parsonage, *The Evolution of Jazz in Britain*; Renoir, *My Life and My Films*; Stratemann, *Louis Armstrong on the Screen*; Walser, *Keeping Time*; Wilson, *Teddy Wilson Talks Jazz*.

NOTES

The *New York Times* could run a story: "American Ragtime Sweeping Europe," *New York Times*, June 28, 1913. **"There is in the Southern Syncopated Orchestra":** E[rnest] Ansermet, "Sur un orchestre nègre," *Revue Romande*, October 1919, quoted in Walser, 111.

"Doing its best to murder music": *Star*, April 19, 1919, quoted in Parsonage, 131. **The vulgar expression:** Parsonage, 45.

"We would suggest your giving these to Louis": Allan W. Fitzock, letter to E. A. Fearn, September 3, 1926, LA, scrapbooks, AA. **Three dozen of them were in circulation:** *LAS*, 159.

"Really good nigger style": Quoted in Goddard, 169. **"The king of all trumpet players"**: "New York's 'Star' Musicians," *Melody Maker*, November 1929, LA, scrapbooks, AA. **A brown-colored mask and a kinky-haired wig**: Brown, 224. **A "raving fan"**: *LAS*, 159. **The "greatest dance trumpeter on earth"**: Nat Gonella, "Imitation without Apology," *Melody Maker*, July 1932, quoted in Parsonage, 230.

European jazzmen **"learnt all we knew about jazz"**: Hughes, 104–5.

Unable to book LA in New York: LA says in *STM* that he played at the Lafayette Theatre in Harlem before going to California (97). None of the New York papers indicates that he fulfilled the engagement, and George James specifically recalled that the band's New York performances had to be canceled "because of the gangsters" (James). The only verifiable occasion on which LA and the band appeared in the New York area during the first part of 1932 was when they filmed *A Rhapsody in Black and Blue* at Paramount's Astoria studios. **"For some time past"**: "Louis Armstrong Coming to London," *Melody Maker*, July 1932, quoted in *LAS*, 160.

He "shook my hand": *LAS*, 48. **Doubt has since been cast**: A month after LA's arrival, Ingman reported that he referred to his trumpet as "'Satchmo,' a contraction, I am told, of 'Satchel Mouth'" (Dan S. Ingman, "England's Welcome to Louis Armstrong," *Melody Maker*, August 1932, quoted in Berrett, 55). A Selmer ad in the same issue stated that "'Satch'-Mo' is a Selmer 'Challenger' Trumpet." No prior use of "Satchmo" in print is known. Ingman later claimed that Percy Brooks "certainly did not meet Louis at Plymouth and say 'Hello Satchmo'." On the other hand, Edgar Jackson of the *Melody Maker* told Max Jones that Brooks "had for some time known Louis as Satchmo from having heard him called that in 1928 by the American musicians in Fred Elizalde's dance orchestra at the Savoy." Asked at the end of his life about these conflicting statements, LA replied, "Percy Brooks deserves all the credit for my new name. . . . [T]o me it was Percy first called me Satchmo, and I love it" (*LAS*, 49–50).

"Eight famous hotels": Ingman, "England's Welcome to Louis Armstrong," quoted in Berrett, 53. **"He does not know who I am"**: Robert Goffin, "The Best Negro Jazz Orchestras," in Cunard, 181–82. **"All swing men can talk together"**: *STM*, 100. **"Sloppy" and "makeshift"**: Feather, 10. **"King of the Trumpet"**: The poster is reproduced in Driggs and Lewine, 216.

"Each one was received with tumult": Ingman, "England's Welcome to Louis Armstrong," in Berrett, 54–55.

"Top *F*'s bubble about all over the place": Ibid. **"The extreme economy of means"**: "Mike," *Melody Maker*, August 1932, quoted in Parsonage, 239. **"His face drips"**: Goffin, "The Best Negro Jazz Orchestras," in Cunard, 182. **"His actual presence"**: Joe Crossman, "What I Think of Armstrong," *Melody Maker*, October 1932, quoted in Parsonage, 239. **"The stageshow Armstrong"**: Larkin, 197. **"The sweating, strutting figure"**: Quoted in *LAS*, 163.

LA **"worked a little more piano"**: *Variety Music, Stage and Film News*, July 27, 1932, quoted in Parsonage, 241. **"Not all of the 28 houses were full"**: *LAS*, 163–64. **Tomatoes were thrown at LA**: Philippe Brun, quoted in Goddard, 183.

"Five out of six people seated in a row": Hannen Swaffer, "I Heard Yesterday," *Daily Herald*, July 25, 1932, LA, scrapbooks, AA. **"This savage growling"**: *Daily Express*, July 20, 1932, quoted in Parsonage, 245. **"The whole show"**: "The Armstrong War," *Rhythm*, September 1932, quoted in Parsonage, 245.

"I, myself, am entirely against": Quoted in Parsonage, 252. **"A lithe, small-ish but power-packed figure"**: *LAS*, 164.

"An artist like Louis Armstrong": Lambert, 187.

"I'll never forget England and its people": *LAS*, 240. **William Walton and William Primrose**: Ibid., 176. **"I didn't see how all of these people"**: *STM*, 101.

"Collins suddenly said": *LAS*, 176–77.

LA "must be worth a lot of money": Ibid., 178.

"Louis was now a star": Goffin, 298. **"A pretty poor revival"**: John Hammond, *Melody Maker*, January 1933, quoted in *LAS*, 172. **LA's name did not appear in the news columns of the *New York Times* until 1935**: "Night Club Notes," *New York Times*, October 19, 1935. The first *Times* story devoted exclusively to LA was Leonard Feather's "Trumpeter's Jubilee: Louis Armstrong Rounds Out Twenty-five Years as a Hot Jazz Wizard," published on October 26, 1941.

"His trumpet virtuosity is endless": Irving Kolodin, "All God's Chillun Got Fun," *Americana*, February 1933, quoted in Giddins, 116. **"A shock and a shiver"**: Mezzrow and Wolfe, 259–60.

"It was a privilege": Nat Hentoff, "Dr. Jazz and His Son, the Professor," *New York Times Magazine*, April 14, 1974.

"No good at all": Wilson, *Teddy Wilson Talks Jazz*, 14. **"Putrid"**: Franklyn S. Driggs, "The Story of Harry Dial," *Jazz Journal* 11, no. 12 (1958) (hereafter cited as "'Dial'"). **"He was always right"**: Wilson, oral-history interview. **"Always friendly with the band"**: Ibid. **"All day in the bus"**: Ibid. **LA earned $1,500 a week**: Wilson, *Teddy Wilson Talks Jazz*, 15. According to *Variety*, LA had been making $2,500 a week early in 1932, a year before Wilson joined the band. The same article claimed that Duke Ellington made $5,000 a week ("Desperation Salaries: 80 'Name Acts,' $2K or More," *Variety*, March 8, 1932).

"You could still get a room": Dance, 211. **The "OKeh Laughing Record"**: LA's record collection contains three copies of the original 78 (AA). **A formal-sounding cadenza**: The source of the cadenza is a 1920 violin solo by Minnie T. Wright called "Love-Song" (Vince Giordano, personal communication). **"We made one particular record"**: Johnson.

LA was still playing 250 or more high Cs: "Louis hit about 250 high C's, just *tch, tch, tch*, which will tear a man's chops to pieces. Man! Then he hit that high F, and held it, and made the walls tremble! The people just looked up at the roof" (Budd Johnson, quoted in Dance, 212). **"My collar was all down"**: "Dial." **"My, my, they all look so tired and sleepy"**: Johnson.

"Saccharine": Quoted in *LAS*, 174. **"As a soloist, as a performer"**: Hammond, 107.

"I went on stage": Ernie Anderson, "Joe Glaser & Louis Armstrong: A Memoir, Part 1: Early Days," *Storyville*, December 1, 1994 (hereafter cited as "Anderson 1").

"When Louis Armstrong completes his present European tour": "Armstrong and His Manager to Part," *Melody Maker*, August 19, 1933.

"One night [Collins] got very drunk": Hammond, 105.

"Listen, cocksucker, you might be my manager": Berrett, 85–86. **"Always something would be wrong"**: *SP*, 45. **"This one's for you, Rex!"**: LA told the story repeatedly in later years. See "People," *Time*, May 21, 1956, and *LAS*, 226. He later gave the gold-plated horn to Lyman Vunk, a trumpeter with Charlie Barnet's band, whose widow presented it to the Armstrong Archives in 1995.

"All I remember": *STM*, 112. **Filmed on a Danish sound stage**: Stratemann, 31. **A group of off-the-air live recordings**: Recordings of "Chinatown, My Chinatown," "You Rascal You," and "On the Sunny Side of the Street" were made by an engineer during an October 28 broadcast from a Stockholm auditorium.

"A new act": Quoted in Chilton, 97. **Hawkins had disliked LA**: According to Cootie Williams, "Coleman hated Louis. It was when I was in the Fletcher Henderson band that I learned about this. I knew Hawk then and he just couldn't even stand the name Armstrong. I used to love Louis so much and when I'd speak about him Hawkins didn't like it at all" (ibid., 30–31). **"Hawk didn't think that I was big enough"**: LA, tape 426, AA. **"I've figured it out"**: *Melody Maker*, May 5, 1934, quoted in Collier, 265. **"An acute attack of artistic temperament"**: "Louis Armstrong Quits: Concert Wrecked," *Melody Maker*, April 14, 1934. **The two men later smoothed over their differences**: "In 1957, when Louis and Hawk were both at the Newport Jazz Festival, I enjoyed seeing them together briefly. Then one of the rare festival thunderstorms broke out, and I was in a position to see Louis's band bus in the parking area, which was pretty dark. There were bolts of lightning, and lo and behold, thus illuminated, I saw the two old friends sitting side by side, smoking a joint" (Dan Morgenstern, personal communication). **"That's just *great!*"**: Johnny Simmens, "Coleman Hawkins in Switzerland 1935/6/8," *Storyville*, October 1974.

"A very hard year": *STM*, 113–14. **"In England on the stage"**: *SP*, 39. **Reports in the British press**: *LAS*, 179–80.

"The greatest of all hot soloists": Panassié, 51, 64.

"My brother! My brother!": Dregni, 54. **"Armstrong, preoccupied by his toilet"**: Delaunay, 73. **"It must have been about five in the morning"**: Ibid. According to Mabel Mercer, LA also played trumpet at the session: "I remember one morning Louis Armstrong with his trumpet and Django Reinhardt with his guitar were playing for each other. I went home and to bed. I got up around noon for some milk or something, and they were still there playing duets" (William Livingstone, "Mabel Mercer," *Stereo Review*, February 1975).

"The entrance of Louis on stage": Panassié, *Douze années de jazz*, quoted in Berrett, 65. This description is from Panassié's 1946 account of the concert. He felt differently at the time, however, writing in the American edition of *Le jazz hot* that "Louis Armstrong gave two concerts in Paris in November, 1934, and, despite his apparent success, my fears have been realized: the French public did not see the musician at all" (Panassié, 62). **"Rubber-mouthed and consummately rhythmic"**: Marshall Sprague, "Lou Armstrong Scores Hit," *New York Herald*, November 11, 1934. **"Overwhelming"**: Panassié, *Douze années de jazz*, quoted in Berrett, 68. **A "triumph"**: Renoir, 79. **"My friend, there is nothing more to say"**: Panassié, *Douze années de jazz*, quoted in Berrett, 69.

"Very 1920, very 1920": Ibid., 67. **"It could be rather curious"**: Ibid., 72. **"Mr. King of Jazz and man-eater offspring"**: Quoted in Hägglöf.

"I got such a big hand": *STM*, 114.

"A push, and not an attack": Briggs. **"As hard as a piece of wood"**: Goddard, 287.

A front-page story: N. J. Canetti, "Armstrong Flees to U.S.A.," *Melody Maker*, February 2, 1935.

Lil was suing LA: *LAS*, 188. **"Maintenance" that Johnny Collins had neglected to remit**: Lucille Armstrong claimed that "Collins had neither paid his taxes nor sent anything to Lil" (Collier, 263). **"Never, never, never"**: Ibid., 181. **"From January of 1935 to May"**: *STM*, 115. **"When I come back"**: *SP*, 45.

SOURCES

DOCUMENTS

LA, VOA series; George Avakian, interview, January 21, 2005; Jack Bradley, interview, July 7, 2008; *The David Frost Show,* TV show, February 10, 1971 (Group W); Charlie Holmes, oral-history interview, IJS; Budd Johnson, oral-history interview, IJS; *Pennies from Heaven,* film (Columbia); John Simmons, oral-history interview, IJS; Trummy Young, oral-history interview, IJS.

BOOKS

Albertson, *Louis Armstrong;* Barnet, *Those Swinging Years;* Bergreen, *Louis Armstrong;* Bigard, *With Louis and the Duke;* Carmichael, The Stardust Road *and* Sometimes I Wonder; Chilton, *Ride, Red, Ride;* Clarke, *Wishing on the Moon;* Collier, *Louis Armstrong;* Coward, *The Noël Coward Diaries;* Dahl, *Morning Glory;* Evans, *Follow Your Heart;* Feather, *The Jazz Years;* Ferguson, *The Otis Ferguson Reader;* Foster, *Autobiography;* Giddins, *Bing Crosby;* Gordon, *Live at the Village Vanguard;* Harrison et al., *The Essential Jazz Records;* Jones, *Jazz Talking;* Panassié, *Louis Armstrong;* Stratemann, *Louis Armstrong on the Screen;* Sudhalter, *Henry "Red" Allen;* Wilder, *American Popular Song;* Zwerin, *Close Enough for Jazz.*

NOTES

"Asking me about Joe": "Joseph G. Glaser Is Dead at 72; Booking Agent for Many Stars," *New York Times,* June 8, 1969. **"My dearest friend":** *LAS,* 16. **"I'm Louis and Louis is me":** "Louis the First," *Time,* February 21, 1949. **"They couldn't be in the same room":** Collier, 160. **"You don't know me":** "Joseph G. Glaser Is Dead at 72." **In bed each night by ten o'clock:** Gordon, 82. **"A painting of the antebellum South":** Nat Hentoff, "Louis: Black and Blue and Triumphant," *JazzTimes,* October 2000. **"Now look, don't get me wrong":** Clarke, 101. **"He acted like a crook":** Dahl, 105. **"The most obscene, the most outrageous":** Gordon, 79. **"A brisk little Jewish go-getter":** Noël Coward, diary entry, December 3, 1954, in Coward, 247. **"If I have Joe Glaser's word":** "Joseph G. Glaser Is Dead at 72."
He was running Capone's South Side nightclubs and whorehouses: "He was frank to say he had worked for Capone, who eventually put him in charge of the brothels and music joints on the Chicago South Side" (George Avakian, personal communication). **"She wore make-up":** "Plantation Café Owner Gets Ten Years in Prison," *Chicago Defender,* February 11, 1928. **"All the court records ... had been 'lost or destroyed' ":** Ernie Anderson, "Joe Glaser & Louis Armstrong: A Memoir, Part 2: The All-Stars," *Storyville,* March 1, 1995 (hereafter cited as "Anderson 2").
"He killed a guy": Johnson.
"Broke and very sick": "Manager Joe Glaser on Louis," *Life,* April 15, 1966 (hereafter cited as " 'Glaser' "). **"He had always been a sharp cat":** Anderson 1. **"I'm going to get Joe Glaser":** Johnson. **"Pops, I need you":** "Everybody's Louie."
"You get me the jobs": Anderson 1. **A fifty-fifty split:** This was what Lucille Armstrong told James Lincoln Collier (Collier, 346). **"I never tried in no way":** "Satchmo Story," 116. **As late as 1937:** *SP,* 49.

"The way he treated his help": *SP*, 45. **"*Dipper*, As long as you live"**: Letter to Joe Glaser, August 2, 1955, in *IHOW*, 160.

"I always said I didn't believe": Young. **"Louis has never failed"**: "Glaser." **"There ain't but one guy"**: VOA series. (This statement by LA is the only evidence that Glaser had any formal knowledge of music.) **"Our first contract was for ten years"**: *LAS*, 240.

"Joe hired and fired everybody": Bigard, 117, 115.

"Joe Glaser, the way he'd talk": Young. **"Long time admiration"**: "Jewish Family," 8, 6.

A six-figure insurance policy on LA: "Glaser." Glaser bought out Johnny Collins: *LAS*, 238. Glaser "saved me from the gangsters": Avakian.

"My chops was beat when I got back": " 'My Chops Was Beat — But I'm Dyin' to Swing Again' — Louis Armstrong," *Down Beat*, June 1935.

Glaser "would buy food along the way": "Daddy, How the Country Has Changed!" The Immerman brothers were no longer running Connie's Inn: "Both of 'em went broke. . . . They had New York sewed up. And then the gangsters broke them before they died," LA says with vengeful relish on a tape of a conversation recorded in the fifties (LA, tape 255, AA). **"I enjoyed all the moments that I spent"**: LA, tape 426, AA. **"I was very proud 'n' happy"**: "Open Letter to Fans," in *IHOW*, 185. **"That [solo] was a half a tone off"**: Ernest Borneman, "Bop Will Kill Business Unless It Kills Itself First: Louis Armstrong," *Down Beat*, April 7, 1948.

College students and musicians: Eli Oberstein, deposition in *Louis Armstrong, Plaintiff*. **"The substantial following"**: Charles Edward Smith, "Collecting Hot," *Esquire*, February 1934. **"An entertainer, singer, and musician"**: "Glaser." **"Joe Glaser could realize I could play with white boys"**: LA, tape 346, AA. **"For many years I blew my brains out"**: "Everybody's Louie."

"Those big lips of his": Carmichael, 140. **"Utterly mad, hoarse, inchoate"**: *STM*, xvi. **"A subtle mix of showmanship and artistry"**: Feather, 26.

An exquisitely well-honed appreciation: For a concise account of Jack Kapp's career, see Gary Giddins's *Bing Crosby*, 365–78. All quotes by or about Kapp in this chapter are from this source.

"He loved melody": Collier, 40.

"Armstrong's small-group recordings of the 1920s": Harrison et al., 340–42. **"Before, he was seeking — and finding"**: Panassié, 108.

"Every word of it was my own": *IHOW*, x.

"A two-fingered blip": Ibid., x–xi.

"A nice easy book": Otis Ferguson, "Speaking of Jazz: I," *New Republic*, August 2, 1939, quoted in Ferguson, 186.

"Every night between their outfit and our outfit": LA letter to unknown recipient, ca. 1967 (AA). **"I've never been invited to the home of a movie star"**: "Daddy, How the Country Has Changed!" **"I never met anybody"**: Bing Crosby, transcript of undated radio interview with Humphrey Lyttelton (IJS). **"The *Boss of All Singers*"**: LA letter to unknown recipient, ca. 1967 (AA).

"I got the boys together": *Pennies from Heaven*.

LA recited the 7 percent scene: *The David Frost Show*. **"Those scenes I had with Bing"**: Ibid. **"Best bit"**: "The New Pictures," *Time*, November 23, 1936. **"Best individual impression is by Louis Armstrong"**: *Variety*, December 16, 1936, quoted in Stratemann, 43.

LA appeared in seven more Hollywood feature films: Crosby also invited him to play a larger role in a 1937 film called *Doctor Rhythm*. LA's scenes were cut from the film and are now lost. **"Each year I also have a fine part"**: Letter to the editors of the *Melody Maker*, December 21, 1946 (IJS). **"A wonderful rhythm song"**: Wilder, 399.

"Regarded less as artists": "The New Pictures," *Time*, April 12, 1943. **"The Uncle Tom slant"**: *Down Beat*, September 15, 1943.

"While Miss Raye is under cork": *Variety*, August 4, 1937, quoted in Stratemann, 51. **"Martha Raye, thinly burnt-corked"**: Dudley Glass, *Atlanta Georgian*, quoted in *Variety*, September 15, 1937, ibid.

$7,500: Bergreen, 416. **The first black to host his own network-radio variety show**: The NBC Artist Record Cards on file at the Library of Congress indicate that LA's show was "the earliest example of an African American performer hosting a network variety program" (Elizabeth McLeod, personal communication). ***Harlem:*** NBC's records state that the show was officially known as *Harlem Radio Review*, but airchecks show that the network's in-house announcers called it *Harlem*. **"Sponsored by the makers of Fleischmann's Yeast"**: *Billboard*, April 17, 1937.

The series **"could only be recommended"**: *Variety*, April 28, 1937, quoted in Bergreen, 385.

"When Pops booked me": Letter to Leonard Feather, September 18, 1941, in *IHOW*, 147–48.

"Once we jumped from Bangor, Maine": Foster, 186. **"I mean, you see"**: Holmes.

"You stay tired, dirty and drunk": Barnet, 117. **"You skim more than read"**: Zwerin, 32. **LA encouraged his musicians to smoke pot**: Bradley. **"He never worked with it"**: Simmons.

"Other trumpet players": Holmes.

"SATCHMO'S UNDERSTUDY": See the 1937 ad reproduced in Sudhalter, 15. **"Louis gave Red an hour's time"**: Holmes. **"It was no fault of Louis'"**: Chilton, 96–97.

"That band could play": Jones, 24. **Alpha rode in a chauffeured Packard**: Holmes. **Two hundred cotton handkerchiefs**: Ernie Anderson, "Louis Armstrong: A Personal Memoir," *Storyville*, December 1, 1991. **"Every night"**: Evans, 67.

"Alpha was all right": "Dark Women." **"What's Wrong Here"**: LA, scrapbooks, AA. **"Louis didn't really want"**: Albertson, 26–27.

"The glow of her deep brown skin": "Dark Women." **"Strict attention"**: "Open Letter to Fans," in *IHOW*, 187.

"She spoke in a very proper English": Bradley. **"You keep running from me"**: Collier, 283.

9. "The People Who Criticize"

SOURCES

DOCUMENTS

LA, VOA series; Phoebe Jacobs, oral-history interview conducted by researchers for Ken Burns's *Jazz* (transcript available online at www.pbs.org/jazz/about/pdfs/Jacobs.pdf); Cliff Leeman, oral-history interview, IJS; Joe Muranyi, interview, September 1, 2007; *Satchmo*, TV documentary (WNET); John Simmons, oral-history interview, IJS.

BOOKS

Agee, *Agee on Film*; Balliett, *American Musicians II*; Bechet, *Treat It Gentle*; Benamou, *It's All True*; Bergreen, *Louis Armstrong*; Berrett, *The Louis Armstrong Companion*; Bigard, *With Louis and the Duke*; Blesh, *Shining Trumpets*; Bradbury, *Armstrong*; Britt, *Long Tall Dexter*; Charles and Ritz, *Brother Ray*; Chilton, *Ride, Red, Ride*; Chilton, *Sidney Bechet*; Cogswell, *Louis Armstrong*; Collier, *Louis Armstrong*; Dance, *The World of Earl Hines*; Ellington, *Music Is My Mistress*; Feather, *From Satchmo to Miles*; Feather, *The Jazz Years*; Firestone, *Swing, Swing, Swing*; Foster, *Autobiography*; Friedman, *Jackson Pollock*; Gleason, *Jam Session*; Harrison et al., *The Essential Jazz Records*; Hentoff, *The Jazz Life*; Holiday, *Lady Sings the Blues*; Jones, *Jazz Talking*; Levinson, *Trumpet Blues*; Miller, *Louis Armstrong*; Porter, *There and Back*; Prial, *The Producer*; Ramsey and Smith, *Jazzmen*; Shapiro and Hentoff, *Hear Me Talkin' to Ya*; Stratemann, *Louis Armstrong on the Screen*; Teague, *Shakespeare and the American Popular Stage*; Thomson, *A Virgil Thomson Reader*; Wald, *Escaping the Delta*.

NOTES

"That number started off": Quoted in Firestone, 148.

"Hot jazz cultists": "Dixieland," *Time*, June 15, 1936. **"His trumpet solos . . . are as important"**: "Whoa-ho-ho-ho-ho-ho!" *Time*, January 20, 1936.

"For many years I was Number One": Jelly Roll Morton, "'I Created Jazz in 1902, Not W. C. Handy,' Declares Jelly Roll Morton," *Down Beat*, August 1938.

"I'm still out of work": Quoted in Frederic Ramsey Jr., "King Oliver and His Creole Jazz Band," in Ramsey and Smith, 89–90.

"Absolutely perfect": Letter to William Russell, October 3, 1939, Hogan Jazz Archive, Tulane University, New Orleans. **"Louis would steal off from home"**: Park Breck, "This Isn't Bunk; Bunk Taught Louis," *Down Beat*, June 1, 1939.

"The Old Dixieland Jazz Band": STM, 10. **"Sydney Bachet"**: Ibid., 14. **"You're a little ahead of your time"**: Charlie Carpenter, quoted in Dance, 148.

"The greatest drummer": LA, tape 249, AA. **"A big man with so much finesse"**: Porter, 31.

"The highly publicized Negro jazz bands": Quoted in Prial, 116. **"It isn't that Louis is playing bad trumpet nowadays"**: John Hammond, "Hot Discs Reviewed," *Rhythm*, February 1936. **"If I may say so"**: John Hammond, "Swing Stuff," *Rhythm*, April 1936. **A successful campaign**: "Song Suppressed," *Time*, June 24, 1940.

"A master of musical art": Virgil Thomson, "Swing Music," *Modern Music*, May 1938, in Thomson, 31. **Swing Music (Louis Armstrong)**: The painting is reproduced in Miller, 46.

"How can they possibly vote for me": Quoted in Levinson, 34. **"First, I'll name my boy Bunny Berigan"**: "Berigan 'Can't Do No Wrong,' Says Armstrong," *Down Beat*, September 1941. **"Theres two trumpet players"**: Letter to the editors of *Melody Maker*, December 21, 1946 (IJS). **"That white boy"**: Ibid. **"Most of the people who criticize"**: *LAS*, 220.

"Louis, it seemed like he was wanting": Bechet, 176, 175.

"The agents and everybody": Shapiro and Hentoff, 187. **"In 1937 my band went to Savannah"**: *SP*, 48–49.

LA received a piteous letter from Bunk Johnson: Foster, 191. **"Your old boy is down":** Gleason, 111–12.

"Man, if Old Shakespeare could see me now": Feather, *From Satchmo to Miles*, 20. **"On the toilet":** LA, tape 238, AA.

Swingin' the Dream: The most detailed account of the show is in Teague, 120–32. **"An uneven show":** Brooks Atkinson, "The Play: Swinging Shakespeare's 'Dream' with Benny Goodman, Louis Armstrong and Maxine Sullivan," *New York Times*, November 30, 1939. **"As a show, it falls flat as a pancake":** "New Musical in Manhattan," *Time*, December 11, 1939. **LA never played "Darn That Dream" again:** "Louis not only didn't record it, he never played it again, and he said to me that it was because he wanted to forget the whole incident" (Dan Morgenstern, personal communication).

"Hard to get along with": Quoted in Chilton, *Ride, Red, Ride*, 110. **"When Joe Glaser took over":** George Hoefer, undated *Down Beat* clipping (IJS). **"Glaser fired the whole band":** Foster, 192. **"I used to have a lot of youngsters":** VOA series.

An inventory of the records: Wald, 277–80. **LA "did more to entertain me":** Charles and Ritz, 71.

"She has that routine down": Letter to Leonard Feather, October 1, 1941 (IJS). **"Brother Winch":** Letter to Walter Winchell, January 19, 1942, Hogan Jazz Archive, Tulane University, New Orleans. **"Louis, Wife Out of Tune":** *Down Beat*, February 14, 1942. **"To believe that Alpha turned out":** "Goffin Notebooks," 99.

"In fact it dawned on me": "Open Letter to Fans," in *IHOW*, 185. **"Just a little small Chorus Girl":** "Early Years with Lucille," in *IHOW*, 139–41.

"My honeymoon was eight months of one-nighters": Collier, 284. **"As nice + sweet + wonderful":** Letter to Joe Glaser, August 2, 1955, quoted in Collier, 159. **"We get along real well":** "Dark Women." **"The Average woman would have 'Quit' my ol ass":** Letter to Joe Glaser, August 2, 1955, in *IHOW*. 159. **LA would "eye Lucille up":** Jacobs. **"That trumpet comes first":** *Times* obituary.

"We finally went to bed": Hentoff, 26.

"I must *set* Lucille down": "Early Years with Lucille," in *IHOW*, 143. **The price tag of the house was sixteen thousand dollars:** Ernie Anderson, "Louis Armstrong: A Personal Memoir," *Storyville*, December 1, 1991.

"*One* look at that big *fine* house": "Early Years with Lucille," in *IHOW*, 144.

"I have partial vision on purpose": *LAS*, 168.

"Someday You'll Be Sorry" refers to LA's marriage: It has also been speculated that the song "wasn't about any love affair, but Louis's response to the once-admiring musicians who now branded him passé" (Dan Morgenstern, personal communication). **"It wasn't just that song, man":** Anderson 1. **"Of all his wives":** Muranyi. **Leeman said nothing about his affair with Alpha:** Leeman.

"A mediocre band": Britt, 49. **Eleven dollars a night:** Simmons. **A well-connected viper:** Dexter Gordon, interview, *Satchmo* (WNET).

"Louis read his part with ease": Feather, *The Jazz Years*, 107.

LA's "ability, not much reflected by his recordings": Harrison et al., 530.

"I had eighteen men": Feather, *From Satchmo to Miles*, 25.

"Their tunes were old": "Jazz? Swing? It's Ragtime," *Time*, November 5, 1945. **"You can hear from the first note":** Leonard Feather, "Lombardo Grooves Louis!" *Metronome*, September 1949.

"He could play funeral marches": Park Breck, "This Isn't Bunk; Bunk Taught Louis," *Down Beat*, June 1, 1939. "A few moments on the trumpet": *Variety*, October 3, 1942, quoted in Bergreen, 419. "Louis Armstrong could conceivably return to jazz": Blesh, 283.

"Most of 'em couldn't stand the gaff": Barry Ulanov, "Louis and Jazz," *Metronome*, April 1945. "The greatest jazzman": "Reverend Satchelmouth," *Time*, April 29, 1946.

"I want to do the history of jazz": Ellington, 240.

Down Beat ran a story in August: Charlie Emge, "Orson Welles Jazz Movie Will Star Louis Armstrong," *Down Beat*, August 15, 1941. "The forthcoming Orson Welles documentary picture": Leonard G. Feather, "Trumpeter's Jubilee: Louis Armstrong Rounds Out Twenty-five Years as a Hot Jazz Wizard," *New York Times*, October 26, 1941. A script called "The Story of Jazz": Benamou, 29. A month-long engagement: Stratemann, 146.

Down Beat told its readers: "Welles Jazz Film May Be Shelved, Louie May Never Be Immortalized in Great Movie," *Down Beat*, May 1, 1942.

A six-page letter outlining the story of LA's life: Letter to Orson Welles, ca. 1945, Orson Welles Collection, Lilly Library, Indiana University.

"I'll be playing a maid": Feather, *From Satchmo to Miles*, 77. "I didn't feel this damn part": Holiday, 119–20. "Ornery": Bigard, 94. "I finally finished making the film": Letter to Madeleine Berard, November 25, 1946, quoted in Berrett, 129–30.

"More cohesive": Feather, *The Jazz Years*, 109.

"The big brassy jazz bands": "'Sincere Sounds,'" *Time*, December 23, 1946. "Promoters all over are going broke": Joe Glaser, letter to Joe Garland, July 25, 1946, quoted in Cogswell, 171. "I'm going to control everything": Collier, 290. "The fee for the 16-piece band": Anderson 1. "My boss (Mr Glaser) so anxious": Letter to the editors of the *Melody Maker*, December 21, 1946 (IJS).

"Playing with his peers": Anderson 1.

"The only other really creative thing": Friedman, 88.

"A bimonthly series": "Jive for Epicures," *Time*, November 23, 1942. "A full and noble expression": Ibid.

"I tell you I was scared to death": Jones, 115.

"We don't have to rehearse": Anderson 1. He showed up at Jimmy Ryan's: Chilton, *Sidney Bechet*, 195. Teagarden and Hackett were sober: *LAS*, 201.

"I work with two bands": Bradbury, 230. "He reined in the obstreperous": Balliett, 206.

"I was particularly struck": Quoted in *LAS*, 201.

Anderson had arranged to have the concert recorded: The complete recording was commercially released on LP by RCA France in 1983. *Down Beat's* review: "Satchmo's Genius Still Lives," *Down Beat*, June 4, 1947. "All the freshness and vigour": Peter Tanner, "Louis Is Still Tops," *Melody Maker*, June 7, 1947. Glaser signed Teagarden to a long-term contract: Anderson 1.

A "series of concert appearances": *Variety*, May 28, 1947, quoted in Stratemann, 234.

"A crime": James Agee, *Nation*, August 2, 1947, in Agee, 271. "Put it down as a fizzle": Bosley Crowther, "'New Orleans,' Study in Jazz, at Winter Garden — Two Other Movies Have Local Premieres," *New York Times*, June 20, 1947.

SOURCES

DOCUMENTS

LA, VOA series; George Avakian, interview, January 21, 2005; *Be My Guest,* TV show, July 2, 1968 (BBC); Barney Bigard, oral-history interview, IJS; Jack Bradley, interview, July 7, 2008; Dick Cary, oral-history interview, Hogan Jazz Archive, Tulane University, New Orleans; Cozy Cole, oral-history interview, IJS; Will Friedwald, liner notes for *The Wonderful World of Louis Armstrong,* sound recording (Time-Life); Dan Morgenstern, liner notes for *The Complete Decca Studio Recordings of Louis Armstrong and the All Stars* (Mosaic); Joe Muranyi, interview, September 1, 2007; *Philco Radio Time,* radio show, March 16, 1949 (ABC); Joe Showler, liner notes for *Louis Armstrong and His All Stars Live at the Hollywood Empire 1949,* sound recording (Storyville); *Stage Show,* TV show, August 21, 1954 (CBS); Trummy Young, oral-history interview, IJS.

BOOKS

Balliett, *American Musicians II;* Bigard, *With Louis and the Duke;* Bradbury, *Armstrong;* Chilton, *Let the Good Times Roll;* Collier, *Louis Armstrong;* Crosby, *Going My Own Way;* Dahl, *Morning Glory;* Dance, *The World of Earl Hines;* Darensbourg, *Jazz Odyssey;* Ellington, *Music Is My Mistress;* Evans, *Follow Your Heart;* Feather, *From Satchmo to Miles;* Firestone, *Swing, Swing, Swing;* Giddins, *Satchmo;* Goffin, *Horn of Plenty;* Goffin, *Souvenirs avant l'adieu;* Hammond, *John Hammond on Record;* Hinton and Berger, *Bass Line;* Jones, *Jazz Talking;* Jordan, *Rhythm Man;* Lyttelton, *Second Chorus;* Traill and Lascelles, *Just Jazz;* Travis, *An Autobiography of Black Jazz.*

NOTES

"The first really cosmopolitan club": Sonny Criss, interview with Bob Porter and Mark Gardner, *Jazz Monthly,* April 1968. **$2,500 a night:** Anderson 1.

"A show-business invasion": Anderson 2. **"I don't need no rehearsals":** "Satchmo Comes Back," *Time,* September 1, 1947.

"Louis Armstrong had forsaken the ways of Mammon": Ibid.

"At first it was going to be two weeks": Bigard, *With Louis and the Duke,* 96. **"Joe makes it sound like a basketball team":** Anderson 2.

The All Stars crisscrossed the United States: Showler. **"I resented Joe Glaser's attitude":** Travis, 281. **"Them days off are bad":** Lyttelton, 151. **"We don't have no days off":** *SP,* 44. **"That's when Louie needed me":** Collier, 284.

"Louis' most trusted companion": Anderson 2. **"When we were doing one-nighters":** Quoted in Bradbury, 110. **"Each member of the band":** Sinclair Traill and Gerald Lascelles, interview with Jack Lesberg, *Jazz Journal,* September 1970. **Weekly salaries ranging from $150 for Cary to $500 for Teagarden:** Cary. Louis Jordan, who was at the height of his popularity in 1947, was paying his sidemen $300 a week, while Duke Ellington was offering $100 to new recruits (Chilton, 136).

"A real ass-hole": Bigard, *With Louis and the Duke,* 116. **"He didn't like anyone":** Hinton and Berger, 197. **"Gee, I hate to see that":** Darensbourg, 166. **"It was perhaps a pity":** Peter Tanner, "Louis Is Still Tops," *Melody Maker,* June 7, 1947.

"**Wonderful, everywhere but Memphis**": LA, interview, *Record Changer*, July–August 1950. **Glaser always took care to keep the All Stars racially mixed:** Teagarden came down with pneumonia in 1949 and was briefly replaced by a black trombonist. This appears to have been the only time that LA appeared in public with an all-black band after 1947. **"Charged with trying to smuggle marijuana":** *Time*, January 11, 1954. See also Hinton and Berger, 198–201. **"Glaser would scream":** Jack Bradley, quoted in Giddins, 107. **"A drug addict":** Cary. **"We don't want junkies with the star":** Bradbury, 109.

"**I never pick my own bands":** Traill and Lascelles, 4. **"He didn't have a big ego":** Hinton and Berger, 207. **"Like a family affair":** Darensbourg, 163.

Dirty jokes: LA's papers include a bound typescript of blue jokes and pornographic stories that he collected over the years (AA). **"Sid's personality reflected his playing":** Balliett, 210.

"**He got so he played everythin' except the drums":** Traill and Lascelles, 7.

"**He never got angry about anything":** Bigard, *With Louis and the Duke*, 100. **"Louis can't do anything wrong":** John Tynan, "Teagarden Talks," *Down Beat*, March 1957. **"Like a holiday":** *SP*, 27.

"**If we played a long engagement":** Bigard, *With Louis and the Duke*, 101. **"Warm but distant":** Ibid., 739. **"If I don't have enough":** Cary.

"**A happy-go-lucky girl":** Dance, 104. **"A 250-lb. lady":** "Reverend Satchelmouth," *Time*, April 29, 1946. **"Wait'll you see Velma's split":** LA, tape 211, AA. **"Velma wasn't a great singer":** Young.

"**Always a little bit distant":** Avakian. **"He would complain a lot":** Dance, 104. **"He had that woody tone":** Ellington, 115.

"**The one thing was that they never really hit it off":** Bigard, *With Louis and the Duke*, 104–5.

"**Tore down the house":** John S. Wilson, "'Hard Times, Good Times' of Marty Napoleon," *New York Times*, March 23, 1984. **"Everybody in the All Stars got a chance":** Bradbury, 92. **"It sits good on the chops":** George Avakian, personal communication.

"**I say, people got all those records":** *SP*, 43. **"Well, y'know it's a real consolation":** Traill and Lascelles, 5. **One of LA's bones of contention with Hines:** VOA series. **"It's like calling Tchaikovsky a bum":** Quoted in *LAS*, 208.

"**What we played with Louis wasn't Dixieland":** Dance, 107. **"A New Orleans type of band":** Bradbury, 102.

"**Louis had been instructed":** Leonard Feather, "Remembering 'Pops' — Salute to Satch," *Down Beat*, July 15, 1965.

"**I wouldn't call them Dixieland":** Feather, 32. **"The film called *New Orleans*":** *LAS*, 202. **"I should know what I'm doing":** Letter to the editors of the *Melody Maker*, December 21, 1946 (IJS). **"You couldn't tell him what to do":** Joe Sully, quoted in Collier, 201.

"**He disliked bad notes":** LA, tape 426, AA. **"Don't fuck with my hustle!":** Muranyi.

"**Did you ever hear that story":** LA, tape 426, AA.

Bop "doesn't come from the heart": George T. Simon, "Bebop's the Easy Way Out, Claims Louis," *Metronome*, March 1948. **"That out-of-the-world music":** Ernest Borneman, "Bop Will Kill Business Unless It Kills Itself First: Louis Armstrong," *Down Beat*, April 7, 1948.

"**This is the sort of stuff":** *Down Beat*, April 22, 1946. **LA always acknowledged that Dizzy Gillespie was a first-class musician:** Gillespie's "'Bout to Wail" was one of the sides he played on the 1956 Voice of America broadcast devoted to his favorite recordings (VOA series). **"Very personally, I don't care for most bop"**: *Down Beat*, July 15, 1949. **"Give this son of a gun *eight* stars!"**: Leonard Feather, "Lombardo Grooves Louis!," *Metronome*, September 1949.

"Overdoing the jazz situation": LA, tape 14, AA. **"I guess musicians would dig this"**: Feather, "Lombardo Grooves Louis!"

"A black rascal raised in a waifs' home": "Black Rascal," *Time*, June 13, 1932. **"Louis says: 'Jazz and I grew up'"**: "Louis the First," *Time*, February 21, 1949.

Seven other popular musicians had been so honored: They were George Gershwin (1925), Morton Downey (1931), George M. Cohan (1933), Irving Berlin (1934), Richard Rodgers (1938), Crosby (1941), and Cole Porter (1949). **"I got a big charge"**: *Philco Radio Time*.

"We'd use Louis to cover the hits": Collier, 315. **"As soon as Louis"**: Morgenstern.

"Louis came in town": Chilton, 156.

"Madame Lucille": *Be My Guest*.

"He used to say": Morgenstern. **"I don't know if they told Louis"**: Friedwald.

"Man, don't pay Louie any mind": Cole. **"A real New Orleans drummer"**: Traill and Lascelles, 8.

"He explained that when he had married Lucille": Anderson 2. **"The pope was such a fine little old fellow"**: LA, tape 17, AA. (Some sources incorrectly state that this exchange took place during LA's 1968 audience with Pope Paul VI.) Ernie Anderson supplied a little-known footnote to this oft-embroidered story, claiming that when he, LA, and Lucille got into the limousine that was to take them to Castel Gandolfo, "Louis took a bomber [i.e., a large stick of marijuana] out of an inside pocket and said, 'Let's light up'" (Anderson 2).

"He approaches his work with thought and pride": Howard Taubman, "Satchmo Wears His Crown Gaily," *New York Times*, January 29, 1950.

"I take a little swig": *SP*, 51–52. LA's special salve, originally known as Ansatz-Crème, was later renamed "Louis Armstrong Lip-Salve" in honor of its most famous user, and Armstrong bought it in five-hundred-dollar lots. "I live by your Lip Salve and I hope that I will never run out," he told the manufacturer in a 1970 letter (letter to "Mr. Kaufmann," April 5, 1970, private collection). The recipient of this letter was an employee of Franz Schüritz, the trombone player who manufactured Louis Armstrong Lip-Salve.

"He didn't care who or how many came": Hinton and Berger, 207. **"These musicians, old friends from New Orleans"**: Bigard, *With Louis and the Duke*, 113–14. **"Ham & eggs"**: "Louis the First," *Time*, February 21, 1949. **"If he came to your house"**: Collier, 336. **"If someone pushed into the end"**: Lyttelton, 150.

650 reels of tape: For an analysis of LA's tape collection, see Ben Alexander, "'For Posterity': The Personal Audio Recordings of Louis Armstrong," *American Archivist*, Spring/Summer 2008. **"I have all my records on tape"**: LA, tape 159, AA. **"One of his two valets"**: Hinton and Berger, 207–8. **His sidemen learned to request rooms on other floors**: Leo Ball, "Allegro Interviews Marty Napoleon," *Allegro*, December 2002.

"It's up to you": LA, tape 5, AA.

"My Sweetheart + secretary": Letter to Joe Glaser, August 2, 1955, in *IHOW*, 159–61. The "secretary" in question was Velma Ford. **"Sweets"**: LA's private tapes identify her as Lucille Preston, another of his "secretaries" (LA, tape 17, AA).

"Oh, he was walking around": Bigard, oral-history interview. This story suggests either that LA was impotent with Lucille (for which there is, to put it mildly, no evidence) or that she suspected him to be sterile, a possible consequence of his use of marijuana, a drug now known to decrease fertility in men who smoke it regularly. It has been speculated that LA was the natural father of Clarence Armstrong, but he never said that he was, and it would have been uncharacteristic of him not to say so had it been true. The Australian jazz vocalist Herb Armstrong has claimed without substantiation in interviews and on his Web site (www.herbarmstrong.com) to have been fathered in New Orleans by a hitherto-unknown natural son of LA (see Kathleen Noonan, "Blowing the Trumpet on the Legacy of Louis," *Brisbane Courier-Mail*, August 31, 2007).

"I wouldn't dare": *SP*, 52. **"Picked down by the tracks"**: *LAS*, 135. **"When it was time to come back"**: Evans, 69–70.

"I'd say Louie played about 80 percent of the time": Cole. **"All hotels are alike"**: *SP*, 55. **LA "put out the same amount of energy"**: Crosby, 226.

"Sometimes when he had a few days off": Bradley. **"Sometimes them big crowds can spook you"**: "Everybody's Louie." **"Don't like to keep my friends waiting"**: Howard Taubman, "Satchmo Wears His Crown Gaily," *New York Times*, January 29, 1950. **"I absolutely forbid it"**: Anderson 2. **"I can make it in New York without trouble"**: David Halberstam, "A Day with Satchmo," *Jazz Journal* 10, no. 8 (1957). **"I figure why should I go out"**: VOA series.

"I had had a contract": Dance, 105. **"Earl Hines and his big ideas"**: Don Freeman, "We'll Get Along Without Hines' Ego, Says Armstrong," *Down Beat*, February 22, 1952.

"I am sure you know": Dahl, 229. **"We had a big repertoire"**: Interview, *Cadence*, May 1985, quoted in Bradbury, 106. **"When I got with Louis"**: Young.

"He can raise hell": Bigard, oral-history interview. **"His implacable, ruthless hostility"**: Lyttelton, 145.

"A gregarious man": Hammond, 315.

"Waiting around": Firestone, 378.

"Louis decided that his part of the show": Hammond, 316. **"Who the fuck do you think you are?"**: Firestone, 378.

"He sounded terrible": Ibid., 379. **"Louis could well have asked"**: Hammond, 320. **"How's the TKO artist today?"**: Jones, 120.

"I love to talk to him": Tallulah Bankhead, "The World's Greatest Musician," *Ebony*, December 1952.

"There may be several spots": Letter to Robert Goffin, May 7, 1944, in *IHOW*, 78.

"I was astonished by the high quality": Goffin, *Souvenirs avant l'adieu*, 26. **"Louis's hand grasped hers"**: Goffin, *Horn of Plenty*, 169. **"Goffin's Horn Fluffs Aplenty"**: Quoted in Collier, 251. **"A detailed, colorful picture"**: Lucy Greenbaum, "Saga of 'Satchmo,'" *New York Times*, May 4, 1947.

"Cashing in on his gift of gab": "Music Is Music," *Time*, May 22, 1950. **"One of the finest stories"**: "Stomping Piano Man," *New York Times Book Review*, June 18, 1950.

"Bunk didn't actually teach me anything": "Bunk Didn't Teach Me," "as told by Louis Armstrong," *Record Changer*, July–August 1950, in *IHOW*, 40–41. In conversation with friends he put it more bluntly: "Bunk didn't teach me shit" (LA, tape 219, AA). **"I have my tape recorder"**: Letter to Betty Jane Holder, February 9, 1952, in *IHOW*, 155.

"In a fall when we are going to have": Cleveland Amory, "Straight from the Trumpet's Mouth," *New York Times Book Review,* October 10, 1954.

"Joe . . . and all them people": "Everybody's Louie." **"I've been writing all down":** *LAS,* i. **A fragmentary continuation:** This is the manuscript on deposit in AA and published in *IHOW* as "The Armstrong Story." **A separate manuscript:** This is the manuscript on deposit in AA and published in *IHOW* as "The Satchmo Story." **"Louis gave his writings to Joe Glaser":** Giddins, 20.

The surviving typescript: A carbon is on deposit at IJS. It was typed by a secretary, indicating that LA may have dictated some parts of *Satchmo* to Velma Ford, whom he describes in a letter to Joe Glaser as "my sharp Chick whom you met while she was helping with my Satchmo story. She's very good at taking Dictation, etc." (August 2, 1955, in *IHOW,* 161).

"I think we should get together on the tempos": *Stage Show.* LA told other versions of this story, but this one is authentic.

11. "The Nice Taste We Leave"

SOURCES

DOCUMENTS

LA, VOA series; George Avakian, "How It Began in 1954," liner notes for *Louis Armstrong Plays W. C. Handy,* sound recording (Columbia/Legacy, 1997 CD reissue version); George Avakian, interview, January 21, 2005; Jack Bradley, interview, July 7, 2008; W. C. Handy, interview with George Avakian, November 19, 1956 (included on the 1997 reissue of *Louis Armstrong Plays W. C. Handy*); *Louis Armstrong: The Portrait Collection,* DVD (Multiprises); Dan Morgenstern, liner notes for *The Complete Decca Studio Recordings of Louis Armstrong and the All Stars* (Mosaic); Joe Muranyi, interview, September 1, 2007; Trummy Young, oral-history interview, IJS.

BOOKS

Bechet, *Treat It Gentle;* Berrett, *The Louis Armstrong Companion;* Bigard, *With Louis and the Duke;* Boujut, *Louis Armstrong;* Chambers, *Milestones;* Chilton, *Let the Good Times Roll;* Chilton, *The Song of the Hawk;* Collier, *Louis Armstrong;* Crow, *Jazz Anecdotes;* Darensbourg, *Jazz Odyssey;* Davis, *Miles;* Early, *The Sammy Davis, Jr., Reader;* Gillespie, *To Be or Not to Bop;* Jones, *Jazz Talking;* Lyttelton, *Second Chorus;* Morgenstern, *Living with Jazz;* Nicholson, *Ella Fitzgerald;* Schuller, *The Swing Era;* Stratemann, *Louis Armstrong on the Screen;* Traill and Lascelles, *Just Jazz;* Travis, *An Autobiography of Black Jazz;* von Eschen, *Satchmo Blows Up the World;* Wein, *Myself among Others;* Williams, *Jazz Panorama.*

NOTES

LA was "playing just like he did": Quoted in Chilton, *The Song of the Hawk,* 282.

"Miles changed the tone of the trumpet": Chambers, 199. **"That sonofabitch is bad for jazz":** Ibid., 191.

"I love his approach to the trumpet": Ibid., 209. **"A long time ago, I was at Bop City":** Morgenstern, *Living with Jazz,* 221.

"I always hated the way they used to laugh and grin": Davis, 83.

"These cool cats": *SP*, 56.

"There is no need for a man as great as Louis": George T. Simon, "Armstrong, Commercialism and Music," *Metronome*, October 1949.

The deal was done: LA's Decca recording contract was still in force in 1954, but Glaser obtained a release from Decca so that the trumpeter could record *Louis Armstrong Plays W. C. Handy*, and LA agreed to sign a two-year exclusive contract with Columbia (Avakian interview).

"For years I had planned": George Avakian, personal communication. "You choose the tunes": Avakian interview. "I'm laying over in Chicago": Avakian, "How It Began in 1954." "Louie came in with no music": Avakian interview.

"I can't remember when I felt this good": Avakian, "How It Began in 1954."

"Intense, quiet": "The Man on Cloud No. 7," *Time*, November 8, 1954.

"Oh, I'm going to *love* doing this!": Avakian interview.

"Dig, man, there goes Mack the Knife": This line and the climactic "*Take it, Satch*" were overdubbed by LA the next day. The introductory line, Avakian recalled, was "inspired by Lotte Lenya's first line in the show, at the end of the street singer's aria: 'Look—there's Mack the Knife!'" (ibid.). "Satchmo plays a lilting chorus": "New Jazz Records," *Time*, November 21, 1955. Bobby Darin's hardswinging cover version: "One of my lowest moments came in 1958 when some idiot congratulated me on my cleverness in having Pops cover Bobby Darin's 'Mack the Knife'" (Avakian interview).

The "most effective ambassador": Felix Belair Jr., "United States Has Secret Sonic Weapon—Jazz," *New York Times*, November 6, 1955. A long series of government-sponsored jazz tours: See von Eschen, passim.

An album by the All Stars: Though *Ambassador Satch* was advertised as a concert recording, the performances on the album, which was taped in Milan and Los Angeles, are studio recordings that contain applause and crowd sounds overdubbed in order to give the impression that they had been recorded live at LA's European concerts. "It was the same morning": Anderson 2. "Pops never let on to me that he had a stash in the attaché case!" (George Avakian, personal communication). "A lot of them Russian cats": "This Trumpet Madness," *Newsweek*, December 19, 1955.

"The only thing I regret": Boujut, 115.

"Well, we had a lot of fun": LA, tape 28, AA. "I have never seen a reception like that": Travis, 281.

"Ninety-seven straight one-nighters": Ibid. "Simply not top-drawer": "The New Pictures," *Time*, August 6, 1956. Bosley Crowther's *New York Times* notice: "No 'Philadelphia Story,' This; 'High Society' Lacks Hepburn Sparkle," *New York Times*, August 10, 1956. "He demonstrated with finality": Quoted in Dan Morgenstern, "Satchmo and the Critics," *Village Voice*, June 6–12, 2001.

"Oh yeah, that first group of All Stars was a good one": Traill and Lascelles, 4–5.

"I don't listen to fanatics": VOA series.

"We had all kinds of plans": Avakian interview.

"When she made the album with Louis": Nicholson, 164.

"I always got [Armstrong] under the worst conditions": Ibid., 175. The unsuitably glossy orchestral arrangements of Russ Garcia: LA told George Avakian that he disliked Garcia's arrangements but added, "Don't quote me—it's not his fault. He was just wrong for the job" (personal communication).

"**We would need all the great tunes**": Morgenstern, liner notes for *The Complete Decca Studio Recordings of Louis Armstrong and the All Stars*.

"**There is an unquenchable fire**": John S. Wilson, "Jazzmen Doubling as Narrators," *New York Times*, September 29, 1957. "**The album . . . should give latter-day jazz fans**": "New Pop Records," *Time*, October 7, 1957.

"**Which delivered, in a manner**": Whitney Balliett, "Musical Events: Jazz," *New Yorker*, July 20, 1957. "**Armstrong's stage presence**": Whitney Balliett, "Jazz Records: The Three Louis," *New Yorker*, September 28, 1957.

"**Whenever the band bus left**": Dan Morgenstern, personal communication.

"**Armstrong is astonishing**": Martin Williams, "Louis Armstrong," in Williams, 115. "**I had gone . . . to write a twilight-of-career piece**": Halberstam, "A Day with Satchmo." "**Man, you don't pose, never!**": Lyttelton, 154.

"**There was something in that voice**": Handy.

"**All of the members of the Zulus**": Letter to Betty Jane Holder, February 9, 1952, in *IHOW*, 151–52. "**There's a thing I've dreamed of all my life**": "Louis the First," *Time*, February 21, 1949.

"**It is the ambition of every big guy in New Orleans**": Bechet, 197.

A "**plantation character**": *Down Beat*, July 1, 1949, quoted in *IHOW*, 166.

"**God bless Louis Armstrong!**": Dan Morgenstern, personal communication. This remark, which Morgenstern overheard, has since been quoted in other, less authentic versions (see, for instance, *LAS*, 207).

"**I think that I have always done *great* things**": "Jewish Family," 9. "**Some folks, even some of my own people**": "Daddy, How the Country Has Changed!"

"**I wanted to give my whole life**": Chilton, *Let the Good Times Roll*, 65, 192.

"**I have my own ideas about racial segregation**": "Armstrong Indignant over Race Ban Story — Says He Loves Race," *Pittsburgh Courier*, July 28, 1956. "**I don't socialize with the top dogs of society**": "Daddy, How the Country Has Changed!" "**I don't want to do nothing**": *SP*, 42.

"**A greater attraction among whites**": "Armstrong Indignant over Race Ban Story." "**One time he did a gig**": Bradley. "**What do you want me to call those black sons-of-bitches**": Bigard, 123–24. Bigard claimed to have heard LA make this remark, but the clarinetist did not play on the recording session in question. Surviving takes from the session confirm, however, that LA did in fact sing *darkies*, then replaced the offending word with *people*. "**See, now, what's wrong with 'Shine'?**": VOA series.

"**The majority of white people, two-thirds of 'em [don't like] niggers**": LA, tape 230, AA. "**This ofay, he wasn't nothing but a call boy**": LA, tape 219, AA.

"**As time went on**": "Everybody's Louie." "**The [road] manager and I**": Travis, 283.

"**When we hit Savannah**": Halberstam, "A Day with Satchmo." "**That's all right**": "Louis Armstrong Quips as Bomb Rocks Concert," *Los Angeles Examiner*, February 20, 1957.

LA listened in silence: Dan Morgenstern, personal communication. "**Who's your daddy?**": Wein, 180.

"**He could be the greatest, most generous guy**": Muranyi.

A journalism student: Larry Lubenow, personal communication. Lubenow spoke for the first time in public about his interview with LA on September 18, 2007, in a presentation sponsored by AA. This account is based in part on the presentation.

"Trumpet player Louis Armstrong said last night": "Louis Armstrong, Barring Soviet Tour, Denounces Eisenhower and Gov. Faubus," *New York Times*, September 19, 1957.

"Hounded me so much": "Four Negro Notables Join Satchmo in Knocking Ike," *Arkansas Gazette*, September 20, 1957. **"I ain't gonna say no more":** Ibid. **"Lacking in leadership":** Ibid. **A "man without a soul":** Ibid.

"For years Louis Armstrong has been important": "Sammy Davis, Jr., Says Satchmo No Spokesman," *Pittsburgh Courier*, October 12, 1957, quoted in Early, 233. **"Now the people who've been calling him":** Evelyn Cunningham, "Give 'Satchmo' the Spingarn Medal," *Pittsburgh Courier*, September 28, 1957, quoted in Early, 236.

"DADDY IF AND WHEN": *IHOW*, 194.

"I think it was what Louis said": Quoted in *LAS*, 206.

"I wouldn't take back a thing": *Pittsburgh Courier*, September 28, 1957, quoted in *IHOW*, 193–94. **"They treat me better":** "Why Louis Armstrong Can't Go Home Again: 'Unconstitutional' Law Nixes Satchmo's Mixed Band," *Jet*, November 26, 1959.

"I have been with Joe Glaser too many years": "Armstrong Indignant over Race Ban Story." **"My life is music":** "Louis Armstrong Scores Beating of Selma Negroes," *New York Times*, March 11, 1965.

An attempt by the Ford Motor Company: See Stratemann, 356.

A cartoon: *New Yorker*, April 19, 1958. **"The reason I don't bother with politics":** Leonard Ingalls, "Armstrong Horn Wins Nairobi, Too," *New York Times*, November 7, 1960.

"Hell, I had my own way": Gillespie, 295–96.

"To take two or three others": Anderson 1. **"Glaser signed both me and Hot Lips Page":** Quoted in Crow, 212. **"He'd make believe he's representing you":** Jones, 117. **"When he felt Glaser was getting ahead of him":** Anderson 2.

"Infirm and short-breathed": Schuller, 197. **"I've got more alma maters than anybody":** *Jet*, April 17, 1958 (AA).

"Louis was on *The Tonight Show*": Dan Morgenstern, personal communication.

"A bad congestion problem": Young. **"I don't know why they're taking me to the hospital":** Collier, 326. **He was "seriously ill":** "Armstrong Very Ill; but Physicians Differ on Exact Details of Sickness," *New York Times*, June 26, 1959.

"I have never felt better": "Louis Armstrong Back; Trumpeter Says He Feels Fine after Pneumonia in Italy," *New York Times*, July 3, 1959. **"Ole Doc Schiff":** Letter to Dizzy and Lorraine Gillespie, July 1, 1959, quoted in Berrett, 156. **"The Italian doctors said":** *SP*, 46. **"You can eat from soup to nuts":** LA and Lucille Armstrong, "Lose Weight the 'Satchmo' Way," quoted in Berrett, 100. **"When I first went with Louis":** Young.

"They're home boys": LA, tape 123, AA.

"Hundreds of different kinds of flowers": *STM*, 19.

"We get just as big a hand": 1961 interview.

"When I joined the band": Darensbourg, 168. **"Everybody was forever trying":** Ibid., 167.

"Today, one good word spoken for Louis Armstrong": "The Beautiful Persons," *Time*, June 28, 1963.

12. "I Don't Sigh for Nothing"

SOURCES

DOCUMENTS
George Avakian, interview, January 21, 2005; Jack Bradley, interview, July 7, 2008; *Desert Island Discs*, radio show, July 1968 (BBC); *The Dick Cavett Show*, TV show, February 22, 1971; Phoebe Jacobs, oral-history interview conducted by researchers for Ken Burns's *Jazz* (transcript available online at www.pbs.org/jazz/about/pdfs/Jacobs.pdf); *Jazz*, auction catalog (Guernsey's, 2005); Mickey Kapp, interview, September 19, 2008; *Louis Armstrong 1900–1971*, TV show, July 9, 1971 (CBS); *Louis Armstrong: The Portrait Collection*, DVD (Multiprises); Dan Morgenstern, liner notes for *Louis Armstrong: Rare Items*, sound recording (Decca); Joe Muranyi, interview, September 1, 2007; Arvell Shaw, oral-history interview, IJS.

BOOKS
Balliett, *American Musicians II*; Bigard, *With Louis and the Duke*; Brookhiser, *Right Time, Right Place*; Brower, *Satchmo*; Citron, *Jerry Herman*; Cogswell, *Louis Armstrong*; Collier, *Louis Armstrong*; Darensbourg, *Jazz Odyssey*; Miles Davis, *Miles*; Ossie Davis, *Life Lit by Some Large Vision*; Sammy Davis Jr., *Hollywood in a Suitcase*; Ellington, *Music Is My Mistress*; Fates, *What's My Line?*; Feather, *From Satchmo to Miles*; Giddins, *Satchmo*; Gourse, *Wynton Marsalis*; Heller, *Ruthless*; Jones, *Jazz Talking*; Kempton, *America Comes of Middle Age*; Larkin, *Jazz Writings*; Larkin, *Selected Letters*; Levin, *Classic Jazz*; Levinson, *Trumpet Blues*; Lyttelton, *Last Chorus*; Miller, *Louis Armstrong*; Mingus, *Beneath the Underdog*; Morgenstern, *Living with Jazz*; Nalepa and Knight, *Fodor's New Orleans 2008*; Richmond, *Fever*; Russo, *Supermob*; Schuller, *Early Jazz*; Schuller, *The Swing Era*; Steele, *A Bound Man*; Sudhalter, *Lost Chords*; Teachout, *A Terry Teachout Reader*; Thiele, *What a Wonderful World*; Wein, *Myself among Others*.

NOTES

"That was for President Kennedy": Giddins, 184.

"Jack came to see my dad": Kapp. Milt Gabler later told James Lincoln Collier that "Hello, Dolly!" was originally recorded as a publisher's demo, then sold to Kapp Records (Collier, 321–22). According to Kapp, "It was not a demo — it was always meant to be a single release. There may have been a demo, but Armstrong didn't do it."

LA **"shook his head in dismay"**: Jack Bradley, quoted in Giddins, 189.

"I asked him to change the first line": In the show the first line of "Hello, Dolly!" is sung to a pair of characters named "Harry" and "Louis" (pronounced "Louie").

"Listen to that, Cork, it's a fucking hit": Collier, 322. **Kapp discreetly sweetened the mix with a touch of overdubbed strings**: He also edited out an instrumental passage following LA's first-chorus vocal, leaving an audible splice in the version that was commercially released. "The reason for the splice was that after the vocal, Louis had to take some time to get the mouthpiece seated on his lips," he explained. "He wasn't young anymore, and by then it wasn't as easy for him. But once he finally got it in place, he *played!*"

A representative from E. H. Morris: Citron, 102.

"The best musical of the season thus far": Howard Taubman, "Hello, Dolly!" *New York Times*, January 17, 1964.

"Couldn't find it": Darensbourg, 183. According to Darensbourg, LA first played the song on stage in San Juan on New Year's Eve. He claimed that "we were working in Puerto Rico and people began requesting 'Hello, Dolly!' We didn't know the record had come out — and it was a hit!" (Levin, 44). It is unlikely, however, that a recording made in the first week of December would have been familiar to Puerto Rican audiences three weeks later. Arvell Shaw, who rejoined the band in mid-January, told a more plausible version of the same story: "We were out somewhere in the wilds of Ioway and Nebraska doing some one-nighters, you know, way out there, you know. So every night the audience would be calling, 'Hello, Dolly!' 'Hello, Dolly!' So Louie didn't, he ignored it for the first couple of nights . . . Louie asked Billy Kyle, 'Say, what's that "Hello, Dolly"?' And Billy said, 'Hey, Pops, remember that date we did in Chicago [*sic*] a few months ago? Well, one of the tunes is from a Broadway show that's called *Hello, Dolly*.' And the first time we put it in the concert, pandemonium broke out. And we were so far out in the woods we didn't realize he had a hit record" (Shaw). "Hello, Dolly!" entered *Billboard*'s Hot 100 chart on February 15. **What's My Line? invited LA to make his second appearance as mystery guest**: Fates, 84–85. Fates misidentifies the variety show on which LA was to sing "Hello, Dolly!" as *The Perry Como Show*, which went off the air in 1963. In 1964 Como was hosting an occasional series of *Kraft Music Hall* TV specials, but LA is not known to have appeared on any of them that year. His next TV appearance after *What's My Line?* was the episode of *The Hollywood Palace* that aired on May 30, 1964. He sang "Hello, Dolly!" on the program, but it is not known whether he was paid his full fee.

"Incredible though it may seem": John S. Wilson, "Still the Champ; Satchmo Beats Beatles with Pop Best-Sellers," *New York Times*, June 21, 1964.

Three million copies: Citron, 102.

Five-figure fees: "Armstrong commands top money — $20,000 to $25,000 — for guest shots on television" ("Everybody's Louie").

"At this time it would not serve the best interest": "Louis Armstrong Barred by Alabama University," *New York Times*, December 7, 1964. **A restaurant owner in Connecticut**: "We set out on a bright warm Saturday afternoon headed north, with everyone in a good mood. The [band] bus did not have a toilet, so somewhere in Connecticut we stopped in order for Louis to go to the bathroom. I was stunned when the owner of a restaurant, clearly on the basis of race, refused him use of the otherwise available facilities. I will never forget the look on Louis' face" (Herb Snitzer, quoted in Nat Hentoff, "Louis: Black and Blue and Triumphant," *JazzTimes*, October 2000). **A fourteen-page interview**: Richard Meryman, "An Interview with Louis Armstrong," *Life*, April 15, 1966. **"I don't sigh for nothing"**: *SP*, 57.

"Pops loved to play the horn": Dennis Mclellan, "Danny Barcelona, 77; Longtime Drummer in Louis Armstrong Band," *Los Angeles Times*, April 9, 2007. **"Louis was itching to go back to work"**: Darensbourg, 167–68. **"So now I do Dolly"**: "Everybody's Louie." **"Hell, Pops hasn't made less than a half-million bucks"**: Charles L. Sanders, "Louis Armstrong — the Reluctant Millionaire," *Ebony*, November 1964.

"By whatever definition of art": Schuller, *Early Jazz*, 89.

"For the rest there is a wasteland": Ibid., 133.

"The River Mississippi, pure like its source": Kempton, 356. **"The end was not what it should have been"**: Schuller, *The Swing Era*, 196.

"**Musicians and dyed-in-the-wool Armstrong devotees**": Morgenstern, liner notes for *Louis Armstrong: Rare Items.*

"**I did my [most] interesting work**": "Good-bye to All of You," *Esquire*, December 1969. "**During the deepening national traumas**": Thiele, 3–4. Thiele claimed to have cowritten "What a Wonderful World" with George Weiss, but Weiss told George Avakian that it had been his work alone: "Thiele strong-armed Weiss into agreeing to list him as a co-composer. This meant that he would collect 50 percent of the composer share of copyright royalties. My guess is that he agreed to bring the song to Glaser with the proviso that he would get a piece of the action if Pops recorded it" (Avakian, personal communication).

"**The real meaning of the tune to Pops**": Muranyi. All quotations from Joe Muranyi in this chapter are from my interview with him.

"**A wonderful cameo**": Sammy Davis Jr., 67. "**A specialty act salted with social protest**": "Message with Music," *Time*, August 19, 1966.

"**No, man, we can't do that shit no more**": Quoted in Ricky Riccardi, *The Wonderful World of Louis Armstrong*, December 31, 2007 (online blog, available at www.dippermouth.blogspot.com).

"**Some little spot . . . where you just come in**": 1961 interview.

"**My man Bobby Hackett**": *Desert Island Discs.* Hackett had joined Joe Oliver, Bunny Berigan, Bix Beiderbecke, and Harry James in LA's personal pantheon of trumpeters. "I'm the coffee, and he's the cream," he said (Sudhalter, 642). Asked on another occasion whether he preferred the playing of Hackett or Billy Butterfield, he replied, "Bobby. He got more ingredients" (Balliett, 145). "**Right outa the old spirituals**": "Everybody's Louie."

"**Two meals a day**": *LAS*, 221.

"**He practically ran out of my office**": Collier, 328. "**Mr. Louis Armstrong decided he wanted**": Feather, 35.

"**Intermission**": Jacobs. "**Now all I got to do is scan my life back**": LA, tape 388, AA. "**For all his popularity**": Darensbourg, 165. "**Hey, man, I gotta tell you something**": Bradley.

"**Cork, if I go to Louie with this**": Collier, 329. "**I went down to see him**": Ibid., 330.

"**I am just waiting — resting — blowing**": Letter to Leonard Feather, June 28, 1969, quoted in Feather, 35–36. "**Reverential to the point of idiocy**": Vincent Canby, "On Screen, Barbra Streisand Displays a Detached Cool," *New York Times*, December 18, 1969. "**I could tell it was Lucille's**": Avakian.

"**When my wife Lucille + I moved into this neighborhood**": "Our Neighborhood," in *IHOW*, 176–78.

"**He didn't like me to put him ahead of anybody**": Jim O'Grady, "What a Wonderful Shave," *New York Times*, November 5, 2003. "**The whole neighborhood**": "Our Neighborhood," 177. "**In the wintertime**": Jacobs. **Lucille was unwilling to supervise the day-to-day care of Clarence**: According to Jack Bradley, she found Clarence to be "an embarrassment." **A marriage-like relationship**: Bradley. After Hadfield died, Clarence was moved to the Hebrew Home for the Aged in the Bronx. He died there in 1998. **He rarely read books**: "I saw him reading a biography of Fats Waller once on the bus. And the Bible. But that was about it" (Muranyi). "**My hobbie is to pick out the different things**": Letter to Marli Mardon, September 27, 1953 (AA). According to Marty Napoleon, LA was "constantly cutting up newspapers, *Jet* and *Life* magazines and anything that he wanted to remember. He would cut out pictures, words, headlines, etc. and paste them all together in little notebooks that he carried around. It was a hobby of his. We'd see him in between sets — cutting and pasting these bits together" (quoted in Miller, 209). More than two hundred of LA's collages are reproduced in Brower. See also Cogswell, 70–82.

"*God Bless you* for looking out for my *interest*": Letter to Oscar Cohen, "Jan. 21/23," 1970, reproduced in *Jazz*, 14–17.

"The greatest for me": Letter to Little Brother Montgomery, July 29, 1969, Hogan Jazz Archive, Tulane University, New Orleans. **"When we started, we both had nothing"**: Wein, 300.

"*King Spook* don't even own fifty per cent": Mingus, 189–90. **"Did you hear what happened to Joe?"**: Anderson 2.

"Sidney functioned as a gangster": Russo, 71. **"In 1962, according to court documents"**: Seymour M. Hersh, "Major Corporations Eager to Seek Korshak's Advice," *New York Times*, June 29, 1976. **The news of the takeover came as a surprise**: George Avakian and Jack Bradley, for instance, knew nothing of Korshak's ownership of Associated Booking until after LA's death. Glaser is not mentioned in Korshak's FBI file, nor is Korshak mentioned in LA's FBI file, whose contents are innocuous. (LA's file can be viewed online at www.theblackvault.com.) In response to a Freedom of Information Act request filed by the author in 2007, the FBI stated that it has no file on Glaser. **"Sid and Joe were very close"**: Russo, 256. **"A mob company"**: Heller, 214, 222.

Jules Stein loaned Glaser one hundred thousand dollars: Russo, 45. **"Everyone knew that Stein worked for Al Capone"**: Ibid., 43.

"I'm waitin' for some word from the doctor": Al Aronowitz, "Retropop Scene: Pop's [*sic*] Last Birthday Bash," *Blacklisted Journalist*, July 1, 1996 (www .blacklistedjournalist.com/). **"His personality was developed"**: "Roses for Satchmo," *Down Beat*, July 9, 1970. **"If it weren't for Louis"**: John S. Wilson, "Jazzmen at Newport Hail King Louis," *New York Times*, July 12, 1970. Gillespie's tribute was not entirely respectful, for he performed "Pops' Confessin'," the Armstrong parody that he had recorded in 1952. "I bet Dizzy is going to do that imitation of me that I hate," LA said to George Wein before the concert (Wein, 293).

"Ain't nobody played nothing like it": Israel Shenker, "'Just Plain Old Satchmo' Turns 70 Sweetly," *New York Times*, July 4, 1970.

"The always jaunty, stiff-limbed walk": Lyttelton, 174. **"You know, Louie's been quite sick"**: *The Dick Cavett Show*.

"Doc, that's all right": Collier, 331.

LA saw an unfavorable review: Ibid., 332. **LA "blows his trumpet sparingly"**: John S. Wilson, "Louis Armstrong Takes to Horn in His Comeback at the Waldorf," *New York Times*, March 7, 1971. **LA soiled himself**: Bradley.

Three days later: "Armstrong in Hospital," *New York Times*, March 19, 1971. **"Armstrong Has Setback"**: *New York Times*, March 25, 1971. **"Armstrong Has Relapse"**: *New York Times*, April 3, 1971. **"Armstrong Gains Slightly"**: *New York Times*, April 4, 1971. **On May 7**: "Armstrong Leaves Hospital," *New York Times*, May 8, 1971. **"As soon as my treaders get in as good shape as my chops"**: *Times* obituary. **The last tape box LA decorated**: Cogswell, 78. **"Lucille told us that she hadn't given him anything"**: Bigard, 136. According to Jack Bradley, "Lucille told me that he wanted to make it [i.e., have sex] with her but that she put him off because the doctor said it wouldn't be good in his current state of health. An hour or two later, he died."

"He didn't look right without it": Levin, 226. **"A couple of middle-aged black guys"**: Dan Morgenstern, personal communication. **"He said if he had one band"**: Joseph Lelyveld, "Friends Bid Louis Armstrong a Nostalgic Farewell at Simple Service," *New York Times,* July 10, 1971. Lucille asked Lee to perform, knowing that LA had been a fan of her singing. "Man, if you can't swing quarter notes, you ain't going to swing," he said. "Peggy can swing quarter notes and all the rest — behind the beat, on the beat, in front of the beat" (Richmond, 320).

"A friend to all people": *Louis Armstrong 1900–1971.*

"It's been hard goddam work": *Times* obituary.

"The disciplined craftsman": "Louis (Satchmo) Armstrong," *Washington Post,* July 9, 1971. **"Minstrel-show appearance"**: "Last Trumpet for the First Trumpeter," *Time,* July 19, 1971. **"He was born poor, died rich"**: Ellington, 236.

LA's net worth: Bergreen, 494. **LA's estate was subsequently estimated at twice that amount**: Michael Cogswell, personal communication. **"He loved Harry"**: Levinson, 254.

"She still wore the rings": Chris Albertson, "Lil Armstrong: A Fond Remembrance," *Saturday Review,* September 25, 1971.

"Get yourself another man": Muranyi.

"Maybe in a hundred or two years": Jones, 146. **"It is already accepted"**: Philip Larkin, letter to Charles Monteith, August 3, 1971, in Larkin, *Selected Letters,* 443. **"An artist of Flaubertian purity"**: Philip Larkin, "Satchmo Still," *Guardian,* October 21, 1971, in Larkin, *Jazz Writings,* 81. **Three extended autobiographical accounts**: The principal source for LA's contributions to *LAS* was a tape he made for Max Jones on August 15, 1970 (LA, tape 426, AA). **"Before long there is bound to be a volume of his letters"**: Larkin to Monteith, August 3, 1971, in Larkin, *Selected Letters,* 443.

"One of the most important figures": Collier, 3. **"Failed his talent"**: Ibid., 345. **"A sense of his own worthlessness"**: Ibid., 202. **"This is all profoundly depressing"**: Philip Larkin, "Pleasing the People," *Observer,* March 25, 1984, in Larkin, *Jazz Writings,* 110.

"An artist who happened to be an entertainer": Giddins, 32. **"I had never really tried"**: Gourse, 104–5.

"Be very careful when wandering": Nalepa and Knight, 50. **A list of "all-American" modernists**: Terry Teachout, "The Return of Beauty," *U.S. Society and Values* (April 2003). See also Teachout, xvi.

"Most of the fellows I grew up with": Ossie Davis, 161–62 (ellipses in the original). **"I don't think there has been a musician"**: Tom Scanlan, "The Impeccable Mr. Wilson," *Down Beat,* January 22, 1959. **"As I watched him and talked with him"**: Quoted in Morgenstern, *Living with Jazz,* 89.

"The relentlessly beaming smile": Steele, 61. **"Bach said everything is in its place"**: Brookhiser, 174. **"My whole life has been happiness"**: *LAS,* 15.

"Years ago I was playing": "Everybody's Louie." For a different description of what appears to have been the same encounter, see LA, tape 115, AA (a transcript of the relevant passage is in Cogswell, 185–86).

Agee, James. *Agee on Film*, vol. 1. New York: McDowell, 1958.

Albertson, Chris. *Louis Armstrong*. Notes on the music by John S. Wilson. Alexandria, VA: Time-Life Records, 1978.

Allen, Walter C. *Hendersonia: The Music of Fletcher Henderson and His Musicians.* Jazz Monographs No. 4. Highland Park, NJ: privately published, 1973.

——— and Brian A. L. Rust. *King Joe Oliver.* Jazz Monographs No. 1. Belleville, NJ: privately published, 1955.

Amis, Kingsley. *Memoirs*. New York: Summit, 1991.

Anderson, Ernest, ed. *Esquire's 1947 Jazz Book: A Yearbook of the Jazz Scene.* New York: Esquire, 1947.

Anderson, Gene H. *The Original Hot Five Recordings of Louis Armstrong.* CMS Sourcebooks in American Music. Hillsdale, NY: Pendragon, 2007.

Armstrong, Louis. *Louis Armstrong, in His Own Words: Selected Writings.* Edited by Thomas Brothers. New York: Oxford, 1999.

———. *Louis Armstrong: A Self-Portrait.* "The interview by Richard Meryman." New York: Eakins, 1971.

———. *Satchmo: My Life in New Orleans.* Reissued with a new introduction by Dan Morgenstern. New York: Da Capo, 1986.

———. *Swing That Music.* Music section edited by Horace Gerlach. London: Longmans, Green, and Co., 1936.

Balliett, Whitney. *American Musicians II: Seventy-two Portraits in Jazz.* New York: Oxford, 1996.

———. *Collected Works: A Journal of Jazz 1954–2000.* New York: St. Martin's, 2000.

Barker, Danny. *A Life in Jazz.* Edited by Alyn Shipton. London: Macmillan, 1986.

Barnet, Charlie, with Stanley Dance. *Those Swinging Years: The Autobiography of Charlie Barnet.* Baton Rouge: Louisiana State University Press, 1984.

Bechet, Sidney. *Treat It Gentle: An Autobiography*. Reissued with a new preface by Rudi Blesh. New York: Da Capo, 1978.

Benamou, Catherine L. *It's All True: Orson Welles's Pan-American Odyssey*. Berkeley: University of California Press, 2007.

Bergreen, Laurence. *Louis Armstrong: An Extravagant Life*. New York: Broadway Books, 1997.

Bernhardt, Clyde. *I Remember: Eighty Years of Black Entertainment, Big Bands, and the Blues*. Philadelphia: University of Pennsylvania Press, 1986.

Berrett, Joshua, ed. *The Louis Armstrong Companion: Eight Decades of Commentary*. New York: Schirmer, 1999.

———. *Louis Armstrong and Paul Whiteman: Two Kings of Jazz*. New Haven: Yale University Press, 2004.

Berton, Ralph. *Remembering Bix: A Memoir of the Jazz Age*. New York: Harper & Row, 1974.

Bethell, Tom. *George Lewis: A Jazzman from New Orleans*. Berkeley: University of California Press, 1977.

Bigard, Barney. *With Louis and the Duke: The Autobiography of a Jazz Clarinetist*. Edited by Barry Martyn. New York: Oxford, 1986.

Blassingame, John W. *Black New Orleans 1860–1880*. Chicago: University of Chicago Press, 1973.

Blesh, Rudi. *Shining Trumpets: A History of Jazz*. New York: Knopf, 1946.

Boujut, Michel. *Louis Armstrong*. New York: Rizzoli, 1998.

Bradbury, David. *Armstrong*. London: Haus, 2003.

Britt, Stan. *Long Tall Dexter: A Critical Musical Biography of Dexter Gordon*. London: Quartet, 1989.

Brookhiser, Richard. *Right Time, Right Place: Coming of Age with William F. Buckley Jr. and the Conservative Movement*. New York: Basic, 2009.

Brooks, Edward. *The Young Louis Armstrong on Records: A Critical Survey of the Early Recordings, 1923–1928*. Lanham, MD: Scarecrow, 2002.

Brothers, Thomas. *Louis Armstrong's New Orleans*. New York: Norton, 2006.

Brower, Steven. *Satchmo: The Wonderful World of Louis Armstrong*. New York: Abrams, 2009.

Brown, Ron, with Cyril Brown. *Georgia on My Mind: The Nat Gonella Story*. Portsmouth (England): Milestone Publications, 1985.

Bryant, Clora, ed. *Central Avenue Sounds: Jazz in Los Angeles*. Edited by the Central Avenue Sounds Editorial Committee. Berkeley: University of California Press, 1998.

Carmichael, Hoagy. The Stardust Road *and* Sometimes I Wonder: *The Autobiographies of Hoagy Carmichael*. Reissued with a new introduction by John Edward Hasse. New York: Da Capo, 1999.

Chambers, Jack. *Milestones: The Music and Times of Miles Davis*. New York: Da Capo, 1998.

Chandler, Raymond. *The Raymond Chandler Papers: Selected Letters and Nonfiction, 1909–1959*. Edited by Tom Hiney and Frank MacShane. New York: Grove Press, 2000.

Charles, Ray, and David Ritz. *Brother Ray: Ray Charles' Own Story*. New York: Da Capo, 1998.

Charters, Samuel. *A Trumpet around the Corner: The Story of New Orleans Jazz*. Jackson: University Press of Mississippi, 2008.

Chilton, John. *Let the Good Times Roll: The Story of Louis Jordan and His Music*. Ann Arbor: University of Michigan Press, 1994.

———. *Ride, Red, Ride: The Life of Henry "Red" Allen*. London: Cassell, 1999.

———. *Sidney Bechet: The Wizard of Jazz*. New York: Oxford, 1987.

———. *The Song of the Hawk: The Life and Recordings of Coleman Hawkins*. London: Quartet, 1990.

Citron, Stephen. *Jerry Herman: Poet of the Showtune*. New Haven: Yale University Press, 2004.

Clark, Andrew. *Riffs & Choruses: A New Jazz Anthology*. London: Continuum, 2001.

Clarke, Donald. *Wishing on the Moon: The Life and Times of Billie Holiday*. New York: Viking, 1994.

Clayton, Buck, assisted by Nancy Miller Elliott. *Buck Clayton's Jazz World*. New York: Oxford, 1986.

Cogswell, Michael. *Louis Armstrong: The Offstage Story of Satchmo*. Portland, OR: Collectors Press, 2003.

Collier, James Lincoln. *Louis Armstrong: An American Genius*. New York: Oxford, 1983.

Condon, Eddie. *We Called It Music: A Generation of Jazz*. Narration by Thomas Sugrue. New York: Henry Holt, 1947.

Copland, Aaron. *A Reader: Selected Writings 1923–1972*. Edited, with an introduction, by Richard Kostelanetz. Assistant editor, Steve Silverstein. New York: Routledge, 2004.

——— and Vivian Perlis. *Copland: 1900 Through 1942*. New York: St. Martin's/Marek, 1984.

Corbusier, Le. *When the Cathedrals Were White*. New York: McGraw-Hill, 1964.

Coward, Noël. *The Noël Coward Diaries*. Edited by Graham Payn and Sheridan Morley. London: Methuen, 1982.

Crosby, Bing. *Call Me Lucky: Bing Crosby's Own Story*. As told to Pete Martin. New York: Simon & Schuster, 1953.

Crosby, Gary, and Ross Firestone. *Going My Own Way*. Garden City, NY: Doubleday, 1983.

Crow, Bill. *Jazz Anecdotes*. New York: Oxford, 2003.

Cunard, Nancy, ed. *Negro: An Anthology*. Edited and abridged with an introduction by Hugh Ford. New York: Continuum, 1996.

Dahl, Linda. *Morning Glory: A Biography of Mary Lou Williams*. Berkeley: University of California Press, 2001.

Dance, Stanley. *Earl Hines*. Arlington, VA: Time-Life Records, 1980.

———. *The World of Earl Hines*. New York: Scribner's, 1977.

———. *The World of Swing*. New York: Da Capo, 1974.

Darensbourg, Joe. *Jazz Odyssey: The Autobiography of Joe Darensbourg*. As told to Peter Vacher. Baton Rouge: Louisiana State University Press, 1987.

Davis, Miles, with Quincy Troupe. *Miles: The Autobiography*. New York: Simon & Schuster, 1989.

Davis, Ossie. *Life Lit by Some Large Vision: Selected Speeches and Writings*. With editorial notes and a foreword by Ruby Dee. New York: Atria, 2006.

Davis, Sammy, Jr. *Hollywood in a Suitcase*. New York: Berkley, 1981.

Delaunay, Charles. *Django Reinhardt*. London: Cassell, 1961.

Dodds, Baby. *The Baby Dodds Story*. As told to Larry Gara. Revised edition. Baton Rouge: Louisiana State University Press, 1992.

Dregni, Michael. *Django: The Life and Music of a Gypsy Legend*. New York: Oxford, 2004.

Driggs, Frank, and Harris Lewine. *Black Beauty, White Heat: A Pictorial History of Classic Jazz 1920–1950*. New York: Da Capo, 1996.

Early, Gerald, ed. *The Sammy Davis, Jr., Reader*. New York: Farrar, Straus, & Giroux, 2001.

Ellington, Duke. *Music Is My Mistress*. Garden City, NY: Doubleday, 1973.

Evans, Joe, with Christopher Brooks. *Follow Your Heart: Moving with the Giants of Jazz, Swing, and Rhythm and Blues*. Urbana: University of Illinois Press, 2008.

Evans, Philip R., and Linda K. Evans. *Bix: The Leon Bix Beiderbecke Story*. Bakersfield, CA: Prelike Press, 1998.

Fates, Gil. *What's My Line? The Inside Story of TV's Most Famous Panel Show*. New York: Prentice Hall, 1978.

Feather, Leonard. *From Satchmo to Miles*. With a new introduction by the author. New York: Da Capo, 1984.

———. *The Jazz Years: Earwitness to an Era*. New York: Da Capo, 1987.

Ferguson, Otis. *The Otis Ferguson Reader*. Edited by Dorothy Chamberlain and Robert Wilson. Highland Park, IL: December Press, 1982.

Firestone, Ross. *Swing, Swing, Swing: The Life and Times of Benny Goodman*. New York: Norton, 1993.

Foster, Pops. *The Autobiography of Pops Foster, New Orleans Jazzman*. As told to Tom Stoddard. Interchapters by Ross Russell. Reissued with a new foreword by Ron Carter. San Francisco: Backbeat, 2005.

Freeman, Bud. *Crazeology: The Autobiography of a Chicago Jazzman*. As told to Robert Wolf. Urbana: University of Illinois Press, 1989.

———. *You Don't Look Like a Musician*. Detroit: Balamp, 1974.

Friedman, B. H. *Jackson Pollock: Energy Made Visible*. New York: McGraw-Hill, 1972.

Giddins, Gary. *Bing Crosby: A Pocketful of Dreams — The Early Years, 1903–1940*. Boston: Little, Brown, 2001.

———. *Satchmo*. Produced by Toby Byron/Multiprises. New York: Dolphin/Doubleday, 1988.

Gillespie, Dizzy, with Al Fraser. *To Be or Not to Bop*. Garden City, NY: Doubleday, 1979.

Gleason, Ralph J. *Celebrating the Duke, and Louis, Bessie, Billie, Bird, Carmen, Miles, Dizzy and Other Heroes*. Foreword by Studs Terkel. New Introduction by Ira Gitler. New York: Da Capo, 1995.

———, ed. *Jam Session: An Anthology of Jazz*. New York: Putnam's, 1958.

Goddard, Chris. *Jazz Away from Home*. New York: Paddington, 1979.

Goffin, Robert. *Horn of Plenty: The Story of Louis Armstrong*. Translated from the French by James F. Bezou. New York: Allen, Towne, & Heath, 1947.

———. *Souvenirs avant l'adieu*. Charleroi (Belgium): Institut Jules Destrée, 1980.

Gordon, Max. *Live at the Village Vanguard*. New York: St. Martin's, 1980.

Gourse, Leslie. *Wynton Marsalis: Skain's Domain, a Biography*. New York: Schirmer, 1999.

Gushee, Lawrence. *Pioneers of Jazz: The Story of the Creole Band*. New York: Oxford, 2005.

Guttridge, Leonard E. *Jack Teagarden*. Notes on the music by John S. Wilson. Alexandria, VA: Time-Life Records, 1979.

Hadlock, Richard. *Jazz Masters of the Twenties*. New York: Collier, 1974.

Hammond, John, with Irving Townsend. *John Hammond on Record: An Autobiography*. New York: Ridge, 1977.

Hampton, Lionel, with James Haskins. *Hamp: An Autobiography*. New York: Warner, 1989.

Harrison, Max, Charles Fox, and Eric Thacker. *The Essential Jazz Records*. Vol. 1, *Ragtime to Swing*. London: Mansell, 1984.

Heller, Jerry, with Gil Reavill. *Ruthless: A Memoir*. New York: Simon & Schuster, 2007.

Hentoff, Nat. *The Jazz Life*. New York: Dial, 1961.

Hinton, Milt, and David G. Berger. *Bass Line: The Stories and Photographs of Milt Hinton*. Philadelphia: Temple University Press, 1988.

Hirsch, Arnold R., and Joseph Logsdon, eds. *Creole New Orleans: Race and Americanization*. Baton Rouge: Louisiana State University Press, 1992.

Hodes, Art, and Chadwick Hansen, eds. *Selections from the Gutter: Portraits from the Jazz Record*. Berkeley: University of California Press, 1977.

Hoffmann, Franz. *Jazz Advertised 1910–1967*. Vol. 1, *Out of the New England Negro Press 1910–1934*. Berlin: privately published, 1989. Vol. 4, *Out of the Chicago Defender 1910–1934*. Berlin: privately published, 1980. Vol. 7, *Out of the New York Times 1922–1950*. Berlin: privately published, 1989.

Holiday, Billie, with William Dufty. *Lady Sings the Blues*. New York: Doubleday, 1956.

Hughes, Spike. *Second Movement: Continuing the Autobiography of Spike Hughes*. London: Museum Press Limited, 1951.

Jackson, Jeffrey H. *Making Jazz French: Music and Modern Life in Interwar Paris*. Durham, NC: Duke University Press, 2003.

Jones, Max. *Jazz Talking: Profiles, Interviews, and Other Riffs on Jazz Musicians*. New York: Macmillan, 1987.

——— and John Chilton. *Louis: The Louis Armstrong Story 1900–1971*. Reissued with a new preface by Dan Morgenstern. New York: Da Capo, 1988.

Jonson, Rich J., with Jim Arpy and Gerri Bowers. *Bix: The Davenport Album*. Barnegat, NJ: Razor Edge Press, 2009.

Jordan, Steve, with Tom Scanlan. *Rhythm Man: Fifty Years in Jazz*. Ann Arbor: University of Michigan Press, 1991.

Kaminsky, Max, with V. E. Hughes. *Jazz Band: My Life in Jazz*. Reissued edition of *My Life in Jazz*. New York: Da Capo, 1981.

Kappler, Frank K. *Johnny Dodds*. Notes on the music by Bob Wilber. Alexandria, VA: Time-Life Records, 1982.

Kempton, Murray. *America Comes of Middle Age: Columns, 1950–1962*. Boston: Little, Brown, 1963.

Kenney, William Howland. *Chicago Jazz: A Cultural History, 1904–1930*. New York: Oxford, 1993.

———. *Jazz on the River*. Chicago: University of Chicago Press, 2005.

Lambert, Constant. *Music Ho! A Study of Music in Decline*. London: Hogarth, 1933.

Larkin, Philip. *All What Jazz: A Record Diary 1961–1971*. Revised edition. New York: Farrar, Straus, & Giroux, 1985.

———. *Jazz Writings: Essays and Reviews 1940–84*. Edited by Richard Palmer and John White. London: Continuum, 2001.

———. *Selected Letters of Philip Larkin, 1940–1985*. Edited by Anthony Thwaite. London: Faber & Faber, 1999.

Lees, Gene. *Portrait of Johnny: The Life of John Herndon Mercer.* New York: Pantheon, 2004.

Levin, Floyd. *Classic Jazz: A Personal View of the Music and the Musicians.* Foreword by Benny Carter. Berkeley: University of California Press, 2000.

Levinson, Peter J. *Trumpet Blues: The Life of Harry James.* New York: Oxford, 1999.

Liebling, A. J. *Liebling at Home.* New York: Wideview, 1982.

Lion, Jean Pierre. *Bix: The Definitive Biography of a Jazz Legend.* Translated from the French by Gabriella Page-Fort with the assistance of Michael B. Heckman and Norman Field. New York: Continuum, 2005.

Lomax, Alan. *Mister Jelly Roll: The Fortunes of Jelly Roll Morton, New Orleans Creole and "Inventor of Jazz."* Reissued with a new preface by the author. New York: Pantheon, 1993.

Long, Alecia P. *The Great Southern Babylon: Sex, Race, and Respectability in New Orleans 1865–1920.* Baton Rouge: Louisiana State University Press, 2004.

Lopes, Paul Douglas. *The Rise of a Jazz Art World.* Cambridge: Cambridge University Press, 2002.

Lyttelton, Humphrey. *Last Chorus: An Autobiographical Medley.* London: JR Books, 2008.

———. *Second Chorus.* London: Jazz Book Club, 1949.

Magee, Jeffrey. *The Uncrowned King of Swing: Fletcher Henderson and Big Band Jazz.* New York: Oxford, 2005.

Manone, Wingy, and Paul Vandervoort II. *Trumpet on the Wing.* Foreword by Bing Crosby. Garden City, NY: Doubleday, 1948.

Marmorstein, Gary. *The Label: The Story of Columbia Records.* New York: Thunder's Mouth, 2007.

Marquis, Donald M. *In Search of Buddy Bolden, First Man of Jazz.* Baton Rouge: Louisiana State University Press, 1978.

McBride, Joseph. *Hawks on Hawks.* Berkeley: University of California Press, 1982.

McCarthy, Albert. *Louis Armstrong.* Kings of Jazz. London: Cassell, 1959.

McDonough, John. *Coleman Hawkins.* Alexandria, VA: Time-Life Records, 1979.

Meckna, Michael. *Satchmo: The Louis Armstrong Encyclopedia.* Westport, CT: Greenwood, 2004.

Meredith, Anthony, and Paul Harris. *Malcolm Arnold: Rogue Genius.* Norwich (England): Thames/Elkin, 2004.

Mezzrow, Mezz, and Bernard Wolfe. *Really the Blues.* New York: Random House, 1946.

Milhaud, Darius. *My Happy Life.* Translated from the French by Donald Evans, George Hall, and Christopher Palmer. London: Marion Boyars, 1995.

Miller, Marc H., ed. *Louis Armstrong: A Cultural Legacy.* New York: Queens Museum of Art, 1994.

Mingus, Charles. *Beneath the Underdog: His World as Composed by Mingus.* Edited by Nel King. New York: Knopf, 1971.

Morgenstern, Dan. *Living with Jazz: A Reader.* Edited by Sheldon Meyer. New York: Pantheon, 2004.

Nalepa, Michael, and Christina Knight, eds. *Fodor's New Orleans 2008.* New York: Fodor's Travel/Random House, 2008.

Nicholson, Stuart. *Ella Fitzgerald: A Biography of the First Lady of Jazz.* New York: Scribner's, 1994.

Orenstein, Arbie, ed. *A Ravel Reader: Correspondence, Articles, Interviews.* New York: Columbia University Press, 1990.

Osborne, Richard. *Herbert von Karajan: A Life in Music.* London: Chatto and Windus, 1998.

Panassié, Hugues. *Hot Jazz: The Guide to Swing Music.* Translated from the French by Lyle and Eleanor Dowling. New York: M. Witmark, 1936.

———. *Louis Armstrong.* New York: Scribner's, 1971.

Parsonage, Catherine. *The Evolution of Jazz in Britain, 1800–1935.* Burlington, VT: Ashgate, 2005.

Percy, Walker. *The Moviegoer.* New York: Knopf, 1961.

Pinfold, Mike. *Louis Armstrong: His Life and Times.* New York: Universe, 1987.

Pleasants, Henry. *The Great American Popular Singers.* New York: Simon & Schuster, 1974.

Porter, Roy, with David Keller. *There and Back: The Roy Porter Story.* New York: Continuum, 1990.

Porterfield, Nolan. *Jimmie Rodgers: The Life and Times of America's Blue Yodeler.* Urbana: University of Illinois Press, 1979.

Prial, Duncan. *The Producer: John Hammond and the Soul of American Music.* New York: Picador, 2006.

Ramsey, Frederic, Jr., and Charles Edward Smith. *Jazzmen.* New York: Harcourt, Brace, 1939.

Reich, Howard, and William Gaines. *Jelly's Blues: The Life, Music, and Redemption of Jelly Roll Morton.* New York: Da Capo, 2003.

Renoir, Jean. *My Life and My Films.* Translated by Norman Denny. New York: Atheneum, 1974.

Richmond, Peter. *Fever: The Life and Music of Miss Peggy Lee.* New York: Henry Holt, 2006.

Rose, Al. *Storyville, New Orleans: Being an Authentic, Illustrated Account of the Notorious Red-Light District.* Tuscaloosa: University of Alabama Press, 1974.

Royal, Marshal, with Claire P. Gordon. *Marshal Royal: Jazz Survivor.* New York: Continuum, 1996.

Russell, Bill. *New Orleans Style.* New Orleans: Jazzology, 1994.

Russo, Gus. *Supermob: How Sidney Korshak and His Criminal Associates Became America's Hidden Power Brokers.* New York: Bloomsbury, 2006.

Schuller, Gunther. *Early Jazz: Its Roots and Musical Development.* New York: Oxford, 1968.

———. *The Swing Era: The Development of Jazz, 1930–1945.* New York: Oxford, 1989.

Shapiro, Nat, and Nat Hentoff. *Hear Me Talkin' to Ya: The Story of Jazz as Told by the Men Who Made It.* New York: Rinehart, 1955.

Singer, Barry. *Black and Blue: The Life and Lyrics of Andy Razaf.* Foreword by Bobby Short. New York: Schirmer, 1995.

Smith, Jay D., and Len Guttridge. *Jack Teagarden: The Story of a Jazz Maverick.* London: Cassell, 1960.

Steele, Shelby. *A Bound Man: Why We Are Excited about Obama and Why He Can't Win.* New York: Free Press, 2007.

Stewart, Rex. *Boy Meets Horn.* Edited by Claire P. Gordon. London: Continuum, 1995.

———. *Jazz Masters of the Thirties.* New York: Macmillan, 1972.

Stratemann, Klaus. *Louis Armstrong on the Screen.* Copenhagen (Denmark): Jazz-Media ApS, 1996.

Sudhalter, Richard M. *Henry "Red" Allen.* Notes on the music by John Chilton. Alexandria, VA: Time-Life Records, 1981.

———. *Lost Chords: White Musicians and Their Contribution to Jazz, 1915–1945.* New York: Oxford, 1999.

———. *Stardust Melody: The Life and Music of Hoagy Carmichael.* New York: Oxford, 2002.

——— and Philip R. Evans. *Bix: Man and Legend.* With William Dean-Myatt. New Rochelle, NY: Arlington, 1974.

Teachout, Terry. *A Terry Teachout Reader.* New Haven: Yale University Press, 2004.

Teague, Frances. *Shakespeare and the American Popular Stage.* Cambridge: Cambridge University Press, 2006.

Thiele, Bob. *What a Wonderful World: A Lifetime of Recordings.* As told to Bob Golden, with a foreword by Steve Allen. New York: Oxford, 2005.

Thomson, Virgil. *A Virgil Thomson Reader.* With an Introduction by John Rockwell. Boston: Houghton Mifflin, 1981.

Traill, Sinclair, and Gerald Lascelles, eds. *Just Jazz.* London: Peter Davies, 1957.

Travis, Dempsey J. *An Autobiography of Black Jazz.* Chicago: Urban Research Institute, 1983.

Untermeyer, Sophie Guggenheimer, and Alix Williamson. *Mother Is Minnie.* Garden City, NY: Doubleday, 1960.

Von Eschen, Penny M. *Satchmo Blows Up the World: Jazz Ambassadors Play the Cold War.* Cambridge: Harvard University Press, 2004.

Wald, Elijah. *Escaping the Delta: Robert Johnson and the Invention of the Blues.* New York: Amistad, 2004.

Walser, Robert, ed. *Keeping Time: Readings in Jazz History.* New York: Oxford, 1999.

Waters, Ethel, with Charles Samuels. *His Eye Is on the Sparrow: An Autobiography.* Garden City, NY: Doubleday, 1951.

Wein, George, with Nate Chinen. *Myself among Others: A Life in Music.* New York: Da Capo, 2003.

Wilder, Alec. *American Popular Song: The Great Innovators 1900–1950.* Edited and with an introduction by James T. Maher. New York: Oxford, 1972.

Willems, Jos. *All of Me: The Complete Discography of Louis Armstrong.* Lanham, MD: Scarecrow, 2006.

Williams, Martin, ed. *Jazz Panorama: From the Pages of* The Jazz Review. New York: Crowell-Collier, 1962.

Wilson, Teddy, with Arie Ligthart and Humphrey Van Loo. *Teddy Wilson Talks Jazz.* London: Cassell, 1996.

Wyatt, Robert, and John Andrew Johnson, eds. *The George Gershwin Reader.* New York: Oxford, 2004.

Zwerin, Mike. *Close Enough for Jazz.* London: Quartet, 1983.

Photo Credits

About the Author

TERRY TEACHOUT is the drama critic of the *Wall Street Journal*, the chief culture critic of *Commentary*, and the author of "Sightings," a column for the Saturday *Journal* about the arts in America. He blogs about the arts at www.terryteachout.com.

Teachout's books include *The Skeptic: A Life of H. L. Mencken*, *A Terry Teachout Reader*, and *All in the Dances: A Brief Life of George Balanchine*. He wrote the libretto for *The Letter*, an opera by Paul Moravec that was premiered in 2009 by the Santa Fe Opera. He contributed to *The Oxford Companion to Jazz* and Robert Gottlieb's *Reading Dance* and wrote the introductions to *William Bailey on Canvas*, Elaine Dundy's *The Dud Avocado*, and Paul Taylor's *Private Domain*. In 1992 he rediscovered the manuscript of *A Second Mencken Chrestomathy* among H. L. Mencken's private papers and edited it for publication by Alfred A. Knopf. He was appointed to the National Council on the Arts in 2004.

Born in Cape Girardeau, Missouri, in 1956, Teachout attended St. John's College, William Jewell College, and the University of Illinois at Urbana-Champaign. From 1975 to 1983 he lived in Kansas City, where he worked as a jazz bassist. He now lives in New York City and Connecticut.